SUPER HIGHWAY

SUPER HIGHWAY

SEA POWER IN THE 21ST CENTURY

CHRIS PARRY

First published 2014
by Elliott and Thompson Limited
27 John Street
London WC1N 2BX
www.eandtbooks.com

ISBN: 978-1-90873-984-1

9 8 7 6 5 4 3 2 1

A catalogue record for this book is available from the British Library.
Typesetting by Marie Doherty
Picture credits: see page 348
Illustrations: Maltings Partnership, Derby

Printed in the UK by TJ International

For John Jenkyn Parry – *mae'r tad gorau yn y byd.*

Contents

Introduction   1

1.   Globalisation and Sea Power   9
2.   Today's Global Super Highway   35
3.   Sea Power Today   63
4.   A Changing Seascape   107
5.   New Opportunities   135
6.   New Technologies   167
7.   Security at Sea   213
8.   Strategic Competition   257
9.   Maritime Warfare   279
10. What's a Country to Do?   315

Select Bibliography   341
Acknowledgements   347
Picture Credits   348
Index   349

Introduction

This book is not intended to be, and cannot be, an authoritative history or definitive account of sea power. Nor is it a theoretical primer or doctrinal guide for budding naval commanders. There are books that fulfil those functions well;[1] this one simply seeks to identify and illuminate some major themes associated with the use of the sea as a source of geopolitical power in the twenty-first century.

The sea is the World Ocean, the connected body of salt water that covers 70 per cent of the Earth's surface. It is important in regulating and moderating the Earth's climate, in providing food and oxygen, in its enormous diversity of life and for navigation. The sea can be used as a medium – for transport and warfare – and as a resource. Just as in earlier periods of history, technological advance is enabling further progress in the use of the sea, not only in terms of transport this time, but also with regard to its exploitation. Most importantly, it is largely the common heritage of mankind and available for use by anyone capable of mastering and employing the technical requirements.

Anyone who goes down to the seashore is looking at an unbroken mass of water that stretches around the whole world. Every drop or molecule of seawater forms an unbroken chain of continuity and connectivity with all the others on the planet. The tiny portion of sea in view is directly linked to waves rolling onto a beach in Japan or to currents streaming under the Arctic ice.

In 1929, a team of German scientists set out to track the journey of a bottle that had been dropped in the southern Indian Ocean with a note

---

[1] Notably, but not exclusively, Geoff Till, *Seapower: A Guide for the Twenty-First Century* (2004).

inside asking the finder to record the location where it washed up and to throw it back into the sea. By 1935, when it was found and retired in East Africa, it had rounded the world and travelled approximately 25,750 km (16,000 miles), the longest recorded distance travelled by an inanimate object.

In fact, 1935 was a good year for messages in bottles. Chunosuke Matsuyama had been stranded on a coral reef in the Pacific in 1784, without food or water, after his fishing boat was wrecked. Before his death, he carved an account of what had happened on a piece of wood, which he sealed in a bottle. In 1935, 151 years after it had been set afloat, the bottle finally washed up in the small Japanese village where Matsuyama had been born.

The point is that any of us could this very instant sail, without let or hindrance, to anywhere in the world that is connected to the sea – to the 150 or so countries with a coast – and without anyone's approval, license or sanction, unless we wished to land. This 'open architecture' of the sea is much like the Internet; in their respective physical and virtual ways, both enable the connectivity, interdependence and extraordinary economic vitality of our world.

Globalisation as it is typically understood today is an expression of the many ways in which people worldwide are connected with each other. This non-physical globalisation – the exchange of information, ideas, images and resources – results in physical expressions of worldwide connectivity, such as human contact, the trade in goods and services, and warfare. The indirect, *virtual* component of globalisation is almost exclusively associated with communications and information systems, while the direct element, involving physical connectivity, relies on the ability to use the sea as an indispensable physical medium across, through and above which all human interaction and exchange takes place. The integration of the world economy and the interdependence of increasing numbers of countries on international trade and access for their continued security, social stability and prosperity mean that the security and environmental sustainability of the sea, and its integrity as a system, are of critical importance to the peace and economic health of the world.

A more interconnected world, allowing an ever-expanding and interdependent interchange of goods, services and people, has meant that sea power today is expressed and employed in more subtly diverse ways than it was in the past. In particular, sea power is used in a permissive international system, in which cooperative political and collaborative economic considerations predominate, mainly because the current situation suits the purposes of the majority of states and corporations. It seems certain that increased use of the sea in the twenty-first century is likely to mirror and parallel the revolutionary consequences and continuing growth of the new age of virtual communication and progress.

Thus, the sea acts as a super highway that allows us to pass over it upon our lawful occasions, as the British naval prayer has it, granting us access to a watery worldwide web. Preserving the 'freedom of the seas', allowing universal and global access to the sea both as a means of transport and trade, and as a means of extracting resources, is crucial to the global economy and international relations between states.

For states, the ability to use the sea freely – unlike airspace, which is subject to the rules and regulations of the states below it – allows governments to intervene militarily in situations at a time and place of political choice, in order to influence events and decisions in the national interest. As the British admiral and noted stentorian, Jacky Fisher, had it, 'the whole principle of naval fighting is to be free to go anywhere with every damned thing the Navy possesses'.[2] Translated into the modern political vernacular, it means the ability of a state, or group of states, to influence a part of the world wherever and whenever it wants. And not just in terms of the ability to coerce: 'Whosoever commands the sea, commands the trade; whosoever commands the trade of the world commands the riches of the world, and consequently the world itself.'[3] No other strategic medium, as yet, offers this freedom of choice and action.

From any historical perspective, the importance of sea power to a country's sense of itself and ability to get its way in the world are evident. Sea power is most commonly associated with the might of naval forces but, in reality, it is based on two simple concepts: the ability of a state, group, company or individual to use the sea for its own benefit (for political, commercial or private reasons) and, if required, to deny its use to others. The

---

[2] Sir John Fisher, *Memories* (1919).
[3] Sir Walter Raleigh, 'A Discourse of the Invention of Ships, Anchors, Compass, etc.' in *The Works of Sir Walter Ralegh, Kt.*, vol. 8 (1829, reprinted 1965).

critical tension is between forces that are trying to achieve sea control and those that are attempting to deny them that control.

There are two main types of sea power in operation today. Hard sea power is associated with the ability to threaten or employ violence and coercion as an instrument of policy. Soft sea power is generally associated with exploitation of the sea's resources and the movement of goods along sea lines of communication. In some cases, as is the case with China, the difference between the state and private sectors is indistinguishable. Here, hard power and soft power are wielded together.

In both its hard and soft forms, sea power covers at least four elements: the control and practice of international trade and commerce; the use and control of ocean resources; the operation of maritime forces in war; and the use of navies and maritime economic power as instruments of diplomacy, deterrence and influence in peacetime. In this regard, appearances can be deceptive: the most powerful navy in the world is that of the USA; the largest merchant fleet is held by the Greeks; the largest fishing fleet, by volume and activity, is the Chinese; and the biggest commercial shipping company is Danish. In this sense, sea power is diffused.

Sea power does not have to be legal in its expression and use and is not always the preserve of states or corporations. Traffickers – of drugs, exploited people and other illicit goods – routinely abuse the freedom of the seas, and pirates demonstrate sea power when engaging in armed robbery and ransoms. Conversely, navies and law enforcement authorities, in the right hands, could perhaps be said to function as the equivalent of an anti-virus and anti-malware protection for the international system. At one end, they deal with pirates, traffickers and terrorists (the seagoing equivalent of malware) and at the other with adventurous states and opportunist regimes as one would with major cyber-attacks. Most of the time, computer users are unaware of their anti-virus systems working; they are usually only alerted on those occasions when there is a serious attack. So it is with navies. It is difficult to know what might happen if they were not there; these situations are Conan Doyle's (sea) dogs that didn't bark in the night.[4]

From the earliest periods of recorded history, sea power, and its use to further political and economic objectives, has always been the litmus test of a

---

[4] In *Silver Blaze* (1892).

great power, one whose reach and influence extended beyond its immediate horizon and local region. With more than 70 per cent of the globe covered by sea, and 90 per cent of trade, by weight and volume, moving by sea, the effective deployment of maritime power confers the political and economic leadership of the known world. The sea is also the indispensable means by which any armed force or humanitarian response can cross to other continents in strength and in bulk; and it is the only means of reaching an opponent or community if access to air routes and forward bases for aircraft are denied or unavailable. There is simply no substitute for sea power. Without being able to access the sea in some way, an economy is not likely to benefit in any meaningful way from globalisation. While the sea is the medium of globalisation, sea power provides its engine, fuelled by states and commercial companies in the pursuit of their own interests, in response to risks and opportunities.

The freedom and connectivity of the seas have only survived over the centuries because states have been strong and self-interested enough to preserve the principle that innocent passage and lawful exchange at sea should be respected and safeguarded. It is a familiar saying that peace at sea does not keep itself and it should be recognised that, in the modern world, globalisation and the freedom of the sea are guarded and guaranteed by the political will, vigilance and fighting power of the USA, specifically through the agency of the US Navy and its sister Services. Along with its allies and partners, who also have an interest in the secure, uninterrupted use of the sea, the maritime power of the USA has been exercised, since the end of the Cold War, in the absence of any significant threat to its dominance.

At the start of a century that is already witnessing significant changes to the balance of power in the international landscape, the only certainty is that countries will continue to make decisions on the basis of their own interests, with regimes (whether democratic or authoritarian) determining which policies will preserve or extend their legitimacy in the eyes of their elites or populations. Therefore, states may operate either inside or outside the system depending on the balance of risk or advantage. Experience has shown that it would be prudent for both navies and shipowners, thinking strategically, to prepare for both eventualities.

A casual glance at the current maritime scene suggests that competition and cooperation by states within a globalised international system will continue to define the opening decades of the twenty-first century. The sea will maintain its role as an indispensable medium of global exchange and access. Nevertheless, there are indications that, over the next ten years, we will inhabit a progressively more complex, challenging and unpredictable world, shaped by the reality and uneven impact of climate change, resource competition and intensifying globalisation. There will also be ongoing risks associated with the political and economic imbalances, social inequalities and perceived injustices in every aspect of human life. Challenges to governance and order, rapid advances in knowledge and innovation and fluid attitudes to identity and interest will further complicate the geostrategic tensions, likely to be caused both by the projected imbalance between population and resources and by severe regional demographic pressures.

In parallel, states are beginning to exert increasing levels of control over their littoral regions and the resources of their exclusive economic zones, encroaching on the rights of innocent passage traditionally associated with the freedom of the seas. Many are also investing significantly in military and naval capability. China, in particular, seeks sovereign rights over much of the South China Sea, well beyond its maritime entitlements as designated in international maritime agreements.

There is also likely to be a 'scramble' by states and commercial enterprises in the high seas and the deep oceans. Here, the prospect of diminishing edible fish stocks and (as technology delivers viable extraction solutions) the appeal of commercially viable, exploitable natural resources will encourage states to encroach on what until now has been seen as international space. It is probable that there will be an increasing incidence of arbitrary and contested actions as states, especially totalitarian and marginally democratic regimes, and commercial organisations seek to assert unilateral claims, pursue their own interests or prevent others from doing so.

All these factors have implications for those states that rely on an open trading system and the freedom of the seas for the security of their homelands, the health of their economies and the promotion of their interests. They will also challenge existing notions about the way in which the sea is used. New relationships and responsibilities with regard to governance on the high seas and in the littoral regions of the world are likely to emerge in the coming years. Without a credible universal regulatory regime, an era of residual claims, uncertain jurisdictions and competing interests is likely to present countless opportunities for confrontation and conflict, especially in the ungoverned, poorly regulated coastal areas of weak or failed states, as well as in the 'scramble' to control and exploit the resources of the high seas.

Those states with an interest in maintaining the international order, for their own advantage, will use their naval power to ensure access not only for their own commerce, but also for that of the world in general and their economic partners in particular. Conversely, other countries that benefit less from an ordered international trading system – for example, aspiring regional or economic powers or restrictive regimes – are likely to want to find ways to restrict or close down parts of the international system or to control it for their own benefit.

As a result, modern maritime forces will still be required to ensure national security and secure the sea in terms of access and trade, especially for natural resources and energy products. They will also be expected to act in those circumstances when state or international authority is weak or ineffectual, in response to the threats from irregular activity, lawless behaviour and naturally induced extreme weather or other events.

Given emerging conditions and trends, it is likely that America and its friends will be increasingly challenged at sea by aspiring regional powers in the years ahead, both commercially and militarily. In addition, their capacity to prevent infractions of international law may become more difficult as states and companies take unilateral action in responding to opportunities presented by local and regional political, economic and demographic conditions. There is also a risk that the USA will tire of ensuring the security of an international system that is upheld not only for the benefit of its own trade, security and prosperity, but also for the benefit of its economic and strategic challengers.

Globalisation has been seen to ebb and flow; historians have spoken of waves and storm surges of globalisation, in response to major changes, discontinuities and imbalances in the international system. In the worst case, globalisation could ebb again and the world would revert to competing – and conflicting – regional, ideological or trading blocs. In this scenario, just as some states (such as China and other restrictive regimes) have done with the Internet, powerful states and assertive corporate players could threaten to make the universal access and freedom enjoyed today on the high seas a thing of the past. Renewed attempts to impose *mare clausum* ('closed sea', under the jurisdiction of a particular state), at the expense of *mare liberum* ('free sea', open to all countries), would not only overturn the trading system that has sustained globalisation for over 500 years, but also determine the balance of power and advantage in the twenty-first century. In these circumstances, history and emerging conditions suggest that the twenty-first century is unlikely to remain quiet for those who 'pass on the seas upon their lawful occasions'.[5]

---

[5] A Prayer to be used at Sea, from the *Book of Common Prayer*.

CHAPTER ONE

Globalisation and Sea Power

*'When man ceased to look upon streams, rivers, and seas as
barriers and learned to use them as highways, he made a
giant stride toward civilization. The waterways of the world
provided a new mobility – to man himself, later to the products
of his toil and skill, and at all times to his ideas.'*[1]

Until the early modern period, oceanic travel was the exception rather than
the rule, with only the Arabs and the Chinese venturing beyond the coastal
regions of their known and familiar horizons, and not far beyond. Apart
from the Mediterranean Sea and the Black Sea, Europeans had made the
Atlantic coast of their continent the limit of their ambition, with settlement
of Greenland and Iceland and what proved to be unsustainable ventures
beyond into the vastness of the North Atlantic.

This situation changed in the wake of the Ottoman capture of
Constantinople in 1453 and the 'Reconquista' of the Iberian Peninsula in
1492, leaving the Western European monarchies free from the threat of
external predators (if not struggles among themselves) and able to speculate about what the Atlantic might offer. The voyages and explorations of
Columbus, Magellan and da Gama, at the start of the early modern period,
kicked off the process of globalisation as Europe began to reach out across
the oceans and the world became increasingly connected through the
medium of the sea. As these maritime ventures continued to expand, states
were able to take advantage of the new opportunities opening up in terms
of trade routes, the exploitation of resources and the ability to exert military

---

[1] E. B. Potter, *Sea Power: A Naval History* (1960).

influence on the oceans. The fortunes of states became linked to their ability to access and exploit the seas, with globalisation, hand-in-hand with the development of sea power, becoming the driving force for imperial ambition and economic success.

The period led to the formation and growth of successive world-spanning maritime empires. Great Britain built and maintained an extensive empire through the maintenance of a network of markets and colonies, fuelled by trade, whose security and integrity were guaranteed by the barrels of naval guns and the cutlasses of its semi-mythic naval heroes. Although the maritime empires of Spain, Portugal, then the Dutch, French and English faced opposition and challenge in turn, not least from each other, no other power outside Europe or the Americas had the technical, organisational and industrial capacity to break the monopoly of sea power held by the Western world. The only non-Western power that ever came close to establishing a maritime-based empire, but only on a regional basis, was Japan in the Second World War. Its success was temporary and dependent on the peculiar conditions that prevailed while Britain and the USA were distracted by the necessity of defeating Nazi Germany and its Axis allies in Europe. Western maritime dominance resumed, this time led by the USA, although the European empires did not long survive the austerities that afflicted the home countries and the nationalist aspirations of their former colonies.

THE PRE-MODERN ERA

Until the time of the great oceanic voyages of the fifteenth century, maritime dominance had been always regional in its extent and ambition, constrained by the limitations of naval technology, an imperfect understanding of oceanic weather patterns and the presence of substantial regional powers determined to hold their own against interlopers. The limited maritime operations of the Greeks and Romans in the Mediterranean, with their extensions into the Black Sea and Red Sea and onto the Atlantic coast, disappeared amid the collapse of the classical world. In the ensuing fragmentation and instability, the idea of a securely navigable, accessible and interconnected world suffered something of a setback as both maritime and intellectual horizons closed down considerably. These gave way to contested sea-spaces and trading routes in the Mediterranean and around the Atlantic coast, occupied by no single dominant power and menaced by raiders, predatory warlords and dynastic rivalry.

The next phase, from the ninth century, was characterised by the rise of Italian maritime city-states (notably Venice, Genoa and Pisa), successively trading with the Levant and helping themselves to the spoils of the Crusades and the break-up of the Byzantine Empire. The key to sea power in the pre-modern era was the ability to maintain a balance between the need to sustain a profitable trading fleet in times of peace and stability and the ability to generate sufficient fighting power in wartime. Meanwhile, the Red Sea and Indian Ocean were controlled without serious opposition or competition – apart from the threat from pirates – by the warships and merchants of Islam, whose coercive power dominated the Red Sea, the western Indian Ocean and whose commercial reach extended to India and China.

Further East, Chinese imperial regimes, notably the Song and Ming dynasties, held most of what we now know as South East Asia and East Asia in a tribute-based political and economic system, whose power at sea was built around intricate trading networks, a huge fleet of powerful warships and the resources of the world's largest economy. Chinese ships at the time of the Ming emperors were rightly famous and remarked upon by European commentators. At about 120 m (400 ft) in length, with up to nine masts, watertight bulkheads and innovative technologies, they dwarfed comparable Western models, both in scale and sophistication. Such was the maritime dominance of the Ming dynasty fleets that, in the early fifteenth century, the great Ming Navy consisted of 3,500 vessels, 2,700 of which were warships stationed along the length of the coast of China.

Any account of China's maritime heritage has to mention Zheng He, a eunuch admiral, who commanded powerful 'treasure' fleets, comprising warships and merchantmen, on a succession of wide-ranging tribute-collecting, exploratory and trading voyages between 1405 and 1433. The scope of his operations extended to the Gulf and East Africa in the west, to all of South East Asia and to the Malaysian and Indonesian archipelagoes. Gavin Menzies in his book 1421 would have us believe that he went even further than that, but the argument would appear to become progressively more circumstantial, though no less engaging, the further the book, and its hero, travel from China.

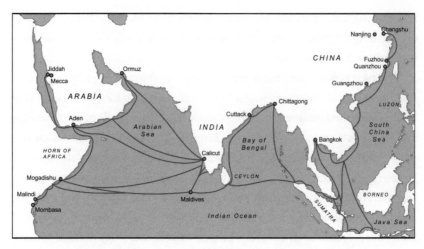

The expeditionary voyages of Chinese Admiral Zheng He, 1405–33.

However, Chinese maritime dominance only effectively extended to the South China Sea and coastal waters. Expeditions and trading that took in East Asia, the Indian Ocean and East Africa were less controllable and secure, as much of the trade was in the hands of Muslim merchants, who had a particularly strong grip on the Indian Ocean and the routes to the Indies. The Chinese never sought to challenge Muslim control of this trade; forward bases or emporiums were never established to offset the logistical challenges of projecting and sustaining power so far away. The Chinese knew about Europe, but were emphatically a regional power; they did not need anything from beyond their region, except what they chose to import on their own terms by means of middlemen.

Chinese sea power foundered on ideology and political partisanship. The philosophy of Confucianism emphasised the virtue of agriculture and was decidedly sniffy about the benefits to be gained from commercial activity and trade, while condemning the baleful consequences of contact with culturally inferior foreigners. As a result, even under the first Ming emperor, who was a strong believer in sea power, maritime trade and some foreign goods were banned and tribute was the only commodity that could legally be carried into Chinese ports by foreign ships. Other reasons for the decline of such a formidable ocean-going capability were linked to the power politics within the Imperial Court and economic stresses. Indeed, they have a familiar modern ring to them and present an instructive parable to our ears today. Factional disputes at court (party politics) and a hostile Confucian bureaucracy eventually scuppered the sea expeditions, limiting ship size and civilian participation in overseas trade (over-regulation), with the result that shipyards for large ocean-going junks were closed (industrial decline and loss of sovereign capacity) and Chinese naval technology lost its momentum (loss of research and development). By the sixteenth century, few shipwrights knew how to build the large ocean-going ships (loss of industrial expertise and skills). The development of guns and cannon also slowed, allowing the European powers to outmatch the Chinese in firepower. Finally, the expenditure on Chinese naval capability could not easily be justified in the absence of an opponent that presented a similar level of threat (also eerily familiar). As a result, the Chinese progressively lost their technological edge over the West, never to regain it.

The decline of Chinese maritime power and presence left the seas open for Europe. In 1453, the Turks captured Constantinople (Istanbul) and for eighty years they and their co-religionists along the North African littoral fought with Christian Europe for maritime supremacy in the Mediterranean. By the closing years of the sixteenth century, this struggle was effectively over – in the short run, after the Turks were firstly repulsed at Malta in 1565 and then defeated in the last major fleet action involving galleys at Lepanto in 1571 and, in the long run, once technically and tactically superior types of vessels, guns and technologies were introduced by the Europeans.

Thus, at almost exactly the same time as European seamen started to expand their horizons and probe the possibilities offered by oceanic travel, the pre-eminent maritime power and presence of the time, Imperial China, made a strategic decision to turn its back on globalisation and sea power and withdraw into a state of self-regarding self-sufficiency. Two centuries or more later, China would be wrenched into the global system, like it or not, according to the will of those maritime powers that did grasp the opportunities – and overcome the challenges – of globalisation.

THE BEGINNINGS OF GLOBALISATION

Amid this pattern of regionally based political, cultural and economic systems, at what point do we identify the first inkling of globalisation, the earliest moment at which most of the people in the world knew that they were capable of being connected to most of the other people in the world? At what point in time did humanity gain an understanding of the global nature of its existence and an awareness of the existence and shape of most of the inhabited land masses? Adam Smith, with his good sense about most things, probably got it right: 'The discovery of America and that of a passage to the East Indies by way of the Cape of Good Hope are the two greatest and most important events recorded in the history of mankind.'[2]

It is clear that the super highway really gets going in the late fifteenth and early sixteenth century, a remarkable period in the history of globalisation and sea power, with attempts by the Europeans living on the Atlantic coast to gain access by sea to Oriental markets that overland were dominated by hostile powers, Italian middlemen and high prices. It is worth remembering that, before those events, no one is recorded as having any meaningful knowledge of the existence and extent of the north and south halves of the American continent. When the early explorers set out from late medieval Europe, they travelled more in hope than in expectation. Indeed, in 1492, when Christopher Columbus, the 'discoverer' of America, landed on an even now unidentified[3] island in the Bahamas, he thought that he had reached China. He quickly realised that he had discovered an island and his next expedition from there set out to prove that he could *still* reach China by sea. He was still not aware that America was in the way and continued to be remarkably steadfast in his original pursuit of a direct route to China. If the giant land mass of America and its offshore islands had not been in the way, we probably would never have heard of Columbus again, except as a footnote in the history of the joint reign of Ferdinand of Aragon and Isabella of Castile.

Oceanic routes had not been attempted before because technology and the accumulated store of human knowledge did not encourage extended voyages to be undertaken with confidence. There were also insufficient incentives to bypass familiar trade routes, by risking life and fortune on the high seas. In this sense, it is significant that Columbus was the first seafarer to demonstrate the viability of linking continents by oceanic travel. All previous trading and movements of people had occurred over land or

[2] Adam Smith, *The Wealth of Nations* (1776).
[3] Probably Watling Island.

along coastlines by ships probing short distances at a time, as with Vasco da Gama and the Portuguese explorers. As far as possible, they had maintained close contact with the land or had used known features to navigate from point to point all the way down the west coast of Africa and into the Indian Ocean. This willingness and ability to navigate successfully across the oceans represented the point at which trade went intercontinental and viral and the process of globalisation began. The oceans were the decisive facilitator of globalisation.

Oceanic travel and trade were made possible for Europeans by the arrival of sturdier ocean-going ships, new arrangements of sails and more reliable compasses and charts, which enabled voyages to reach out further into the Atlantic and along the African coast. Significant improvements to cannon and firearms arrived at just the right time to deal with any hostile or uncooperative elements that might be encountered. With their experience of life at sea in the Mediterranean, the Spanish and the Portuguese knew that if they wanted to trade, they needed to be prepared to fight. There were hostile potentates, pirates and brigands out there, not to mention various terrors of the deep (all graphically illustrated in the blank areas and margins of charts) that might require some careful handling. Coupled with the sailing characteristics of their late fifteenth-century ships, this technological edge gave European seamen in remote, uncharted waters a decided superiority in terms of manoeuvre and in the use of organised violence in support of their trading and other speculative ventures. It is an edge that Western countries have been careful to preserve throughout the centuries.

The subsequent age of exploration and colonisation saw countries becoming richer and more powerful through increasing levels of exchange. In a competitive market, it was always likely that power struggles would break out between the maritime rivals. When sea powers clashed, the country with the most skilled seamen and the most effective, innovative use of its ships and guns usually prevailed. In particular, the possession of relatively rapid-firing, reliable guns and more manoeuvrable designs of fighting ship saw the progressive defeat of countries that relied on boarding and fighting land battles at sea. Ships were now able to stand well clear of their opponents and either sink or pound them into submission. Thus, the English were able to defeat the Spanish in the Armada year of 1588 and in a whole series of running fights the length and breadth of the Americas, just as the Portuguese had defeated the forces of Islam at the Battle of Diu in the Indian Ocean earlier in the century.

INTRODUCING INTERNATIONAL MARITIME LAW

Increasing levels of bitter rivalry and power struggles between the European nations, as they all continued to attempt to exert their power on the seas, had resulted in serious demarcation disputes and highlighted the need for some form of international agreements regarding access to the seas, trade and transport. In the marginal balance of risk and reward, conditions of anarchy and free-for-all in the remote regions of the sea were not in any country's interest, least of all those with what would now be called 'first-mover advantage'.

. In 1494, the Pope, in the Treaty of Tordesillas, allowed Spain and Portugal exclusive rights to travel and trade globally to the west and east respectively of an arbitrary and geographically doubtful line drawn down the Atlantic. The treaty was of course only applicable and enforceable if the two countries had the will and power to prevent intrusions and infractions. The determination and ability of the English, the French and the Dutch over the next century to circumvent the cosy Iberian arrangement reflected a combination of entrepreneurial initiative, religious zeal (after the Reformation began to take hold) and commercial opportunity, as well as the complicity, indifference and occasional energetic and clumsy reprisals of the colonial authorities and mother countries. Interlopers were always liable to be caught out under the 'catch me if you can' principle, and outright war from time to time complicated things still further. There was good money to be made where legal theory came up against commercial impulse, private ambition and consumer demand in an environment that was indifferently policed. Legal theory came off decidedly worse.

On 25 February 1603, three ships from the Dutch East India Company seized an anchored Portuguese merchant ship, the *Santa Catarina*, off the coast of what is now Singapore. As Portugal had been absorbed into the Spanish crown in 1580 and the Netherlands was at war with Spain, the Dutch presumably did not take long to assess that the ship was fair game. This view was probably encouraged by the likelihood that she was carrying valuable cargo. Having captured her after a stiff fight of a few hours, it transpired that the *Santa Catarina* had 1,200 bales of Chinese raw silk and a substantial amount of musk on board. A quick calculation established that the value of this cargo would more than double the capital of the Dutch East India Company.

The problem was that under Dutch law the capture of the prize and its cargo was of uncertain legality, and international (and some Dutch) opinion, in its ponderous pre-modern way, was not entirely happy with the Dutch keeping what were considered ill-gotten gains. There were also considerable doubts about whether the Dutch should be in the East Indies in the first place, in defiance of Portuguese claims to a monopoly on trade with the region, and whether the war should have been carried on between merchant ships far away from the main theatre of conflict.

At this point, the Dutch East India Company called on Hugo Grotius, a jurist, who was counsel to the Company and one of the few authorities on these issues, to justify the action and secure the retention of the captured cargo. In a commendable feat of intellectual gymnastics, Grotius chose to concentrate his attention not on the inconvenient circumstances of the case, but on a new general principle, which he called 'the freedom of the seas'. This he outlined in a book, called *Mare Liberum* (*The Free Sea*), which comprehensively demolished the Portuguese – or any other state's – claims to exclusive rights to trade at sea.

With a dramatic flourish, Grotius called in aid the 'most [hitherto unknown] specific and unimpeachable axiom of the Law of Nations, called a primary rule or first principle, the spirit of which is self-evident and immutable'. The sea was not like the land, he claimed, but like the air: 'it is not susceptible of occupation; and, second, its common use is destined for all men. For the same reasons, the sea is common to all, because it is so limitless that it cannot become a possession of any one, and because it is adapted for the use of all.'[4]

As a result, Grotius maintained, every nation was free to travel to every other nation, and to trade with it. As clear as day, it was a right according to natural law. Therefore, the Dutch were entirely justified in going to the Indies, trading with the locals and, by the way, keeping the loot from the *Santa Catarina*.

---

[4] Hugo Grotius, *The Freedom of the Seas* (1609).

With an alternating cavalier and compliant approach to legal restraint at sea, England opposed the Dutch position and supported the existing restrictions imposed and implied since the Treaty of Tordesillas (even though the English had long repudiated the authority of the Pope). England's own particular circumstances – which increasingly included seeing the Dutch as maritime rivals and worrying about English interests in the Americas – somewhat tempered its enthusiasm for upsetting the Spanish and Portuguese. In his 1635 work *Mare Clausum* (*The Closed Sea*), the English scholar John Selden tried to prove that the sea was in practice as capable of appropriation as land or territory.

However, after almost a century of dispute between England and its near neighbour and Protestant co-religionist, including three maritime trade wars, both countries settled on the principle of the freedom of the seas. A formula[5] was agreed that only limited the sovereignty owing to a state to 3 nautical miles (nm) (5.6 km) offshore, the range at which a cannon could theoretically fire. It was implicit that maritime claims were only valid in practice to the extent that they could be enforced and rights protected, quite literally at gunpoint. Elsewhere, the ships of all countries could – in theory – undertake peaceful navigation and innocent passage.

Despite blatant breaches of this generous principle, especially in the blurred area between war and peace, which inconveniently complicated the rights of neutrals and the actions of belligerents, this generally agreed arrangement for international maritime practice persisted through to the twentieth century and survived two world wars and the Cold War. In more recent years, new international conventions have been introduced, as we will see, but the basic concept of freedom of the seas has prevailed.

SEA POWER AND EMPIRES

As long as public and private interests continued to coincide, investment in the sea proved both commercially profitable and politically popular. Those countries that had excess agricultural or industrial output could find ready markets for their goods, alongside those with the skills and daring at sea to turn a profit in the service of the state or on their own behalf. It was the

---

[5] Cornelius Bynkershoek in *De Dominio Maris* (*Concerning the Ownership of the Sea*) (1702).

accumulated national experience of securing free access to the sea, venturing capital and exploiting trade, transport and naval power that enabled the creation of empires and growing national wealth.

The British, for example, secure in their island home from the worst excesses of conflict in Europe, were able to seize opportunities to establish their maritime pre-eminence on trade. This ascent started at a time when it was believed that there were winners and losers in trading and that only one side could profit substantially from a transaction, the supplier or seller. Often, countries sought to assert monopolies, both in terms of access to markets and goods and in their intolerance of the goods imported from, and carried by, other states. This mercantilist approach led to a succession of wars and strategic friction between the major powers, with Britain throughout its early modern and modern history more or less continuously engaged in competitive trade wars and disputes over market access. Also evident from an early stage was the close connection between trade and armed force: 'You should well know from experience that in Asia trade must be driven and maintained under the protection and favour of your own weapons, and that the weapons must be wielded from the profits gained from trade; so that trade cannot be maintained without war, nor war without trade.'[6]

In the early modern period, British sea power under the Tudor and Stuart monarchs had grown as a result of the country's need to defend itself against hostile powers (notably Spain), the search for new markets for English goods and a determination to share in the trade and opportunities of an expanding world. In the reign of Elizabeth, both private and royal ships that were needed to defend in war could only be afforded if they were able to turn a profit and be put to good use in the intervals between bouts of fighting. In the absence of sufficient capacity on the part of Spain and Portugal to supply and service the needs of their new colonies in the Americas, this took the form of the provision of goods (manufactures and raw materials) and of what would now be called services, in the form of slaves and privateering.

At this stage, in the Atlantic Ocean, most trade was carried out by private merchant vessels (armed to a greater or lesser degree), with very little investment or interest by the state, except in the levying of tolls and customs

---

[6] Jan Pietersz Coen, quoted in C. R. Boxer, *Portuguese Conquest and Commerce in Southern Asia 1500–1750* (1985).

dues. Sea power was primarily expressed by the actions of merchants and privateers. The state simply sanctioned them, financed them when it was advantageous to do so and taxed them; it also contracted their services in wartime. It protected them from the jealous attentions of other states and dealt with local problems as well, such as pirates and belligerent potentates, when they assumed a level of inconvenience greater than that with which commercial enterprises could cope. And it took out the competition whenever war or local circumstances allowed.

Trade at this time meant exploiting commercial gaps in the market and illicit opportunities where they could in the margins of the restrictions imposed, however imperfectly and unevenly enforced, by the Treaty of Tordesillas and by subsequent strictures about trade with the Americas in particular. Needless, to say, these were more honoured in the breach than in the observance, by both sides, until the Spanish attempted to enforce their trading monopoly against what were now considered Protestant heretics, as well as commercial interlopers. These measures, which included open fighting between English ships and the Spanish authorities, notably involving John Hawkins and Francis Drake, resulted in a period of unrestrained irregular warfare against Spanish interests in the Atlantic and the Americas. Whether it was piracy or entrepreneurial activity depends on your point of view.

The Elizabethans knew about globalisation.[7] They thrilled at Drake's exploits; they traded in goods from as far afield as Persia, India and the Moluccas. They had ambitious plans to develop the New World. The period culminated in Drake's highly profitable sortie into the Pacific and his circumnavigation of the world between 1578 and 1580. The systematic attacks on Spanish shipping by numerous English freebooters and the support given to Dutch rebels by Elizabeth resulted in open warfare with Spain, and a succession of Armadas sent against England, the most famous of which in 1588 was defeated by English tactical shrewdness, superior technology (ships and guns) used in context and, perhaps more decisively, the geography of the English Channel and a 'Protestant Wind'.

Military successes at sea served to defend the country and extend English commercial reach to North America, the West Indies, Muscovy and the

---

[7] Not for nothing was William Shakespeare's most famous theatre called the 'Globe'.

Baltic, to Constantinople (modern-day Istanbul) and into the Indian Ocean. This habit of success established the English in their own minds as a maritime nation. The significant trends of this period were the close alignment of the country's commercial and military interests, a system of private financing and joint stock companies for commercial ventures and the recognition that the use of the global super highway needed warships to protect British activities. The navies established and maintained under Charles I and, more importantly, the Commonwealth, were built in response to a realisation that a standing, professional government-financed and operated fleet would be required to project military power in support of government policy and to protect British commercial and colonial interests, which were expanding rapidly in North America throughout the seventeenth century.

In the late seventeenth and eighteenth centuries, the technical improvements in ship design, the rigging of vessels and their armaments ensured the continued dominance of the Europeans at sea, increasing the speed, efficiency, agility and fighting power of ocean-going vessels. More precise navigational techniques and the production of more accurate specialist instruments, notably in the field of timekeeping, also enabled safer, more reliable transits of great distances in general and the calculation of longitude in particular.

In the century before the American Revolution of 1776–83, British sea power in all its forms had been deployed to support commercial and speculative ventures and to deal with the ambitions and hostility of European peer competitors. Major wars against the Dutch in the seventeenth century, the Spanish and French in the early years of the eighteenth century and the French in the Seven Years' War of 1756–63 had resulted in not only control of Canada and India, but also the acquisition of a range of overseas bases, markets and possessions, mostly in the West Indies. This had allowed the expansion of British trade and the acquisition of an extensive trading and basing network, both across the Atlantic and to India. Trade was reinforced by naval power, the adroit apportionment of private investment and credit and government war expenditure, which stimulated exchange but relied on extensive public borrowing. Britain had also acquired a very substantial naval organisation and supporting infrastructure that benefited from the vastly improved productivity, technological sophistication and innovation made available through the Industrial Revolution. By this time, the idea of 'Great'

Britain had become synonymous with its relationship with the sea, as typi-
fied by James Thomson's 'Rule Britannia'[8] (set to music by Thomas Arne).

In 1783, Britain's claims to empire and maritime supremacy suffered
a serious setback with the loss of the thirteen North American colonies in
the American War of Independence. On this occasion, Britain's inability to
dominate the sea everywhere, all the time, in the face of a coalition of forces
that included the French, the Spanish and the Dutch, as well as more than
1,700 American privateers (who captured 2,283 ships), was decisive in its
defeat. However, Britain generally continued to hold its own elsewhere,
most notably in the hugely profitable islands of the Caribbean, and acquired
settlements in New South Wales, Sierra Leone, Trinidad, Mauritius and the
Cape Colony. It also exerted an increased control over Bengal, Madras and
the Indian hinterland.

British enterprise, in terms of trading networks and naval power, provided the investment, ships, commercial impetus and migrants to hold these
disparate possessions together. Like other European powers, although more
successful, Britain had developed the ability to use the oceans as the means
by which trading systems and military power could be used on a global scale.
Empires on which the sun never set were crucially dependent on the free
use of the sea as the basic connector. Rather like cyberspace, the sea was
the vital gateway and enabler for a more interconnected world – an imperial web, if you like. Indeed, between 1760 and 1850, the British – and to
a lesser extent the other European powers – were vital agents of globalisation, bringing together, through administrative and technological means,
territories and new sources of economic growth, while circulating people,
credit, goods, services and innovation between Europe and the networks of
colonies and markets.

Despite these high levels of interchange and energy, the period of the Age
of Sail cannot be seen as true globalisation, as it is commonly understood

---

[8] The lyrics are explicit, as seen in verse five:

'To thee belongs the rural reign;
Thy cities shall with commerce shine:
All thine shall be the subject main,
And every shore it circles thine.
"Rule, Britannia! rule the waves:
"Britons never will be slaves."'

today. Goods carried needed to have a high value to weight ratio, without the threat of competition in the home countries, in order to justify the expenditure and risks involved in oceanic trade and travel – hence the attractions of spices, tea, silk and sugar. Intercontinental maritime trade was not yet a global free market; piracy, privateering, commerce and trade were all considered part of what was, in essence, an extension of the normal rivalry between states and dynasties for the accumulation of commodities and assets. States and companies acted on the basis of what they could get away with, relative to their commercial power and leveraged naval strength, both in overall terms and in numerous distant, remote parts of the world.

THE EMERGENCE OF MODERN GLOBALISATION

It would not be until the end of the long cycle of persistent warfare in 1815 that anything approaching the modern system would start to evolve. Once Britain had achieved superpower status on the back of its protected and privileged commerce and its naval strength, it made the world safe for free trade and abolished its navigation acts[9] and other restrictive, mercantilist practices.

For Britain, the remainder of the nineteenth century was a period of unchallenged naval supremacy, in which the appearance of its warships was usually decisive in dominating a situation or resolving a crisis. The Royal Navy was instrumental in wringing concessions – sometimes at gunpoint – from China, in suppressing pirates and ending the slave trade from Africa to the Americas. In addition, the unrivalled and unchallenged access provided by the sea enabled Britain to extend the reach of its empire, exploit new markets and to apply pressure to recalcitrant or uncooperative regimes and potentates. Above all, it gave the leading industrial power a distinct competitive advantage in the ability to exchange goods on time and with the assurance of delivery, even in the face of instability or disorder in various parts of the world.

It is difficult to underplay the importance of the building of the Suez Canal in 1869 and the Panama Canal in 1914, both of which significantly

[9] Navigation Acts, pioneered by the British (from 1651), were used to severely restrict foreign shipping in the trade between England and its colonies. Such policies can be imposed by any country, to its advantage, but they invite retaliation in kind.

improved the volume and speed of the global super highway. The Suez Canal expanded and exemplified Britain's control of the super highway and its dominant industrial and trading power, by providing a fast, continuous route to its possessions and markets in Asia. The Panama Canal enabled the USA to integrate the economies of its east and west coasts and was a key stimulus for investment and exports. An indication of its breakthrough importance is that, by the time of the Great Depression of 1929, the USA accounted for 48 per cent of the world's industrial output. Furthermore, the canal allowed the US Navy to operate as a single entity (not as two separate fleets, unable to support each other quickly) in the face of an overwhelming threat appearing in either the Atlantic or the Pacific. This ability to transit quickly between the east and west coasts was to become critical later, in the early years of the Second World War (that is to say in the period after Pearl Harbor), when America had to rush both ships and resources into the Pacific to contain Japanese expansion.

Britain's empire had been built, and was reliant on, sea power to maintain its integrity and security. The crippling cost of victory in the First World War and its huge burden of war debt meant that Britain's capacity to sustain the world's largest navy shrank significantly. Under the 'ten-year rule' (the theory that major war was unlikely within a decade), provision for the Royal Navy, which in 1918–19 had been £356 million, dropped to £188 million in 1919–20 and just £52 million in 1923. Britain's politicians had voluntarily surrendered its naval supremacy in the Washington Naval Treaty of 1922, in a move both to contain the cost growth of its own navy and in an attempt to maintain a balance between the Royal Navy, the United States Navy and the Imperial Japanese Navy (in particular, in the Asia-Pacific region. As a result of the 5:5:3[10] agreement, Britain could still project substantial power at sea in support of its empire and in the event of major conflict, but it could no longer prevail anywhere and everywhere against major regional powers, without the material and military assistance of its imperial partners and allies.

An indication of the inherent vulnerability and fragility that this situation produced was demonstrated when its relative, deployable power in

---

[10] This allowed the USA and Britain to maintain a ratio of five major warships each in relation to Japan's three.

the Asia-Pacific region was overwhelmed by Japanese naval capability in the Second World War. Just as German U-boats sought to disable British access to the super highway, both for trade and reinforcement (as they had attempted in the First World War), the Japanese severed Britain's connectivity with the ocean, isolating and taking over the various territorial components of Britain's empire in the Asia-Pacific region. It was reminiscent of what Britain had inflicted on the French for over three centuries. The lesson of maritime warfare, time and again, was that success or failure depended on the balance between opponents of relative, readily available combat power in the region in which belligerents are operating. It's not what you have at home, but what you can bring to the party.

While the fortunes of Britain, and much of Europe, declined in the aftermath of the austerities and sheer effort required in the Second World War, for the USA, overwhelming victory in the war and the economic benefits that accrued from being both the arsenal and banker of democracy led to it becoming the pre-eminent superpower and champion of the free world. In addition, the threat of domination by an authoritarian state that had also achieved overwhelming victory in the same war, but not similar economic growth or access to nuclear weapons, meant that the USA was largely able to dictate the basis on which the free world would be sustained and run, in terms of strategy, recovery and economics.

The North Atlantic Treaty Organization (NATO) was formed to link the countries of North America and Western Europe in opposition to the threat posed by the Soviet Union and its allies. NATO's strategy was predicated on the use of the sea – not for nothing was it called the North *Atlantic* Treaty Organization. The peculiar geopolitical alignment of the alliance, involving the expanse of the Atlantic Ocean and Europe's configuration as a peninsula – framed by the Mediterranean and Black Sea on its right flank and the Baltic on its left, with links to the Norwegian and the Barents seas – determined that the Alliance would adopt a maritime-based containment strategy with regard to its opponents.

In addition, there was a general acceptance that the credibility of NATO's conventional strategy relied on the Central Front in Europe being held long enough to allow reinforcement across the Atlantic by the USA and Canada. This required the Soviet Northern Fleet either to be contained in its northern fastnesses in the Kola Peninsula and the Barents Sea or confronted by powerful battle groups in the Atlantic, able to punch through any Soviet war-ships or submarines that had been able to make their way into the Atlantic. The Far East, Black Sea and Baltic Sea fleets would be fixed in place locally. This would enable the resupply and reinforcement of western Europe to arrive in good time with suitable weight to throw back a Soviet assault and avoid recourse to nuclear weapons as part of strategies successively called, depending on how successful things had been, Mutually Assured Destruction or Flexible Response.

The US geographic position was critical in the struggle with the Soviet Union. It was able to deploy naval and air forces across the Pacific and Atlantic at will, while the fleets of its adversary were constrained in their free-dom of manoeuvre by ice-bound ports for much of the year or the simple fact that America or its allies controlled the main routes and exit points through which the Soviet Navy had to pass. A dozen or so carrier battle groups and defence expenditure that varied in value between those of the next twenty and ten leading military countries together ensured that US supremacy at sea remained unassailable.

MODERN DEVELOPMENTS
IN INTERNATIONAL MARITIME LAW

Since the end of the Cold War, the sea has been implicit rather than explicit in NATO's strategy, as it has taken on expeditionary, coercive and peace-keeping roles that have involved the deployment of predominantly land forces to distant theatres of operation. The security of the sea lanes across the Atlantic has been largely taken for granted, in the absence of a threat to their integrity, as have the routes to and from NATO's newer out-of-area commitments, such as Afghanistan and Iraq. Meanwhile, a large number of other countries have taken advantage of declining or containable threats to their land borders to invest in both hard and soft sea power.

Throughout the latter part of the twentieth century, the changing scen-ery of international activity at sea meant that new regulations were needed to ensure the continued protection of the freedom of the seas. The British and the USA, in particular and in turn, had always been especially keen on upholding the idea, in association with their support of free trade. President Woodrow Wilson specifically championed 'Absolute freedom of navigation upon the seas, outside territorial waters, alike in peace and war, except as the seas may be closed in whole or in part by international action for the enforcement of international covenants', as number two of his famous '14 Points'.[11]

During the Cold War, the US Navy was especially active in demonstrating its (and everyone else's) right to conduct innocent passage in waters that were deemed by the Soviet Union to be its exclusive domain. This was despite Karl Marx's 1861 doctrinal statement that, 'The sea as a general highway of all nations cannot be under the sovereignty of any power.'[12] Soviet and US warships frequently tried to ride each other off – playing brinkmanship to see who could gain the advantage within the international traffic regulations and who would back down in close quarters situations.

Nevertheless, by the late twentieth century, technological progress, security considerations and the broader interests of states resulted in adjustments to existing conventions. After several false starts, complex negotiations and extensive legal scrutiny, the United Nations Convention on the Law of the Sea (UNCLOS) was drawn up as an international agreement that was finalised after its third phase of discussions in 1982, when it replaced four previous treaties. Abbreviated as UNCLOS III and in force from 1994, the 1982 Convention established a legal framework that governs the use of the sea. More importantly, it defined and codified the rights and responsibilities of states in relation to the sea, the environment and the management of marine natural resources.

All those countries that have ratified (162 and the European Union) the Convention are subject to its provisions. A number of countries have signed, but not ratified it, including the USA, whose Senate has not yet produced the two-thirds majority necessary for ratification. However, America does generally observe and adopt the principles on which the Convention is based. Indeed, in the modern era, along with the freedom of the seas, the USA, with mostly tacit support from its allies, has robustly asserted the principle of the sea as a 'global commons'– the common heritage of mankind – enshrined in UNCLOS III and continues to do so.

Arbitration and dispute resolution have been provided over time by the International Court of Justice (ICJ), but, since 1996, disputes arising

---

[11] On 8 January 1918.
[12] K. Marx and F. Engels *Works* (2nd Edition), Volume 15 (1986).

out of the interpretation and application of the Convention have also been handled by the International Tribunal for the Law of the Sea (ITLOS) in Hamburg. Nevertheless, the UN has no enforcement role in implementing the Convention or the judgments of these courts. Organisations such as the International Maritime Organization (IMO) and the International Seabed Authority (ISA) have a share in some aspects of implementation, but the absence of a single implementation and enforcement authority limits the effectiveness of the Convention (for a discussion of global governance, see Chapter 7).

UNCLOS provisions

In broad terms, UNCLOS III divided the waters of the world into five legal regimes that are measured from a baseline, established as the low-water line on a coast, but inevitably it is the basis for any number of disputes.

- Internal waters are on the landward side of the baseline, such as small, enclosed bays, rivers or lakes. Foreign vessels may not enter these waters without the consent of the state, unless forced to do so or in an emergency.
- Territorial seas extend out to 12 nm (22 km) from the baseline within which states exercise sovereignty and jurisdiction, but with the exception that ships are allowed innocent and transit passage.
- The contiguous zone extends 24 nm (44 km) out from the baseline. Here states can exercise control that is needed to enforce laws regarding customs, fiscal, immigration and sanitation matters that affect their territory or territorial sea.
- The exclusive economic zone (EEZ) extends 200 nm (370 km) from the baseline. States can regulate activities such as the exploration, exploitation, management and conservation of natural resources in the water, seabed and subsoil. However, they may not limit the traditional high seas freedom of navigation enjoyed by all states.
- The high seas, upon which all states enjoy freedom of navigation as long as they do not interfere with the freedom of others (and subject to other international agreements, laws and conventions that prohibit the proliferation of weapons, trafficking slaves or mining of the seabed).

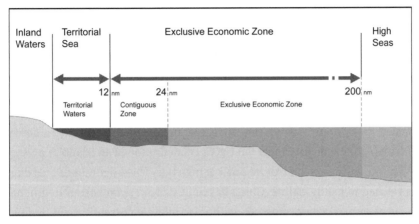

The five main zones established by UNCLOS III.

One other important provision concerns the continental shelf, which is defined as the 'natural prolongation of the land territory to the continental margin's outer edge', or 200 nm (370 km) from the coastal state's baseline, whichever is the greater. However, it may not be greater than 350 nm (650 km) from the baseline; or 100 nm (190 km) beyond the 2,500-m (8,200-ft) contour. Coastal states have the right to exploit mineral and non-living material in the subsoil of their continental shelf, to the exclusion of others. They also have exclusive rights to living resources (fish) that are 'attached' to the continental shelf, but not to those in the water column beyond the EEZ.

With regard to entitlements, UNCLOS III makes important and interesting distinctions between islands, rocks, 'low-tide elevations' (those that are uncovered at low tide) and artificial islands. They are important because zones (and their resources) can be claimed on the basis of their precise status:

- Islands are entitled to the same maritime zones as land territory.
- Rocks are only entitled to a 12 nm (22 km) territorial sea.
- Low-tide elevations are not entitled to any territorial sea of their own, but can be used as base points to measure the territorial sea if they are within 12 nm (22 km) from the mainland or an island. Reclamation does not entitle them to be islands.
- Artificial islands are entitled to no maritime zones, except for a 500 m (1,640 ft) safety zone.

Of course, definitions are everything in law. The state with sovereignty over an island has the sovereign right to explore and exploit all the living and non-living natural resources in and under the island's EEZ. If, on the other hand, a feature is only a low-tide elevation or an artificial island, the state with sovereignty does not have any right to the natural resources in or under the waters adjacent to the low-tide elevation or artificial island. Thus states, for obvious reasons, have a distinct interest in making any remotely insular-looking feature meet the UNCLOS definition of an island as a naturally formed area of land above water at high tide. These definitions are being stretched to justify claims. China has built structures on barren fragments of geology and stationed people on them to indicate possession, although in theory rocks posing as islands have to be able to 'sustain human habitation or economic life of their own'. The idea was that tiny, uninhabitable features should not justify disproportionate resource entitlements.

Claims and disputes

The article in UNCLOS III that permits states to make representations and claims to the Commission for the Limits of the Continental Shelf (CLCS), in order to qualify for the benefits of the 'prolongation' out to 350 nm (650 km), and possibly beyond, set a deadline of 13 May 2009. As a result, several countries have submitted claims to CLCS. For example, the UK has submissions in play with CLCS regarding the continental shelf limits in the Celtic Sea and Bay of Biscay (with Spain and France), Ascension Island, the Falkland Islands, South Georgia and the South Sandwich Islands and the Hatton Area near Rockall.

The Hatton Area dispute is between the UK, Ireland and Denmark and centres on a land feature called Rockall. The clue to Rockall is in its name – it is a 784-sq-m (8,442-sq-ft) stump of the core of an extinct volcano. It lies 162.7 nm (301.3 km) west of Soay in the St Kilda archipelago off the coast of Scotland. The UK judged it wise to claim the island/rock in 1955 and annexed it in 1972. In an attempt to prove it habitable, a former SAS soldier, Tom McClean, lived on Rockall for five weeks in 1985 to reinforce the UK's claim. However, in 1997, the UK ratified UNCLOS III and, despite Tom's efforts, had to give up its claim to an EEZ of 200 nm (370 km) extending onwards from the freshly 'outed' rock. Happily, as Rockall is within 200 nm

(370 km) of both St Kilda and North Uist, it remains within the EEZ of the United Kingdom and has territorial waters 12 nm (22 km) around it, with all the sovereign privileges that brings.

However, that was not the end of the international dispute. Although the Irish agreed that Rockall was part of the UK's area, they have now made a submission to CLCS with regard to the continental shelf limits, as have Denmark (on behalf of the Faroe Islands, claiming it relates to the Southern Continental Shelf of the Faroe Islands and the Faroe-Rockall Plateau), and Iceland. It seems that the recent discoveries of substantial amounts of methane hydrates below the waters around Rockall have revived proprietorial claims.

The international law of the sea is supposed to reflect the desire and need to maintain a medium that is safe and secure for commerce and human intercourse on a global scale. Unfortunately, it is not at all certain that the law will be sufficient to protect the rights and liberties 'for such as pass on the seas upon their lawful occasions' in the face of narrow political and commercial interests. This is partly because of the inadequate enforcement powers, but also because international law is not the expression of a global political will or universal rights. It is the legitimisation of states' rights and the formalisation of obligations between them. As such, although it supposedly represents consensus, in practice states jealously guard their sovereign authority and their decisions about cooperation and collaboration are based on a reasonable assessment of the balance of risk and opportunity in relation to their interests. This has implications for the enforcement of international maritime laws both on states and on illegal activity at sea. For example, it proved extremely difficult in the face of political and economic interests to eradicate slavery even after it had been declared 'a traffic repugnant to the principles of natural justice and of the enlightened age in which we live'.[13] Existing conventions and laws are routinely challenged and flouted (in the absence of enforcement authorities), and in order to gain the initiative and protect the freedom of the seas, international maritime law, as it evolves, will need to take into account the demands placed on it by commerce, warfare and conflicting interests, whether national or private.

---

[13] An additional article in the 'Extract from the definitive treaty of peace between Great Britain and France signed at Paris the 30 May 1814'.

MARITIME AND ECONOMIC GLOBALISATION

Currently, the maritime scene is generally peaceful and permissive, but contains vast tracts of ungoverned and unregulated space, where localised, seemingly intractable disputes between states and criminal and terrorist activity will persist. Overall, the international system at sea will be shaped in the near term by the economic rise and 'great power' ambitions of China, the prospect of a reviving, more assertive Russia and a more expansively minded Japan, as well as the steady accumulation of modern, sophisticated capabilities and accelerating economic output of a host of other increasingly confident states such as India, South Korea, Turkey and Brazil. This context indicates that the sea will again be the medium for a dynamic mix of alternating competition and cooperation.

Part of this picture is an interesting mirror image of the fifteenth century, with China seeking to export its manufactures and goods worldwide, in exchange for the 'tribute' of currency and raw materials. However, the one big difference in the twenty-first century is the active participation of the Americas in the international system, including the preponderant power and prosperity of the USA, which will continue to be a major consideration in calculations of relative power in the current and emerging world.

The lessons from history, and the experience of Britain, tend to emphasise the intimate connection between the economic health of a country (its economic efficiency and productivity and, in most cases, its trade by sea) and its capacity for providing the resources required for expenditure on naval power. The two are, in most cases, mutually supportive. It is axiomatic, as historian Paul Kennedy has convincingly shown,[14] that great maritime powers rely for their strength on a thriving economic base and the acknowledgement by the political establishment of the benefits of sea power. Economic vitality and maritime power used to be expressed in regional terms until the late fifteenth century; from then on, they progressively came to be associated with global opportunities and markets, as more countries became connected to the world economy through their investment in the sea.

However, the mere possession of power (in the form of either military assets or capital) is not sufficient for supremacy or market leadership; it is

14 In his *Rise and Fall of the Great Powers* (1988).

the way in which power is applied in relation to ends that deliver strategic benefit. Great powers generally cease to dominate when they no longer use their power for strategic purposes or fail to deal with challenges or threats to their status, whether commercial or military. Indeed, it seems to be the fate of dominant maritime powers that a period of armed struggle for supremacy is succeeded by hegemony and a role as guardian of the prevailing international system, until new challengers to the status quo appear. They fail to adapt as more agile, aggressive and ambitious powers seek to rise at their expense. As in business, as in warfare, when everything else is moving fast, constant adaptation and innovation are the only ways to sustain advantage. When the sources of commodities or the markets change, then so must the routes that connect them; if the hardware – the ships and infrastructure – cannot be changed overnight, then the approach and attitudes have to evolve quickly in response to changing contexts. As Charles Darwin never wrote, but perhaps, should have, 'it is not the strongest of the species that survives, nor the most intelligent that survives. It is the one that is most adaptable to change. In the struggle for survival, the fittest win out at the expense of their rivals because they succeed in adapting themselves best to their environment'.[15]

Modern trends in globalisation are being shaped by changes in energy flows and market dynamics, as well as periodic disruptions to traditional trade routes and subtle tilts in balances of power, which all continue to influence the ways in which decisions about the resourcing of sea power are made. Similarly, the operation of new trade routes, fresh technological solutions and changes in the interpretation and enforcement of international law are determining how sea power can be applied. Strategy, which defines the military capabilities, commercial priorities and partnerships required to exploit this kaleidoscopic context, has to be constantly reviewed and adjusted to reflect these changes or it becomes irrelevant. It is no place for ideological approaches or short-termism. Countries need to be prepared for the long haul and the long view, in anticipation of risks and opportunities.

---

[15] The unattributed quotation, which seems to have achieved the status of a meme among motivational speakers and business 'gurus', cannot be found in the corpus of Charles Darwin's works or recorded sayings.

CHAPTER TWO

Today's Global Super Highway

*'A modern fleet of ships does not so much make
use of the sea as exploit a highway.'*[1]

The sea has much in common with the Internet. It is an environment in which humans cannot yet live, except in a virtual or temporary sense. Both are used for global access, communication, business and trade. Those elements that pass virtually over the Internet by e-commerce pass in reality, to a large, very real and irreplaceable extent, by sea. Of course, packages of bytes move around the Internet at the speed of light (about 162,000 nautical miles/300,000 km per second), while physical packages of goods travel by sea at a more leisurely 15 m (48 ft) per second.

For centuries, the sea was regarded as a place apart – a virtual world that had its 'geeks' and specialists who understood the mysteries of the medium and how best to exploit it. One could almost say that they understood the programming rules (the winds, waves and tides) that conditioned the flow of vessels around the world. Sea warfare was as alien a concept to the general population as cyber warfare is today.

As mankind took to the oceans with more enthusiasm, the sea became a more familiar part of our cultures and societies, and countless nautical idioms have found their way into everyday English usage: 'room to swing a cat', 'a square meal', 'crossing the bar', 'shaking a leg'. Sea imagery is especially prevalent in the terminology of the Internet ('surfing' and 'navigation') and that other globalising medium, space. Space 'ships' tend to be commanded by captains (from a 'bridge'), and space fleets by admirals; their subordinates

---

[1] Joseph Conrad, *The Mirror of the Sea* (1906), Chapter XXII.

also have naval ranks. Port and starboard are frequently used, especially when spaceships are 'under helm' and people pass between 'decks'.

The sea was, and continues to be, the perpetual motion engine of globalisation; the technical complexity of the Internet is matched by the changing moods of the physical, watery worldwide web, manifested by global supply chains, trade protocols, port and harbour facilities and the vast apparatus of production and distribution. Similarly, the liquidity of the world's financial system is mirrored in the physical liquidity of the trading system that relies on the sea. It is the world's pre-eminent strategic medium (military manoeuvre space) and worldwide means of communication (oceanic transport and human contact), connecting resources and markets.

Just as the cost of moving electronic packages on the Internet is cheap, so too is the movement of real packages by sea. It varies from product to product, but is always small compared to other means of transport. For example, transport costs from China to Europe for a $700 television set would be around $10, while 15 cents would pay for a $15 kilo of coffee or a $50 bottle of Scotch whisky and a $1 can of beer costs just 1 cent. Further up the scale, the cost of transporting crude oil from the Middle East to a petrol pump in the USA or Europe is less than 1 cent per litre (0.2 gallon). A ton of iron ore from Australia to Europe by sea would cost about $10, while a 6-m (20-ft) container from Asia to Europe with 20 tons of cargo would travel for the same price as an economy class passenger by air on the same route.

Goods can, of course, also go by air when time is crucial and the value to weight ratio of the goods, including humans, is high (as was the case with sea transport in the fifteenth century). But the laws of physics and simple economics dictate why the sea is the lifeblood of trade and transportation: the average value of 1 kg (2.2 lb) of containerised cargo arriving at the Los Angeles/Long Beach port complex in 2013 was $6.34; at LAX airport it was $102.78. That is why sea trade represents about 90 per cent of global intercontinental and regional trade by volume and between 70 and 80 per cent by value.

The same is true for military hardware, whether for export or for military campaigns – if you need to get it there quickly, send it by air, as long as aircraft can carry it, or have it pre-positioned offshore; if you want to sustain a serious campaign, over time and with bulk items like armoured vehicles and ammunition, the sea is the only option. If you live on an island (or on another continent) and have to take the war to an enemy, 97 per cent of all the munitions that are used in combat have to go by sea. As such, the sea will still be required for almost all forms of serious exchange and heavy lifting for some time to come, whether for peaceful, benign or coercive purposes.

International trade and movement rely on the stability, security and shared understanding of the freedom of the seas, and an acknowledgement of them as one of the 'global commons'. The commons are usually defined as those unclaimed and ownerless natural spaces that lie beyond national or private jurisdictions, which also include the atmosphere, space, cyberspace and the electromagnetic spectrum. The expression derives from English customary law, in which the 'commons' referred to a piece of land shared in common by a community for the good of all. The 'tragedy of the commons' is an expression referring to situations in which common resources (such as fish) are overexploited or exhausted because no authority has the power or inclination to manage them in a sustainable way.

Significantly, landlocked states (11.4 per cent of the world and 6.9 per cent of the world's population) have the same rights of access to the freedom of the high seas and the global commons as those states with a coastline, even though they have no exclusive economic zones (EEZs). It has long been recognised in modern times that landlocked countries would be severely limited in their ability to trade with the rest of the world if some arrangement were not made. The 1982 United Nations Convention on the Law of the Sea (UNCLOS) made provision for landlocked countries to be able to maintain access – by river, lake, railway, road transport or on foot – to the sea through 'transit states' (those that separate them from the coast). If a landlocked state and a transit state agree, pipelines, gas lines and means of transport can also be used. It is sometimes claimed by competitors that these landlocked countries are geographically protected by natural tariff barriers, which shield them from cheap imports, but it is significant that nine of the twelve countries with the worst Human Development Index are landlocked. They would probably want a coast, and all the advantages such access would bring, if they could get one.

TRAFFIC FLOWS

No nation can be fully self-sufficient in today's interdependent world; all are in the process of selling the excess produce they have, and acquiring what they lack. While ships can, in theory, travel anywhere on the world's oceans, the most efficient means of getting from one point to another by sea have remained fairly constant for more than a hundred years. In spite of technological advances in all forms of transport, the prevailing winds, ocean currents and weather patterns, as well as the geographical configuration of the land and sea, still determine the safest and most efficient maritime trade routes, or sea lines of communication/commerce.

Ships facilitate transport goods between producers and markets along shipping routes that are determined by trade patterns, economic profitability and the most trouble-free steaming. In the past, these have been characterised by consistent trends, centred on major commodities, such as coal from Australia, southern Africa and North America to Europe and the Far East. The major routes are now predominantly defined by the flow of oil and gas to established markets in North America, Japan and Europe, as well as to India, China and Asia generally. They are supplemented by large amounts of consumer products from China and Asia passing them in the opposite direction, bound for Europe, North and South America and, increasingly, Africa. World seaborne trade figures vary, but the weight of transported goods currently stands at over 9 billion tons annually, with a current growth rate of 4.7 per cent.[2] Developing countries account for the largest share of global seaborne trade: 60 per cent of goods loaded and 56 per cent of goods unloaded.

The trade and economic health of the world depend on free flow through a limited number of so-called 'choke points'. These are locations where shipping is constrained either by geographical features, like narrow straits or canals, or by a high volume of traffic, again much like choke points on the Internet, which occur where the sheer volume of traffic exceeds the carrying capacity of the bearers through which content, especially high-grade video, is transferred.[3]

In the real world, 80 per cent of marine traffic passes through eight major choke points. These are: the Strait of Hormuz, between Oman and

---

[2] United Nations Conference on Trade and Development (UNCTAD), '*Review of Maritime Transport 2013*'.

[3] These choke points are where the networks that comprise the Internet are physically connected, such as Verizon's facility in Miami, which is a physical junction for more than 200 networks, and Google's 8th Avenue New York, which introduces hundreds more networks to each other.

Iran at the entrance to the Gulf; the Strait of Malacca, between Malaysia and Indonesia; the Bab-el-Mandeb passage from the Arabian Sea to the Red Sea; the Panama Canal, connecting the Pacific and Atlantic Oceans; the Suez Canal, connecting the Red Sea and Mediterranean Sea; the Turkish Straits/Bosporus, linking the Black Sea (and oil coming from the Caspian Sea region) to the Mediterranean; the Strait of Gibraltar (Gibraltar); and Cape Horn and the Cape of Good Hope.[4] These are the enduring choke points, but others can rise to prominence by virtue of their position astride trade routes that are important in relation to a particular time and context. No one would doubt the importance of the English Channel as a key choke point, or the entrance into and out of the Baltic. In the future, possibly the Northern Sea Route and the Northwest Passage (see Chapter 5) will become significant choke points depending on the nature of the traffic that passes along them.

The world's economy today depends on stable trade routes through the Indian Ocean. In 2012, some 19,800 ships passed through the Suez Canal. More than half of the world's annual merchant fleet tonnage transits the Strait of Malacca, the Sunda Strait and the Lombok Strait, with the major-ity continuing on into the South China Sea. Tanker traffic out of the Strait of Hormuz through to the Strait of Malacca leading into the South China Sea is more than three times greater than Suez Canal traffic, and well over five times greater than that of the Panama Canal. Major trading countries – China, Japan, Singapore, India and South Korea – are heavily reliant on these routes for energy and raw materials. More than 80 per cent of China's oil imports transit the area. Loose talk and threats about the closure of vital seaways, such as the Strait of Hormuz or the Suez Canal, or pirate attacks on ships in the Indian Ocean, have immediate and unpredictable effects on the commodity and energy markets. Chinese attempts to assert jurisdiction over the South China Sea are a direct result of a desire to control not only strategic, but also economic access to East Asia.

For all users of the sea, the tautly connected character of global trade and the 'just enough, just in time' mentality that underpins modern supply chain efficiencies have resulted in a system that is fragile and vulnerable to

---

[4] The size of merchant ships is limited by whether they can squeeze through the Panama and Suez canals or through the Malacca Strait – the so-called Malaccamax size constrains a ship to dimensions of 470 m (1,540 ft) in length and 60 m (200 ft) wide.

disruption. It is prone to abrupt and unanticipated shocks, such as extreme weather events, geopolitical instability, pirates and states implicitly or explicitly threatening to deny the use of major shipping straits or routes, such as the Strait of Hormuz. The persistent survival, and rude health, of the territorial state, even in the face of powerful multinational entities and companies, internationalist sentiments and the erosion of borders, both real and imagined, is another complicating factor for maritime commercial and military operations. As the state has survived, so has its primary responsibility for deterring and defeating threats to its sovereignty and security, as well as protecting and promoting its interests. Here, it retains substantial power, in relation to external opponents and to its citizens, and for intervening along the super highway of the sea.

CONTAINERS

The advantage of what are known as 'intermodal'[5] freight containers lies in their suitability for transporting products and raw materials by sea, rail and road around the world, minimising transfer times between types of vehicle. There are approximately 17 million such containers in use globally. Their standard size is 6 m (20 ft) long and 2.5 m (8 ft) wide. The twenty-foot equivalent unit (TEU) is the unit of cargo capacity often used to describe the capacity of container ships and terminals.

Prior to containers, freight had been carried by sea in either loose freight or wooden crates, which required loading and unloading by large numbers of dockside workers or stevedores. The process was subject to the vagaries of berthing arrangements, labour disputes and widespread crime and corruption. Ships could spend more time alongside waiting to load or unload than at sea, with goods unable to move to or from their ports because of the need to wait for suitable transport. In response to his frustrations at the overhead costs and delays, Malcolm P. McLean, an American trucking entrepreneur, invented the container in 1956, which became one of the transforming innovations and critical enablers of globalisation at sea.

When the first containers were introduced, the throughput costs of

---

[5] 'Intermodal' refers to standardised facilities or objects that can be used on any form of transport: sea, rail, road and air.

loading and unloading fell from $5.83 per ton to $0.16 per ton, while theft and insurance rates also diminished. More importantly, the amount of commodities or inventory tied up in ports and warehouses reduced drastically – in effect, transferring the warehousing from the land to ships at sea and in transit. Increasing mechanisation of the process also enabled the rapid transfer of goods at a shrinking number of key hub ports.

It has been calculated that containerisation caused a 790 per cent increase in volume of bilateral trade among the leading twenty-two industrialised countries over twenty years, more than all the free trade agreements combined. As such, the use of containers has increased the volume and flow of traffic on the seas – much like the online move from dial-up to broadband. Ports have grown in size, if not in number, and the costs of trading have reduced markedly across a wide range of products and commodities. 'Just enough and just in time' processes have reduced inventory costs and allowed producers to be more responsive to customer requirements. The container and its associated infrastructure also led to the achievement of low entry costs for newcomers to global markets: rather than having to develop complete industries from scratch, they could simply join and exploit existing supply chains. China, India and other rising economies have clearly benefited from the rise to world domination of the container, and it is perhaps no coincidence that the most successful modern manufacturers of dockside container-handling equipment and systems are Chinese.

Containerisation has completely transformed the way in which cargo is loaded and unloaded in ports, and also the character and livelihoods of the ports themselves. London, Liverpool and San Francisco are classic examples of how traditional ports declined once the need for extensive wharves and segmented warehousing disappeared. Containers underpinned the corresponding rise of Felixstowe and Rotterdam, as well as new facilities in China, to handle the huge trade boom in manufactured and consumer goods associated with the last twenty-five years.

Broadly speaking, ports inland on estuaries and rivers and subject to tidal restrictions are not able to take increasingly deep draft ships. This puts them at a significant disadvantage in the lean world of modern commerce. Little wonder that DP World chose to build its newest port (London Gateway) in the UK at the mouth of the Thames estuary, opposite the Dutch coast. With intermodal containers, the task of breaking down and packing containers can be performed far from the port. Dockers and longshoremen, twenty to twenty-five of whom were once needed to load and unload an average cargo ship, are no longer required.

Improved cargo security is another important benefit of containerisation. Cargo is not visible to the casual viewer and is less likely to be identified for theft; container doors are usually sealed so that tampering is more evident. Some containers are fitted with electronic monitoring devices and can be remotely monitored for changes in air pressure, which happens when the doors are opened. This has effectively reduced the mass theft and overheads that had long plagued the shipping industry.

Approximately 90 per cent of non-bulk cargo worldwide is transported by container and, as a class, container ships now rival crude oil tankers and bulk carriers as the largest commercial vessels, along with cruise liners. A. P. Møller–Maersk is the leading container shipping company, transporting more than 2.6 million TEUs a year (15.9 per cent of global market share). At any one time, there are 5–6 million shipping containers in transit across the world's oceans. It appears that they fall overboard at regular intervals: a protest group claims that this happens at a rate of one every hour, on average (10,000 a year). The shipping industry estimates roughly one every five hours (2,000 a year). On balance – if you will pardon the pun – the proportion of lost containers is not very high.

UNDERWATER CABLES

We have seen that 95 per cent of the world's tradable goods by volume are transported by sea. Coincidentally, over 95 per cent of Internet traffic and communications travels along the 232 (and counting) undersea cables that cross the world's connected seabed.

The Internet can also be accessed at sea by using geostationary telecommunications satellites in orbit at a height of 35,000 km (22,000 miles). Taking advantage of this (largely) assured access, military satellite communications provide a high-volume, fast, reliable and secure means of access to the full range of web and Internet-based products. It is possible to command and control forces at every level, either on exercise or in combat, using only satellite-enabled secure communications, without the risk of interception by opponents that is always implicit in the use of terrestrially based radio and data communications. Nevertheless, satellite time is expensive and sometimes the bandwidth[6] and positioning of individual satellites do not allow continuous access and global coverage, especially near the North and South Poles.

Also, submarine cables are able to convey terabits per second, while satellites, having gigabit levels of capacity, can scarcely manage megabits per second, along with significantly greater delays and latency. A message or data package sent across the Atlantic takes about eight times longer to arrive by satellite and it would cost substantially more to send it. Non-satellite Internet traffic passes along cables contained in tubes that are laid on land and, mostly, at sea to link up myriad servers, multiple nodes and exponentially growing numbers of users. The reliability of submarine cables is extremely good and, just like the Internet itself, alternative routeing paths can be used in the event of a break or malfunction in a cable.

Heralding and enabling the modern burst of globalisation between 1870 and 1914, the first transatlantic cables were laid in the 1860s. Messages were transmitted at six to eight words per minute and were charged at $5 a word – in 1866 dollars, equating to $73 dollars a word in 2014. By 1900, there were ten Atlantic cables, with two more being laid, and the first cables were starting to be positioned across the Pacific. Thirty-six cable ships were used to lay the new cables and maintain the 210,000 km (130,000 miles) of cable already laid.

Submarine cables allowed shipowners and companies to communicate with their ships and suppliers on a regular basis. This enabled significant efficiencies to be introduced in the selection of cargoes, changes in programme and the dispatch of commodities and goods on the basis of more sensitive price and supply information. It was the start of what we would now call supply chain management. Cables were also critical to the administration of the British Empire and the flexible direction of its military and naval forces.

The first transatlantic telephone cable connection (TAT-1) went into service in 1956, with thirty-two channels and two cables (one for eastbound

---

[6] Bandwidth is the range (band) of frequencies that an electronic signal can use within a particular transmission medium. A human voice covers about 3 Khz, while a satellite signal might exploit anything between 3.7 and 300 Ghz.

traffic, the other for westbound). A call cost £3 for three minutes, or £1 a minute at the time, which would represent about £12 ($20) a minute in today's money. TAT-8, the first fibre-optic cable across the Atlantic, was introduced in 1988 (retired in 2002) to provide 40,000 telephone channels. The introduction of optical amplifiers in 1994 allowed the capacity on a single cable to rise to the equivalent of 60 million phone calls.

As of 2014, there are twenty-six cables across the Atlantic, largely the result of the massive investment in digital technologies (resembling the railway mania in the UK in the nineteenth century), associated with the dot.com boom and bubble of the late 1990s. Across the world, underwater cables total 885,000 km (550,000 miles) in length, and have transfer speeds of between 40 gigabits per second (Gbps) and 10 terabits per second (Tbps). The data capacity of a single cable has in effect been increased 80,000 times in less than twenty years. The two busiest Internet hubs are New York City and London, with nine cables linking them. Antarctica is the only continent yet to be reached by a submarine telecommunications cable, owing partly to significant temperature and topographical challenges, but also because there is little economic incentive. All traffic there is relayed by satellite or long-haul radio.

A submarine cable is anywhere between 2 cm (0.75 in) and 6.5 cm (2.5 in) thick, and the armoured sections close to shore have two layers of galvanised wire, a copper sheath and an outside layer of polyethylene insulation to protect the fibre-optic core. They also carry thousands of volts of power and speeds reach between 40 and 60 micro-seconds for a round trip of about 16,000 km (10,000 miles). Each fibre-optic cable is just the width of a human hair, but 3.2 Tb of data pass along every second, each element taking 0.00072 seconds to complete a 6,600-nm (12,200-km) return trip – about a million times faster than the average broadband speed for UK households of 3.6 megabits per second (Mbps).

Owned by Cable & Wireless Worldwide and Alcatel-Lucent, Apollo is the most advanced transatlantic submarine fibre-optic cable system in the world, running from London to New York and from Paris to Washington DC. It has the highest-capacity and highest-speed system on the Atlantic route. Extremely powerful lasers at either end of its cable, one in the UK and the other in New York, accelerate the optical signal along the fibre-optic lines. As no light source can sustain its intensity over thousands of kilometres, electrical repeaters costing £1 million each and powered by a 10,000 volt current in the cable are attached to the cable on the seabed at 50-km (30-mile) intervals, to amplify the signal. The cable handles the equivalent data transfer of 200 million phone calls. It is anticipated that by 2014 the cable system will suffer from significant overloading across the Atlantic, meaning that re-routing will be limited to the capacity available in other cables.[7]

The 232 undersea fibre-optic cables that link the world's telecommunications are largely unprotected and only occasionally monitored, in the physical sense, although they are continuously tested for integrity by electronic means. It is also necessary to take care that these cables are laid carefully to ensure that they are not stretched taut between the peaks and troughs of the ocean floor and become vulnerable to fracture. Despite being armoured and buried just under the seabed close to shore and boldly delineated in navigational charts and publications, cables are damaged by accidents – about ninety times a year – caused by ships dragging their anchors, fishing and extreme events, such as earthquakes. The Fukushima earthquake triggered several underwater landslides, which covered nearby cables with hundreds of metres of rocks and sediment, while the 2006 earthquake in Taiwan damaged several cables that provided communication to Hong Kong, South East Asia and China. Other recent incidents have seen India, the Middle East and Asia disconnected after accidental damage to cables from ships' anchors. Cables are also vulnerable to sabotage and other damage, either by accident or design. A severed cable off the coast of Alexandria in 2008 left Egypt, India, Pakistan and Kuwait without Internet communications, and a recent deliberate or accidental cutting by divers of the undersea cables off Alexandria caused a 60 per cent fall in Internet speeds and led to outages in several East African countries. Cuts on 27 March 2013 to three cables that provided connections between numerous countries in different continents, for example, India and Europe, caused a 21 per cent loss of service.

These incidents highlight the vulnerability of individual undersea communications cables to accidental and deliberate damage. Each cable costs in the order of hundreds of millions of dollars and takes about eighteen months to lay; this level of investment, combined with the strategic importance of

---

[7] The combined capacity of all trans-Atlantic cables is nearly 40 Tbps, but this is likely to be challenged by demand that is projected to rise by 33 per cent per year until 2018.

undersea cables, has led to some states – including Australia – imposing protection zones prohibiting certain types of activity in their vicinity.

Ultimately, the cables cannot be kept under constant surveillance and they are vulnerable to terrorist and criminal activity, except in the vicinity of where cables come ashore near the landing station. Anyone can find out their locations just by looking at a chart. Some telecoms companies and maritime authorities use radar tracking systems to monitor the area in the vicinity of cables, and vessels are warned if they approach too closely. Unfortunately, this also helps those seeking the exact location of cables. In places like Egypt, the Internet is especially vulnerable because of the cluster of fourteen cables connected to both Alexandria and Cairo, eight of which come ashore at Alexandria. These in turn serve as a hub for several other countries in the area, a virtual version of a geographic choke point.

Specialist maintenance and repair ships are permanently on standby to deal with cable breaks and routine malfunctions. A typical specialist ship deals with about thirty repairs a year, with each activation costing about $1 million dollars. It uses remotely operated vehicles (ROVs), down to depths of about 6,000 m (20,000 ft), to survey, cut and repair damaged sections identified by diagnostic software. Beyond that depth, the damaged cable section (or broken ends) has to be hauled up by crane onto the ship and up to 192 fibres rejoined. During the course of the break and repair, traffic is re-routed onto other cables.

Underwater cables have tempted intelligence-gathering organisations since the late nineteenth century. At the beginning of wars, countries have cut the cables of their opponents to redirect the information flow into cables that were being monitored. Britain's experience with cables in the First World War is an interesting indication of what might happen in the event of major war in the twenty-first century, both with the Internet and with existing fibre-optic cables. British officials were concerned that in time of war telegraph lines passing through non-British territory were insecure and could be cut, so not only was a dedicated imperial network, the 'All Red Line', set up, but also plans were made to sever potential enemy cables. In the event, the British managed to cut all five cables that linked Germany with France, Spain and the Azores, and, by extension, North America, using the cable ship, *Alert*. They were never repaired because of the British block-ade of Germany, and the Germans had to rely on wireless communication, presenting opportunities for British intelligence, based on 'Room 40', to intercept. Britain retained uninterrupted, secure coverage throughout.

During the Cold War, the US Navy and the National Security Agency (NSA) succeeded in placing interception devices on Soviet underwater communication lines. There were several attempts by both the USA and the Soviet Union to pull up and exploit traditional analogue underwater cables, but systematic exploitation has required – and still requires – the services of advanced digital processes, convenient access points and substantial computing power. This intercept activity is still going on; we know for certain, thanks to NSA whistle-blower Edward Snowden, that these cables are still subject to the prying eyes and ears of intelligence and security agencies.

In the future, it is likely that undersea cables will be targets for terrorists and criminals, seeking to disrupt global business and gain propaganda value on the one hand or operating extortion or protection rackets on the other. They will also be vulnerable to potentially hostile states, which have the technology to locate, sever and interfere with cables, for either denial of service or manipulation. However, the tactics of both state and irregular forces will be tempered by the knowledge that their own operations and activities rely on the use of the Internet and its associate services to a greater or lesser extent.

SHIPPING

Modern shipping is highly specialised, reflecting economies of scale and changes in infrastructural facilities development, technological development and the needs of high-volume exchange.

The main types of shipping today are:

- Tankers – crude oil, petroleum products, chemicals, liquefied natural gas (LNG) and other liquids (including wine and fruit juice).
- Bulk carriers – minerals, ores, coal and agricultural produce, as well as vehicles, arms transfers and machinery.
- Refrigerated vessels (reefers) – perishable items, especially food.
- General cargo ships – mixed loads and for the regional transport of goods.
- Container ships – general cargo on long-haul routes with their distinctive boxes.

- Ferries and liners for recreational and short-haul passenger services.
- Roll-on roll-off (Ro-Ro) ships – with articulated, container-cargo-carrying lorries for short-haul routes.
- Various specialist vessels – oil and gas support, fish factory and cable repair ships and a wide range of other working craft.

A country's merchant navy comprises its commercial and trading ships and their crews. However, the strength of a merchant fleet is difficult to ascertain at any one time owing to variations in registry and ownership. Foreign-owned ships fly the flag of one country but belong to owners in another, while registered ships belong to owners in one country but fly the flag of another. Confused? For all sorts of cost reduction, tax minimisation and other good commercial reasons, you are meant to be.

Ship registries

In order to travel or trade across international borders, international law requires that every merchant ship has to be registered in a country, which is familiarly known as its 'flag state'. The ship is bound by the law of its flag state and is subject to regular inspections of its equipment, crew, safety provision and pollution prevention arrangements. Countries that only register their own ships are called national or 'closed' registries; those that admit foreign-owned ships are known as 'open' registries.

The general principle is that there must be a 'genuine link' between a ship's owners and its flag state – the state must effectively exercise its jurisdiction and control in administrative, technical and social matters over ships flying its flag. This principle was set out by UNCLOS in 1982 and taken forward in 1986, when the United Nations Conference on Trade and Development (UNCTAD) attempted to reinforce it in the United Nations Convention for Registration of Ships. This would require that flag states be linked to its ships either by having an economic stake in the ownership of its ships or by providing seafarers to crew the ships. To come into force, the 1986 treaty requires forty signatories, but, so far, only fourteen countries have signed the treaty.

The increasing spread of 'open' registries has allowed shipping companies to combine relatively low capital costs in industrial countries with low labour costs for seafarers from developing countries like the Philippines. By changing to an open registry, shipowners can avoid very costly regulations such as national labour, standardisation and employment laws. It is hardly surprising, therefore, that the top ten open and international registries account for about half of the global merchant fleet. In 1950, this figure was only 5 per cent. The largest shipping registries are Panama, Liberia, Greece, the Marshall Islands and the Bahamas. Registries are linked to flags of convenience (FOCs), which are flown by ships that are registered in one country and owned in another.

The UK merchant marine is a case in point, in terms of ownership and the use of FOCs. In 2010, it had 504 ships. However, when the foreign-owned ships were added there are 271 more and an additional 308 that are registered in other countries. Meanwhile, as of 2014, China's merchant marine totalled around 2,030, with 22 foreign-owned and 1,559 registered in other countries (including 500 in Hong Kong).

So by registration and gross tonnage (GT),[8] the countries with the biggest fleets are Panama (201,264,453), Liberia (106,708,344), the Marshall Islands (62,011,182), Hong Kong (55,543,246) and the Bahamas (50,369,836). Of course, if Hong Kong is added to China (34,705,141), the total propels them together into third place. The UK and the USA weigh in at numbers 13 (16,477,909) and 17 (11,941,087) respectively.

When considered from the countries where the owners are based, the perspective changes: again in gross tonnage, it is Japan (131,955,001), Greece (118,089,051), Germany (85,371,604), China (67,156,101) and the USA (42,982,683). Once again, China and Hong Kong (23,427,839) together would reach third place, while the UK (40,700,626) is sixth and Denmark (26,445,159) ninth.

The problem with FOCs is that some countries' registries demand only minimal safety and environmental standards and safeguards. Inspection and training regimes are significantly less rigorous, and ships that register with FOCs only have to comply with the international conventions that have been ratified by the state of registry. Flag states are supposed to adopt the regulations issued by agencies such as the International Maritime Organization

---

[8] Gross tonnage (GT): internal measurement of a ship's open spaces, according to a set formula in the IMO Tonnage Convention.

(IMO) and the International Labour Organization (ILO) by ratifying individual treaties, but often do not ratify or enforce them, either through policy
or lack of resources. These loopholes mean that a range of conventions can
be ignored or imperfectly enforced in ships flying a FOC.

In turn, the situation allows an owner to take advantage of cheaper registration fees, low or non-existent tax regimes and the ability to employ crews
on low pay, long working hours and with poorer working and living conditions. There are about 1.5 million seafarers, with widely varying conditions
of service, pay and health and safety provision. In particular, the income
and welfare packages available to seafarers show a marked disparity, with
some seafarers working in conditions equivalent to bonded labour as victims of people trafficking. On average, in 2012, for example, Filipino and
Chinese able seamen earned between 7 and 10 per cent of the wages of their
US equivalents. In August 2013, ILO's Maritime Labour Convention was
introduced. If enforced, it should lead to higher standards of engagement
and employment, as well as improvements in living conditions, welfare
provision and legal protection. It is likely to lead to a narrowing of the gap
between employment offerings in developed and developing countries, as
well as removing the competitive advantage from unscrupulous owners and
operators.

Not surprisingly, FOC ships have been associated with some notable
marine environmental disasters, such as the Maltese-flagged MV *Erika*, the
Bahamian-flagged MV *Prestige*, and the Liberian-flagged MV *Amoco Cadiz*
and MV *Sea Empress*. FOCs have also been engaged in criminal activity,
drugs trafficking, illegal, unreported and unregulated fishing (IUU), people
smuggling and the evasion of UN sanctions.

However, in an increasingly fierce competitive shipping market, each
new FOC is forced to promote itself by offering the lowest possible fees and
the minimum of regulation. In the same way, shipowners are tempted to
look for the cheapest and least regulated ways of running their vessels in
order to compete, and FOCs provide the solution. For over forty years, the
cruise ship company Carnival registered its cruise ships in Panama. In 2011,
the *New York Times*[9] reported that this manoeuvre resulted in the avoidance

---

[9] David Leonhardt, 'The Paradox of Corporate Taxes in America', www.nytimes.com,
1 February 2011.

of some $10 billion in taxes. Until it registered in Delaware recently, it had paid only 1.1 per cent of its cumulative $11.3 billion profit in tax in the previous five years. Significantly, some 60 per cent of cruise ships are registered in Panama, Liberia and the Bahamas.

Ratifying states have formed various organisations to monitor, inspect and audit ships flying FOCs when operating within their jurisdictions. The Paris Memorandum of Understanding on Port State Control (Paris MOU) was established in 1982, setting port state control standards for working conditions for twenty-six European countries and Canada. Similar MOUs exist in other regions around the world; some publish black, white and grey lists of flag states, based on the shortcomings, defects and detentions of ships; others maintain a list of poorly performing flag states.

Of course, flag states like Panama, the Marshall Islands and Liberia can only thrive in benign environments guaranteed by major powers like the USA and the European states; they are less viable in a more disordered region or world, from an insurance or risk point of view. When flag states are unable to mobilise protection and security, they are distinctly vulnerable. During the 1980–88 Iran–Iraq War, for example, many vessels were reflagged to the USA.

Increasing sizes

Worldwide, at the end of 2012, the total tonnage[10] of ships with a capacity above 100 GT reached 1.09 billion GT, spread around 86,300 ships. The heaviest ships by tonnage are the four TI-class ultra-large crude carriers (owned by a pooling company, Tankers International), weighing in at 234,006 GT and 441,585 deadweight tonnage (DWT).[11] They can carry 3.2 million barrels of oil. Only two remain mobile, but cannot squeeze through even the new Panama Canal locks; the other two are now used as floating storage and offload vessels, off Qatar.

---

[10] Tonnage is the amount of cargo a ship can carry, originating from the tax paid on *tuns* or casks of wine or other merchandise.

[11] Deadweight tonnage (DWT) is how much weight a ship is carrying or can safely carry, comprising the total weight of cargo, fuel, fresh water, ballast, stores, passengers and crew. It is mostly simply expressed as the weight that would load a ship to its Plimsoll line, although might indicate the notional tonnage of a ship not loaded to capacity for other reasons.

The world's largest ship ever built when combining deadweight tonnage (564,765 DWT), gross tonnage (261,000 GT) and length (458.45 m/1,504 ft) was a tanker called *Seawise Giant*. She could not pass through the English Channel, the Suez Canal or the Panama Canal. Seriously damaged in the Strait of Hormuz in the Iran–Iraq War, she was repaired and appropriately renamed the *Happy Giant*, and then the *Jahre Viking, Knock Nevis* and finally *Mont*. She became a static floating storage and offload vessel until 2010 when she was broken up in India. The cruise industry is also deploying some monster ships, most of which are operated by Royal Caribbean International. The biggest, and second only to the TI class in terms of gross tonnage, is Royal Caribbean's *Allure of the Seas*, at more than 225,000 GT.

In the future, the need for coal, iron ore and other commodities is likely to push the size of ships upwards. Brazil is seeking to acquire six ultra-large ore carriers, of 400,000 DWT each. A 600,000 DWT design for a very large ore carrier is being considered in China for use between South America and China. One can also confidently expect the current fashion for leisure at sea, especially on board large cruising ships, to continue to expand. Some ships whose proportions approach the size of floating artificial islands are likely to make their appearance as cruise companies and tourists seek to combine the advantages of contained environments, in which all facilities, including suitable weather and amenities, are provided in one place. Some of these vessels are likely to assume the character and scale of theme parks, operating close offshore, remaining largely static or moored and moving only to seek agreeable weather or environmental conditions, or in support of major sporting and prestige events.

Shipping lines

In the roller-coaster world of shipping, the Danes are the understated, high-achieving denizens of the marine industry, with several successful shipping lines and maritime enterprises. The largest shipping company in the world is A. P. Møller–Maersk, based in Copenhagen. It employs more than 120,000 people and sits comfortably at around the 100 mark in the Fortune Global 500. Maersk Logistics provides supply chain management, intermodal freight transport and retail outlets, and other subsidiaries are engaged in activities such as shipbuilding, offshore oil and gas exploitation.

Competition is particularly intense in the container shipping business, with the top twenty companies representing the bulk of global capacity. Maersk Line is the biggest and leads the way owing to its ability to call on the strategic resources of its parent group and the speed with which it translates innovation into operation. It demonstrates the value of a diversified approach to the marine sector, with investment being allocated to the most profitable and least loss-leading elements, when crisis or falling margins strikes a particular section of the business.

The backbone of its fleet has been – and for now continues to be – ships like the *Maersk Eleanora*, which were specifically designed and built to work the routes between Asia and Europe. The ship is indicative of the way in which shipping companies are investing in ever larger, more fuel-efficient and lean-manned ships to reduce the costs per container per nautical mile and remain competitive. It is simply a question of economies of scale. In the case of the *Maersk Eleanora*, that means a propulsion system that delivers an average speed of 17 knots at a rate of 3 grams per nautical mile. The crew is anything between thirteen and twenty, relying on high levels of remote sensing and automation to control the ship, monitor its performance and manage its systems.

Staying competitive is particularly important in the face of falling demand or cut-throat competition, indicated by two long-term trends: the slowing of offshoring and outsourcing of manufacturing to countries in Asia and the fact that there are few goods that do not already go by container. The situation was exacerbated by the volatility and falling demand of the Asia–Europe route, which saw break-even levels at $1,200 per TEU fall to $400 at one stage in 2011–12. Agile companies had to lower operating costs by using less fuel at slower speeds and cheaper routes (shorter, with reduced port and canal fees).

As might be expected, Maersk Line responded aggressively, with extensive cost cutting and a shift in emphasis from shipping to oil, drilling rigs and ports, in an attempt to increase margins. Then, at the height of the crisis (early 2011), the company placed a $3.7 billion order for twenty new Triple-E-class ships capable of carrying an unprecedented 18,000 TEUs, to work the routes between Asia and Europe. The first ten of what are the longest ships in the world were delivered in 2013 (and into 2014); and another ten will be delivered in 2014 and 2015. They are designed to capitalise on

The maiden voyage of the *McKinney-Møller*, the lead ship of Maersk's Triple E class vessels, with the largest cargo capacity at 18,270 TEU (2014).

economies of scale, more streamlined ways of operating and cleaner energy use. It is claimed that the Triple-Es will emit 20 per cent less carbon dioxide than the *Emma Maersk* (previously the largest container vessel in the world) and 50 per cent less than the average emissions per container on the Asia–Europe routes. It means that Maersk Line will have achieved its 2020 target of reducing its fleet-wide CO_2 emissions by 25 per cent from its benchmark 2007 levels. It now aims to reduce emissions by 40 per cent by 2020.

As a sign of the times, other companies have followed suit: Seaspan ordered five 14,000-TEU container ships from Hyundai Heavy Industries, to begin operation in the second half of 2015, at a cost of $550 million; the Chinese shipping company CSCL has commissioned even larger ships from Hyundai in South Korea, with a capacity of 18,400 TEUs, which is 400 TEUs more than the Triple-E ships, though they will be 40 cm (16 in) narrower. They will also be cheaper, at $135 million each, rather than $190 million for the Triple-E ships, which will be the most advanced in the world.

In June 2013, the three largest container ship groups – Maersk Line,

Mediterranean Shipping Company and CMA CGM – formed an operational alliance (the P3 Network) to dominate the Asia–Europe, trans-Pacific and transatlantic routes. As long as it is not deemed anti-competitive under European law, the consortium will start operating together in 2014 with 255 vessels and 2.6 million TEUs. All vessels will continue to be owned by the individual lines, but the companies will set up a joint vessel operating centre and offer customers more frequent services with, for instance, eight weekly sailings between Asia and northern Europe and more direct ports of call.

The oceanic shipping industry is tough and acutely sensitive to the vagaries and variability of the global economic system. As elsewhere at sea, activity is characterised by alternating competition and cooperation, on the basis of compete when you can, cooperate when you must. Maersk is a classic example of how to compete successfully in a cutthroat shipping market. It is anticipated that, in the future, China will mirror Maersk's strategy, both in lowering operating costs and in switching resources between marine business areas (facilitated by the networks of state-controlled banks and companies across the whole marine sector), in order to increase the country's market share and price its rivals out of business.

Emerging trends will affect the requirement and pattern of shipping during the coming decades. The discovery and widespread exploitation of shale and unconventional sources of energy are likely to alter the patterns of shipping around the world, while the increased use of pipelines will offer both strategic and commercial flexibility in terms of risk and price. The greater use of rail and road links within regional markets will also result in less movement by sea. More broadly, local re-shoring and novel manufacturing processes, including the commercialisation of 3D printing and nanotechnology, will alter the way in which trade is conducted around the world. In all cases, though, the vast bulk of goods and commodities will continue to travel by sea between continents, and on inland and in coastal waters when it is more economical or effective to do so.

PORTS

On a computer, a port is associated with an IP address of the host and it allows the computer a single physical connection point to connect with a variety of different applications or processes. Similarly, maritime ports act as hubs that enable access to a wide variety of goods and commodities, allowing them to be distributed within a particular country or trans-shipped to other ports. The most successful are highly specialised, as well as being technologically enabled and organisationally efficient hubs that are priori- tised to handle vast amounts of cargoes, goods and commodities at a very high rate of transfer.

Shipping routes and the activity at ports sensitively reflect the patterns of global trade and consumption and are reliable barometers of change. US ports, for example, have benefited from a dramatic 38 per cent rise in exports since 2009, reflecting largely the demands and growing expectations of the emerging and developing world, especially for agricultural products and vehicles. Domestic oil and gas production has also markedly reduced imports of hydrocarbons to America. In future years, the trade balance will shift further as LNG is exported in increasing volumes from North America to Asia, which currently consumes 63 per cent of all global LNG production.

The strength and economic value of a port is its ability in the shortest time and with the least cost to distribute imports by road and rail within its own country or region and accumulate exports for markets abroad. It is the total cost of the route from the manufacturer or producer to the cus- tomer, not the individual legs of the journey, that determines whether ports thrive or not. Thus, the expansion of the Panama Canal to enable it to take vessels up to 13,000 TEUs (currently 4,400) from 2015 will mean that the East Coast of the USA and the Gulf of Mexico will be able to benefit from faster sailing times to and from Asia and exploit increased direct access to US domestic markets on and near the East Coast, once they have upgraded their facilities to handle bigger ships. This trade will benefit particularly from the rapidly expanding production and shipment of unconventional oil and gas. Meanwhile, trans-shipment ports, such as Singapore, make their living as hubs that quickly handle frequent intercontinental trade, which is then distributed widely within their regions (in this case, the Asia-Pacific) to ports that cannot easily handle extremely high volume container and freight traffic.

The current trend, to match the growth in the size of ships and inter- national trade, is to build larger ports from new and extend the facilities of existing ports. The most extensive, most active port in the world is Shanghai, right in the middle of China's 18,000-km (11,200-mile) long coastline. It handles around 32 million TEUs of containers a year, dispatches 2,000 container ships every month and handles 25 per cent of China's foreign trade. Based on TEUs, the runners-up are Ningbo-Zhoushan (also in China), Singapore, Rotterdam and Tianjin, once again in China. In fact, six of the world's ten busiest container ports are in China. Ranked by container-handling activity, the order becomes Shanghai, Singapore, Hong Kong, Shenzhen and Busan (South Korea).

New modern ports are being built connecting producers with consumers. The United Arab Emirates (UAE) has built a huge facility in Jebel Ali, known as the Dubai Logistics City, designed to compete successfully with the likes of Rotterdam, Shanghai and Singapore. Oman hopes that the huge intermodal complex at Al-Duqm (halfway along its east coast) will act as the leading entrepôt of Arabia and transform the local area. In November 2013, London Gateway, a modern deep-sea container terminal and Europe's largest logistics complex, opened for business at the mouth of the River Thames. It was built and is owned by DP World. Along with Felixstowe and Southampton, it is one of the few UK ports capable of taking the largest container ships, which represent 40 per cent of UK trade with Asia, and adds an additional 3.5 million TEUs to the UK's port capacity. It will not only provide freight forwarding and warehousing facilities, but also operate as an intermodal distribution hub. The future success of Jebel Ali, Al-Duqm and London Gateway will lie in their ability to service an entire region, not just the hinterland of their respective countries.

Other developments typical of the new type of port include Colombo and Hambantota in Sri Lanka, both being developed by the Chinese to access the Indian market. The two ports form part of the so-called 'string of pearls' extending Chinese influence and footprint into the Indian Ocean and beyond. They also include Gwadar and Karachi in Pakistan, a container terminal in Chittagong (Bangladesh) and port facilities in Myanmar (Burma). Overtures have also been made to the Seychelles, Mauritius and several other regional countries.

In March 2013, China also began the $10 billion construction of a new port at Bagamoyo, Tanzania, which will be completed in 2017. It will be the largest port in Africa, handling 20 million containers annually, and will be the gateway to a region that includes landlocked countries like Malawi, Zambia, Democratic Republic of the Congo, Burundi, Rwanda and Uganda.

It and other ports acquired in Egypt and West Africa will serve as conduits for the export of Chinese manufactured goods to Africa and the trans-shipment of raw materials and natural resources from Africa to China. The port development will be accompanied by investment in the connecting transport and distribution infrastructure.

Overall, South East Asia and Africa are continuing to attract Chinese suitors on the back of a trend that seems to suggest that the world will be largely connected by a global network of super-ports able to take the largest ships that squeeze through the various canals and choke points on the various routes.

Ports of the future, if they are not major regional entrepôts or primary trans-shipment hubs, will need to be able to specialise (to maximise competitive advantage) on the one hand and diversify on the other, providing a wider range of offerings beyond marine and maritime services, as the more innovative have already done. These might already include manufacturing, power generation and bulk storage facilities. All will need to adjust their profile and business models to reflect trading patterns, while ensuring relevance and a coherent balance of productive investment and use of assets.

In a globalised world, trade routes and patterns are subject to volatility and ports are vulnerable to geopolitical and geo-economic shifts. New trade routes are opening, notably those between South America and Asia and increasingly between Africa, the Gulf and Asia. It is relevant here that the value of exports from developing countries to other developing countries (the so-called South–South trade) last year exceeded that passing from developing countries to developed countries (South–North). As with shipping, ports will be affected by the rise in local manufacturing, the prevalence of the re-shoring of industrial production and manufacturing and the growth in overland transport.

SHIPBUILDING

Ships that ply their trade along the global super highway have to be built in ways that are cost-effective and make them fit for task. Britain dominated the shipbuilding industry from the 1860s to the 1950s, but lost its leadership after an inability to invest in modernisation and skills after the hardships of the Second World War. Despite its experience in the same conflict, Japan took over the leadership role from the mid-1950s to the mid-1990s, but its competitive power was weakened by an ageing demographic, rising wages, a reduction in the resources afforded to research and development and a sharp rise in the cost of steel. South Korea, which took over the mantle from Japan, is now striving to maintain its competitive edge in the face of rising wages, the high price of commodities and the appreciation of its currency. After ten years of rapid, aggressive growth, China is gaining market leadership in this sector and by tonnage builds the most ships. It benefits from low labour costs (nearly 50 per cent of Japan's and 30 per cent of South Korea's), ambitious growth and investment programmes, joint ventures with leading Western companies and state subsidies.

Factors affecting the shipbuilding industry can be divided into two groups: macro factors (world seaborne trade, oil prices, economic stability and political stability) and market factors (subsidies by governments, scrapping of old vessels, charter rates and vessels on order). Inevitably, though, the shipbuilding industry in most countries is dependent on the iron rule of supply and demand, and states have to determine the extent to which they mediate and moderate the effects of market forces on what many believe, in terms of national capacity, infrastructure and specialist skills, to be a strategic industry. The preference in most countries possessing significant navies tends to lean towards either the sustainability of an existing shipbuilding industry or joint ventures with foreign companies that enable skills, expertise and technology transfer, as well as sharing the burdens of capital investment, research and development and programme risk.

Turkey is a good example where industrial and defence policies combine to produce a fully functioning partnership culture in relation to its foreign suppliers and domestic companies. The country aims to be self-sufficient in defence provision and in the top ten of defence equipment exporters by 2023. As such, every major programme is scrutinised in relation to the potential for Turkish companies to be able to pair with prospective platform and equipment suppliers. For example, the acquisition of new submarines involves the initial delivery of the first two submarines built in Germany, but with systems integrated and in some cases supplied by Turkish firms. The remaining submarines will be fully built and equipped in Turkey. The pattern is repeated across the whole of the defence procurement process and supply chain.

The largest private shipbuilder in the world is Rongsheng Heavy Industries in China. The Chinese shipbuilding industry and Rongsheng demonstrate the risks associated with overambitious projections in an industry that is notoriously sensitive to swings in supply and demand. The boom period of the early years of the twenty-first century saw a demonstrable upsurge in trade by sea and enthusiastic ordering of new hulls in anticipation of continuing prosperity. Following the financial crash of 2008–9 and the subsequent stagnation of the world's economy, which led to significant overcapacity, both in shipping fleets and in shipbuilding yards, Rongsheng lost $93.5 million in 2012. The trend continued into 2013, despite government subsidies of over $200 million, and 8,000 jobs were cut, leading to riots and demonstrations. This decline is symptomatic of China's shipbuilding industry as a whole, with orders down a quarter over the past year, coupled to shortages of liquidity and financing. Inevitably, continued global economic decline is likely to lead to the loss of the less productive yards and diversification into other products, such as offshore rigs, pipelines and marine structures.

Meanwhile, developed-world shipbuilding frequently loses out because of an uneven playing field with regard to trade agreements and labour laws, which means that companies have to compete on productivity, quality and innovation rather than price. In particular, they cannot compete on labour costs. New initiatives should centre on those specialist ships and high-technology systems that will be required in the future in the underwater, Arctic and unmanned sectors. Companies could also usefully pioneer the development of energy efficiency and the production and retrofitting of low-emission ships. Technical innovations like new hull designs, composite surfaces, rudder and propulsion design, LNG-fuelled ships and ballast management all offer possibilities for growth. Europe, in particular, could seek to retain its market leadership in cruise liners and leisure craft and aggressively seek more maintenance, repair, ship conversion and upgrade work. Warships are also likely to be built by the countries operating them or by their close allies, with the opportunities for export sales that benefit from economies of scale, as well as industrial offsets and joint ventures with indigenous companies. There are also opportunities for niche products that are distinctively effective in their own fields: German submarine production is a case in point, as is the Kongsberg Joint and Naval Strike missile in Norway.

In the future, the prospects for shipbuilding are likely to be volatile, reflecting both the overcapacity introduced before the global economic slow-down and competition from countries that afford strategic importance to their shipbuilding industries. Investment and orders will also be determined by economic growth and activity that are proceeding at different rates for advanced, emerging and developing countries. Even now, the South Koreans are making a comeback, with competitive pricing for their ships, achieved through rigorous cost cutting, more competitive sourcing of materials and the streamlining of production processes.

OUT OF SIGHT?

While on passage, especially on oceanic routes, ships used to be largely unmonitored. Not so today. With various regional vessel management systems in place, movement at sea is more visible nowadays and in the future there will be increased awareness of shipping as it transits.

For a start, the IMO's International Convention for the Safety of Life at Sea requires an Automatic Identification System (AIS), used to locate and identify vessels, to be fitted aboard international voyaging ships with 300 or more GT, and all passenger ships regardless of size. The last course, speed and movements of the ill-fated South Korean ferry *Sewol* on 16 April 2014 were faithfully recorded and transmitted by AIS. Meanwhile, maritime border security and offshore surveillance operations by both military and government systems are becoming increasingly capable, sophisticated and integrated. Webcams and countless mobile devices betray activity close to shore, while high above in orbit numerous radar, electronic and high-resolution optical devices are mounted in military satellites, which allow detection and identification to a very high level of accuracy. These intelligence-gathering satellites are categorised as: high-resolution photography or imagery (IMINT), measurement and signature (of emissions) intelligence (MASINT), signals intelligence (SIGINT)[12] and radar ocean reconnaissance satellites (RORSAT).

In addition, there is a rapidly proliferating galaxy of commercial satellite services and imagery now that affordable, easy-use software and access to

---

[12] The technical term for communications intercept and analysis.

satellite imagery databases are available. These can be expected to multiply once cheaper ways of putting satellites into orbit are developed. RapidEye's five satellites can cover 4 million sq km (1.5 million sq miles) a day, with daily revisits to particular areas. In 2009, Google introduced Google Ocean, which offered 3D ocean and, in 2011, high-resolution underwater topography. Thus, vessels are clearly identifiable from space by commercial satellite services except in conditions of poor visibility. Ships captured by Somali pirates were clearly visible during their time at anchor. When the Chinese Navy berthed a new Jin class (Type 094) ballistic missile submarine at Yulin on Hainan Island on the South China Sea in February 2008, it was first identified by a QuickBird satellite and the image released by DigitalGlobe. The search for the missing Malaysia Airlines flight MH370 in March 2014 was spearheaded by the efforts of governments, crowd-sourcing volunteers and people the world over, scanning the images from high-resolution military and commercial satellites, with the crucial locating input from data from the satellite communications company Inmarsat.

Of course, this is all not just a question of control, military necessity or intrusive surveillance. The ability to track vessels, from supertankers to round-the-world yachtsmen, means that operations can be more efficiently conducted, safety and security can be more effectively provided and, when the unexpected happens, emergency and rescue services can be sent rapidly to the scene. Satellite and long-haul communications provide the means by which, even in the remotest parts of the ocean, the Internet and the sea remain linked.

Even so, the use of the sea is fundamental to the efficient functioning of the world's economy, but its smooth operation cannot be taken for granted. Globalisation is fragile, subject to both natural and man-made shocks and interventions. Investment in any aspect of the use of the sea as a highway requires countries and companies to be agile in their management of assets, with the ability to switch resources away from underperforming sectors to more promising areas and then be prepared to switch them back again. It is also clear that a country needs to maintain its grip on – or access to – the benefits and rewards of soft sea power, the ways by which the sea acts as a highway and as an exploitable resource. If it does not, others will, competing not only with soft sea power, but also with hard sea power in the form of military presence and coercive activity.

CHAPTER THREE

Sea Power Today

'I hate your pen and ink men. A fleet of British ships
of war are the best negotiators in Europe.'[1]

Sea power can be best expressed as the combined investment in the sea of the various components and resources of a state or enterprise in the pursuit of favourable outcomes. It is too often viewed simply and narrowly as the benefit gained in a particular time and place by the possession and deployment of naval forces.

American naval officer and academic Alfred Thayer Mahan (1840–1914)[2] is primarily famous for his iconic *The Influence of Sea Power Upon History*, in which he attempted to produce a unified theory of naval warfare. Mahan strongly believed that the fundamental purpose of a navy was command of the sea. He recognised the importance of trade by sea, but asserted that the true role of the navy was the destruction of the enemy's fleet, by means of a decisive naval battle. Once this had happened, the theory went, you could do pretty much what you wanted at sea. Above all, he did not consider any country great that did not have a powerful navy.

Mahan's theories were challenged by Sir Julian Corbett (1854–1922). Corbett was suspicious of enduring principles in warfare, which he believed encouraged military and political leaders to think that they could determine the outcomes of wars. He argued that naval strategy should form part of the overall maritime strategy of the state, taking in maritime power, trade,

---

[1] Horatio Nelson, in a letter to Emma Hamilton, quoted in Walter Runciman, *Drake, Nelson and Napoleon* (1919) and written in March 1801.
[2] The ships that he commanded had an unfortunate habit of colliding with moving and stationary objects.

economics, policy and other factors as well. He rejected the idea of the decisive battle, because the enemy at sea was too hard to find, was not worth the effort or risk involved and, even if located, could easily and rapidly disperse. Conversely, he believed that the main roles of the navy were to protect the homeland and sea lines of communication (shipping routes and trade) and to prevent an enemy from being able to trade and project power at sea. He also saw how offensive and defensive measures were combined to deal with enemy capabilities and to facilitate the projection of power against the land. When taken together, his views have a modern ring to them.

The reality is that sea power can be used both as an instrument of state and as a means of achieving strategic outcomes by a commercial enterprise. In both cases, it is important to recognise that sea power has only one, paramount use – the ability to influence decisions and events on land, because that is where people live.

HARD AND SOFT SEA POWER

Let's look first at hard sea power. This is characterised by those components of sea power that enable an individual, group or state to enforce its will at sea or to influence decisions on land, by the threat or use of force. At the national level, alongside an army and air force, a navy exists as an instrument of national power, to enable its government to intervene at sea or anywhere that can be reached from the sea at a time and place of choice. Its influence and ability to deliver what a government wants are limited by its ability to operate away from its own country and region, in terms of capability and support, by legal considerations and the extent to which the navies of other countries are disposed to allow it to go about its business. By logical extension, any individual or group able to bring force or influence to bear at sea can be said to be demonstrating sea power in one form or another. That includes law enforcement organisations, but also extends to private security companies, pirates and others with access to the use of force.

Soft power, on the other hand – comprising trade, the exploitation of the resources of the sea, humanitarian aid, fishing, tourism and all other maritime activities that do not imply the use of force – can be deployed at sea because of the cooperative, permissive trading environment that exists, secured by international law and the threat of sanction or force against those seeking to disrupt a system that pretty much works for everyone. China and many other 'non-aligned' trading countries have taken advantage of the security of the seas provided by the USA and its allies for some considerable time, calculating reasonably that strategic and commercial interests are best served by acquiescing in the current system. Unfortunately, until recently, they have not contributed much to the licence fee or maintenance costs and China, in particular, has emerged as a significant strategic and economic peer competitor for the USA.[3]

But – and this consideration is a big but – soft power is usable only with the implicit or explicit presence of hard power, to prevent disruptions in the international system by states, criminals or others. Hard power would be required to ensure the safe, secure transit of shipping through the Strait of Hormuz if it had been declared closed by Iran. If it chose, the USA could curtail China's trade, either by threatening the use of its navy or by simply looking the other way when an area critical to the Chinese became unstable or insecure. In the future, China might consider that it would prefer on balance to safeguard for itself not only its economic interests and citizens abroad, but also the lines of communication that connect them.

In the past, those countries able to combine hard and soft power elements, most notably the seaborne enterprises of Spain, Portugal, the Netherlands and England have been able to form empires, found colonies and project military and commercial power around the world. It has been the classic formula of 'flag' and 'trade', in which navies support the commercial elements of a country's productive capacity, while commerce and trade provide the resources, through taxes, finance and economic growth, to sustain a state's military instrument of power. It is a far cry from the merchantmen called up for state service in the medieval period. In an odd reversal of the privatisation trend, commerce has simply contracted out security to the state.

In some cases, the deal does not always work out. In the face of piracy off Somalia between the 1990s and 2014, Danish shipping firms at various

---

[3] Sir Norman Angell (author of the historically controversial book *The Great Illusion*) in *The World's Highway: Some Notes on America's Relation to Sea Power and Non-Military Sanctions For the Law of Nations* (1915) doubted whether solely altruistic motives counted in keeping the world safe for civilisation, arguing that 'England's unquestioned naval predominance ... has given England no privilege not freely possessed by the commerce of all nations.'

stages adopted a variety of measures. Møller–Maersk chose to re-route its ships around the Cape of Good Hope, at a reported cost of $100 million, while others, like Clipper Shipping, took the risk and paid ransoms, as part of an otherwise exemplary approach to the welfare of its crews. More widely, shipping companies sought the naval surveillance and protection capabilities from their own countries or multinational efforts.

However, at first, states were not able or willing to devote sufficient resources to the problem. Nor were they prepared to tackle the issue at source, in Somalia itself. After a spate of ship hijackings and ransom demands, those companies not prepared to take alternative measures, such as re-routeing and paying ransoms, provided their own security in the form of private security companies embarked in the ships themselves. This arming of merchant ships was an echo of the armed merchantmen of the East India Companies, which were armed with cannon and other weapons for just this eventuality in the Indian Ocean. Not surprisingly, it worked, both then and today.

As sea power interacts with such a variety of human activities, including trade, resources and diplomacy as well as naval strength, the sea is a major component and determinant of geography, geopolitics and geostrategy. It can be seen that geography shapes the ways in which sea power can be used because the configuration of land and sea determines the routes and the space available for projecting both hard and soft sea power. In the First World War, geography enabled the Royal Navy to block the routes around the British Isles, both to the north and south, with superior forces, effectively containing the German fleet. Geopolitics – the location of resources and their relationship to human activity, as well as their value and the means of accessing them – is inconceivable without the sea. Similarly, geostrategy is the assessment by individual states about where best to invest their diplomatic, economic, cultural and military capital, as a way of gaining and maintaining power, influence and legitimacy; any such policy would lack coherence and completeness without recognition of the importance of sea power.

The sea power of a state is strategic in its consideration, application and effect, as the means by which its people can acquire wealth through trade and by accessing resources along routes that are predominantly sea-based. Also, the leverage that a state can exert by sea provides security for the state itself, as well as its international traffic, and holds at risk the territorial integrity and trade of others, especially opponents and competitors. It follows from these thoughts that a substantial mismatch between the context in which states have to operate (geopolitics) and the geostrategy they have determined for themselves is likely to lead to loss of power, influence and the ability to increase wealth.

All sorts of sea power today are exerted in those parts of the oceans where there is no other force to oppose their countervailing presence. Thus, fishing takes place in hundreds of places where there is no authority to prevent it. Warships fire cruise missiles and launch aircraft against land targets with impunity because there is no opposition at the range at which they release their weapons or aircraft. Pirates dominate any area of sea they occupy and deny its use to ships that do not wish to face the hazards and costs of the passage, unless there is a power close by to deter or prevent their depredations. Sea power is what you have to hand and can get to sea in the right place and the right time; it can never be an existential power.

MARITIME FORCES AND POWER

Armed forces exist primarily to deter and defeat threats to a country's security, prosperity and interests. Maritime forces consist of those vessels, aircraft, systems and personnel that are equipped, configured and trained to threaten and apply force at sea or from the sea against the land, or indeed any other strategic medium, such as space, cyberspace or the air. Although these normally involve naval forces, this definition includes all those other military capabilities that have the potential to contribute to warfare at sea and from the sea. It does not matter whether an aircraft, submarine, warship or terrorist is involved, or whether it is an air force, navy, marine or army asset. As Sir Herbert Richmond wrote, 'Command of the sea is indispensable to security, but whether the instrument that commands swims, floats or flies is a matter of detail.'[4]

Specifically, naval forces are state-owned, authorised and formally commanded platforms, and personnel are designed to operate at sea – below, on or above the surface. They are instruments of state policy that are able to produce an effect at sea and influence decisions on land. As such, naval

---

[4] *Statesmen and Sea Power* (1946).

power should not simply be considered in terms of its use for deterrence and defence, but also in relation to the positive effects that it can have in promoting and protecting political, diplomatic and economic interests.

Given Sir Herbert Richmond's view about the variety of influences and instruments that can produce an effect at sea, it seems appropriate to express all operational (and commercial) terms associated with *sea* power in terms of *maritime* power, which, in the face of non-existent, negligible or containable opposition, aims at maritime supremacy or maritime control. Sea power represents the strategic theory; maritime power expresses the instrumental ways – the ships, the aircraft and both military and commercial operations – through which the sea power of the state, both hard and soft, is applied. Three main themes shape the way in which maritime power is exercised in the early twenty-first century.

- Maritime security – the ability to maintain the free, safe and secure use of the seas, for trade and other peaceful purposes, either locally or generally. For companies, this would mean the creation and maintenance of a favourable legal, commercial and sufficiently secure environment, for investment and operations.
- Maritime manoeuvre – the use of the sea as manoeuvre space, to deploy maritime and military forces at a time and place of choice. Also, it expresses the means by which commercial companies establish market positioning and competitive advantage through use of the sea.
- Maritime power projection – the capability to determine events and decisions on land through the use of forces operating at sea or from the sea. Power projection includes all those capabilities that enable maritime security and manoeuvre, and the ways in which maritime power enables military capabilities to be used in relation to the land. These would comprise attacks by aircraft and cruise missiles, amphibious landings, the deployment of major ground forces and, at the other end of the scale, humanitarian assistance and disaster relief (HADR). Commercially, it means the targeting of investment and operational effort to achieve market dominance or advantage by the use of the sea.

Advanced technologies and more assertive claims throw up another definitive theme, that of maritime denial, the means by which trading competitors or military opponents can be prevented from achieving maritime security, manoeuvre or power projection. It implies the ability to stop someone else from doing what he wants and is subtly different to the freedom given to a state exercising sea or maritime control, whereby the state can do what it wants in an area *as well as* denying the use to others. In current doctrinal usage, it is expressed as anti-access and area denial and is the capability that the USA supposes China, in particular, has deployed in the Asia-Pacific region.

Countries that do not aspire to achieving maritime control or supremacy, or cannot afford the scale of effort, generally want to deter other states and deny access to their sea areas. They invest in a range of denial platforms and systems, notably mines, submarines and land-based aircraft and missiles. In addition, they can, at the soft end of sea power, and, in conjunction with major conglomerates and companies, seek to exclude foreign forces and competitive commercial activities by the exploitation or use of international maritime law, navigation restrictions and trade agreements. The option is, of course, available for the soft aspects of maritime denial to be backed up by the implicit threat and occasional use of the hard elements.

NAVAL POWER

Naval power specifically and primarily exists to deter and defeat threats to national sovereignty and protect a country's interests. In circumstances short of conflict, it preserves the use of the sea on behalf of its country by ensuring that it can be used as a secure medium for trade, global access and transport. Navies also support state interests through presence in areas of diplomatic sensitivity, to reinforce national foreign policy initiatives and guarantee sovereign rights and jurisdictions. They deal with pirates, terrorists and traffickers, alongside private security companies and law enforcement authorities, for the general good and welfare of the system. However, the harsh reality is that states only support the international system of trade and law based on the sea because it is in the interests of individual states to do so. Nevertheless, at all times, there is the shared, but unspoken understanding that all involved have to deal with a common enemy, the sea, and, short of conflict, there are rules and conventions to be observed. As such, they have in peacetime a vested interest in safety at sea and the security of the overall system, for the benefit of everyone. In wartime, they tend to want to keep the use of the sea to themselves.

The benefits of naval power fall into five main categories: deterrence (and if that fails, operational success), political, economic, diplomatic and cultural.

Deterrence

Deterrence is achieved when a potential opponent is convinced that the disadvantages of taking a course of action outweigh (demonstrably) the likely benefits. In conventional terms, it normally comes down to the amount of attrition that an opponent's armed forces would have to sustain in relation to the political and economic gain envisaged by the resort to force. However, it can also relate to the possibility of wider political, diplomatic or economic impacts. The advantage of maritime power in relation to deterrence is that an opponent can be confronted with the likely consequences of his decisions or actions at any point geographically between his own country and the country against which aggression is threatened. Deterrent and dissuasive force can be dispatched to allow time, both to negotiate from a position of strength and to deploy capabilities in the event of conflict.

That is because, in tension or confrontation, warships allow a certain amount of shadow-boxing, involving the harassment of an opponent's military units, the overt or covert monitoring of his latest technologies, weapon firings or exercises and the deliberate engineering of close quarters situations. In wartime or combat, navies project 'hard power' capabilities needed to achieve the objectives of their own states and inhibit the realisation of objectives by opponents, by interrupting their military and trading activities, diminishing their resources and neutralising and destroying their capabilities to resist.

Of course, nuclear capabilities have a value and weight all of their own in taking most opponents well beyond the point at which any aggression that threatens the vital interests of a nuclear-armed state could be reasonably or rationally assessed as worthwhile. The threshold at which a state or group of states would respond to a threat or attack with nuclear weapons always remains deliberately vague, in order to complicate the calculations of potential opponents. It normally hovers around the point at which it is perceived that a sovereign state or a country's way of life is threatened with extinction. In military terms, the possession of nuclear weapons also affords some assurance against the likelihood of an overwhelming pre-emptive strike (conventional, chemical or nuclear).

Political benefits

Naval forces give politicians flexibility and scope for manoeuvre, allowing them to send subtle, yet uncommitted signals and expressions of interest in particular situations, without the blunt statements of intent implied by the dispatch of fighter aircraft or army formations. Capable of sustained, twenty-four-hour operations, with a range of operational characteristics, warships can gain unhindered access, remain on station for as long as a crisis or situation lasts and position themselves without undue provocation or overt deployment. This benefit accrues simply because they are able to exploit the freedom of the seas and move across and through a medium over which no one country has exclusive jurisdiction. These types of operation entail a low spread of risk and a flexible means of applying pressure or with-drawing at will. As such, they can implement a sequence of escalation and de-escalation to prevent conflict and, if necessary, move quickly to coercive diplomacy and conflict.

This spectrum of response was admirably demonstrated during the 2013 deployment of US warships to the eastern Mediterranean in support of allies (providing theatre ballistic missile defence capabilities) and in advance of operations against Syria (threatening the use of cruise missiles). The flexibility of warship deployment allowed a subtle shift of emphasis in tune with the political process. More generally, warships are able to provoke a variety of reactions, perceptions and expectations. The alternately benign and belligerent character of warships makes them equally effective – and credible – as both ambassadors and unambiguous instruments of fighting power. As the Roman dictator Sulla remarked (in Latin), 'I can either be your best friend or your worst enemy.'

Forward presence, whereby naval forces are regularly stationed beyond a country's immediate region in areas of strategic or economic interest, is often criticised for its expense and lack of impact. However, it provides reassurance to actual and potential markets, demonstrating that a country is in a relationship for the long haul and will not cut and run when the going gets tough. More importantly, it demonstrates solidarity in the face of shared risks and dangers – the presence of a warship is a tangible, yet subtle expression of support to an ally or partner. It is no coincidence that there is a strong US military presence, including warships, in Bahrain on a permanent basis, and a French joint service base in Abu Dhabi. During the Syrian crisis, Russian ships have been berthed at Tartous, one of the country's major ports. Meanwhile, American carrier battle groups are at high readiness in the major oceans of the world to deal with those who seek to do the USA, its interests or its allies and partners harm.

From a military point of view, forward presence is important because it allows forces to prepare for possible action and to gather intelligence about local contexts and potential opponents. Bearing in mind Nelson's good advice that the training ground is the battle ground, it also gives deployed forces familiarity with the region in which they may have to fight, the occasion to forge close links with local countries and to train with likely partners. All these activities deliver political and diplomatic benefits as well. It can also boost local capacity, or even provide implicit protection, until training and local naval acquisitions can make up the shortfall.

Economic benefits

In economic terms, the possession of sea power serves three main functions. Firstly, it enables a state to have a stake in the way in which the international system is safeguarded and managed, in the interests of open access and the freedom of the seas (or not, as the case may be). In this connection, it allows governments to take corrective action in the event of trade being disrupted and the flow of goods curtailed when geopolitical instability occurs. This is the classic 'price at the pump' argument, which denotes the increase in fuel prices that usually occurs as a result of interruptions to the flow of hydrocarbons at sea in cases of political instability, conflict, confrontation or embargo. Hard choices about strategic growth or shrinkage need to be based on the political, economic and diplomatic benefits to be gained from the possession of naval power and the input costs. Too often, states view their national economic health and prosperity simply in terms of domestic criteria. In a globalised world, states are especially dependent on far distant countries and contexts for their economic wealth, political influence and prosperity. As Mahan wrote, 'the necessity of a navy springs from the existence of peaceful shipping'.[5]

Secondly, naval power allows the direct promotion of a state's economic interests worldwide, not just in terms of sales of naval and marine-related platforms, systems and services, but also in support of a wider range of commercial and industrial products. There is also a direct economic benefit to the home country. As an example, over half the value of each British Astute-class submarine is absorbed by the domestic supply chain. Major suppliers include Rolls-Royce, Derby (nuclear plant), Thales Optronics (visual system), Thales Underwater Systems Ltd (sonar), Ultra Electronics (technology and software programmes) and Weir, Strachan & Henshaw, Bristol (the weapon handling and discharge system).

Finally, there is good money to be made from the sea, in the exploitation of its resources, the carriage of goods and the application of a country's soft sea power, represented by the civil engagement with the sea: merchant

The Astute-class nuclear submarine HMS *Ambush* during sea trials near Scotland.

[5] *The Influence of Sea Power on History* (1918).

shipping, shipbuilding, oil and gas exploration, fishing, financing, insurance and the rest. The ability to focus a country's commercial potential and efforts translates directly into strategic advantage, competitive edge and revenue generated with the minimum of duplication and overhead. It is a public-private partnership in which both strategic and commercial objectives are aligned and consistently pursued. At times, hard power can be applied to ensure that competitive advantage and market access can be sustained even in the face of threats (think pirates and rogue states). A navy ensures that a country – and its friends – can benefit from contact with the economic wealth gained from transactions and trade. It maintains the necessary political, commercial and security conditions for globalisation, and the ability and readiness to continue to trade when in harm's way or in the face of threats are likely to confer considerable competitive (and political) advantage in the twenty-first century. A navy can also provide direct protection for one's friends – who might be resource rich, but poor in terms of manpower or operational capability – at a price, either directly or indirectly.

Diplomatic benefits

In diplomatic terms, a warship is a floating chunk of sovereign territory, which enables a country to express an interest in a situation or location. It represents the latent power of the state, deployable to anywhere of significance in the world. It allows political contact with the man on the scene and a demonstration of commitment to both allies and potential opponents that a country is taking a situation seriously. However, the presence of a warship does not have to be escalatory or tie a politician's hands. A warship that is one morning cleared for action can be ready to conduct a good will visit or a humanitarian mission after lunch on the same day. Alternatively, it can withdraw with no harm done and no offence taken. The politician retains a range of options right up until the point that he or she authorises, or the situation demands, the warship to act.

Events and contingencies involving national pride, tests of will and brinkmanship are nearly always more containable at sea than on land. Even though a warship is viewed generally as an embodiment of a country's identity, incidents involving opposing warships tend to maintain tensions at a low level of engagement and, usually, the protagonists at a wary distance.

Except in the most blatant acts of sustained aggression, in which one side is spoiling or planning for a fight, de-escalation seems to have more of a chance when ships can be withdrawn, reinforced or redeployed to send an infinite variety of political and diplomatic messages. Warships usually do not 'occupy ground' in the same way that armies do, allowing for more flexible and considered approaches to the resolution of problems, without necessarily losing face or national prestige.

Even so, some platforms and formations transmit serious intent – the overt dispatch of an aircraft carrier, an amphibious group or nuclear submarines away from their normal pattern of deployment or employment is a clear form of political signalling that a country means business and is concerned. So too, with the commitment of special forces, marines and other elite troops, who, over and above their specialist roles, convey the hint of possible action that enables a framework of understanding for diplomacy and political leverage to play their part. In this way, all the participants in a crisis will have had their perceptions shaped and behaviours influenced by the presence and tangible potential for use of immediately available military power, to be used at a time and place of political choice. As Oliver Cromwell supposedly said (about 150 years before Nelson), 'A man-of-war is the best ambassador.'

The simple fact is that warships, whether from the eighteenth or twenty-first century, are visually and emotionally impressive. The rows of great guns that protrude from the gun ports along the whole length of HMS *Victory* in Portsmouth proclaim fighting power and stir the imagination. Similarly, modern warships with their futuristic designs, clean lines and stealth technology promote an air of mystery, a sense of the unfamiliar and a strong hint of menace. It is difficult for the eye not to be drawn to the sight of a warship, whether at sea or entering or leaving harbour. They are impossible to ignore – they turn heads. They are tangible instruments of state power and a direct reflection of the society that they represent.

Cultural benefits

Finally, there are cultural benefits. A navy is one of the ways in which a country determines how it feels about itself in relation to the rest of the world, demonstrates its confidence and reflects its sense of place in history.

More than an army regiment or an aircraft, a warship is a concentrated embodiment of the country it serves and an object of emotional attachment:

> As night began to fall, it was time to make port in Bergen. The sentries put on body armour and manned the machineguns, in case the Norwegians got any silly ideas. And we were nudged to a standstill by a local tug. When you have only 18 warships in total, you can't risk dinging one in a parking accident.
>
> As I disembarked, I couldn't help turning round for one last look. It may be a government vessel in a government navy. But I can tell you this. It does something no other government operation does: it makes you achingly proud to be British.[6]

THE USA: THE MARITIME HYPER-POWER

Despite recent cutbacks, sequesters and reductions, the USA still has by far the biggest defence budget in the world, considerably in excess in real terms of the sum total of the next fifteen countries. It has a navy that dominates every sea and not only outweighs, but also outclasses any other competitor by a long way. The fighting power and sustained global reach of America are exemplified by the US Navy and all those elements of its formidable capability that it can bring to bear at sea, including the resources and firepower of its other three Services, its Air Force, Marine Corps and Army. This superiority has enabled the USA to protect its own trade, deploy military forces at will for deterrence, coercion and fighting expeditionary wars, and to promote its own interests. Above all, it has preserved – and exploited – the access provided by the sea, both for expressing its interest in almost any part of the world and for promoting the ideals of preferential free trade and universal economic penetration so cherished by the apostles of capitalist enterprise.

Since the end of the Second World War, the control exercised at sea by America has only been seriously and credibly challenged by the Soviet Union during the Cold War. Largely through a policy of rigorous containment of the four main Soviet fleets, as a result of geography, climate and the formidable nuclear and conventional fighting power of the USA and its allies,

---

[6] Jeremy Clarkson, 'Hello sailor. Show me what Britain is made of', *The Sunday Times*, 17 February 2013.

this challenge was countered. Otherwise, America has enjoyed supremacy at sea for the best part of seventy years, allowing it to protect and promote both US interests and the progress associated with intensifying globalisation. The leading, most vocal exponent of capitalism and political freedom has been the guarantor of universal access on the watery worldwide web.[7]

Indeed, in every aspect of naval supremacy – submarine warfare, carrier aviation, assault and attack on the land from the sea, ballistic missile defence and oceanic surveillance – the USA is way out in front of everyone else, and in terms of tactics, techniques and technology it also leads the field. Its carrier battle groups are fearsome projectors of US national power, both as expressions of force withheld (what they could do to you) and also as significant, decisive contributors to the relief of humanitarian suffering and natural disasters (what they could do for you). The USA and its allies can surge decisive fighting power capable of prevailing against an opponent that challenges the maritime status quo in any region of the world.

Perhaps because of that unrivalled pre-eminence, there have been very few classic naval wars since the Second World War. A notable naval clash occurred in 1950 when Chinese Communist forces defeated Nationalist forces (with a flagship named *Eternal Peace*) to take Hainan Island, and there were also scuffles between Royal Navy and Icelandic ships in the 'Cod Wars' of the 1950s and 1970s. However, most have been 'encounter' actions between single units or have been contained skirmishes, such as those between Iran and the USA in the 1980s, which have taken place within a wider confrontation or conflict and have not led to extended engagements at sea. The only significant 'naval' war, which saw a contest for the control of the sea and used a high proportion of the fleets involved, was the Falklands War of 1982 between Britain and Argentina.[8] Mostly, such has been the dominance of the USA and its allies at sea that their power has largely been unchallenged and most naval power has been deployed against the land, as in Korea, the Vietnam War, both Gulf Wars and operations against Libya.

[7] In April 2013, Senator Marco Rubio (R-FL) gave a speech at the Brookings Institute: 'Millions of people have emerged from poverty around the world in part because our Navy protects the freedom of the seas, allowing the ever-increasing flow of goods between nations.'
[8] Until its warships returned to the safety of their coast and ports after the sinking of the cruiser ARA *General Belgrano*.

However, American power to impose its will at sea is declining in aggregate terms and in relation to the ability of rising powers to generate powerful maritime forces. The numbers of its ships are shrinking and their readiness levels appear to have declined, with almost a quarter of US warships failing their operational inspections in 2012. In parallel, US Marine Corps formations have been hard-worked in Iraq and Afghanistan. Its men and equipment are in need of a period of recuperation, with a return to the US Marine Corps' primary role of being the tip of the spear of amphibious capabilities, able to threaten or realise high-impact, low-footprint operations, not to do the US Army's job for it. Both the US Navy and the US Marine Corps are threatened with reducing numbers of personnel and resources while inflation and the cost growth of modern technology and hardware eat away at even the most generous provision. Manpower is also a substantial overhead, both in terms of investment in training and in through-life funding.

SEA POWER IN THE WIDER WORLD

At present, the commercial and naval power of the so-called 'free world' dominates the maritime scene. Apart from the USA, other maritime forces, predominantly North Atlantic Treaty Organization (NATO) members, have substantial individual power projection assets, capable of extended worldwide deployment, with several states, notably the USA, the UK, France and Italy, able to commit powerful, balanced force packages at short notice. Other European countries maintain navies in scale and balance of forces that reflect their resources and domestic commitments, but also their available manpower and their purely national interests in the wider world. They are generally congruent with US capabilities; that is to say, they have similar, symmetrical technological and tactical characteristics, but at a proportionately smaller scale. Very few have balanced forces, combining the full range of capabilities, but enough to service their peacetime requirements, to sustain national prestige and, as members of the European Union (EU) and NATO, maintain a contribution to the common collective effort.

Elsewhere, almost all states with a coastline are increasing their maritime capabilities in response to the need to protect their littoral resources and improve their offshore and coastal security, especially in relation to their maritime borders. Some, like Turkey, are expanding their areas of commercial and diplomatic influence; others, like the Gulf States, assess the need to acquire capabilities in the face of an existential threat from Iran to their political independence and economic interests. Some need naval forces to secure their lines of economic supply, while others worry about the threat from regional instability, overbearing neighbours and rivals. Archipelagic countries, like Japan, Malaysia, the Philippines and Indonesia, are building up, to a greater or lesser extent, maritime security forces, as well as significant maritime denial capabilities, to deter unwanted attention. For a significant number of rising countries, a powerful navy, preferably with aircraft carriers, nuclear submarines and amphibious capabilities, is seen as a defining attribute of a great power and a means of influencing others. And they are right to do regard it as such.

At the conventional level, the majority of countries deploy navies that are defensive in posture and capability, designed to deter potential opponents and defeat both invasive and destructive attacks aimed at their land area and to prevent violations of their sovereignty. These navies deploy anti-access and area denial capabilities. Some have the capacity to operate beyond their immediate offshore zone and prevent the freedom of manoeuvre or passage of other maritime forces or of international trade. They would also be major players in a regional conflict involving their own area.

Those that wish to project power beyond their immediate neighbourhood normally seek to acquire capabilities that offer sustainable reach and sufficient suppressive firepower to be able to force their way past attempts at anti-access and sea denial. Some states (the UK, France – and soon, China, India and Russia) are able to dispatch balanced, expeditionary forces as a major contribution to a coalition, or independently, to confront regional contingencies and conflicts beyond their immediate area.

Expeditionary operations are usually associated with nuclear or long-endurance submarines, aircraft carriers, land-attack cruise missiles and amphibious capabilities that allow attacks on a country's territory and its capacity for making war, as well as precision strikes on its key civil and military infrastructure. They normally include assault forces that enable raids from the sea or forcible entries into a country for the purpose of landing larger follow-on forces, such as major ground forces. They also have sufficient logistic support – in the form of dedicated fuel, munitions and stores, integrated with the warships, as in the case of the UK's Royal Fleet Auxiliary or the US Navy's Fast Combat Support Ships and US Naval Service. Some have extensive deployable repair and maintenance facilities, based around specialist ships and personnel, as well as access to merchant vessels that they can use as auxiliaries or transports.

At the high end of the expeditionary scale and in a league of its own is the USA, which individually is capable of transoceanic, sustained deployment. It can project decisive combat power against opponents at sea or on the land in times and places of its choosing, often in different oceans simultaneously.

All these attributes and aspirations can be seen in a snapshot of activity across the world. Although by no means comprehensive, the countries selected indicate where attention and investment, in both types of vessel and in capabilities, are being placed.

THE ASIA-PACIFIC REGION

The most notable regional build-up of naval power is in the Asia-Pacific region, whose complex geography pattern of archipelagos, peninsulas and island groups gives it a distinctively maritime character. It is framed to the west by the vast bulk of China, and almost all the trade within and in and out of the region goes by sea. Meanwhile, the ten countries of the Association of Southeast Asian Nations (ASEAN) represent a collective market of 620 million people and are home to a young, large and growing labour population. There is also an expanding, confident and increasingly consumption-oriented middle class. The combined GDP of the ASEAN countries was more than $2.3 trillion in 2012, with the prospect that it will double by 2020. ASEAN's five leading countries (and original founding members) alone – Indonesia, Malaysia, the Philippines, Singapore and Thailand – have grown and attracted as much inward investment as any other region since 2008.

'ASEAN plus 3' includes China, Japan and South Korea in the periodic discussions and policy statements, while other adjunct mechanisms contrive to include India, Russia, the USA, Australia and New Zealand. The ASEAN Regional Summit of twenty-seven members, which discusses security in the region, even includes entities as diverse as North Korea and the EU. Meanwhile, Australia, New Zealand, the UK, Malaysia and Singapore are members of the long-standing Five Power Defence Arrangements (FPDA), which promote cooperation and operational understanding between the former imperial and current Commonwealth partners.

Even before the US announcement of a 'pivot'[9] or rebalance towards the Asia-Pacific region, Asian powers such as Malaysia, Indonesia, Vietnam and the Philippines were already demonstrating varying degrees of nervousness and alarm about China's intentions and actions. China has been predictably bullish in dealing with what it consistently calls 'small countries', while attempting to influence their decisions with substantial inward investment, cultural pressure and appeals to Asian solidarity in the face of outside interference. Most countries in the region need and tacitly want the USA to maintain its footprint and restraining influence in the region, as well as its formidable fighting power. As a result, most ASEAN countries and others in the region are conflicted between their economic and strategic interests – trading with and accepting investment from China, but sheltering behind US security assurances. Doubts about whether this difficult balancing act can be sustained have led some countries to invest in modern military capabilities of their own and Asia has more defence budgets growing at more than 8 per cent annually than any other region in the world, including the Gulf.

China

The rapid rise of China from a coastal defence force not so long ago to a maritime power in the twenty-first century means that its capabilities and intentions are of paramount importance to the way in which the balance of power at sea develops over the next decade or so, especially in the Asia-Pacific region. Both as a potential regional hegemon and prospective superpower, its presence and influence at sea will affect all aspects of security at sea, not least its attitude to the United Nations Convention on the Law of the Sea (UNCLOS) and to the current global naval dominance of the USA.

China's strategic priorities in the twenty-first century will be to maintain the Communist Party in power (and by extension social stability and national

---

[9] An undertaking by the Obama administration that the USA would devote more strategic attention and resources to the Asia-Pacific region.

unity); uphold territorial integrity and sovereign claims (including offshore pretensions in the East China and South China seas); sustain growth and economic development; ensure energy security; preserve regional stability and the international system in so far as they support economic growth; modernise its military; assert its foreign policy goals; and generally be regarded as the pre-eminent hemispheric great power. If all these objectives are to be achieved, Premiere Xi Jinping, will need to balance the demands of an increasingly powerful (and vocal) military establishment with the requirement for stability and investment that enable economic growth and maintain social cohesion.

Operationally, China wants to keep any foreign military capability that could threaten China itself as far away from its coast as possible. It wants a free hand in determining what goes on in the bulk of the South China and East China seas and the Yellow Sea (which includes isolating and absorbing Taiwan). It also feels the need to secure the entry and exit points to the open oceans through the choke points of the archipelagos that surround it to seaward, both for its vital energy and goods traffic and for its naval forces. China's coastline is 18,000 km (11,200 miles) long, but its military and civilian traffic has to cross the exclusive economic zones (EEZs) of neighbouring states such as South Korea and Japan to the east and the Philippines and Malaysia to the south. Taiwan sticks in its metaphorical throat just off its coast at the midpoint.

China has also invested a great deal in South East Asia and its immediate region, to the tune of nearly 60 per cent of its outward direct investment. The fifteenth-century world of Zheng He, with its tribute-based system, intricate commercial network and military muscle, seems to be reappearing before our very eyes. The Chinese just need to push the Europeans back beyond the Cape of Good Hope and the Americans as far away as possible. They would then only have to deal with the heirs of the Mongols (the Russians) and the Japanese pirates. The thinking is that China thrived in the fifteenth century, insulated from the challenge and shock of outsiders, and is seeking to recreate that controlled environment, safe from unauthorised activities and outside challenge. With its neighbours overawed and the USA excluded from intervention, China would be able to dictate the terms of trade and security in the region, as well as consolidating its grip on trade routes through the Indian Ocean to the Gulf, Africa and the 'four [other] seas' that are critical to its energy security and markets (the Red, Mediterranean, Black and Caspian seas).

Therefore, China wants freedom of action and strategic depth for itself in the Pacific, with the priority afforded to a zone extending to a 'first island chain' roughly encompassing the East China and South China seas and the Yellow Sea. It would also like to dominate the Sea of Japan. Eventually, it would want to push its area of control out to a 'second island chain', comprising a line running from northern Japan to Guam, the Bonins, the Marianas and the Carolines, and down to Indonesia in the south. In this way, it is trying to limit the operating radius of US air and naval forces, in order to break the linkages and dependencies between regional countries and their allies outside the region, predominantly the USA,[10] but also Australia and the European countries. It particularly wants to isolate and coerce Taiwan into submission and to neutralise Japan.

China's investment in modern combat capabilities, aligned with its economic growth, indicates that it wishes to be able to negotiate about political and maritime differences, especially in its near abroad, from a position of strength. Mindful of its real and imagined past, it would not want the humiliation of having to submit to terms other than those of its own choosing or as a result of coercion. In addition, scale matters to the Chinese. A casual survey of its major infrastructure projects and programmes – such as modern airports and stadiums – confirms that a powerfully impressive navy, including aircraft carriers and nuclear submarines, would be the sort of attributes China expects to possess as a self-perceived great power. The golden age of Zheng He – with its magnificent ships, wide-ranging power projection voyages and extensive naval facilities, not to mention the tribute and respect that it gained – casts a long beam or a long shadow, depending on your point of view. The People's Liberation Army Navy (PLAN) is, however, aware that a misstep involving the use of force is likely to bring in the USA. The threat from US carrier battle groups, especially in relation to the dispute with Japan and Taiwan, is a constant neurosis, which periodically induces bouts of serious paranoia.

---

[10] This is ironic because China is the USA's biggest creditor, with the loans provided by China subsidising the cost of the US armed forces; the interest payments alone on the debt more than pay for China's military expansion.

In response, China has rapidly expanded its spending on defence over the past decade, at a pace that has closely mirrored its economic growth. Between 2001 and 2011, the average annual increase was 10.3 per cent in real terms. China recently announced a 12.2 per cent rise in its defence budget for 2014–15, a declaration which anticipated a second aircraft carrier and more submarines, indicating that China intends to project power and extend its reach beyond its immediate territorial sea. In three years alone, China's defence budget will have doubled, making China the world's second-largest defence spender after the USA – more than Japan, South Korea and Taiwan combined – although it is still only about a third of the US defence budget.

China's submarine fleet now has 65 boats and, by 2030, the total could rise to between 85 and 100 (of which 12 could be nuclear-powered by 2020). That would be more than the USA could commit to the Asia-Pacific region and allow the PLAN to deploy more widely into other areas. Similarly, 28 of the 48 warships currently in China's six destroyer flotillas were accepted into service within the last twelve years. Its one aircraft carrier (*Liaoning*), with her Shenyang J-15 carrier-based strike fighters, could be joined by four more carriers by 2025. New destroyers, corvettes and conventional submarines are being produced in increasing numbers, as well as large amphibious ships, carrier-based airborne early warning aircraft and maritime patrol aircraft. By 2020, it could have eighty major warships.

In addition to modernising its land-based fighter aircraft with stealth and other advanced features, China is developing a range of ballistic, cruise and land-attack missiles, together with satellites and non-space-based sensors and surveillance systems, such as over-the-horizon radar and electronic intercept facilities, in order to improve surveillance and targeting. China has also invested in electronic intercept and disruption technologies, including anti-satellite and counter-unmanned aerial vehicle (UAV) systems. It has improved and extended its chains of reconnaissance and guidance satellites, while also providing facilities for a number of UAV bases and underwater sensor arrays.

Although it is doubtful whether the Dong Feng anti-ship ballistic missile has the supporting imagery and guidance systems to allow its effective use, it does represent a clear statement of intent. As Admiral Mike Mullen, the previous chairman of the US Joint Chiefs of Staff, said, 'I have moved from

China purchased the *Varyag* in 1998, which it rebuilt and commissioned as the *Liaoning*, its first aircraft carrier, in 2012.

being curious to being genuinely concerned.'[11] The scale of ambition has also been reflected by regular Chinese high seas exercises in the western Pacific, involving 140 vessels. The latest of these was a major exercise in December 2013 by the *Liaoning* and her nascent escorting battle group. Although the technology transfer of Russian capabilities or imitation of Western systems has been at the heart of this programme, China has built a credible maritime denial capability.

Of course, America is able to protect – and guarantee itself and its friends – access to the world's resources and deny access to an opponent or other disturber of the international peace. This situation is similar to that put in place by Britain, which asserted control over the routes and access to Asia and America, having succeeded Portugal, Spain and the Dutch in that role. The USA, with its focus turning to the Asia-Pacific region, has convinced China, whether deliberately or not, that it will contain and constrain China in strategic terms. If China wishes to be a great power, with global reach and regional dominance, rather than remaining focused on

[11] Speaking at Arlington National Cemetery on Memorial Day, 31 May 2010.

economic growth and social stability, it has to extend its grip on the sea lanes that connect it to its resources and markets, while keeping the USA at a safe distance.

Japan

History plays a significant part in the thinking of a country that was effectively isolated from its sources of energy before the Second World War, was a notable maritime power in that war and was shorn of many of its island possessions afterwards. Since 1945, it has only been allowed by treaty to have self-defence forces, which cannot be used for offensive operations. Nowadays, the USA is the ultimate guarantor of Japan's security in the event of war with another state or group of states as part of a treaty that enabled the post-war recovery and revival of Japan. However, Japan retains a robust maritime strategy that is designed to deter aggression against its homeland, to safeguard its sovereign rights over a significantly large number (6,800) of dispersed islands and to secure its sea lines of communications and commerce on which its economic prosperity depends.

Japan has the seventh largest EEZ in the world, and is currently on the receiving end of considerable aggravation from China over rights to the Senkaku Islands (often described as rocks), which are 120 nm (220 km) to the North-east of Taiwan and exactly 200 nm (370 km) from both China and Japan (see Chapter 7). The heat of the issue partly reflects the poisonous historical legacy of war and the cultural animosity between the two countries. Practically speaking, the islands are important to China as being part of the encircling 'first island chain' and because, if acquired, they would afford China claims to EEZ rights well out to sea. Possession would also put pressure on Taiwan because they lie on the ocean-facing side of the beleaguered island. Meanwhile, the Russians are also applying pressure with regard to the Japanese Kuril Islands, where Russia sent two naval vessels in 2012.

Japan is being unyielding, yet dignified in the assertion of its rights, but is keen to reduce tensions. In September 2013, China and ASEAN began formal consultations on developing a Code of Conduct for the South China Sea, one which China's foreign minister, Wang Yi, anticipated would be characterised by a 'gradual approach' based (ominously) on 'realistic expectations' (normally code for China getting its way). Despite its extensive trade and investment links with China, Japan feels the tightening grip of China within the Asia-Pacific region and is busy cultivating friends, including the Philippines, India and Vietnam, while exercising and cooperating more frequently with the USA.

Behind the rhetoric, the Japan Coast Guard has more than 350 vessels and 70 aircraft, while the Japanese Maritime Self-Defense Force represents a significantly more powerful capability than one might expect from its understated title. Its naval forces comprise 4 helicopter 'destroyers' (effectively helicopter carriers), 6 anti-air and anti-ballistic missile cruisers, 30 destroyers and frigates, 19 frigates and corvettes, 16 submarines and 29 MCM vessels, all backed up by various auxiliaries and support ships. In addition, Japan possesses eighty maritime patrol aircraft and over one hundred maritime helicopters, as well as rapidly increasing numbers of UAVs. Similarly, its combat air and early warning capabilities, comprising over 500 aircraft, are formidable, both in terms of capability and training.

Since December 2013, Japan has been planning to enhance its surveillance and response forces to oppose threats to its sovereignty, especially around contested sea and airspace. Additional F-15 Eagle fighter jets have been deployed to Okinawa, near to the Senkaku Islands, as well as early warning aircraft and UAVs. More significantly, Japan will also form a specialist Marine Corps, which clearly has amphibious assault on its agenda of potential things to do, as well as bringing into service 27,000 tons of amphibious assault and helicopter ships.

Japan and China are competing hard for influence and partners in the ASEAN region. China is respected for its trade and investment dominance in the region, but feared on account of its ambitions in the South China and East China seas. Conversely, Japan is viewed as a useful diplomatic and possibly increasingly economic counterweight to China, but is handicapped by its historical legacy and close alignment with the USA. For now, ASEAN states will find it useful to be courted by both Japan and China. The complex interplay might lead to more cooperative approaches to maritime and regional issues and the development of a nascent Code of Conduct in the region, as witnessed by the cooperation that sprung up in the wake of the Malaysia Airlines flight MH370 tragedy. On the other hand, regional tensions have the potential to divide the region into two opposing, competing camps.

South Korea

Just across the historically resonant Tsushima Strait[12] is South Korea (the Republic of Korea/ROK), which, like Japan, has for most of its independent history relied on the USA for its broader maritime security. It has had its hands full for much of the past 60 years dealing with incursions, sporadic attacks and the continuous threat of invasion from North Korea. It also occupies a precarious geographic space sandwiched between Japan, North Korea and China. For all practical purposes, it can usefully be considered as an island, which depends utterly on freedom of navigation to ensure the flow of resources and raw materials to its ports and industrial facilities. It has faced frequent irregular attacks from seaward by small North Korean raiding craft and mini-submarines, which culminated in the unprovoked sinking of one of its frigates, the *Cheonan*, in March 2010, by a North Korean submarine-launched torpedo. However, South Korea is less dependent on the USA for its security than it used to be, although America maintains a substantial ground presence and exercises regularly with South Korean forces.

South Korea's leadership is fully aware that maritime disputes involving, among others, its two large neighbours, China and Japan, have the most potential to affect South Korea's broader interests. South Korea has an EEZ that has been largely agreed with China on the median line principle (see Chapter 7), but which has seen more than 4,800 unauthorised incursions by Chinese fishermen since 2001 and several violent incidents. The recent Chinese declaration of an Air Defence Identification Zone (ADIZ) in late 2013, which extended over an islet claimed by both China and South Korea, served to excite public opinion and maintain awareness of the need for strong maritime capabilities. It also provoked ROK into extending its own ADIZ as a counter-measure. Maritime policy is afforded a significant priority in South Korean government planning, and more resources are being devoted to defending the ROK's commercial interests and modernising its navy, in order to deter and defeat threats to its maritime and territorial sovereignty.

South Korea has one of the world's most efficient, productive and cost-effective shipbuilding industries (including Hyundai Heavy Industries), delivering ships of all shapes and sizes (some of the largest in the world, including

---

[12] The scene of an annihilating victory at sea by the Japanese over the Russians in 1905.

the Maersk Triple-Es) and a sophisticated, commercially driven electronics industry (including Samsung). As such, South Korea seeks to make itself economically competitive, but diplomatically cooperative with Japan and China, without being too compliant with them. It wants to be a major maritime hub in East Asia, concentrating on trans-shipment, finance, electronics and shipbuilding. Sea lines of communication and supply will be important.

The ROK Navy has more than twenty destroyers and frigates in service and twelve submarines, as well as an amphibious capability that is headed by two helicopter-carrying assault ships. These are joined by over one hundred patrol craft and corvettes, mining and mine countermeasures (MCM) vessels and an extensive maritime patrol air fleet of fixed wing Orion aircraft and anti-submarine warfare (ASW) helicopters. More impressive still are the South Korean Navy's plans for a complete modernisation of its capabilities. By 2020, it will acquire nine modern air-independent propulsion (AIP) submarines, followed by nine 3,000-ton boats that will be built in South Korea. These will be joined, from 2019, by six advanced destroyers, together with 20–24 multipurpose frigates by 2020. It will also build a large amphibious assault ship and four smaller amphibious vessels, as well as a force of fast combat support ships and new MCM and mining vessels. Its ambition also extends to introducing two light aircraft carriers by the late 2020s, capable of carrying up to thirty F-35B Lightning-type fighter aircraft.

Vietnam

As its economy expands and the country modernises, Vietnam has realised that its prosperity and security rely on its offshore assets and access to the sea. It is in dispute with China with regard to maritime boundaries and various islands (the Spratlys and the Paracels) in the South China Sea. It occupies twenty-nine of the Spratly Islands and has concluded over sixty joint oil and gas exploration and production contracts with foreign companies. Oil exports now constitute more than 30 per cent of Vietnam's GDP.

Its defence expenditure will amount to 2.5 per cent of GDP by 2015. As a result, Vietnam, having accumulated a varied collection of ex-Soviet era corvettes, patrol and missile boats, is modernising its forces rapidly with a programme that includes two Russian-built Kilo-class submarines in service, with four more operational by 2017. They will be armed with torpedoes and

3M-54 Klub-S anti-ship missiles with a range of 160 nm (300 km). Russia also provided two anti-submarine frigates in 2011; another two will be delivered by 2015. Twelve Sukhoi Su-30 MK2 multirole jet aircraft armed with anti-ship missiles will arrive in 2014–15, to add to the twenty already delivered. It is also increasing and improving its patrol and coastguard capabilities, with maritime patrol aircraft and its own Magic Eye UAV. It deploys an integrated, powerful, coastal missile defence system, equipped with, among others, the supersonic and lethal P-800 Yakhont missile, with the likelihood that it will add the Indian Brahmos missile in the near future. This missile system enables engagement against ships at a range of 160–300 nm (300–550 km). These assets will enable Vietnam to project power into its maritime zone in the South China Sea and provide a powerful anti-access and area denial capability, should it come to blows.

Singapore

The high-achieving city-state of Singapore, with its vibrant economy, extensive foreign investments and accumulating sovereign wealth fund, is proud of its sturdy independence and military competence. Consequently, it has a powerful navy, which is designed to not only deter its more populous neighbours (Malaysia, Indonesia and China), but also protect its lines of economic supply in the spirit of forward defence. It has six submarines, six multirole stealth frigates and an assortment of twenty-four powerfully armed corvettes, patrol craft and missile boats. It also has enough amphibious transports to deploy a brigade of fighting troops in one go. Together with a highly capable air force, which contains advanced fighter, patrol and UAV capabilities, Singapore would be a formidable opponent at sea. It also has an extensive armaments and shipbuilding industry that extends to every aspect of its naval procurement, except for some weapon and control systems that are obtained from abroad, as well as being a world-class electronics and avionics provider.

Taiwan

Sitting nervously in China's cross hairs is Taiwan, which does not intend to be surprised or isolated by its acquisitive neighbour. Its navy has more than twenty destroyers and frigates, four submarines and over fifty missile and patrol boats, as well as mining and MCM capabilities. It also has a respectable amphibious capability and a range of patrol aircraft and helicopters optimised for the surveillance and protection of its territorial sea and economic zone.

Australia

Australia has substantial strategic and commercial interests in the Asia-Pacific region. Its largest trading partner is China, taking 29 per cent of Australia's exports, mostly in energy and minerals. However, its political, cultural and social reference points, as well as its security requirements and inward investment, tie its future to the developed world and, in particular, to the USA. Therefore, over the next ten years, Australia has a difficult task in balancing the expectations and requirements of its biggest ally, the USA, on the one hand and its largest trading partner, China, on the other: 'In few countries do history and geography tug in such different directions.'[13] Australia has increasingly productive commercial links with India and shares strategic interests, especially in relation to maritime and trading issues.

Current Australian assumptions are that the margin of US strategic advantage in the Asia-Pacific region is reducing as China rises. As such, Australia will have a strong forward presence in its north and western approaches, for the direct defence of Australia and its associated territories and in support of its partners and trading networks in the Asia-Pacific region. This shift will be complemented by a predominantly maritime-based strategy, which, by 2018, in close cooperation with New Zealand, should be reflected in a reasonably balanced, modern and integrated fleet. This will include a powerful and agile amphibious ready group, comprising two large aviation-capable specialist ships (LHDs) and a large amphibious transport, capable of extensive sea control in its economic zone, the power projection of a Joint Defence Force in its immediate region and the capacity, with appropriate support, of deploying Joint Force packages further afield. Other major force elements will include a powerful destroyer and frigate force of fifteen vessels, new submarines, P-8 *Poseidon* maritime patrol aircraft and

---

[13] 'On the Edge', *The Economist*, 26 January 2013.

long-range and high-endurance UAVs. Australia will also host increasing numbers of US warships and aircraft in its northern ports, as well as basing facilities for US Marines on a rotational basis.

Russia

Russia's economy depends on the export of oil and gas, from which it derives the resources that maintain its economy and its armed forces. Unfortunately for the stability of its procurement plans, these resources fluctuate according to the spot price of hydrocarbons on the world market. Russia has other serious issues, including problems of regime legitimacy, a restless and periodically violent southern border and a declining population. It also has extensive borders, by land and sea, which it has to protect and secure, without the assurance of belonging to a broader collective security organisation. Despite the settlement of land disputes and other issues with China, it still keeps a wary eye on its politically and militarily assertive neighbour, even as it cooperates with it in a range of Asian forums and military exercises.

Russia's regime has an ambivalent attitude to the USA, Europe and the developed world. It is dependent on the West for access to technology, a refuge for many of its richer citizens and for markets for its hydrocarbons, but is anxious about its military strength, its inexorable grip on the world's economic processes and the corrosive power and relentless march of its democratic model. There is also, barely below the surface, a distinct flavour of sour grapes about the outcome of the Cold War, during which it posed a substantial threat to NATO and its maritime security. Russia yearns to be a great power and its political and security elite mourns the passing of the leverage exerted by the Soviet Union on the world stage, even as it has consigned Marxist economic theory to the historic past.

At sea, Russia just about sustained a steady drumbeat of ballistic missile and attack submarine deployments throughout the post-Cold War era and continues to maintain its remaining surface ships at reasonable, if not completely reliable, levels of activity. With access to three oceans and territory facing onto the Baltic, Black and Caspian Seas, as well as its extensive, detailed scientific familiarity with the sea, Russia needs to protect long sea coasts, but will seek to exploit its geographic advantages in the twenty-first century. It will be an increasingly insistent player in the Arctic and the North Pacific and will want to maintain a strong position on the Black and Baltic seas, as well as in the Mediterranean, as part of a general reassertion of its authority and pursuit of respect in its 'near-abroad'.

Its navy, and the related shipbuilding and system engineering industries, have had persistent budgetary, infrastructure and technical problems over the past two decades, but as part of this more expansive approach, the development of a strong and effective navy is now one of Russia's key priorities. It aims to develop a rapidly modernising fleet, which by 2020 aspires to be as technically advanced, professionally structured and operationally proficient as most NATO countries, although other projects stretch out to 2050, including at some stage a new aircraft carrier or two. It will also introduce up to a hundred new surface ships and submarines of different types over the next ten years. It will spend more than 20 trillion roubles ($657 billion) on modernising its armed forces up until 2020 (more realistically 2030, given Russian industry's track record this century).

The programme includes eight of the new Borei-class nuclear-powered ballistic missile submarines, as well as up to twenty-four new nuclear and conventional attack boats, some of which have begun to enter service. These will join an aircraft carrier (*Admiral Kuznetsov*), a nuclear-powered battle cruiser (*Peter the Great*) and several large missile cruisers. The surface fleet is currently being enhanced by the construction of twenty to thirty new frigates, thirty corvettes and several amphibious ships. A new class of fifteen powerful destroyers will be delivered over the next fifteen to twenty years, to provide anti-submarine, anti-surface and anti-air capabilities. The intention is clearly to provide forces suitable for EEZ and homeland protection,

Russian Borei-class submarine *Yuri Dolgorukiy* on sea trials.

by keeping foreign offensive forces as far away as possible, as well as the ability to project maritime power into distant regions.

With its long history of exploration, sacrifice and effort in the Arctic, the Russian approach to the High North is robustly proprietorial. The fact that the Northern Sea Route (see Chapter 5) for the moment passes through its EEZ suits its purposes entirely, in allowing the Russians to dictate the terms of passage and making Russia, with its grip on access and available infrastructure and icebreakers, the only viable partner for oil and gas exploitation in the region. As the twenty-first century progresses, more of the Arctic will become accessible to shipping and exploitation outside Russia's EEZ and there will be tensions between Russia and those states and companies seeking new opportunities. The presence of Russia's powerful Northern Fleet in Murmansk and its immediate area will be a constant reminder of Russia's capacity to intervene and assert its claims.

Russia is also aware that it needs to maintain its hold on the Black Sea, especially in view of its sensitivities about Ukraine, Georgia and other potentially Western-influenced and breakaway southern republics. It is also suspicious of the growing Turkish and NATO presence and influence in the Black Sea, which, most importantly, gives access to the Mediterranean. The imminent prospect of losing Syria as a long-standing ally, a vital repair and maintenance facility at Tartous and a valuable export market galvanised the Russians into reviving their naval presence in the Mediterranean. In addition, it gave the Russians an opportunity to dabble in the politics of the Arab world after the Arab Spring and detach vessels to the Atlantic and to the international counter-piracy effort in the Indian Ocean. The Russians will not have failed to notice that the navies of other aspirational countries have dipped their toes in the Mediterranean in recent years, notably the Iranians and the Chinese.

As a result, a Russian task group entered the Mediterranean in June 2013. This group comprised a destroyer, two amphibious ships, a tanker and, presumably just in case, a tug. They joined a large anti-submarine ship, a frigate and an amphibious ship from Russia's other three fleets. Official announcements indicated that five or six warships and support vessels would be stationed in the Mediterranean on a rotating basis from each of the four fleets – the Black Sea, Baltic, Northern and Pacific fleets – and that nuclear submarines were likely to follow. By December 2013,

Russia's Mediterranean flotilla comprised a nuclear-powered missile cruiser, a missile destroyer and three large landing ships. They were poised to help escort the transit of chemical weapons out of Syria in civilian roll-on roll-off (Ro-Ro) ferries.

In the Asia-Pacific region, Russia has its own interests to protect and promote. It still keeps a wary eye on Japan, with which it is in dispute about its possession of the southernmost Kuril Islands (close to Hokkaido). It also needs to secure its own ice-free routes into the Pacific from its ports and bases in the east and the Arctic. It has allies and trading partners, like Vietnam, in the region, with which it maintains a careful watch on China's ambitions, even as it conducts naval and military exercises with the Chinese. It is significant that Russia's Pacific Fleet is being modernised and increased at a faster rate than its Northern Fleet.

Russia and China have exercised together regularly over the past few years within the framework of the Shanghai Cooperation Organisation. Nevertheless, even though the Russians have provided significant amounts of military materiel to the Chinese, along with advanced technologies, the two countries have low levels of interoperability and joint doctrine. Russia will be wary of closer engagement with China. Large-scale land-based exercises conducted by each side independently of each other (and clearly with each other in mind) in recent years do not suggest that traditional suspicions have dissipated. Nevertheless, at sea, it seems that the Chinese and the Russians are seeking to cooperate more closely and conduct more sophisticated exercises to project and protect their shared strategic interests. It is likely that these joint exercises will begin to take place closer to the territorial seas and vital shipping lanes of other regional countries.

Further afield, Russia has appreciated that its allies and friends need encouragement occasionally. The largest out-of-area deployment by the Russian Navy in recent years crossed the Atlantic to Cuba and in August 2013 visited Havana, in Cuba. The squadron consisted of the flagship of the Black Sea Fleet, the large missile cruiser *Moscow*, a large anti-submarine ship from the Northern Fleet and an accompanying auxiliary. It is likely that the Russians will seek to reinforce their access to countries where they formerly had bases in the Cold War, such as Vietnam, Cuba and in Africa, to ease their lines of communication in South East Asia, the Atlantic and the Indian Ocean respectively.

India

With its steadily, if not spectacularly, rising economy, increasing regional influence and a long period of political stability, India also considers itself as a potential great power. It assesses that in order to be reasonably secure in relation to Pakistan and China, it needs to maintain substantial land forces, while building up its naval power, so that it can exercise maritime control over the Indian Ocean, from the Gulf of Aden to the Malacca Strait. Its strategy recognises that the air and sea routes across the Indian Ocean convey most of the world's trade, not least considerable amounts of oil and gas from the Gulf, mostly bound for Japan, China, the wider Asia-Pacific region and India itself. The Gulf, from where much of India and China's energy supplies will derive in the years to come, will be a keen area of focus for both India and China.

At the same time, much of India and China's commercial activity will overlap in South East Asia, the Gulf and Africa. India needs to counterbalance Chinese penetration of the Indian Ocean in terms of its port developments, its connections with the Gulf and its diplomatic influence. With an eye on China's growing naval capability and capacity, it seeks to act as a restraint on China's expanding influence and increasingly heavy footprint in the Indian Ocean.

In addition, as they compete in the same markets, more than a hint of rising power rivalry between India and China is likely to manifest itself as both vie for strategic space and regional adherents, even though 70 per cent of India's trade by value and 95 per cent by volume travel by sea, a fair proportion of which is with its largest trading partner, China. As such, the relationship is likely to be complex and will require clear boundaries if both countries are to benefit. The likelihood is that the strategic situation at sea will be determined by a mutual respect for each other's geostrategic space, with an unspoken acknowledgement of China's *droit de seigneur* on the Asia-Pacific rim and a tacit acceptance of a similar position for India in the Indian Ocean, as long as the sea routes remain open and secure for each other's trade and energy supply.

Therefore, although India's security policies will remain centred on South Asia (and its complicated politics), they will increasingly widen to include the Indian Ocean and the broader Asia-Pacific region. The growth of India's power projection capabilities will parallel – and probably conflict with – those of China. India worries about the expansion of Chinese port facilities in Sri Lanka, Bangladesh, Myanmar (Burma), Tanzania and, in particular, the port of Gwadar in Pakistan. China, on the other hand, is concerned about potential Indian interdiction of its lines of supply to and from the Gulf and from its markets in Europe and Africa, something that Indian armchair strategists are keen to highlight. India is also promoting naval cooperation with Vietnam, South Korea, Japan and the USA, with whom India conducts more exercises than with any other country.

In support of this policy, the Indian Navy is expanding its capacity to operate throughout the Indian Ocean region and beyond, especially with HADR interventions, anti-piracy patrols and other missions involving naval diplomacy and local capacity building. It is especially active in supporting the security needs of island states like the Maldives, Mauritius, the Seychelles and Mozambique, as well as Sri Lanka, but has also assisted with more distant evacuation and relief operations as far afield as Indonesia, Myanmar (Burma), Lebanon and Syria. It has defence cooperation agreements and joint exercise arrangements in place with Oman and Qatar.

The Indian Navy is investing heavily in modern platforms, advanced technologies and sophisticated surveillance and communications networks in order to acquire a credible oceanic power projection capability, with the intention 'of safeguarding our maritime interests on the high seas and projecting combat power across the littoral', as the Indian Navy's current Vision Document has it. India has committed $95 billion to naval modernisation and expansion by 2028. It plans to have 150 major warships (currently 132) by 2017, with the older hulls being phased out rapidly. Its modernisation programmes centre on new attack submarines, aircraft carriers and maritime patrol aircraft, together with amphibious and escort vessels, all supported by fleet tankers and supply ships. Forty or so warships and submarines are under construction, the vast majority in Indian shipyards.

India's investment in submarines over the next thirty years is particularly impressive. It will build five new 6,000-ton Arihant-class ballistic missile submarines by 2025, with three boats operational by 2018 (one has just started trials at sea). It will also acquire up to twenty-four new conventional submarines to replace its older Sindhughosh- and

Shishumar-class hulls. The Indian Navy has also been leasing a Russian Akula-class nuclear attack submarine and plans to lease a second hull from 2014.

India's power projection and sea control capabilities will be centred around two carrier task groups, with a third carrier in commission to ensure that two carriers are always available. The Russian-built and modernised 45,000-ton *Vikramaditya* was handed over to the Indian Navy in late 2013. A second carrier, the 37,500-ton *Vikrant*, will be built in Indian yards and launched in 2015, while a third will complete in 2018. Four hundred new maritime aircraft will be acquired by 2025, including maritime patrol aircraft, helicopters and forty-five MiG-29K fighters, for service afloat in the carriers and ashore. Three bases already host UAVs that are used for ocean surveillance. India will also substantially increase its amphibious capability with the acquisition of four large assault ships and eight large landing craft. At the same time, the whole destroyer and frigate force is being upgraded or replaced with modern vessels, notably with additional Kolkota-class destroyers and new stealth frigates.

Finally, it has to provide maritime border and offshore zone defence against criminal activities and terrorist attacks from the sea, such as the November 2008 attack on Mumbai. A newly formed coastguard and a network of land, sea and air platforms and sensors are dedicated to tracking and identifying all contacts operating close to and approaching India's coasts. Given the length of India's coastline and the remoteness of some of its access points, this is a formidable undertaking. However, the acquisition of new P-8I *Neptune* maritime patrol aircraft (the Indian version of the *Poseidon*) and the deployment of UAVs have demonstrated serious intent, as well as concerted attempts to track and report all fishing vessels operating in its territorial seas and offshore zone.

As long as economic growth is sustained and no external threat arises on its land borders, India's naval modernisation programme is likely to match or possibly exceed that of China over the next twenty years. If technical delivery, systems integration and skills issues can be resolved, the Indian Navy will be a dominant regional force in the Indian Ocean by 2030, able to secure its own lines of economic activity and deny opponents the freedom to manoeuvre, and capable of sustaining a powerful presence in the Gulf or Asia-Pacific regions.

Iran

In the modern era, Iran has always sought to be strong at sea, with ambitions in the time of the last Shah that reached out into the Indian Ocean. It seeks to deny access to forces that threaten its regime and encroach on its sovereignty. It also likes to scare the living daylights out of its neighbours in the Gulf and would like to control the passage of shipping through the Strait of Hormuz. It has a particular interest in extending its influence into Central Asia and the Caspian Sea and intends to hold onto three Gulf islands,[14] in the western approaches to the Strait of Hormuz, astride major shipping routes, which it seized from Sharjah (United Arab Emirates) in 1974.

Iran has two navies: a traditional naval force of older frigates, patrol craft and three Russian-built Kilo-class conventional submarines, but with new indigenous frigate and submarine hulls being built and the Iranian Revolutionary Guard Corps (IRGC), which employs high-speed attack boats with rapid-fire guns and short-range weapons, as well as mini-submarines and semi-submersible torpedo-firing vessels. The surface craft rely on swarm tactics against both warships and merchant traffic, while the semi-submersibles are designed for clandestine and covert attack. Since the Iranian Revolution of 1979 and until recently (2008), there have been frequent confrontations and armed exchanges between Iranian forces and US warships in the Gulf and Strait of Hormuz, usually involving IRGC fast attack craft.

By and large, the US Navy and international law, in that order, constrain the ambitions of both the Iranian Navy and the IRGC. In addition, the considerable capabilities of the Gulf States within the Gulf and in the Gulf of Oman, those of Oman, constitute a substantial counterweight to Iran's pretensions. The Arab countries of the Gulf region have invested in powerful, modern warships and systems, designed to resist aggression and coercion by any aspiring regional power. They centre on significant sea denial and anti-access capabilities, which deter threats to both territorial and maritime sovereignty, especially oil and gas facilities in the offshore zones. However, in the face of aggression from Iran or another regional hegemon, it is less certain whether on their own they could guarantee freedom of navigation

---

[14] Abu Musa, Greater Tunb and Lesser Tunb.

or the sea lines of communication through the Gulf, without the implicit assurance of support from the USA and its allies.

The constraints of US-inspired sanctions against the Iranian regime have resulted in a certain amount of improvisation with regard to keeping its older capabilities operational and in its procurement policy. Here, Iran has a particularly close commercial and technology transfer relationship with China, in exchange for the export of substantial energy. There is also a wide range of collaborative military programmes with Chinese defence-related industries. Since 2004, it has been developing its own anti-ship missiles, based on Chinese models. For example, Iran deploys the Chinese-derived 65-nm (120-km) range C-802 sea-skimming anti-ship missile in significant numbers and provided the two missiles to Hezbollah that sunk an Egyptian coaster and struck an Israeli corvette in 2006.

Iran has recently been producing a small number of surface craft and submarines. These have included frigates (with helicopters, anti-ship missiles and torpedoes) and missile boats with anti-ship missiles. Two indigenous mini-submarines have appeared, along with Noor anti-ship missiles, with another in development. In February 2011, Iran demonstrated a short-range anti-ship ballistic missile (135–162 nm/250–300 km) named Khalij Fars, which successfully hit a stationary target vessel. The Iranian Navy claims to have an indigenous Hoot high-speed underwater weapon (equivalent to the Russian Shkval 200-knot weapon).

The Iranian Navy also conducts long-range deployments to the Asia-Pacific region, in shows of solidarity with its primary trading partner. Meanwhile, Iran and Russia both support the Assad regime in Syria, as well as having mutual interests in the Caspian Sea and Caucasus region. Iran also provides basing, maintenance and refuelling facilities to Russian warships, either deployed on anti-piracy patrols off the Horn of Africa or transiting between the Pacific Fleet and the Mediterranean.

Iran's position also has to be considered in relation to increasing Chinese – and Indian – dependence and focus on oil and gas exports from the Gulf region, especially as US interest fades as a result of its shale and unconventional deposit-led drive towards energy security and self-sufficiency. China and Iran are already close, but the relationship will be paralleled by India's growing bilateral agreements with Iraq about oil exports and wider trading interests.

Iran has also been steadily building a presence on the Caspian Sea, to press its claims for between 12 and 20 per cent of the surface area as its economic zone. These claims relate to resource exploitation, fish and caviar as well as oil and gas, but also to a desire for more influence in Central Asia. Iran's latest frigate (*Jamaran-2*) was launched there and its deployment, together with mine warfare exercises, would appear to have sent a clear message about Iranian intentions.

Despite sanctions, Iran's merchant marine is active, often operating through obscure beneficial owners and shell companies, to avoid the scrutiny associated with sanctions. It also has an established relationship with Sudan, which involves port visits and trade, but is thought to include the supply of weapons, through informal networks, to Iranian proxies in the wider Middle East. In both 2011 and 2012, the Iranian Navy sent warships into the eastern Mediterranean in a gesture that was clearly designed to appeal to a domestic audience and to annoy Israel. In 2013, Iran said that it would dispatch warships in response to the Syrian crisis and in February 2014 that a destroyer and a support ship would transit the Atlantic. All in all, it would appear that the Iranian regime is appreciating the influence and political leverage that deployable sea power can offer in its quest to become a regional power. It seems to have learned that the mere possession of naval assets is insufficient in this regard; it is how they are used that counts.

South America

One geographical area that still lacks an obviously dominant or maritime hegemon is South America, where Chile and Brazil have the most competent and capable maritime forces. All countries in that region are likely to extend their control over their EEZs in the period leading up to the 2020s, while it is likely that Brazil will continue to develop its maritime capabilities rapidly in the next fifteen years as its interests in offshore oil and gas extraction expand and as its international profile and regional clout grow in the years up until 2020. Brazil already operates the refurbished aircraft carrier *São Paulo*,[15] along with naval A-4 Skyhawk jet aircraft, S-6 Tracker AEW aircraft and Sea King ASW helicopters. Also used to allow Argentinian

---

[15] Formerly the French aircraft carrier *Foch*, built in the early 1960s.

naval aircrew to practice deck landings, the *São Paulo* is likely to be replaced by a new domestically built (or leased) carrier in 2020–22, with modern jet aircraft and unmanned systems. Brazil is also likely soon to acquire modern surface combatants and advanced submarines, to add to its extensive maritime patrol capabilities. Chile, with its extensive coastline will continue to invest in a strong navy, while Argentina, with the benefit of significant discoveries of offshore gas, is likely to invest heavily in maritime forces as soon as its economy reconfigures to reflect this windfall. This shift will alter the balance of power in the South Atlantic and in the Antarctic and will have implications for broader security. Another emerging trend is that China is likely to wish to establish port facilities on the continent, engage more intensively in oil and gas extraction joint ventures and secure its routes in support of its significant investment in commodities and raw materials in South America.

THE EMERGING PATTERN OF POWER AT SEA

Many countries around the world are investing in capabilities that enable them to resist aggression by assertive neighbours, penetration of their maritime borders and encroachment in their offshore zones. This reflects in part an acknowledgement of their vulnerabilities to coercive naval power and commercial and other interlopers. Therefore, countries on the rise are tending to prioritise their investment towards not only maritime patrol vessels and aircraft to protect their EEZs, but also advanced, multipurpose submarines, anti-ballistic missile capabilities and amphibious forces to deter would-be aggressors or robustly maintain claims. The states with more substantial resources and great power aspirations are thinking in terms of aircraft carriers, amphibious capabilities and nuclear-powered submarines as the means of asserting regional primacy and projecting power and influence beyond their immediate neighbourhoods. They also have a general desire to deploy 'soft power' in response to humanitarian events and natural disasters, in a world in which increasing numbers of people and coastal areas will be affected by extreme events.

The distinctive feature of almost all these navies is that they define themselves, in terms of capabilities and resource allocation, in relation to each other or in relation to a specific regional threat, and as a hedge against future uncertainty. In the case of China, imitation of, opposition to or catch up with the USA seems to be the order of the day. As a result, the navies of the leading maritime states are likely to eye each other and each other's capabilities warily; balances of maritime power are likely to emerge, involving regional competition between major emerging powers and countervailing competitors or a combination of like-minded countries. However, European countries and the democracies of the Asia-Pacific region will stand on their own two feet only on the understanding that the USA will be willing and able to project decisive force into their individual regions in the event of serious confrontation or crisis, in relation to Russia and China respectively.

China and Russia and others have an interest in diminishing the dominant role of America at sea, especially to exclude its presence in their spheres of influence and to keep its military power at a respectable distance. China is not keen on US naval presence in the Asia-Pacific region; Russia wants to exclude it from its 'near abroad', notably in the Black Sea, the Baltic Sea and the Arctic; and Iran frets constantly about supercarriers passing through the Strait of Hormuz. More benignly, perhaps, the Indians would just like to be left to look after the Indian Ocean. China and India also wish to reset the terms by which the sea is used and the current international rules are interpreted and applied. China in particular has invested significant resources, technology and training in a range of capabilities that seek to exclude the USA from its areas of vital interest. It is also developing strategic programmes that include expeditionary and power projection platforms that will enable it to operate across many of the world's oceans. Meanwhile, Russia is modernising its maritime capabilities so that its tactical and technical proficiency will be roughly equivalent to that of NATO forces by 2020–25. NATO will remain critical in maintaining equilibrium in the Western hemisphere, just as suitable arrangements for the USA and its allies to provide assurance and to support their friends (and interests) will be critical in the Eastern hemisphere.

Nevertheless, countries will cooperate or compete with other states as it suits their interests over time. Given the diversity and dispersal of political, economic and military power as a result of globalisation, it is probable that relationships will be complex and multi-stranded. The dilemma between various countries' strategic and security preoccupations and their commercial interests will be a constant challenge to simplistic notions about the character of strategic competition in the twenty-first century. Lord Palmerston's views are likely to prevail: 'It is a narrow policy to suppose that this country or that is to be marked out as the eternal ally or the perpetual enemy ... we have no eternal allies, and we have no eternal enemies. Our interests are eternal and perpetual, and those interests it is our duty to follow.'[16]

What is certain is that many other states are investing in systems and technologies that will make it difficult and risky for America and its allies to impose their will or prevail in situations that have been traditionally amenable to the exercise of sea power. They will have to become used to seeing much more of their rivals and competitors at sea, as well as a host of new local and regional powers, all determined to exploit the benefits of maritime power. This is likely to result in a decline of America's relative power to enforce its will in certain regions, but the maintenance of enough fighting power and sustained reach to make its influence felt across whole oceans and continents. As such, the USA looks set to remain the decisive force at sea in the near future – in gross tonnage of warships alone, the USA outweighs both China and Russia by a ratio of thirteen to one.

The situation at sea in the Asia-Pacific region will be shaped by the development and reorientation of trade routes – to reflect the global economy of the twenty-first century – and the pattern of alliances and antipathies that emerges in response to geopolitical imperatives and regional disputes. The interrelationships between the various major players will be important and always in motion. The USA has a treaty with Japan and South Korea, an implied protective arm around Taiwan and a strategic understanding with India. It does not like Iran, has never trusted Russia and feels intuitively that China is up to no good. China has a strategic and commercial understanding with Russia and a close commercial and political relationship with Iran; it is commercially engaged with South Korea and Japan, yet it is culturally and politically out of tune with both. Russia and China do not step on each other's toes at present. Russia has given up for now on India, except for armaments exports and technological cooperation, wants to see the breakup of NATO and continues to see the USA as a strategic competitor, if only as a means of preserving its own identity and regime security; it also

---

[16] Speech to the House of Commons, 1848.

has outstanding territorial disputes with Japan. India is concerned about China on its land border and in the Indian Ocean, especially in relation to Pakistan and its lines of communication to the Gulf. Everyone trades with each other. Nobody likes to mention North Korea. No one expects the USA to depart the scene.

CHAPTER FOUR

A Changing Seascape

*'Oceans are critical, not just to our economy; not just to our
food supply; not just to America's trade and security; but to
the fabric of life itself. Those dark-blue waters are perhaps
the single greatest natural treasure on God's Earth.'*[1]

Natural processes and human activity ensure that the sea is constantly chang-ing its physical appearance, extent and composition. Much of the change takes place, as far as most people are concerned, out of sight and, therefore, out of mind. When considered at all, the sea is usually viewed in abstract or romantic terms or with fascination, fear or incomprehension. Like sea power, most people simply think of the sea in a general sense when it affects the land or in relation to how it either helps or hinders their everyday lives.

This chapter looks at current and emerging changes in the physical character of the sea in the twenty-first century arising from man-made and natural causes. It deals with acknowledged and recognisable trends, along with their likely consequences and outcomes for the sea and everyone on the planet.

THE HUMAN FOOTPRINT

Even a casual observer will have noticed that the seascape of the inshore area has been changing its appearance rapidly as a result of human activity in the modern era. It will be evident from the profusion of renewable energy wind turbines off the coast of Denmark, the proliferation of oil and gas platforms

[1] Al Gore in a speech to the National Ocean Conference, Monterey, California, 12 June 1998.

off the United Arab Emirates (UAE) or the extensive engineering projects that hope to forestall and mitigate rising sea levels in the Netherlands that mankind is going energetically offshore. Although for centuries the shallow waters of the littoral regions have been subject to extensive colonisation and expansion, mostly in response to climatic and topographical changes, the absence of suitable technological solutions and sufficient economic incentives have limited the extent to which offshore development took place. The pace has now quickened.

In addition to hosting the extraction of oil and gas deposits, the littoral regions of the world are becoming increasingly complex and densely covered with fixed features. In order to create more space in certain areas for human activity, especially in crowded cities, major engineering works have been undertaken in coastal zones to develop habitation, industrial facilities, aquaculture, renewable energy generation and transportation.

The most tangible change takes the form of land reclamation or the construction of artificial islands, notably off the eastern seaboard of the USA and around Japan. For centuries, reclamation of land has been the principal peaceful means by which countries and densely populated cities have been able to extend their territories, build large infrastructure projects, such as airports and power generation facilities, and expand economic activity. The process is particularly active in the vicinity of high-value, urban developments and in states where there is too little space to sustain population and economic growth in tandem.

Major land reclamation in the UAE, though a relatively recent phenomenon, has significantly changed the geography of the coastline. Abu Dhabi has implemented extensive land reclamation programmes (at Yas, Al-Reem and Lulu islands), by filling in coastal salt flats and wetlands, on which extremely large industrial, recreational and port facilities have been built. Similarly, in Dubai, reclamation has seen the construction of the iconic Palm and World Islands, the Dubai Marina and the Burj Al-Arab hotel. The Palm Islands alone add 520 km (320 miles) of water frontage to the Emirate.

Singapore has grown by nearly 30 per cent since the 1960s, driven by population pressure and economic necessity, to accommodate housing, commercial development, industrial space and a range of transport requirements, including port and airport facilities. By 2030, the land area will have increased by roughly another 100 sq km (40 sq miles). Hong Kong has been growing ever since the second century BCE. In more recent times, a succession of major reclamation schemes were started in the nineteenth century; in 1890, 240,000 sq m (287,000 sq yd) were added and the process has continued since then. Major commercial, recreational and transport facilities, such as the Hong Kong Disneyland Resort and Hong Kong International Airport, were all built on reclaimed land, and a new three-runway airport scheme will reclaim a further 6.5 sq km (2.5 sq miles).

The country with the shortest coastline in the world is trying to move up the league table. Having rejected schemes for large, artificial offshore habitable islands, Monaco will extend its Fontvieille district into the Mediterranean to produce another 0.05 sq km by 2014, at a cost of £10.5 billion.

With the prospect of 9 billion people on the planet by 2045, it is likely that more intensive colonisation of the coast will occur in those places where commercial interests and demographic pressure justify the investment for land reclamation, to provide habitation and sites for industrial installations such as oil rigs, renewable energy plants and aquaculture. More intense use of the coastal zone will introduce vulnerabilities and challenges, especially for security and defence, not least because of the numbers of people and the inherent fragility of urban infrastructure and integrated utilities in the face of disruption and attack, whether by a conventional opponent or a terrorist group.

CLIMATE CHANGE

Let's get one thing straight from the start. Climate change is happening; the climate has always changed and it always will. It is part of the natural cycle of our planet.

Right now, the planet is assessed to have been warming for some time and carbon dioxide has been absorbed into the atmosphere at an appreciable rate. Beyond that, the problem for the man on the street is that debate and policy development with regard to climate change have taken place predominantly at the political, ideological and emotional levels. The balance of evidence and reasoned judgement seems to have taken a back seat; everyone has an agenda. The extent to which humans are responsible for changes on a planetary scale has become a matter of interpretation in the face of a mass of conflicting evidence. As such, we mortals can only realistically deal with trends affecting the biosphere that we can clearly see are already under way and from which we can deduce tangible and likely consequences.

Let us agree about something else: the liquid volume of the sea is increasing, for two main reasons. Firstly, the Arctic ice cap[2] is reducing in size and pouring masses of fresh water into the oceans, where it is joined by freshwater run-off from the land through rivers and melting glaciers. The second cause is thermal expansion – the warmer water becomes, the more its volume increases. As a result, sea levels are rising (although not at a uniform rate on account of local and regional variations in topography). In addition, there are detectable changes under way in the salinity and chemical composition of the water column.

The bottom line is that changes in the world's climate are affecting the sea. As the sea is a major participant in the way in which the planet operates and regulates its functions, any change in its character will have consequences for all life on Earth. Regardless of what is being done to arrest, mitigate or reverse climate change, mankind will have to adapt to the changes that are taking place, just as previous generations have done. We just need to be careful that our assessment of the underlying science and the human engagement in complex processes are appropriate and proportionate, remembering that sometimes, in 'striving to better, oft we mar what's well'.

Ocean warming

Overall, the world's oceans are warmer now than at any point in the last fifty years. This is important because the sea contains and retains significantly more heat than the atmosphere. In particular, the top layer of the ocean has been warming at a rate of about $0.1°C$ ($0.2°F$) per decade. Not only has this caused thermal expansion of the oceans, but changes in temperature have also led to significant shifts in both the sedentary behaviour and migratory patterns of all living things in the sea. The biological consequences are hard to predict with confidence, but some species are likely to find themselves in

---

[2] The volume, of course, is not increased by the ice floating on the surface of the sea, but by water from glaciers and ice fields that overlie the land (Archimedes' Principle).

areas where their normal diet does not exist or where their usual breeding and nursery habitats cannot be sustained.

Already, many species are moving to higher latitudes to seek more congenial temperatures, while other creatures are adapting to their new environments. It is estimated that fish will move 27–35 km (17–22 miles) closer to the Poles between 2014 and 2050. This process of warming and migration looks set to continue, both in the shallow surface layer and in deeper waters, as animals move to those areas that best suit their chances of survival, procreation and well-being.

Static species and those that are not able to move easily or far are being seriously affected. Coral growth has slowed and is sometimes killed off by minor changes in temperature because reefs 'bleach' and fail to absorb algae. Krill reproduce in significantly smaller numbers when the surrounding sea temperature rises, with consequent effects all the way up the food chain, notably to penguins and seals.

Warmer water also holds less oxygen, a problem for fish as they need to absorb oxygen from water to grow. Larger fish require correspondingly more oxygen so the decline means that they will stop growing at a younger age. This will also have an impact on breeding cycles and fertility as smaller fish generally produce fewer, smaller eggs and overall their resistance to over-fishing and pollution would be reduced. Modelling suggests that by 2050 fish in the Indian Ocean are likely to shrink by 24 per cent, in the Atlantic by 20 per cent, and in the Pacific by 14 per cent. [3]

Acidification

About 30–40 per cent of the carbon dioxide in the atmosphere dissolves naturally into oceans, rivers and lakes. The sea is a natural carbon dioxide sink, with marine life such as phytoplankton happily absorbing significant amounts of carbon. In the past 300 years, carbon dioxide has been absorbed in increasing amounts (up to 30 per cent more) in the oceans. To maintain chemical equilibrium, some of that carbon has reacted with the water to form carbonic acid, causing the sea to become progressively more acidic – or less alkaline, if you prefer.

---

[3] *Nature Climate Change*, published online 30 September 2012.

Verifiable readings taken since only the 1980s indicate that there has been a 12 per cent rise in acidity levels in the oceans since then. Informed opinion avers that acid levels could have risen by 25 per cent since the start of the Industrial Period and might almost double by 2100. This process of acidification not only alters the chemical content of the water, but also hinders or, in the worst cases, dissolves the shell and skeletal development of certain sea creatures, such as molluscs and corals. Antarctic pteropods, whose life cycles are particularly sensitive to changes in acidity and alkalinity, are regularly held up by the scientific community as being in the front line of acid attack, but oysters, clams, sea urchins, jumbo squid and calcareous plankton are also at risk. As the planktonic larvae of these and other creatures are an essential part of the marine food chain, there are concerns that variation in their growth patterns and distribution on this scale could have an adverse impact on edible fish as well. It is worth reflecting that seafood generates about 16 per cent of the protein that sustains almost two-thirds of the world's population as part of an industry that is worth over $200 billion a year.

Shellfish also play an important role in removing substantial amounts of carbon from the ocean as it is accumulated and stored in their shells, which then descend into the deep ocean after they die. Therefore, a collapse of some populations would further aggravate and accelerate the acidification process.

On the other hand, just as on land, marine algae and plants thrive on absorption of carbon dioxide, which they exploit during photosynthesis. In addition, it is thought that acid enables algae and plants to trap nitrogen and convert it into protein. This would be good news for areas of ocean that are sterile as a result of too much nitrogen. As the oceans' plant life provides about 52 per cent of the oxygen in the atmosphere, increasing activity by various sea flora could prove beneficial overall.

It is clear that there could be winners as well as losers, as a result of increasing acidity in the oceans. On the available evidence, it seems reasonable to suggest that some species are likely to decay and die out as a result, while others will positively thrive. Nevertheless, there is some evidence to suggest that species are more resilient and resistant to changes caused by temperature variations and acidification when they are healthy. Here, the encouragement and maintenance of balanced and sustainable eco-systems would appear to lie at the heart of long-term remedial measures.

It is perhaps also worth noting in passing that in the past carbon dioxide has formed a higher proportion of the Earth's atmosphere than it does today, and the geological record shows clearly and unambiguously that life flourished at the time, both in the oceans and on land.

The Arctic

The most dramatic changes in the physical composition and appearance of the sea are taking place in the High North, at the top of the world. No precise definition for the term 'Arctic' is universally recognised, but it is generally taken to mean the land contained within the Arctic Circle (75 degrees North latitude). The Arctic accounts for a sixth of the world's total land mass, and it supports 4 million permanent inhabitants, as well as numerous other land and sea species, including significant numbers of photogenic polar bears.

Before 1990, more than 80 per cent of the Arctic Ocean was covered by a solid ice sheet that had thickened year-on-year. Research published over the last ten to fifteen years shows that Arctic sea ice has been gradually shrinking and thinning over the last few decades. The National Snow and Ice Data Center at the University of Colorado reported in 2013 that since 2007 sea ice had fallen by 70,000 sq km (27,000 sq miles). Currently, the Arctic region is losing about 155,000 sq km (60,000 sq miles) of ice annually, roughly equivalent to the size of the US state of Georgia. There are uncertainties regarding the pace and pattern of the melting, and predictions of future sea ice melt and ice cover differ greatly, but scientists do more or less agree (amazingly) that the Arctic is warming faster than the rest of the planet.

In September 2012, Arctic sea ice reached its lowest extent since satellite records began, a level of loss blamed on the decline of a mechanism called albedo, the ability of the Earth's surface to reflect sunlight. Snow-covered sea ice has a high albedo, which reflects up to 85 per cent of sunlight, but the land and sea do not reflect as much. Most studies accept that there has been a 3 per cent decline in albedo in the Arctic in the past thirty years, with the most rapid drop every August. The reflectivity of the remaining ice is also being affected by the unwelcome presence of industrial soot or black carbon.

On balance, it seems possible that, over the next twenty years, the volume of Arctic sea ice will decrease by approximately 40 per cent and the lateral extent of sea ice will be reduced by at least 20 per cent in summer. The loss of ice is most noticeable at the end of each northern summer (September), when sea ice shrinks to a minimum, as part of its seasonal cycle. Climate models also suggest that summer sea ice in the Arctic Basin will retreat further and further away from most Arctic land masses, opening new shipping routes and extending the navigation season on the Northern Sea Route (the passage across the top of Russia) by between two and four months, an issue which will be explored further in the next chapter.

SEA LEVEL RISE

Thermal expansion and melting ice increase the volume of the world's oceans and cause sea levels to rise. This phenomenon is widely considered to be the greatest threat to humans posed by climate change and is reckoned to be the clearest indicator of a warming planet.

But sea levels change all the time. Everyone knows that over the centuries of the historic record, sea levels have risen and fallen. In England, William I (the Conqueror) landed on the seashore at Pevensey in Sussex in 1066. He would find it difficult to do so today, as the place is 3 km (2 miles) inland. There are many other places around the world that exist today only because of a previous retreat of the sea, which can be caused by a variety of factors, including changes in climate and variations in the motion and rotation of the Earth. It is all very complicated and scientists have not been able to unravel the complexities of what has clearly not always been a linear process. In any case, reliable data for the evidence of previous sea level variability is not available.

The major land ice formations – Greenland and the Antarctic – contain huge amounts of fresh water, around 70 per cent of all the fresh water on the planet. Estimates suggest that, if the land-based Greenland ice sheet were to melt away completely, sea levels would rise about 6 m (20 ft). If the similarly land-hugging West Antarctic Ice Sheet (WAIS) were to melt, you could add another 6 m (20 ft). If the East Antarctic Ice Sheet (EAIS) melts, life would look and feel a lot different, as that would mean a rise of about 70 m (230 ft). A 1 per cent loss in ice from these three sources would produce a likely rise in sea levels of about 76 cm (30 in). The theoretical potential for sea level rise is spectacular and takes us into some scenarios that would spur Noah into action. Add in the routine thermal expansion, and the predictions become a lot higher – and certain coastal cities like New Orleans and Miami would be joining Atlantis and Port Royal.

Forecasts rely on models that contain a high number of variables: the rate of atmospheric warming (which varies from region to region), the pace of glacial and polar ice melting and the absorption rate of carbon dioxide by the sea. Regional projections are highly unreliable, with each model producing widely varying results based on little more than interpolation from general or global trends. All this uncertainty does not help strategic planning and investment in places such as London, the Netherlands or Miami, places where routine storm surges, inundation and flooding are likely to accompany any appreciable rise.

For example, the Intergovernmental Panel on Climate Change (IPCC), while hedging about the uncertainty, reckoned in 2007 that the sea would rise 18–59 cm (7–23 in) by 2100. That was of course if current trends in polar melt and glacier flow continued and the planet warmed by 5.4°C (9.7°F), despite the fact that elsewhere the report thought that it would be 6.4°C (11.5°F). In 2013, the estimate was updated, and the sea level rise is now set at 26–82 cm (10–32 in) by 2100.

Traditionally, measurements of sea levels have been taken by tide gauges, which recorded the height of a water level relative to a fixed, specific point on land. They are affected by several influences, such as seasons, astronomical tides and storm surges, so there is a large margin of error, but on average they showed that, between 1870 and 2004, global average sea levels rose 195 mm (7.7 in). From 1950 to 2009, measurements showed an average annual rise in sea level of 1.7 mm with satellite data showing a rise of 3.3 mm per year from 1993 to 2009 – almost twice the long-term average.

Since satellite altimeters were placed in orbit in 1992, they have shown that sea levels have risen at 3.2 mm per year. On this basis, by 2100 they could have risen to average levels of 50–150 cm (20–59 in). Recent projections assessed by the US National Research Council in 2010 suggest a possible sea level rise over the twenty-first century of 56–200 cm (22–79 in). Although the estimates for future increases vary, both tide gauge and satellite data show that sea levels are indeed rising. The bottom line is, you choose the rate of sea level rise, but you can't deny that it *is* rising, and apparently at a faster rate than at any other time in the previous century.

Also affecting sea levels are the routine incidence of storm surges, extreme events, high tides and other meteorological assaults on the land, such as hurricanes, typhoons and tsunamis, and general rising temperatures. Models suggest that there will be increases in the frequency and strength of high-end temperature extremes by the end of the twenty-first century, while cold extremes will decrease. These indicators suggest that the occurrence of extreme events (hottest days) will increase from one in twenty years to one in five or one in two, and will also rise on average by 1–3°C (1.8–5.4°F) by the mid-twenty-first century and 2–5°C (3.6–9°F) by the late twenty-first century.

As well as rising sea levels, warmer oceans are thought to be contributing to a big increase in evaporation from the surface of the seas, which in turn leads to heavier rains and potentially more severe storms, as well as the possibility of longer cyclone seasons in some parts of the world. Taken together, these two issues – vertical movement of the sea upwards and horizontal movement during extreme events – add up to a potentially 'perfect storm' for coastal settlements in topographies that are already vulnerable to the violence of the sea.

Even though sea level rises will not be uniform, owing to local topography and weather patterns, there is little doubt that the most serious effects will be witnessed in the Asia-Pacific region, with low-lying areas subject to extensive inundation and land loss. Without remedial action, this scale of devastation towards 2050 and beyond will certainly lead to depopulation, migration and starvation on a massive scale. A 20-cm (8-in) rise would mean extensive depopulation in certain areas such as Nigeria (up to 600,000). Thailand's floods from July 2011 to January 2012 resulted in $46 billion in damage, much of which could have been mitigated with adequate infrastructural defences. Island states in the Indian Ocean and Pacific are particularly vulnerable – Tuvalu and the Maldives could be uninhabitable by 2100. The nature of the evidence is such, though, that even this assessment is open to question because of conflicting evidence associated with storm-derived coastal erosion and local geological contexts.

In the Netherlands (appropriately also known as the Low Countries), 80 per cent of the population live below sea level in a country that has seen a 20-cm (8-in) rise in sea level over the past century. The people of the Netherlands, used to a pragmatic relationship with the sea, are prepared for up to a third of the country being threatened with inundation in future.

Floating houses in Groningen, the Netherlands.

They are working on the assumption that the North Sea will rise by up to 1.3 m (4.3 ft) by 2100, and 2–4 m (6.5–13 ft) by 2200. In 2008, the Dutch assessed their infrastructure requirements in anticipation of these rises,[4] and the recommendations included plans for permanent evacuations to the east, as well as €100 billion (£83.5 billion) of spending up to 2100 to strengthen coastal dunes, flood certain areas and construct new sea and river dykes to complement the massive engineering and flood control schemes that are already in place. There are also schemes for floating housing and utilities that would link to form anchored communities of up to 50,000 people.

Similar studies are taking place to determine the vulnerability of eastern England and the Thames Estuary to rising sea levels and to the frequency and strength of storm surges in the area. Given current projections, it is unlikely that the current Thames Barrier would be able to cope. Places such as Sheerness, at the mouth of the River Thames, face rises of just under 1 m (3 ft) by 2100, which complicates decisions about existing and future infrastructure and settlement. The flood barriers that protect London only expect to be breached once every 1,000 years. A 1-m (3-ft) rise in sea levels

---

[4] *Delta Commission (Deltacommissie)* (2007), led by Dutch politician Cees Veerman.

would result in the flood protection defences in the Thames being breached during storms once every ten years on average. Some perspective is required, though, as a 1-m (3-ft) rise would be five times the rate that has been estimated for the twentieth century.

Meanwhile, the *New York Times* produced a series of maps and sea level rise projections that graphically illustrated the likely impact on cities in the Continental USA.[5] It demonstrated that, in the event of a 1.5-m (5-ft) rise, 7 per cent of New York; 32 per cent of St Petersburg, Florida; 68 per cent of Galveston, Texas; and 94 per cent of Miami Beach would be flooded.[6] If the sea goes higher, to 3.5 m (12 ft), the entire Miami downtown area would be submerged.

The effects of these changes would be magnified and complicated by the high, and accelerating, level of urbanisation in the coastal regions of the world. By 2045, it is anticipated that 70 per cent of the world's population will be living in cities compared to 51 per cent in 2014. These changes will pose further problems for those countries with nuclear power generation plants, which need access to plentiful amounts of coolant, and thus are sited close to the sea in coastal regions. The Fukushima nuclear disaster in 2011, when the plant was hit by a tsunami, was a salutary reminder of the peculiar vulnerabilities of nuclear plants in the face of extreme events and the difficulties of containing the complex fallout (literally). The fact that significant numbers of nuclear power generation plants are also situated in an area of significantly elevated risk (the Pacific 'Ring of Fire') with regard to earthquakes, extreme weather and tsunamis should be a cause of international concern.

Rising sea levels and the impact of extreme events are affecting insurance premiums and the willingness of insurers to provide cover for certain areas. The insurance company Allianz estimated that as much as $28 trillion in coastal infrastructure would be at risk by 2050, with just a 0.5-m (1.6-ft) sea level rise. It is clear that governments will need to make strategic judgements about investing in infrastructure and works to deal with the effects of climate change or plan a programme of managed retreat. They will also

[5] 'What Could Disappear', www.nytimes.com, 24 November 2011.
[6] The percentages represent dry, habitable land within the city limits that would be permanently submerged.

need to invest in flood defences and tighten building restrictions in risky locations to mitigate the collateral damage from extreme weather hazards. Hurricane Sandy, which struck in October 2012, cost the US economy about $65 billion (£39 billion), second only to Hurricane Katrina, at $108 billion (£65.5 billion).

The prospect of changing topographies caused by sea level rise means that realistic consideration is being given to the siting of living space and facilities on artificial platforms, floating structures or moored communities, to support significant numbers of people. Floating communities already feature in parts of the Great Lakes in North America and (as we have seen) in the Netherlands. The Makoko floating and stilted community off Lagos in Nigeria, which has existed for more than 120 years, contains about 12,000 vessels and structures and accommodates over 90,000 people. Although Makoko is being broken up as part of a slum clearance programme, there are plans to replace it with floating and moored eco-friendly, sustainable dwellings and facilities, to help relieve a city that is projected to increase from 21 million in 2014 to 40 million by 2035.

We will all have to accept that coastal topographies and the familiar features of our shorelines are going to change, as they always have, in response to the volume, motion and temperature of the sea. The reality is that countries need to be prepared for changes in the physical character of their coastlines and have plans and precautions in place to deal with whatever Mother Nature has in store. History is probably a good guide to where inundation and flooding are likely to occur and a careful watch on the tide gauge and the best estimates of sea level trends would seem a reasonable investment, even if the data never seems definitive enough for democratic policy decisions and hard resource investment. Not everyone is convinced of the need for action: North Carolina's legislators have outlawed 'scenarios of accelerated sea-level rise unless such rates are ... consistent with historic trends'[7] and a survey by the Massachusetts Institute of Technology found cities in America among the least likely, globally, to have plans for adapting to changing weather.

---

[7] Kieran Mulvaney, 'North Carolina to Sea Level Rise: Go Away', www.news.discovery.com, 15 June 2012.

EXTREME WEATHER

Many extreme weather and climate events continue to be the result of natural climate variability that has been recorded for some considerable time. Significantly large changes in climate do lead to changes in the frequency, intensity, geographical footprint and seasonal timing of extreme weather and climate events, and can result in unprecedented extreme weather and climate events. However, many extremes are the result of an accumulation of normal, regular weather or climate events that are not considered extreme on their own. There is little doubt that, as the temperature of the atmosphere increases, its capacity to hold water increases, leading to stronger storms and higher rainfall amounts. This natural variability has to be recognised as a key factor when assessing whether increasing amounts of carbon dioxide and other 'greenhouse gases' in the atmosphere have an appreciable effect on the frequency and intensity of extreme events.

Climate models claim to predict that the number of intense hurricanes will increase in certain parts of the world. Globally, however, the IPCC says it is likely that the number of tropical cyclones will 'either decrease or remain essentially unchanged'. It is difficult to make predictions about these types of storms as the processes involved occur on much smaller scales than climate models can replicate.

There is a popular misconception that the world is today subject to increasing levels and incidence of severe and extreme weather events. This is perhaps based on the fact that nine out of ten of the costliest hurricanes, in terms of damage, in the USA have occurred in the last decade (with Katrina and Sandy heading the list). The statistical evidence, however, suggests that this is not the case. A brief look back at the twentieth century reveals a trail of similar, if not greater, destruction, including three Category 5 hurricanes; we can continue all the way back to the Great Hurricane of 1780, which was reported to have stripped the bark from the trees (supposedly requiring wind speeds of 320 kmph/200 mph). In November 2013, at its height, Hurricane Haiyan sustained wind speeds of 314 kmph (195 mph), gusting to 378 kmph (235 mph), but it was still only the fourth strongest tropical cyclone in world history.

The simple truth seems to be that in more recent years, increasing numbers of people are settling in coastal zones and developing areas, which

Mother Nature never intended for intensive human occupation. Another accentuating factor is the instant availability of televised reportage and extensive Internet chatter about these types of events, which tend to exaggerate the severity of modern extreme events at the expense of established evidence of fierce weather recorded in the past. Overall, it is difficult to escape the conclusion that, when it comes down to it, the world is not experiencing any more frequent or more intense extreme events than in the past.

One natural process that does determine the likelihood and intensity of storms and floods of biblical proportions is the El Niño phenomenon. This occurs on occasions when a body of unusually warm ocean water temperatures develops off the western coast of South America and causes climatic changes across the Pacific Ocean. In the El Niño–Southern Oscillation (ENSO) phase, there are two linked variations: El Niño is a warm water component, which leads to high air surface pressure; its sister, La Niña is the cold water component, which leads to low air surface pressure. The phenomenon occurs randomly at periods of two to seven years, and lasts nine months to two years, although the average incidence is about five years.

When it gets going, El Niño is characterised by a substantial rise in surface pressure over the Indian Ocean, Indonesia and Australia, with a corresponding decrease in air pressure over Tahiti and the rest of the central and eastern Pacific Ocean. The trade winds in the South Pacific weaken or blow eastwards; warm air rises near Peru, causing rain in the northern Peruvian deserts, and warm water flows from the western Pacific and the Indian Ocean to the eastern Pacific. It is accompanied by rain, causing extensive drought in the western Pacific region and unseasonable, unexpected rainfall in the eastern Pacific region, whose land is normally dry at this time.

Sometimes, the circulation associated with El Niño and La Niña evaporates huge amounts of water out of the oceans and dumps it onto the land, notably in Brazil and Australia. This results in extensive flooding, as was witnessed in dramatic fashion in Brisbane and eastern Australia in 2011 and at lower levels of intensity every year since then, but also causes a relative, momentary drop in sea levels because so much water is retained on the land. Data from 2005 to 2011 shows that two big associated La Niña events in this period caused sea levels to rise more slowly than the long-term trend would have suggested (about 2.4 mm per year instead of 3.1 mm).

So, it would seem that typhoons and hurricanes will continue to inflict themselves on mankind much as they have done in the past. However, it is likely that their impact will grow in relative terms as more people settle in coastal areas, many of which are densely urbanised, that are susceptible to these types of event. It is already apparent that more resources will need to be made available to forecast and prepare for natural disasters and extreme events, and that responses will also need to improve, from more secure buildings, resilient infrastructure and coherent defences to evacuation routines and contingency planning and preparations, all underpinned by simulation technologies and specifically allocated resources.

Navies have a key role to play both in anticipation and during these crises, as formed, equipped and trained bodies of available manpower. They are important not only as a humanitarian response, but also as a key component of diplomacy, on the basis that a friend in need is a friend indeed. For example, during the hurricane season, in case of an emergency, the Royal Navy maintains a frigate and/or a replenishment ship on station in the Caribbean, which has been used on many occasions. More recently, the contribution of specialist platforms, such as aircraft carriers and amphibious ships, able to carry a wide range of stores and supplies as well as provide a source of command and medical and logistics facilities, has been critical to all major emergency situations in the last decade. The aircraft carriers USS *Abraham Lincoln* and USS *Carl Vinson* were at the centre of relief efforts in Indonesia and Haiti respectively. In particular, the ability to deploy helicopters and amphibious craft and vehicles, including hovercraft, has proved invaluable.

Such disaster relief is most effective, however, when these vessels are positioned and coordinated in anticipation of extreme events. Before Hurricane Katrina, the amphibious ship USS *Bataan* had been positioned close to New Orleans and the Gulf Coast ahead of the hurricane's landfall on 29 August 2005, but it took a further five days before a large amphibious group arrived and six before the supercarrier USS *Harry S. Truman* hove into view. In 2012, Hurricane Sandy attracted significantly more effort at an earlier stage, with twenty-seven US Navy and Coast Guard ships, aircraft and various other specialist units involved.

POLLUTION

An area of concern likely to attract cooperation and collaboration on a global scale will be the constant struggle to limit and eliminate pollution in the sea. As all exclusive economic zones (EEZs) are connected to the world ocean it is in everyone's national and international interest that the seas should remain safe, clean, healthy and productive.

Unfortunately, it has been an article of faith among commercial and illicit users of the sea that the sea, in its immensity and depth, is capable of absorbing unlimited amounts of refuse, effluent and inorganic matter. The slogan, 'the solution to pollution is dilution' appears to be the default answer to calls for tighter regulation. All over the world, contamination and degradation of the sea's water quality and of shorelines are continuously taking place, not only as a result of discharges at sea, but also because of the effluent from industrial processes, rapidly expanding cities and intensive agriculture. Harmful contaminants include pesticides, herbicides, chemical fertilisers, detergents, oil, sewage, plastics and other solid materials, all of which introduce alien elements into ecosystems. Many pollutants sink to the seabed and are absorbed by small marine organisms, before entering the global food chain.

Many of these contaminants originate on the land and arrive in the ocean through the discharge of rivers into the sea. Nitrogen-rich fertilisers, phosphates and other chemical-based products feed massive blooms of algae that extract the oxygen from the sea. This process results in 'dead zones', of which more than 400 have been identified around the world, amounting to 260,000 sq km (100,000 sq miles) in total – a tenfold increase since the Second World War. Most of these dead zones are in the littoral regions and in enclosed seas, but they also occur on the high seas in areas where increased temperatures inhibit water mixing and produce oxygen levels insufficient to support marine life. This aspect is already affecting major species and poses a significant threat to others in the future.

The most notorious are the wide dead zone that forms off the Mississippi Delta every year and several off the major Chinese rivers, mainly caused by the accumulated fertilisers and other noxious matter running off agricultural land into the rivers. The areas just about recover before being hit by the next year's deluge. The impacts are compounded in enclosed seas like the

Baltic and Black Seas, the Mediterranean and the Caribbean. Here, the economic and social impact can often be devastating, leading to significant loss of local and regional resilience and sustainability.

On the positive side of the issue, the historical evidence demonstrates that, despite the serious short-term impacts of oil and other pollution on water quality, wildlife and local habitats, the sea, in general, has remarkable powers of recovery in those places where oceanic circulation is not constrained and ecosystems have not been totally destroyed. Happily, major transnational efforts have seen action taken to eliminate the dead zone that used to form in the Black Sea as a result of run-off accumulated during the long route (2,800 km/1,750 miles) of the river Danube to the sea.

But there is another problem that the oceans are struggling to accommodate. Every year a vast amount of solid debris and manufactured waste is deposited in the sea. In particular, the sea is being seriously polluted by plastic objects either dumped from shipping and platforms, in bulk and as casual litter, or from the land, from landfill sites and industrial waste.[8] Organic matter decays, but non-biodegradable objects, such as those made from plastic and other toxic materials, persist in finding their way into the digestive systems of birds, mammals and fish. Fragments of man-made material can be found suspended in the water column, in sediments and in reefs, but can also form vast accumulations of detritus and debris because of the pattern of interconnected oceanic currents, or gyres. One of the best known is the North Pacific gyre, which acts as a massive spinning mechanism, either sucking in material or pushing it out and spreading it around the oceans. It is here that the Great Pacific Garbage Patch, a mass of plastics, chemical waste and other debris, accumulated. At its greatest extent, it stretched across an area of 675 by 450 km (420 by 280 miles) in 2010.

Also in 2010, two other notable garbage patches associated with plastic debris were discovered in the Indian Ocean (4,800 km/3,000 miles in length), and the North Atlantic, where the patch is estimated to be hundreds of kilometres across in size, with a density of over 200,000 pieces of debris per sq km. The debris zone shifts by as much as 1,600 km (1,000 miles)

---

[8] The substantial amount of debris floating, even in the remote region of the southern Indian Ocean, was highlighted by aircraft searching for the missing Malaysia Airlines flight MH370 in March 2014.

north and south seasonally, and drifts even further south during the El Niño-Southern Oscillation. These garbage patches should not be thought of as similar in appearance to landfill sites or islands of rubbish, but, as described by Anna Cummins, co-founder of the 5 Gyres Institute, as 'a thin plastic soup'.[9] The micro-plastic elements, less than a millimetre in size, readily enter the food chain through bivalves and shellfish, which have been shown to suffer hormonal changes as a result. The guts of fish types higher up the benthic chain, like mackerel and cod, have also been found to contain plastic and micro-plastic fragments, although it has not been fully established whether these fragments affect the edible flesh.

Marine sanctuaries and protected areas have proved effective in stimulating conservation measures and imposing discharge limits, as well as enforcement mechanisms. As a result, habitats have been restored, species have recovered and sea-based economies have flourished. However, these areas have generally been positioned in areas of national jurisdiction; beyond these regions designation, monitoring, surveillance and enforcement have proved difficult to establish and maintain.

As might be expected, despite the existence of numerous, overlapping national laws, common regulatory measures and international agreements, notably brokered through the United Nations' International Maritime Organization (IMO), compliance and enforcement have been generally patchy outside national jurisdictions. Widespread dumping of toxic waste has been happening in international waters and in poorly monitored national economic zones for decades and continues to occur. The IMO has had to resort to introducing initiatives that encourage states to cooperate in reducing human effects on water quality.

Emission control

The IMO is the United Nations' specialised agency charged with taking responsibility for the safety and security of shipping and the prevention of marine pollution by ships. It has achieved a good deal more on the pollution and emissions front than it has in its other areas of responsibility, mostly owing to the difficulties of securing consensus from member states. As a

[9] 'Plastic Soup', www.shiptalk.com, 12 August 2010.

result, it has energetically taken up the issue of emissions from ships and the control of alien species, which regularly hitch a ride in the ballast tanks of vessels and migrate to new habitats, which they promptly devastate.

The IMO has also introduced limits to the noxious emissions that are produced by shipping and other users of the sea. It is estimated that shipping emits about 2.4 per cent of the carbon and other polluting elements that make up the global total and, by 2025, this figure could be as high as 4 per cent. In particular, IMO has focused on sulphur and nitrous oxide emissions for which specific control measures are already in place, especially within emission control areas (ECAs) associated with North American and European waters. It has mandated that by 2020, sulphur content will have to be reduced to 0.5 per cent globally (from 4 per cent in 2011) and from 1 per cent to zero in the ECAs. These measures restrict the types of fuel that can be used. While ships are also being obliged to introduce fuel economy measures in order to reduce emissions, the IMO has introduced stringent requirements in relation to the discharge of ballast and so-called 'grey water' from ships, in order to limit the spread of alien species and the introduction of pollutants into the water column.

These measures point towards significant, escalating costs for the shipping industry, which is already experiencing pressure. A report by the UK Chamber of Shipping in 2012 calculated that the measures would result in the loss of 2,000 marine-related jobs and the unexpected consequences of more carbon emissions from land transportation and increases in the cost of passenger and container route rates. In any case, economic considerations and environmental concerns have already prompted concerted efforts to cut fuel consumption and find alternatives. Ship operators are introducing systems to 'scrub' emissions, remove noxious elements and filter discharged water. As usual, Møller-Maersk has pioneered ways of reducing fuel costs and emissions across the whole of its fleet, not least by slower steaming and the introduction of more fuel-efficient ships.

Innovations in machinery design and advanced technical applications have also helped. A modern large crude oil tanker, for example, is able to transport the same amount of cargo twice the distance using the same amount of energy that it would have done in 1995. Marine diesel engines, the prime mover of the world merchant fleet, have improved in efficiency; modern engines installed in 2010–14 use about 10–15 per cent less fuel per kilowatt-hour as compared with engines installed in the 1990s. Ships powered by liquefied natural gas (LNG) are already featuring as a means to reduce emissions. Norway, in particular, has a variety of LNG-powered passenger ferries and other vessels in operation, while two LNG-powered roll-on roll-off (Ro-Ro) cargo vessels entered service in late 2013. As a result, ports are now beginning to develop the necessary infrastructure for LNG refuelling.

Noise

The sea is noisy enough already, as any submariner will tell you, but it is becoming progressively a lot noisier as a result of increased levels of human and mechanical activity. Tangible sound pollution, from high-powered military sonars, offshore platforms, shipping and even natural causes such as earthquakes can cause distress and disruption to the migration, communications and reproductive patterns of many marine animals, especially mammals. Even telecommunications and electrical cables give off discrete sounds that can be detected by sensitive instruments and even more sensitive sea creatures. From the military perspective, high levels of ambient noise, especially in the shallow waters inshore, significantly reduce the ranges at which sonars are able to detect potential opponents, mines and other submarines, although it is possible that advanced processing and increased amounts of computing power will enable sensors to be more effective in the future.

HERITAGE

The term 'underwater cultural heritage' (UCH) refers to all remains of human activities lying on the seabed, on riverbeds or at the bottom of lakes. It includes shipwrecks and other objects lost at sea, as well as prehistoric sites, sunken towns and ancient ports that were once on dry land, but were eventually submerged as a result of climatic or geological changes.

International organisations, states and people are becoming more concerned about their underwater cultural and historical heritage in the face of the threat of progressive decay and commercial exploitation, especially in their EEZs. As such, increased importance and attention is being attached to the recording, preservation and recovery of historically and archaeologically significant vessels and artefacts. The rapidly increasing sophistication of underwater techniques and technologies means that there will be a greatly improved ability to locate and survey sites which in the past would have been too deep or too inaccessible for conventional methods of exploration and excavation.

Wrecks

Wrecks are well out of sight to most users of the sea (unless they happen to hit them). The systematic search for wrecks is motivated principally by the prospect of gain (precious metals and artefacts). Archaeologists and historians come a long way behind in terms of resources, technology and access to legal clout. Countries and the international community are only now waking up to the consequences of the loss of both cultural heritage and significant material riches that have hitherto lain undisturbed on the ocean floor. One can reasonably expect that, as technology for underwater access improves, the motivation to explore and exploit wreck sites will rise, both for archaeological and commercial purposes. This trend is likely to lead to an increase in the demand and need for regulatory and other oversight provision. There are huge numbers of wrecks on the seabed. It is estimated that there are up to 100,000 shipwrecks in the Baltic alone, of which at least 6,000 are deemed of significant archaeological and historical significance.

Current exploration in this area falls into three main categories. Firstly, there are the treasure hunters, whose motivation derives from the commercial value of the contents of the wreck sites. Then, there are the trophy hunters, concerned with locating and probing the secrets of famous wrecks like the *Titanic* and *Bismarck*. Finally, there are the conservationists and archaeologists who seek to preserve as much of the historic record as possible, for the benefit of both current and future generations. One might call this sustainable heritage.

Of course, the motivations of all three main operators in this area overlap and the categories are not exclusive. Nevertheless, there has been sufficient evidence so far to indicate that the profit motive looms large in considerations of investment in the exploration of underwater wrecks and the sites are difficult to police and protect.

The jurisdiction of coastal states under the United Nations Convention on the Law of the Sea (UNCLOS) extends only to objects found within 24 nm (44 km) of the coastline. Objects found on the high seas are not subject to any state's jurisdiction. Some countries have introduced legislation in respect of the wreck sites that lie within their territorial seas. The UK, for example, has a series of Acts, which prohibit or restrict access to more than one hundred historically important wreck sites. The Protection of Wrecks Act of 1973 allocates an exclusion zone around approximately fifty-six historically, archaeologically or artistically important wrecks. It is an offence, in the absence of a licence, to tamper with, damage or remove any objects or part of these vessels. Other wrecks are designated by virtue of their actual or likely contents; diving and exploration on these is strictly prohibited.

Military aircraft and naval vessels that crashed or sank after 4 August 1914 are covered by the Protection of Military Remains Act 1986, which makes it an offence to interfere with the wreckage of any military aircraft or designated vessel without a licence. All crashed military aircraft receive automatic protection, but vessels must be individually designated. Although diving is not prohibited on a designated aircraft or vessel, it is an offence to conduct unlicensed diving or salvage operations to tamper with, damage, remove or unearth any remains or enter any hatch or other opening. Controlled sites are specifically designated areas that cover the remains of a military aircraft or a vessel sunk or stranded in military service within the last 200 years and similar rules about tampering apply.

Finally, the Ancient Monuments and Archaeological Areas Act 1979, which was intended for land sites, is now used for the scheduling of marine sites 'of national importance' for protection at sea. Access is not restricted, but, once again, it is an offence to demolish, destroy, alter or repair it without scheduled monument consent. Effectively, diving on maritime scheduled monuments is permitted on a 'look but don't touch' basis.

Seafarers are also bound under the Merchant Shipping Act of 1995 to report to the Receiver of Wreck all wreck material recovered from UK territorial waters and any wreck material brought into the UK from outside UK territorial waters. This includes wreck material found in or on the sea, washed ashore in tidal waters or recovered from a wreck site, specifically 'jetsam, flotsam, lagan and derelict'.[10]

---

[10] Jetsam: goods cast overboard to lighten a vessel in danger of sinking; flotsam: goods lost from a ship that has sunk or otherwise perished (goods are recoverable because they remain afloat); lagan: goods cast overboard from a ship that afterwards perishes (goods are buoyed so they can be recovered); derelict: property, whether vessel or cargo, which has been abandoned and deserted at sea by those who were in charge without any hope of recovering it.

Similarly, the USA has the Abandoned Shipwreck Act (ASA). Under ASA, the federal government acquires title to any abandoned shipwrecks found in the territorial waters of the USA and immediately transfers title over such wrecks to the state in or on whose submerged lands the shipwreck is located. In granting to the USA title to all abandoned wrecks found within its territorial waters, the law specifically abrogates the law of finds and the law of salvage by preventing the finders of abandoned shipwrecks from acquiring title.

UNCLOS addresses the issue of shipwrecks found on the high seas. It invites all states to protect objects of an archaeological and historical nature found at sea, for the benefit of mankind as a whole, with particular regard being paid to the preferential rights of the state or country of origin. Then it goes on to say , '[n]othing in this article affects the rights of identifiable owners, the law of salvage or other rules of admiralty, or laws and practices with respect to cultural exchanges'. Essentially, UNCLOS provisions concerning shipwrecks in international waters do little to impinge on the law of finds and the law of salvage.

UNCLOS also does not effectively secure the preservation of wrecks found on the high seas. While Article 149 discusses preservation, it fails to define 'objects of an archaeological and historical nature'. Moreover, since Article 303 cannot affect ownership rights, it cannot effectively operate in the presence of an ownership claim. Equally, the goals of preservation conflict with the property rights affirmed in Article 303.

As far as preservation is concerned, under UNCLOS, it is clear that the best protection any state can offer a sunken vessel in international waters is a statute that protects the shipwreck from its own nationals and encourages governments to broker treaties with other countries to respect the archaeological value of wrecks.

The most comprehensive legal instrument available at present for ensuring the protection of UCH beyond territorial waters is the Convention for the Protection of Underwater Cultural Heritage, introduced by the United Nations Educational, Scientific and Cultural Organization (UNESCO) in 2001. This sought to extend state regulation over cultural resources to the length of the continental shelf or EEZ (whichever is widest) and introduce a system of penalties and confiscatory powers for material culture recovered in a manner not consistent with good archaeological practice. As of June

2013, forty-three nation states have signed the Convention, an insufficient number for ratification.

One of the most active and technically successful companies operating in this area is Odyssey Marine. Trading as Odyssey Marine Exploration, Inc., it is possibly the leading deep-ocean speculator, using advanced and unmanned technologies to locate historic and modern shipwrecks and exploit seabed minerals. In 2003, Odyssey Marine discovered the SS *Republic* (American Civil War era) about 160 km (100 miles) south-east of Savannah, Georgia, and recovered more than 51,000 coins and nearly 14,000 artefacts from a site 518 m (1,700 ft) deep.

However, the company's tendency to 'follow the money' and attempts to profit from its pioneering work in locating these wrecks provoked substantial resistance from countries claiming ownership of both the wrecks and their contents, as well as from cultural and historical heritage groups. During the course of its exploration and exploitation of underwater heritage sites, it has had a roller-coaster ride in the ambiguities of international and national law. Between 2007 and 2012, it fought and lost a protracted legal battle over the ownership of the *Nuestra Señora de las Mercedes* (sunk by the British in 1804), containing 600,000 silver coins weighing more than 17 tons, hundreds of gold coins and other precious artefacts. Ultimately, the boat was judged to have still belonged to Spain and Odyssey Marine had to pass the recovered goods to the Spanish authorities.

During the course of extensive legal battles with both international and national authorities, the company would appear to have worked out compromise solutions with national authorities that enable exploration and recovery of finds to mutual benefit and with archaeological best practice enshrined in its operations, working, for example, with the UK's Maritime Heritage Foundation. In turn, this enables the excavation and recovery of objects from British shipwrecks, such as HMS *Sussex* and HMS *Victory*, so that Odyssey Marine is reasonably compensated for its work and responsible survey, excavation and recording of the site takes place.

As a result, in an agreement with the British government, Odyssey Marine recovered 48 tons of silver bars from the SS *Gairsoppa*, a British steam merchant ship that was sunk by a German U-boat in 1941. With the wreck being found 5.5 km (3 miles) deep, it was the heaviest and deepest recovery of precious metals on record. A second recovery effort in 2013 yielded another 1,574 silver ingots (62 tons), resulting in a total of 110 tons of silver, 99 per cent of all the silver that was on board. In accordance with the contract with the British government, Odyssey Marine will retain 80 per cent of the value of the silver, estimated at $210 million.

We can expect to see more determined attempts by countries to preserve and acquire title to the material and historical treasures of wrecks as far out to sea as they can legally and practically assert. States are likely either to extend the use of marine protected areas (MPAs) to nationally significant historical wreck sites or seek to use the UNESCO convention as a vehicle and a pretext for extending other sovereign rights into their EEZs. At the same time, in the absence of definitive international law, there is likely to be a marked increase in exploratory and exploitative activity on the high seas, as technology develops and allows, and a straightforward scramble to locate and exploit wrecks, especially those that can justify a significant return on investment, probably to the detriment of the historic and cultural record.

GEOENGINEERING

Over the past decade or so, there has been a great deal of excitement with regard to the prospects of being able to reverse climate change through what have become known as geoengineering initiatives. These conceptual ideas have ranged from giant sun shields in space to mechanical and absorptive systems that suck the carbon out of the air. The sea has also been the subject and object of various geoengineering schemes, to intervene and counteract climate change and its impact.

One of the most popular schemes (depending on your point of view), with about fifteen practical demonstrations, has been the iron fertilisation of the ocean, which involves the deposit of vast quantities of iron fragments in the sea, on the basis that they would stimulate photosynthesis in phyto-plankton. The idea is that the phytoplankton convert the ocean's dissolved carbon dioxide into carbohydrate and oxygen gas, some of which would sink into the deeper ocean before oxidising. The process actually works and experiments have shown that photosynthesis in phytoplankton can be increased by up to thirty times.

The downside would appear to be that, while the process reduces the amount of ocean acidification at the surface, it tends to increase it in the deep ocean. There is also the chance that, apart from stimulating vast amounts of plankton blooms, iron fertilisation could also markedly increase the incidence of anoxia (the absence of oxygen) in the areas in which it is implemented.

Geoengineering schemes are still in their infancy and clearly need to be subjected to rigorous scrutiny with regard to their impact on complex natural processes and eco-systems, through empirical study and reliable modelling, to allow their safe implementation. Indeed, the international community has had doubts about the wisdom of allowing unrestrained geoengineering enthusiasm. As a result, the IMO has subjected marine geoengineering, mostly centred on ocean fertilisation, to the provisions of the 1996 Protocol to the Convention on the Prevention of Marine Pollution by Dumping of Wastes and Other Matter (1972). Future geoengineering activity that involves altering the composition of the water column will require authorisation and a licence.

FUTURE PROSPECTS

Geoengineering is an example of where there is simply not enough definitive science to support one opinion or another. Policy makers and publics alike are bombarded with a constant barrage of expert assessments and opinion that rarely produce either scientific consensus or policy proposals. It is the nature of scientific inquiry to have a community that supports a range of opinion. Assessments are based on the known facts and a host of variables that together deliver complex, blurred pictures of what is actually going on in the oceans and what is likely to happen. As usual, the public is confused about what it is supposed to think and about what is really going on.

Nevertheless, it is probably safe to accept that certain trends are under way: the climate is changing, fish stocks are being depleted, sea levels are rising, acidification is occurring and the Arctic ice is shrinking. However, opinion about the timeline, scale and extent of the impacts of these processes, especially on different parts of the globe, remains conflicted or obscure, making it difficult for politicians and investors to be precise in their risk assessments and policy development. It is also a recipe for inertia and global indifference in the face of worldwide problems that rely so much on international collaboration and cooperation to resolve.

The physical appearance of the world's oceans is certainly going to change, with a seascape festooned with artificial structures, especially in the littoral regions, including oil and gas platforms, man-made islands and a wide range of power and infrastructure networks. Closer inshore are likely to be floating facilities of increasing complexity and size, servicing energy production and distribution and urban developments. All these factors will have implications for the ways in which states and cities seek to exploit, regulate and secure their economic zones, while balancing social, economic and environmental requirements in the interests of sustainable development.

Similarly, the underwater environment will host increased levels of power generation and distribution systems, alongside wind farms, wave and tide generators, intensive aquaculture, an expanding network of oil and gas pipelines and communications cables, and transport infrastructure that will either pass through tunnels or through tubes on the seabed. Integrating this infrastructure with existing hardware and sites of natural and historical importance will be a significant challenge.

At the same time, the effects of changing topographies and sea levels, especially with regard to critical national infrastructure and nuclear installations, need to be monitored and factored into future plans. As can be readily seen, the littoral and coastal zones will present significant challenges to states and port operators, if they are to preserve and enhance their security and prosperity. Not only are there traditional navigational, security and safety issues, but also the considerable pressures and spatial difficulties caused by the incorporation and integration of complex infrastructures, social requirements and industrial ventures. For military operators, the complexity of these inshore land- and seascapes will make operations much more complicated; it will seem to be more like operating on land in built-up, urbanised areas. Civilian authorities will face a constant struggle to balance social, economic and environmental factors in the interests of sustainable development and in de-conflicting, regulating and licensing significantly increased amounts of human activity.

CHAPTER FIVE

New Opportunities

'Four things never come back: the spoken word, the sped arrow, time past, the neglected opportunity.'[1]

We have seen that the coastal regions of the world will be subject to continual changes in their topographies and character in the twenty-first century. Just as rising sea levels threaten, to a greater or lesser extent, human settlement and development in the coastal zone, mankind is going offshore in the search for living space and economic opportunities. Enabled by new technologies and emboldened by the intense competition for resources, mankind is also venturing further out into the deep oceans, with the intention of exploiting the natural resources that are becoming increasingly accessible and recoverable.

The phrase 'sea control' is usually defined in military terms, but increasingly, in the twenty-first century, it is also likely to be expressed as the ability to gain and maintain access to the resources of the sea. There is likely to be an identifiable 'front line' where soft sea power competes for resource exploitation in both settled and disputed sea areas. This already happens on a daily basis between fishermen of various countries, and the confrontations look likely to increase in the sphere of oil and gas extraction and mineral exploitation. It is already occurring in the South Atlantic, between the UK and Argentina, and threatens to erupt in the East China and South China seas and in the eastern Mediterranean. Nevertheless, for now, it seems appropriate to look at the opportunities rather than the risks.

---

[1] Arabian proverb.

OIL AND GAS

The next 20 years will see fossil fuels continuing to dominate global energy demand for some time to come, with annual increases of 7 million barrels per day (mbpd) up to 2020 to reach over 100 mbpd of annual consumption in 2035, representing a rise of more than a third in that time. Global patterns of consumption and trade are set to change over the next decade, however, as the USA and Canada exploit sources of shale gas, tight oil, oil sands and biofuels. Indeed, North America's emergence as a net oil exporter within about 15 years will reverse the direction of the international oil trade, as China, India and the greater Middle East will account for 60 per cent of all growth in consumption. Almost 90 per cent of Middle Eastern oil exports, as well as a proportion of those from Russia, Nigeria and Venezuela, will go to Asia by 2035, while American and Canadian imports of oil and other liquid fuels are likely to reduce considerably, from the 8 mbpd of 2010 to about 1 mpbd in the same period.

In addition, the USA should become a net exporter of natural gas by 2020 and almost self-sufficient in energy, in net terms, by 2035. Regional gas markets will become more integrated as liquefied natural gas (LNG) becomes more transportable and useable. Gas will increase its share of the energy mix, as demand increases by 50 per cent to 5 trillion cubic metres (176 trillion cubic ft) in 2035. Nearly half the increase in production over this period will be from conventional sources, mostly from the USA, Australia and China, but with significant unconventional and offshore sources in most parts of the inhabited world. Coal is also likely to increase in demand, with an expected growth of 21 per cent by 2030.

It is hardly necessary to mention the opportunities for hydrocarbon extraction and exploitation that exist at sea. All over the world, notable offshore oil and gas fields are to be found in places as far afield as the North Sea between the UK and northern Europe; the Gulf of Mexico; the Santa Barbara basin in California; the Caspian Sea (primarily off Azerbaijan); the Campos and Santos Basins, off the coast of Brazil; Newfoundland and Nova Scotia (Atlantic Canada); West Africa, most notably west of Nigeria and Angola; South East Asia and Sakhalin, in Russia; and the Gulf such as Safaniya, Manifa, Marjan and Abu Dhabi.

New fields are continuously being discovered as well, particularly associated with major gas finds. Evidence of extensive deposits is emerging off East Africa, Brazil, Argentina and in the South China Sea, with many others yet to be located. At the top of the world, fresh discoveries are being made in the Arctic, along with significant amounts of methane contained in the permafrost and as hydrates below the ocean floor. Current indications are that there are 90 billion barrels of oil and 47 trillion cubic m (1.7 quadrillion cubic ft) of natural gas within the Arctic Circle. In total, the US Geological Survey has calculated that the Arctic contains 13 per cent of the world's undiscovered conventional oil and 30 per cent of undiscovered gas reserves.

However, the costs of venturing into remote areas, unconventional environments and even greater depths to explore and exploit hydrocarbon resources are high. The deepest floating facilities are currently operating at depths of about 2,500 m (8,200 ft), including one operated by Royal Dutch Shell in the Gulf of Mexico, which cost $3 billion. The *Financial Times*[2] highlighted a large drillship, the *Bob Douglas*, which operates down to depths of 3,000 m (10,000 ft) of water, drills a further 9,000 m (30,000 ft) and is quoted as costing $618,000 a day – more than twice the cost of the hire of an Airbus A-320 for a month. The technology development and installation costs have reached $600 million and the price of this type of vessel has tripled in ten years.

The CLOV project (named after the Carnation, Lily, Orchid and Violet fields), off the coast of Angola, is an interesting example of a shared enterprise, with Total holding a 40 per cent share as the operator of the block; Statoil a 23.33 per cent share; ExxonMobil 20 per cent; and BP Exploration Angola 16.67 per cent. Extracting oil in water depths of about 1,400 m (4,600 ft) at a range of 75 nautical miles (140 km) from the coast, it will start production of 160,000 barrels per day (bpd) from 2014, based around a floating, production, storage and offloading (FPSO) vessel, connected to thirty-four wells, with 1.8 million barrels of storage capacity. It will also be able to process 6.5 million cubic m (230 million cubic ft) of gas per year.

A noticeable new feature of the physical infrastructure associated with the sea will be the construction and proliferation of terminals capable of handling LNG. This expansion reflects the increased use of gas around the world, especially over distances to markets where pipelines are uneconomical. The

[2] Sylvia Pfeifer and Guy Chazan, 'Energy: More buck, less bang', 11 April 2012.

largest suppliers will be Australia and Qatar, followed by Nigeria and off-shore sources in East Africa, especially Mozambique. China wants to double its imports of natural gas to 80 billion cubic m (bcm) (2.8 trillion cubic ft) by 2015, to achieve an energy mix of 8 per cent, and now has six import LNG terminals, with a total receiving capacity of 21.9 million tons per year, with another twelve in construction, which will have a capacity of 59.4 million tons/80 bcm (2.8 trillion cubic ft) per year.

In August 2013, the China National Offshore Oil Corporation (CNOOC) also announced that it would be developing China's first float-ing terminal for LNG in Tianjin; it will have an annual receiving capacity of 2.2 million tons/3 bcm (106 billion cubic ft). A second phase of the project would see the construction of a more normal onshore LNG ter-minal, with an annual receiving capacity of at least 6 million tons/8 bcm (2.8 billion cubic ft).

Meanwhile, Shell has seen the keel laid for the world's first floating liquefied natural gas (FLNG) project, Prelude FLNG, at Samsung Heavy Industries' Geoje shipyard in South Korea. Once complete, the 600,000-ton facility will be almost 500 m (550 yd) in length, longer than four soccer fields, and will displace six times as much water as the largest aircraft carrier, although it is still only a quarter of the size of equivalent plants on land. It will be moored and connected to an undersea infrastructure, about 475 km (300 miles) north-east of Broome, Western Australia. The FLNG project will allow Shell to produce natural gas at sea, turn it into LNG and then transfer it directly to the ships that will transport it to markets.

At the same time, Total is pioneering the siting of various facilities and processes on the seabed, including gas compression and liquid-liquid sepa-ration, both vital for maximising recovery from mature oilfields. Other inno-vations include Subsea Works Inspection and Maintenance with Minimum Environment ROV (SWIMMER), which comprises a pre-programmed autonomous underwater vehicle (AUV) with its own remotely operated vehicle (ROV). The AUV descends to a docking station on the seabed and releases its ROV, which under guidance by an operator on the surface sets to work within a radius of 200 m (650 ft) around the station. Meanwhile, the AUV inspects pipes and other equipment as it swims from one docking station to another up to a distance of 50 km (30 miles). The assembly is designed to stay on the seabed for up to three months.

Oil and gas companies, such as ExxonMobil, Royal Dutch Shell and BP, are dominant energy players at sea, exerting a powerful influence (and considerable soft sea power) in developing wide tracts of the offshore zones of the world. The existing arrangements and power balance at sea are being challenged and complemented by major Chinese companies that both compete and combine with the established major players in aggressively seeking market share. China has three major energy companies that already dominate its national industry and continue to expand: CNOOC, the China National Petroleum Corporation (PetroChina or CNPC) and the China Petroleum & Chemical Corporation (Sinopec).

While it is anticipated that Chinese consumption of oil will double by 2020, to match that of the USA, CNOOC is on track to becoming one of the biggest oil companies in the world by 2030. It concentrates on the exploitation, exploration and development of crude oil and natural gas offshore of China and is heavily engaged in joint venture deep-sea projects in China's offshore zone and the South China Sea. It is China's largest producer of offshore crude oil and natural gas and one of the largest independent oil and gas exploration and production companies in the world. At the end of 2012, the company owned net proved reserves of approximately 3.49 billion Barrel of Oil Equivalent (BOE),[3] and its average daily net production was 935,615 BOE. The company holds interests in oil and natural gas blocks around Indonesia, Australia, Nigeria, the USA and Canada.

Overall, fossil fuels will continue to dominate global energy demand for some time to come. Taken as a whole, the exploitation of unconventional oil and gas reserves both onshore and offshore over the next decade and beyond will transform geopolitics, trade balances, the pattern of commercial exchange by sea and the priorities for sea power. These discoveries have also extended the time that was forecast for the depletion of gas and oil, by anything up to eighty years, allowing opportunities for the development of further technical solutions to the increasing demand for energy from a steadily modernising, relentlessly urbanising and rapidly expanding world population.

[3] A unit of energy based on the approximate energy released by burning one barrel (160 litres/42 gallons) of crude oil.

THE ARCTIC

There is likely to be a veritable scramble for commercial and strategic opportunities in the Arctic, just as soon as the ice releases its grip and technology allows exploitation in the decidedly challenging weather conditions. The first area that is likely to see development is in the European approaches to the Northern Sea Route (NSR – previously known as the Northeast Passage), which is likely to transform the economies of northern Europe and Russia. For example, Iceland is pondering whether to build an Arctic port in Finna Fjord in association with Bremenports, which would be ice-free all year. There are oil and natural gas deposits with considerable economic potential to the north and west of Iceland and the country wants to profit from the cruise shipping business in Arctic waters. Meanwhile, mineral resources will soon be mined in Greenland, which is thought to have extensive deposits of rare earth metals, and licences have already been granted to Chinese and other Asian companies. On the other side of the world, within a generation, much of Alaska's coast will be ice-free during the summer, and is likely to become a more attractive proposition in terms of resource exploitation, shipping access and human settlement. Canada will gain additional agricultural land as the permafrost relaxes its grip. Most countries will be interested in the rich reserves of gold, tin, lead, nickel and copper, as well as extensive oil and natural gas deposits that exist in the Arctic.

The five countries with the most direct interest in the Arctic are the 'coastal' states – Russia, the USA, Canada, Denmark (by virtue of Greenland and the Faroe Islands) and Norway. These, together with Iceland, Sweden and Finland, comprise the Arctic Council, which agrees policy and the way ahead for the Arctic region. Observer status, which affords countries the right to listen to meetings, as well as proposing and financing policies, extends to China, Japan, India, South Korea, Singapore and the EU.

When China achieved observer status on the Arctic Council in May 2013, it immediately followed up with an intensive diplomatic mission to Finland, Sweden and Denmark to stimulate trade and cooperation, including proposals for an expanded research and scientific polar institute that would study climate change and its implications for Arctic policies and legislation. Having been invited to witness proceedings, it appeared that China was determined to play an active part in shaping future Arctic decision-making.

A number of commercial initiatives also emerged. CNOOC announced a deal with Iceland's Eykon Energy to explore off Iceland's south-east coast, and the state-owned Sichan Xinue Mining agreed to finance operations at Greenland's Isua iron-ore field, which would supply China with 15 million tons of iron ore a year. It would require a team of 3,000 Chinese workers, adding more than 4 per cent to the country's population of 57,000. If this investment is successful, other Chinese mining companies will start prospecting for gold and copper, alongside aluminium smelting.

China has also set up agreements with with Rosneft and Gazprom to explore for oil and gas in the Arctic. Rosneft contracted to triple the size of current oil deliveries to China to 900,000 bpd and accepted loans of $25–30 billion for development funding, as well as allowing the acquisition of oil and gas assets in Russia by Sinopec. This loan substantially increased the indebtedness of Russia to China, which, along with the proliferating Chinese footprint in Russia, will give it considerable leverage in the region.

There are indications that Russian indebtedness and Chinese investment in Arctic energy resources will continue to grow in future years. In return for loans, Russia is likely to mortgage future production, as shown by a recent loan of $2 billion to Rosneft in exchange for twenty-five years of oil supply. In addition to its commercial and energy advantages, China gained a foothold and stake at the top of the world that will enable it to have a strong voice in setting the terms on which any future regional or climate agreements are based. It will be particularly interested in securing rights of access and in the regime that is established for the NSR. It also is able to add substance to its claims to be a 'near-Arctic state' and 'Arctic stakeholder'.

It is reasonable to ask how long Russia will tolerate the commercial invasion of its backyard by its 'strategic partner' and the loss of control over its Arctic hydrocarbon and mineral resources, at the same time as it seeks to open up the NSR to transnational trade from Europe to Asia. Also, as investment opportunities grow in Greenland, Denmark may come under pressure to grant full independence, despite the considerable autonomy that the territory already enjoys, encouraged in part by those countries seeking partnerships to exploit its natural and mineral wealth. It is clear that the Arctic will no longer be a sideshow in the strategic deliberations of major countries. The prospect of both navigational access and commercial partnerships with

Arctic countries to exploit resources seem likely to dominate strategic and economic calculations well into the century.

THE ANTARCTIC

At the other end of the world, things are entirely different. In the first place, as Stephen J. Pyne wryly observes, 'The Arctic is a true ocean surrounded by continents; the Antarctic a continent surrounded by oceans'.[4] Several countries would like to assert sovereignty in Antarctica and many more maintain scientific and other research stations there. However, nature and science have been given free range and national ambitions have been contained by the Antarctic Treaty, which came into force on 23 June 1961 after ratification by the twelve countries that at the time had scientific involvement with Antarctica.[5]

The Antarctic Treaty covers the area south of 60 degrees South latitude and remains in force indefinitely. Forty-six countries are signed up and all those conducting scientific research in Antarctica (currently twenty-eight) have consultative (voting) status in formulating policy and conventions. Any UN member state can accede to it. Commendably short (just 14 articles), the treaty effectively forbids the militarisation of Antarctica, the conduct of nuclear tests, the disposal of radioactive waste and any activity that would compromise its use for peaceful purposes only. It encourages international scientific cooperation in Antarctica and, most importantly, sets aside disputes over territorial claims and sovereignty, blocking any consideration of exclusive economic zones (EEZs).[6] Supplementary protocols have since been added to cover environmental protection as well, such as the Convention for the Conservation of Antarctic Living Resources in 1980.

The Treaty stipulated that any party could call for a review conference after thirty years. In 1991, no one bothered and the regime continues, with annual Antarctic Treaty consultative meetings (ATCMs) to determine by

---

[4] *The Ice* (2004).
[5] Argentina, Australia, Belgium, Chile, France, Japan, New Zealand, Norway, South Africa, United Kingdom, United States and USSR.
[6] However, no activities will enhance or diminish previously asserted positions with respect to territorial claims. The Treaty also provides that no new or enlarged claims can be made and makes rules relating to jurisdiction.

consensus how activities, such as tourism, should be conducted, while safe-guarding national interests and Antarctica's implicit status as 'the common heritage of all mankind'. The continuing consensus seems to be that the Antarctic belongs to everyone, and no one – for now.

One troubling issue is that the Southern Ocean is more accessible than the Arctic, where the huge costs of operations have been no bar to exploita-tion when the potential commercial rewards have been high enough. The prospect of significant oil and gas deposits in the Southern Ocean and the continent continues to exert a powerful attraction. Despite the fact that the US Geological Survey stated baldly in 1983 that 'no known petroleum or mineral resources occur in Antarctica', there is some evidence that consider-able reserves do exist on the continent and on the adjacent continental shelf. In the 1970s, the *Glomar Challenger* discovered evidence of methane and other suitably indicative elements in the Ross Sea. However, no systematic surveys have taken place, no oil or gas has been discovered and the obstacles to exploitation presented by the climate and remoteness, without the prom-ise of return on investment, are formidable, meaning that development in these areas is unlikely for now.

That will not stop exploitation nearby, which has already begun in the (marginally) more benign conditions, shallower waters and lower latitudes of the Falkland Islands and off Chile and Argentina. Plans for legislation, environmental measures and infrastructure – and assertion of claims – are already being implemented. The fishing grounds to the north of 60 degrees South are also attracting increasing numbers of high-volume fishing vessels, mostly from Asia, and the Falkland Islands makes a tidy living from the sale of fishing licences relating to their offshore zone. The waters to the south are likely to attract increasingly covetous attention, as the population of the world demands more protein in the years ahead.

SEA LANES AND ROUTES

At this stage, it is necessary to mention the opening up of new shipping routes, which will present new opportunities as the patterns of trade and exchange continue to evolve. The prospect of US shale-gas output, for exam-ple, is expected to increase traffic through the Panama Canal for large ships working the US East Coast and Gulf Coast–Asia route. Conveniently, the expansion of the Panama Canal will double its capacity by 2015 by allowing increased throughput and enabling larger ships to transit along a third lane and a new set of locks. The availability of the new locks means that the size of vessels passing through the canal will increase and will save them the 7,500-nm (13,900-km) trip around Cape Horn. It is anticipated by the Panama Canal Authority (ACP) that cargo volume going through the canal will increase by an average of 3 per cent per year, resulting in a doubling of the 2005 tonnage by 2025. The new arrangements will allow the transit of higher cargo volumes with fewer transits and less water and power use.

Traffic flow and growth are expected to continue to rise on the basis of the US imports from China passing through the canal en route to ports on the US East and Gulf coasts. The new canal system will benefit from the export of US and Canadian shale and unconventional oils and gas from the US East Coast to Asia. It remains to be seen whether changes in trade patterns in China, reflecting a shift towards a more balanced, less export-driven model, will affect the volume of traffic.

Both the Panama and Suez canals are likely to face competition in the future from the opening up of the Arctic routes. The NSR and the Northwest Passage (NWP), which both give access to the Pacific, are likely to be open for the transit of shipping for significant periods every year. Later in the century, it might even be possible to navigate across the middle of the ice cap, right across the North Pole.[7]

In 2012, the NSR was open for transits for around six months a year, with an ice-strengthened LNG carrier crossing from Norway to Japan, with icebreaker assistance, as late as November, and that window may open to eight months by 2025. Optimists believe that, within five years, the NSR will be open to non-ice-strengthened vessels for at least two months each summer and the NWP for at least one month. Also, within the same time frame, the Sea of Okhotsk and the Sea of Japan could potentially remain ice-free all year.

Scientific opinion is more reserved. The most consistent forecasts indicate that the NSR will be the only viable Arctic passage for Polar class 6

---

[7] The NSR runs to the north of Norway and close to the coast of Russia; the Northwest Passage runs to the north of Canada; the Transpolar Route would run straight across the North Pole.

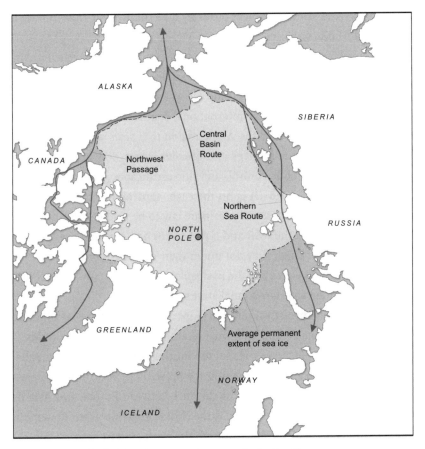

As the ice melts, new routes across the Arctic will open up,
and the NSR and NWP will be open for longer periods during the year.

(PC6) vessels and Open Water (OW) vessels in the near term. By the middle of the century (2040–59) OW vessels, the overwhelming majority of ocean-going ships, should be able to complete September transits along the NSR more often, with a 95 per cent probability of getting through. They may also be able to pass during other summer months, but may need ice-breaking assistance and the journey may take longer.

PC6 ships will be able to transit for many more months of the year, and by mid-century new routes through the central Arctic Ocean and the NWP should also be open for them. The sea ice will be sufficiently thin for ships with moderate ice-breaking capability to use the shortest distances on the great circle routes. In the same time frame, more northerly routes, notably near Norway and Greenland, will probably take traffic away from the NSR and Russia's EEZ.

Even once the issue of sea ice is out of the way, however, Arctic transits are still likely to be problematic, owing to a decided lack of local services and infrastructure, high insurance and escort fees, and sparse mapping and communications facilities. The international community also needs to sort out a governance regime for the Arctic region that deals with navigational safety, search and rescue services and broader issues, relating to environmental standards, pollution controls and ship certification. The International Maritime Organization (IMO) is on the case, apparently. There are also a couple of issues of international maritime law to be resolved. Both Russia and Canada claim that the NSR and NWP routes pass through their territorial seas and EEZs (which they do) under their exclusive control; however, the USA and others believe that the navigable routes (especially in the NWP) should be classified as international straits.

But why would anyone want to sail ships along these routes when there are perfectly reasonable and well-tried alternatives in warmer latitudes to the south? The simple answer is that the northern routes allow substantial savings in time and fuel; the melting ice presents opportunities for new shipping routes that will reduce the distance between Europe and Asia by thousands of kilometres. For example, the NSR sailing time from Rotterdam to Kobe, in Japan, using a route through the Bering Strait between Siberia and Alaska, would be twenty-three days compared with thirty-three days via the Suez Canal. The distance to Busan, in South Korea, via the Suez Canal is 12,400 nm (23,000 km) with a transit time of thirty-eight days at 14 knots. On the NSR, the distance is 6,220 nm (11,520 km) with a twenty-day transit at 12.9 knots. The NSR also cuts the distance to China from Europe by about a third. In an average cargo or container ship that burns around 30 tons of fuel per day, priced at $600 per ton, the daily saving is $18,000, yielding $360,000 over twenty days.

Even as it is melting and thinning, navigation in the Arctic still presents formidable challenges that require the services of specialist icebreakers, for both routine and emergency operations. The strategic advantage is likely to reside with those countries that have access to heavy icebreakers. They have strengthened hulls, whose shape is optimised for ice penetration, as well as powerful engines to provide the necessary momentum and force. Typical is

The Russian vessel *50 Let Pobedy*, the largest nuclear-powered icebreaker in the world (2014).

the US Coast Guard Cutter (USCGC) *Mackinaw*, which operates on the Great Lakes and breaks up to 82 cm (32 in) of level ice at speeds of 3 knots ahead or 2 knots astern and 36 cm (14 in) of ice at a speed of 10 knots ahead. But this is dwarfed by the Russian nuclear-powered icebreaker *50 Let Pobedy* at 160 m (524 ft) and 25,480 tons, and a top speed of 21.4 knots. It can smash through ice 2.8 m (9 ft) thick. In fact, Russia maintains a decided advantage in Arctic operations in its ownership of icebreakers, currently operating seven nuclear-powered civilian vessels and nineteen diesel-powered variants, with six more planned in the near future.

When it happens, the opening up of the Arctic will have the same effect on world shipping as the construction of the Panama and Suez canals, with knock-on effects for both those, literally, ground-breaking enterprises as they look to compete with the new routes.

Other routes are constantly revealing themselves, reflecting the distribution of resources and markets. New shipping routes are emerging between the Gulf and East Africa, repeating a historic relationship dating from the medieval period, and commodity traffic from South America and Australia across the Pacific is also increasing markedly. One of the biggest changes in shipping routes elsewhere will occur because of the reorientation of oil and gas suppliers and consumers as a result of the development of shale and unconventional sources. As we have seen, massive amounts are being discovered, which are feeding the economic booms of countries not particularly concerned about mitigating climate change. They are much more concerned about economic growth, social development and political stability. Similarly, other countries are thriving on the imbalance of labour costs, safety standards and environmental limitations between the developed and developing worlds.

These imbalances amount to significant competitive advantage in the maritime and marine sectors, notably with regard to seafaring in the merchant and fishing communities, shipbuilding and offshore development. Either more uniform regulation and enforcement will need to apply or countries are likely to introduce environmental, social or energy premiums to imported goods (effectively stealth tariffs). Alternatively, countries will need to make pragmatic choices about their adherence to commitments to climate change targets and other asymmetric conventions and regulations in order to preserve legitimacy with their electorates and growth in their economies.

FISH

A major component of most countries' soft sea power is their capacity to catch, process and market fish and fish products. Thomas Huxley, the President of the Royal Society, speaking in 1883, expressed the view that, 'probably all the great sea fisheries are inexhaustible; that is to say that nothing we do seriously affects the number of the fish'. His view clearly did not anticipate the effects of technology on fishing and the massive increase in the demand for protein by a world population that has grown from 1.55 billion to 7.1 billion.

Seafood plays a vital role in food security. Protein from fish provides 16 per cent of the animal protein that is consumed by humans, either directly or indirectly (by feeding other edible animals). Over 30 per cent of the world's population absorbs about 20 per cent of their animal protein from fish.

The problem is that human beings are munching their way through the sea's food chain, to the extent that about 80 per cent of the major fisheries are either at or beyond the point at which they are sustainable. The industrial scale of fishing activity, coupled with advanced detection technologies that enable the systematic capture of increasing numbers of fish, means the world is in imminent danger of depleting a global resource beyond the point at which it can recover, resulting in a true 'tragedy of the commons'. The fish at greatest risk are the open ocean, migratory species, like tuna, cod and swordfish, which are dangerously close to the point where they will not recover and only 13 per cent of oceanic fish stocks are in the 'not fully exploited' category (from 40 per cent in 1974).

One aspect to the problem is that governments pay subsidies and financial incentives to maintain local economies and employment levels. Governments around the world invest $16 billion annually in their fishing industries, including $4 billion in fuel subsidies, of which developed countries spend $10 billion and $2 billion is spent by China, whose catch is nearly three times that of the next closest country, Indonesia. Fishing is also a case of diminishing returns – overall engine power for the world fishing fleet has grown tenfold (twenty-five-fold in Asia) since 1950, while the total catch has grown only five times. In simple terms, vessels use double the energy today to catch a ton of fish as they did in the 1950s.

China has the largest deep-water fishing fleet in the world, with annual catch of 4.6 million tons in 2012, worth around $10 billion. There are over 1,300 boats operating in the South Pacific alone, which are heavily subsidised in terms of labour and operational costs, in particular diesel fuel. The rest are smaller regional and coastal private companies that could not survive without subsidies.

The Chinese are in the process of building higher-capacity, higher-endurance boats, as part of a current five-year plan that increases its officially registered fishing vessels from just under 2,000 to 2,300 by 2015. It is calculated that this would increase output by 1.7 million tons, equating to about $2.6 billion. However, without government support for catching fish in other countries' EEZs and in international waters, many Chinese fishing companies would most likely fail. Meanwhile, industrial development and land reclamation have left China's coastal waters virtually uninhabitable for fish. A 2009 inspection demonstrated that industrial concerns were discharging 14 million tons of heavy metals into its seas, degrading the ecosystem and ruining the inshore fishing industry. Although the Chinese are trying to clean up their waters, this means that they are likely to be more aggressive in fishing in both international waters and in disputed areas in future.

The business of fishing also has extensive links to organised crime, involving subsidy, quota and grant aid fraud, 'fish-laundering', human trafficking and widespread evasion of national, regional and international legislative arrangements and sanctions. It is assessed that about 20 per cent of all fishing on the seas is illegal, unreported and unregulated (IUU). IUU fishing is the major obstacle to the achievement of sustainable world fisheries and is estimated to be worth $10–23 billion per year. That creates a direct loss to legal fleets, a reduction in tax revenues for governments and destruction of the global resource.

A wide range of techniques are employed: fishing deep inside exclusion zones, disguising fishing vessels, the use of flags of convenience (FOCs), false registration, the use of banned fishing equipment, illegal trans-shipment, the corruption of local officials and enforcement officers and refusals to obey local environmental and conservation measures. IUU fishing is prejudicial not only to fish stocks, but also to the livelihoods of poorer countries and attempts to maintain law and order at sea. Illegal fishing has been widely blamed for the rise in Somali piracy, while the commoditisation of fish and the illegal trans-shipment of catches originating in the Barents Sea has been a source of revenue for organised crime.

One of the most active areas for illegal fishing is off West Africa. Here, in the absence of local or regional capacity to monitor fishing activity, the trans-shipment of fish from one vessel to another on the high seas creates the conditions for fish 'laundering' to take place and the fish to enter legitimate markets. Fish are regularly caught by vessels accredited to export fish to the EU, the world's largest importer of fish and fish products with a market value of €14 billion annually. It has been estimated that about 10 per cent of seafood imports (over €1.1 billion) are derived from illicit sources, within an overall assessment that IUU fishing could constitute between 35 and 50 per cent of all catches. Up to 2020, this will amount to €10 billion of lost catches, over €8 billion of lost stock value and over 27,000 jobs lost in the fishing and processing industries.

What can be done?

Clearly, there is a considerable imbalance between the size of the world's fishing fleet and the amount of fish that can be sustainably caught. Right now, the world's fisheries are in a precarious state. However, with the implementation and enforcement of suitable measures and safeguards, such as restricting gear types, lowering the total allowable catch and dividing shares of catches among registered fishermen, fisheries have been known to recover. There are grounds for cautious optimism.

The UN's Food and Agriculture Organization (FAO) assessed that the world's wild fish harvest was 90 million tons in 2012, a 4 per cent drop from the record 94 million tons in 1996. The catch per person dropped from 17 kg (37.5 lb) per person in 1988 to 13 kg (28.7 lb) in 2012. At the same time, aquaculture (fish farming) has rapidly expanded from 24 million tons in the mid-1990s to about 67 million tons in 2012.[8] About 600 aquatic species are raised in captivity in about 190 countries, and the industry supports 200 million jobs worldwide.

If our consumption of fish protein continues to increase, growth will almost certainly have to come from more disciplined and systematic management of fisheries. More to the point, if sustainable wild fisheries are to be achieved and maintained, much more rigorous supervision of regional and international waters needs to be established. This can only be effective by means of a collaborative approach between governments, producers and consumers, to ensure tighter, end-to-end control of fishery management and its economic cycle.

Clearly, it is essential that individual countries establish legislation within their own economic zones. Those that cannot should be prime candidates for assistance in managing their fisheries. In both developed and developing countries, it is vital to introduce the idea that fishermen should be farmers of fish rather than hunters.

Most importantly, overcapacity in fishing fleets needs to be addressed. The total number of fishing vessels in the world was about 4.36 million in 2010. The fleet in Asia is the largest, consisting of 3.18 million vessels or 73 per cent of the global fleet. The FAO has estimated that there are about two and a half times too many fishing vessels operating at sea. Secondly, about 15 per cent of the world's largest fishing vessels are flying FOCs or listed as 'flag unknown' to evade the rules and make enormous profits. This

---

[8] When farmed aquatic plants and non-food products are included, world aquaculture production in 2012 was 79 million tons, worth $125 billion.

practice severely limits the ability of responsible countries and regional fisheries management organizations (RFMOs) to manage fisheries on the high seas and eliminate IUU fishing. The EU and Taiwanese companies are the biggest exploiters of this loophole. It is evident that more standardisation between flag states and registries needs to be adopted or imposed to ensure common adherence to conventions and laws.

However, the most difficult problems occur in areas beyond national jurisdiction (ABNJ), defined as those parts of the sea where no one country has the specific or sole responsibility for management. Here, 250,000 tons of about sixty deep-sea species, worth more than $400 million, are fished every year by at least twenty-seven flag states. The ABNJ are a common resource, comprising 64 per cent of the surface of the sea and, interestingly, nearly 95 per cent of their volume. Sustainable management of fisheries and conservation of the preservation of biodiversity are problematic in these areas, to say the least, in the face of all types of unregulated activity, such as pollution, deep-sea mining and fishing. The warming and progressive acidification of the sea do not help matters either.

The UN's collaborative 'Common Seas' programme up to 2018 seeks to promote global sustainable fisheries management and biodiversity conservation in the ABNJ. The programme will also encourage states to meet their obligations under the United Nations Convention on the Law of the Sea (UNCLOS), with regard to the conservation and management of living resources and ecosystems on the high seas. The UN's efforts are aided by RFMOs, made up of states that agree to cooperate in the common interest. Other regions are starting to introduce collaborative mechanisms along the same lines. In September 2011, the EU and the USA undertook to cooperate bilaterally to combat IUU fishing, to keep illegal fish out of the market and strengthen fisheries management capacity.

Another way of helping fisheries to be more resilient is in the elimination of 'by-catch' or discards. These are living creatures, both mammals and fish, that are inadvertently caught by fishermen looking for other species and which die as a result. Non-discriminating fishing equipment, such as trawlers, gill nets and some longlines, can result in huge amounts of by-catch, including birds, dolphins, sea turtles and other edible fish. In extreme cases, the catch of 1 kg (2.2 lb) of prawns can result in over 120 kg (265 lb) of dead by-catch. Discards and by-catch also occur when regional quota systems, as in the EU, forbid the catching and landing of species not speci-fied. Fortunately, from 2012, reform of this EU policy was under way, with a ban on discards of mackerel and herring before 2014 and a phased ban on discards of cod, haddock, plaice and sole fully in operation before 2018. The reform also includes a commitment to fishing policies that related to the stocks available by 2020, based on scientific evidence and the principle of maximum sustainable yield (MSY).

Limiting the opportunities for fishing also helps. Immediately after each of the world wars, it was discovered around Europe that fish stocks had undergone a remarkable recovery in terms of numbers, biomass and resil-ience, owing to the markedly reduced numbers of fishermen working at sea. Nowadays, the designation of 'no-take' zones and marine protected areas (MPAs), in which human activity has been restricted to protect the natural environment, is having a similar effect.

In areas where fishing is excluded, there has been on average a doubling of fish stocks and similar increases in sizes. Fish populations have also increased outside the MPAs. In response, Australia has designated a third of its waters as MPAs. However, although 8.1 million sq km (3.1 million sq miles) of MPAs have been assigned around the world, this is only 2.3 per cent of the global ocean, of which a tiny proportion is the high seas, whereas more than 12 per cent of the Earth's land surface is protected. Although MPAs are increasing, only a small number are true marine reserves, where no extractive or polluting activities are allowed.

An ambitious scheme was initiated in 2011, to create 127 marine con-servation zones (MCZs) around the UK (about 25 per cent of the sea area), each tailored according to local conditions. It was proposed to exclude fishing activity, especially trawling (which is particularly injuri-ous to ecosystems and seabed life), and limit other forms of commercial operations, energy infrastructure and recreational use. It was intended that these zones would allow fish stocks to recover and preserve ecosys-tems that were vulnerable to human activity. Similar schemes were envis-aged for the areas around British Overseas Territories such as Pitcairn Island, Ascension Island, the Falklands, South Sandwich Islands and South Georgia, representing about 1 per cent of the world's oceans. In the end, in December 2012, the UK designated just thirty-one MCZs after consideration of the costs and practicalities of enforcing compliance in these zones, and accepted that some fishing might be permitted even in these zones.

The formation of these marine 'national parks' is evidently a viable method for protecting ecosystems and fish stocks. However, they are constantly under pressure from conflicting demands, with regard to resource use and access. Of course, fishing vessels transfer their activities elsewhere or concentrate their technology and attentions on the fringes of the MCZs. Nevertheless, control measures do work if they are uniformly and responsibly enforced. A good example of where control and conservation, based on practical measures and scientific analysis, have been seen to work is in the North Sea. Today, cod have made a remarkable recovery after being threatened with serious collapse because of overfishing between 2000 and 2010. The spawning stock biomass had risen to 75,000 tons by 2012, about the level required to provide sustained growth and prevent further species collapse. Success has been achieved through strict enforcement of science-backed quotas, the use of nets that allow smaller fish to escape and a reduction of the number of dead fish thrown back as by-catch. As a result, it is hoped that the North Sea cod spawning stock biomass will soon rise to 150,000 tons.

Aquaculture

One solution that offers significant potential is aquaculture, which has emerged as a major source of animal protein. In fact, it is poised to overtake beef in terms of total tonnage. FAO estimates indicate that world seafood demand will increase by 40 per cent by 2030, with the majority of fish consumed by humans likely to come from farmed sources by the 2020s, notably aquaculture.

Aquaculture is one of the most technically efficient, but environmentally challenging ways of farming fish. The practice has picked up a bad reputation because it requires large amounts of fishmeal (typically a farmed fish requires more than five to six times the feed that a wild fish does), but also because fish tend to acquire and spread disease and bacteria when they are in confined water. Other negative factors are the threat posed to sensitive ecosystems, such as mangrove swamps and wetlands, by coastal fish farms that in Asia have taken up millions of acres; algal proliferation and dead zones produced by dense aquaculture, depositing nitrate-rich waste products and unconsumed food; and distortions of the gene pool if farmed fish escape and breed with the wild population.

Traditional fish farms typically consist of cages submerged in shallow, calm waters near shore, where they are protected from the weather and easily accessible for feeding and maintenance. Cages must be moved to keep the waters clean and the fish healthy. Technological and economic limitations have dictated that operations are mostly located in sheltered bays or estuaries, where effluent build-up and contact between farmed and wild stocks can cause environmental degradation. Although improved technology and practices have reduced the environmental impact, the establishment of protected areas and conflicts with other inshore users mean that there is still limited real estate for new production.

The best option would seem to be the movement of production offshore and on the high seas, out to 200 nm (370 km) and beyond, where deeper water and stronger currents are more effective at diluting and dispersing the effluent of aquaculture. In addition, oceanic pens and cages offer freely circulating ocean water and the availability of natural food.

The Velella Project off Hawaii is a large offshore aquaculture enterprise, based on a free-floating, drifting pen, stocked with 2,000 hatchery-born fish, called kampachi (related to the yellowtail). The project uses an Aquapod, a spherical structure able to withstand rough seas and reduce the chances of fish escaping. The structure comprises triangular panels covered with vinyl-coated, galvanised steel netting and come in sizes ranging from 8 to 28 m (26 to 92 ft) in diameter.

If deep-water aquaculture is to reduce pressure on and complement wild fisheries, feed has to move away from wild fish derivatives towards more sustainable sources of proteins and oils. Experiments at the Velella Project show that, by using soya protein concentrate and high Omega-3 soya oil, fish can develop on a diet that includes only 12 per cent fishmeal. The nutritional content and weight gain equals or exceeds conventionally fed fish. The fish grow to maturity in half the normal time and survival rates are higher than in traditional pens. The siting of the Aquapods in over 3,600 m (12,000 ft) of water has resulted in very few effects on the water column and other species, with negligible pollution and cross-contamination.

However, regulatory and security concerns will need to be addressed

An Aquapod used by the Velella Project in its offshore aquaculture venture.

in the open ocean, as well as the requirements of navigational safety. Additionally, the cages require more robust construction, remote controls and effective security systems to prevent interference, as well as technological solutions to mitigate the problems of distance from shore, such as pens that are anchored to the seabed, to ensure a continuous flow of water and to prevent random drifting. Remotely controlled, GPS-guided and sustainably powered oceanic fish farms will probably shape the future of aquaculture. An Aquapod cage with 2.4-m (8-ft) propellers to enable it to be moved around has already been developed.

Woods Hole Marine Biological Laboratory has developed an innovative technique that combines both free-range and caged elements. Experiments have taken place with an upturned semi-Aquapod on the seabed in Buzzards Bay, Massachusetts. The fish are able to swim out of the dome, but return to feed in the cage in response to a distinctive sound produced by an emitter.

This would appear to solve the problem of how to harvest the fish, yet allow them a normal feeding and breeding pattern. One technical problem remains – how to stop canny predators massing to devour the fish as they return to feed.

As stated, the situation with fisheries is precarious, but it is not unsalvageable. In reality, an international body is needed to address the lack of effective governance, enforcement and management of the global commons, as well as dealing with transnational problems such as overfishing, habitat destruction, biodiversity loss and the equitable authorisation and licensing of activities. Responsibility for progressing this line of development would appear to fall to the UN and, in particular, the IMO.

POWER FROM THE SEA

One of the most important aspects of the development of the littoral regions of the world is the potential for generating renewable energy, in the form of offshore wind, solar, wide and tide energy. Renewables could become the world's second-largest source of power generation after coal by 2018, but require continued subsidies to overtake coal by 2035. In 2011, these subsidies (including for biofuels) amounted to $88 billion, but over the period to 2035 would rise to $4.8 trillion, over half of which has already been committed to existing projects or is required to meet 2020 emissions targets. All new forms of power generation will rely on complex webs of distribution and smart grids that will link production sites with storage sites and consumers. Consequently, by mid-century, the offshore zone of all countries is likely to be heavily populated with such artificial structures. This is going to present a challenge for planning, licensing and regulation, as well as for security. The investment and criticality of the resource are also likely to provide further reasons why states will choose to exercise increasing control over their EEZs.

The world's first commercial offshore wind farm opened in 1991 in the Baltic Sea off the coast of Vindeby, in Denmark. Since then, offshore wind turbine development has lagged behind similar projects on land because of the costs and difficulties associated with installation offshore and the protective measures needed to withstand the violence of the sea and weather conditions. Until technology enables cheaper alternative ways of providing the machinery, it remains a staggeringly expensive way of generating electricity,[9] and the set-up and operational costs would not be viable without existing levels of governmental subsidy and price guarantees.

That probably explains why global installed offshore wind capacity only stands at 4,620 megawatts (MW), representing about 2 per cent of total installed wind power capacity. More than 90 per cent of that is sited off northern Europe, in the North, Baltic and Irish seas, and the English Channel. The UK and Denmark are the two biggest markets for offshore wind in Europe. Further afield, countries are not so keen; there are two demonstration projects off the east coast of China, which have a capacity of 258 MW, with a target of 5 gigawatts (GW) by 2015, and projects under way in both Japan and South Korea. Legislators in the USA have proved at best reluctant, but mostly resistant.

Underwater renewable energy solutions are based on the motion of the sea, such as waves, which supply energy to wave energy converters, and tidal motion, both vertical and horizontal, which drives tidal barrages, fences and turbines. A wave test facility has existed at Lysekil in Sweden since 2001, with an array of point absorber wave energy devices. It was the first operational wave farm and its first generator was set to work in March 2013. Similarly, a working tidal turbine has been installed off the coast of Northern Ireland, which supplies electricity to the grid. There are problems with the technology though; even the largest wave-powered devices rely on motion that has insufficient energy potential to provide enough reliable power to feed generators. Tides have greater potential, but the technology and infrastructure required to convert the dynamic forces into usable energy are in most cases prohibitively expensive. It is only cost-competitive in areas with high tidal ranges, where the difference between high and low tide is at least 5 m (16 ft). A barrage built across an estuary in Brittany generates 240 MW; another, on Nova Scotia's Annapolis River, produces 50 MW.

There would appear to be some potential for solar power generation at sea, at least for large installations. The surface of the sea absorbs the equivalent of 37 trillion kilowatts (kW) of solar energy every year – 4,000

---

[9] As of 2014, onshore wind has a guaranteed 'strike price' of £90 per megawatt-hour (MW-h), while offshore delivers £155 per MW-h, compared with £50–60 per MW-h for fossil fuel electricity generation.

times the amount of electricity currently used by all humans on the planet. A mere 2.5 sq km (1 sq mile) contains more potential generated energy than 7,000 barrels of oil.

The whole renewable energy sector at sea is beset with unanswered questions about the technical viability of certain technologies, its pricing mechanisms and the environmental impact. Also, in the face of consistently lower prices for hydrocarbons, it will be necessary to demonstrate that the initial upfront costs are justified by the return on capital investment and by long-term, sustainable benefits to both the consumer and society as a whole. The stability of electrical supply is another issue as renewables supply a constantly varying level of power to the grid, and so they have to be backed up by nuclear- or conventionally powered (that is to say oil-, gas- or coal-fired) plants, not to mention the multiple opportunities for power losses as the electricity is transferred. Moreover, the construction of new renewable capacity, in response to subsidies, has far outpaced the building of connections to link it to the grid.

For now, political and public opinion seem set to sustain the momentum to continue to invest in renewable energy at sea, particularly wind turbines, unless the comparative costs between renewable and other forms of energy become excessively wide (beyond those currently experienced) or views on climate change drastically alter. As a result, it seems likely that the shallow waters of most offshore zones will be colonised by a variety of renewable energy schemes and the supporting infrastructure, most of which will probably be constructed on the seabed. This infrastructure would include increasingly internationally connected power grids and long-distance power cables, which would allow the sharing of electrical loads and the distribution of electrical power from where it is generated to where it is needed in the most economical and efficient manner.

A number of grids have already been developed to bring electrical power from offshore to the land. Most involve the laying of high-voltage direct current (HVDC) cables. They are already in use in China, Brazil, the USA and around Europe, with transmission losses of about 3 per cent every 1,000 km (620 miles). To reduce losses, significant technological development is required. The problem might in future be solved by the introduction of superconductors, which, with their demanding requirements for cooling, could be ideally sited on the seabed.

Energy companies are also already developing suitable power grids for running offshore installations in deep water remotely from land, significantly reducing the requirement for production platforms. This approach would envisage the provision of electrical power from the land or from generating platforms on the surface.

As a result, Siemens anticipates the subsea market will double by 2020 from $23 billion last year, and the subsea power grid market, estimated at $800 million in 2009 will be around $2.7 billion by 2020. The company has developed an underwater power distribution system that could convey 100 MW at a distance of more than 110 km (70 miles) from a generating plant, which should be commercialised in 2014.[10] Until now, the delivery of only about 4 MW of power has been possible. The critical technology will be the means by which equipment is joined up to the grid, through so-called 'wet connectors', which until now have not been robust or flexible enough to be connected and disconnected remotely.

More sophisticated electrical grids on the seabed will enable the replacement of hydraulic with electrical controls. Hydraulic failures are the primary cause of underwater equipment failure. Total is working on a range of underwater supply and distribution systems, linked to water depth, transmission distances and power requirements. Other experimentation is taking place to determine whether local renewable sources can be used to produce up to 20 MW.

Of course, the expansion of power grids further out to sea in the littoral regions of the world would significantly assist this process, perhaps allowing power, communications and other applications to be accessed on a plug-and-play basis through mooring points or buoys. Also, the ability to position compression and separation technology on the seabed should improve the efficiency of recovering oil from deep-sea wells. On the ground, Statoil is experimenting off Norway with possible solutions to providing electrical power to the seabed to run a gas compression system.

Another technology to watch out for in future is ocean thermal energy conversion (OTEC), a process that exploits the pressure and temperature difference between cold deep ocean water and warm tropical surface waters, in areas where the ocean has a surface temperature above 25°C (77°F) and

[10] Emily Pickrell, 'Power grid in sea reaches for new depths', www.fuelfix.com, 19 July 2012.

is more than 1,000 m (3,300 ft) deep. Essentially, OTEC plants pump large quantities of deep cold seawater and surface seawater to run a power cycle and produce electricity. As well as power generation, there are also applications for OTEC in air conditioning and refrigeration, while the nutrient-rich deep ocean water can supply aquaculture and other related industries. As a by-product, OTEC can produce desalinated fresh water for irrigation, drinking and other engineering projects. Already proven in theory and at low levels of power production as long ago as the 1930s, the challenge is to be able to generate significantly more power than it takes to run the plant in the first place.

Despite the substantial set-up costs, there are extensive opportunities, especially in the Pacific Ocean, to develop the technology. Lockheed Martin is working on a 10 MW test bed that should be in operation by 2015, with hopes that it will lead to a plant that will deliver 100 MW by 2020. As an idea of scale, a regular nuclear power plant produces about 1,000 MW. Progress is being made at the OTEC test facility at Kailua-Kona in Hawaii, in conjunction with Makei Ocean Engineering. Tests have been going on since the 1990s, including the generation of 255 kW, at the expense of 151 kW used in generation (a world record at the time). As part of renewed interest and investment, turbines are being fitted to the site by early 2014, followed by improved efficiency heat exchangers, en route to operating the world's only operational OTEC plant since 1998. Funded by the Office of Naval Research (ONR), to the tune of about $3.6 million, it is hoped that testing and development of improved heat exchangers (the key to the process) will result in the ability to develop commercially viable, renewable energy supplies for military bases in Hawaii and Guam.

For OTEC to be viable, the future is likely to lie with new kinds of lighter-weight plastic or composite turbines. In addition, even though a series of open-cycle-system modules might together create 10-MW-sized plants, the technology is limited in the power levels that can be generated. Another type of OTEC system, called 'closed cycle', can more easily be scaled up to a larger industrial size; it can theoretically reach 100 MW.

It is also worth mentioning that OTEC would have consequences for ecosystems and the water column. The flow of water from a 100-MW OTEC plant would equal that of the Colorado River. The water would also have undergone a change of about 2.78°C (5°F) in temperature on being passed through an OTEC plant, with resultant effects on seawater temperature, salinity and biological diversity.

SEABED MINING

All coastal countries permit the dredging and extraction of aggregates and minerals in their littoral and offshore zones, both for deepening channels and providing the materials for land reclamation and construction. However, the emergence of advanced technologies and the prospect of profitable mineral extraction are alerting countries and commercial enterprises to the possibilities that lie in deeper waters.

That is because minerals lie in abundance on the ocean floor, mostly in the form of scattered clusters of manganese nodules, both within countries' EEZs and in the deep oceans. They vary in size from a potato to that of a refrigerator and contain manganese, nickel, copper, cobalt and rare earth metals used in electronics. It has been estimated that the Cook Islands' 2 million-sq-km (770,000-sq-mile) EEZ alone contains up to 10 billion tons of manganese nodules.

Also, mineral-rich sulphide deposits, which are formed from hot volcanic eruptions, can usually be found several kilometres deep in the undersea mountain ranges that run along the tectonic fissures caused by continental drift. Typical conditions occur in the Red Sea, where Africa and Arabia are parting company still further, and in the Galápagos Rift off Ecuador, where seawater penetrates cracks in volcanic areas of the ocean floor and is heated by hot, sometimes molten rock. The water dissolves minerals deep in the Earth's crust before erupting from the seabed at temperatures of up to 400°C (750°F). The spouting fluid creates a plume of black smoke (indicating iron and/or sulphur), from which, where it meets cold water, minerals are deposited. These form tall stacks that grow up to 6 m (20 ft) a year; when they collapse, they create fields of high-grade sulphides.

Hydrothermal vents tend to be located about 100 km (60 miles) along the 65,000 km (40,400 miles) of mid-ocean ridge and in volcanic basins behind ocean trenches, where one tectonic plate is sliding beneath another. Many of these basins are in the western Pacific, the 'ring of fire' that runs from New Zealand through Indonesia, the Philippines and Japan, eastwards through the Aleutian Islands and then south along the Pacific coast of North and South America, taking in most of the world's active and dormant volcanoes.

The 1970s saw the start of serious and systematic seabed mining, principally for manganese nodules. UNCLOS III established that the resources of the seabed outside the limits of national jurisdiction constituted 'the common heritage of mankind'. It decreed that coastal states were permitted to explore and exploit resources within a 200-nm (370-km) EEZ. As a result, licences for economic exploitation within EEZs would be required from the relevant littoral state, while an International Seabed Authority (ISA) was established to issue licences in the areas beyond EEZs. It would also ensure that a fair proportion of the benefits would be shared among all countries, especially in support of development in the emerging world.

Commercial companies were slow to respond with investment because technology was unable to offer economically viable solutions to the problems of mining at depth. Even so, various state enterprises, notably Russian and Chinese, have been prospecting over a number of years, while simultaneously surveying areas of possible military interest. Booms in commodity prices as well as soaring costs and environmental opposition in relation to many large onshore mining projects have recently renewed interest in the sector. In addition, now that deep-sea technologies are proving effective in the oil and gas industry, it is likely that seabed mining will pick up again, initially in shallower waters, but later expanding to the deep oceans. The British Prime Minister, David Cameron, estimated in 2013 that the seabed mining industry could be worth £40 billion to the UK economy over the next thirty years, stating, 'we want to make sure we get every opportunity out of this'.

Since 2001, ISA has issued thirteen licences, with another six in prospect. The licences, valid for fifteen years, were bought for $500,000 each by government organisations, state-owned corporations and private companies from countries including China, India, Russia, Japan and South Korea. Interest is likely to centre initially on the mineral deposits in the vicinity of hydrothermal vents. Lying 1–2 km (0.6–1.2 miles) in depth, the sulphide formations contain copper, gold, zinc and silver in highly concentrated forms; they can contain up to several million tons of ore.

China and Russia remain the two major countries leading the charge for sulphides in deep waters, followed by India and South Korea. Russia has found four sulphide deposits of over 10 million tons each and rich in cobalt-bearing ferromanganese minerals, all on the Mid-Atlantic Ridge. China is exploring the southern Indian Ocean and the North Pacific where most of the manganese-nodule licences have been granted.

Several companies have shown serious interest in seabed mining. De Beers, which gathers diamonds washed down by rivers, is operating off the coasts of Namibia and South Africa, in about 100 m (330 ft) of water. UK Seabed Resources, a subsidiary of Lockheed Martin, has started prospecting in the Pacific for nodules, between Hawaii and Mexico, at depths of 4,000 m (13,000 ft). Neptune Minerals is an Australian-based company that applied for a mining licence in 2008 for two deposits in about 1,250 m (4,100 ft) of water near the Kermadec Islands off New Zealand. It has also been granted exploration licences in territorial waters off Papua New Guinea (PNG), the Federated States of Micronesia and Vanuatu. Nautilus Minerals is a Canadian seabed mining firm whose Solwara 1 project in PNG's territorial waters is targeting between 60,000 and 100,000 tons of copper and gold.

Deep-sea mining will accelerate beyond the small scale, once the price of ores makes extraction and refining of seabed minerals commercially competitive. Currently, in a market that has considerable excess of copper and other minerals from land sources, seabed mining is not likely to prove profitable. It has been determined that a ton of discarded mobile phones contains about three times the gold of a ton of typical sulphide ore. When deep-sea mining does start in earnest, it is likely to be in the EEZs of states, where the water is shallower and the regulatory and environmental liabilities are likely to be containable. Commercial miners want both a clear title to their holdings and exclusive rights to exploit them. They also have to answer to shareholders.

The business risks associated with seabed mining were demonstrated in late 2012 when Nautilus Minerals stopped development of specialised seabed mining equipment, claiming that the PNG government, which has a 30 per cent stake in the project, had failed to share the $3–4 million per week costs. The project subsequently stalled until the High Court of Australia judged in Nautilus's favour in September 2013, requiring the PNG government to pay Nautilus $118 million, allowing the world's first seabed vent mine to go ahead.

An additional challenge for mining developers will be to exploit the accessibility of seabed minerals without destroying ecosystems, marine life and environmental balance. Nodules are generally found in sediment 5–15 cm (2–6 in) thick. The mining of hydrothermal vents would be more invasive because it would involve breaking up the uppermost metre of the sea floor and piping the rock fragments to the surface. There are also environmental concerns about the leakage of heavy metals into the water column and marine food chains. Not surprisingly, suction, scooping, bucket dredging and the removal of the minerals themselves all carry environmental and ecosystem liabilities.

METHANE HYDRATES

Possibly the greatest offshore opportunity lies at the edges of continental shelves. It has been calculated that the total global amount of methane contained in hydrate deposits on the seabed and in the permafrost of the north is 1,000 to 5,000 gigatons, which massively exceeds the natural gas reserves in conventional deposits of oil, gas and coal. For every 1 cubic m (35 cubic ft) of methane hydrate, about 160 cubic m (5,650 cubic ft) of gaseous methane can be extracted – enough energy to run an average personal computer continuously for a year.

Methane hydrates occur worldwide, as ice-like solid lumps of methane and water that lie on the seabed. They also exist hundreds of metres beneath the permafrost sediments in the Arctic, where the cold and pressure enable them to form and remain stable. At sea, the methane, which is encapsulated within molecules of water, was formed from microorganisms and plankton that was absorbed by sediments. They are stable at pressures found at depths of more than 350 m (1,150 ft) and at low temperatures of around 0–4°C (32–39°F).

There is a problem though. If the water and the sea floor become warmer, then the hydrates can break down and release methane. Methane, which is itself a strong greenhouse gas, does not escape directly out of the sea; microorganisms oxidise the gas to transform it into carbon dioxide. The process not only releases additional carbon dioxide into the atmosphere, but also uses up oxygen in the seawater, contributing to the acidification of the oceans. Warming oceans and a thawing Arctic mean that this could happen on a massive scale.

In the past the cost of extraction, the absence of suitable technology and the difficulties of commoditising the gas have precluded exploitation. However, it has been estimated that mining hydrates is feasible now in the face of continually rising prices of conventional energy sources, and efforts are under way to develop hydrate deposits, most notably in the EEZs of Japan, China, India, South Korea and Taiwan.

Mining technologies have already been tested in controlled experiments. Natural gas was extracted from methane hydrates onshore in 2008 by scientists in Canada and Japan, and the first offshore trials are currently under way in Japan's Eastern Tankai Trough, where Japanese and Canadian firms have drilled 300 m (980 ft) below the seabed into deposits of methane hydrates. The immediate discovery is thought to hold 1.1 trillion cubic m (40 trillion cubic ft) of methane, equal to eleven years of gas imports, enough to supply Japan's natural gas needs for at least the next eighty years. It is hoped to bring the gas to market on a commercial scale within five years. There was also evidence of rare earth metals.

German scientists are developing technologies that will assist the extraction, based on replacing the methane with carbon dioxide. This offers a particularly satisfying environmental and commercial solution, as the gas will be extracted while enabling carbon to be stored in the deep oceans or permafrost of the north, and carbon dioxide hydrates would be much more stable than methane hydrates, even if the sea warmed. However, the operation risks leaking methane into seawater, so this method could probably only be feasible in sediments that are 70 to 100 m (230–330 ft) below the seabed. The extraction of methane by this method onshore has just started in Alaska.

There is another potential snag – with uncontrolled methane release, which could possibly occur with warmer Arctic waters causing the thawing of the permafrost beneath the East Siberian Sea, which is believed to contain vast deposits of methane. As methane is twenty times more potent than carbon dioxide in the atmosphere, it could, if it escapes en masse without passing through the carbonisation process, have significant effects on climate behaviour, including the accelerated melting of the northern ice sheets and rises in sea levels.

CHAPTER SIX
·····················

New Technologies

'The design of fighting ships must follow the mode of fighting instead of fighting being subsidiary to and dependent on the design of ships.'[1]

History has shown, time and again, that a technological edge, used wisely and decisively, tends to confer an advantage both in warfare and in business, and particularly at sea. Superior ship design and armaments prevailed in the Indian Ocean of the fifteenth and sixteenth centuries, in the face of unknown seas, uncertain weather and the local competition, and continued to do so into the present era. Indeed, alongside nuclear weapons, technological leadership has maintained the geopolitical and military pre-eminence of the USA and its allies for almost seventy years.

The twenty-first century will see a succession of new technologies incorporated into naval and commercial use, in the pursuit of strategic and commercial advantage. But superior technology alone will not guarantee success at sea. Technology should enable a commander or business leader to shape a situation and an opponent to his advantage, but it is the ability of human beings, both singly and collectively, to exploit technology in specific contexts that confers operational success. Some will evolve slowly, advertising their arrival in theory and proofs of concept before being introduced in service without fuss. In the past, these transformational technologies in warfare have conferred a temporary strategic advantage until other countries have been able to acquire, replicate or neutralise the latest innovation. Other technologies will emerge as complete surprises, or even shocks, transforming

---

[1] Admiral of the Fleet Lord Fisher, quoted in Admiral Sir Reginald Hugh Bacon, *The Life of Lord Fisher of Kilverstone Vols 1 & 2* (1929), Vol. I.

the character of warfare and commerce and introducing profound discontinuities and disruptions into conventional ways of operating.

Thus it was with the maritime chronometer, Brunel's block-making
machinery, the screw propeller, the ironclad warship, the submarine, the
aircraft carrier, the atomic bomb and the nuclear-powered submarine. War,
or the threat of war, is a great innovator. In the civilian world, the introduction of roll-on roll-off (Ro-Ro) ships and facilities and the widespread adoption of standardised shipping containers had similarly transformative effects.
Their use has become almost universal.

In our modern era, countries absorb technological innovation at much
the same rate as each other, owing to the open culture of scientific research
and technological inquiry. Also, the interconnected, digitally enabled character of the modern world means that secrets are rarely safe and technology
rapidly proliferates, by legal or illicit means.

The twenty-first century is likely to see an accelerated rate of innovation,
based on near universal accessibility to existing knowledge, exploitation of
Big Data and continued strategic investment in research and development. A
greater proportion of this activity will take place outside the traditional market leaders of Europe, Japan and North America. China is an active investor
in – and notable poacher of – other people's research and development, and
other states such as Israel, South Korea, Singapore and India, have highly
active research sectors. Even so, several European countries, including the
UK, retain highly developed world-class research capabilities. Russia has
world-leading technologies in many areas, such as missile, aircraft, mining
and submarine design and production, which influence how sea power will
be exercised in the future.

The most dramatic advances are likely in Information and Communications
Technology (ICT), based on increases in processing power, data correlation and
services shared among expanding numbers of users. Technology is also breaking down divisions between land, sea and air environments, allowing the similar
systems, sensors and weapons to be employed across all three environments.
Modern digital communications and increasingly common system architectures will provide improved capabilities for widely dispersed military units to
operate as complete, flexible systems or as modular components in a network.

The possibilities offered by worldwide connectivity through satellite
or terrestrially based communications, including linkages to mobile and

wireless solutions, are enabling the processing of vast amounts of actionable information, dynamic decision-making and the near instantaneous cueing of operational responses. Further developments will allow greater synchronisation and integration of a wider range of activities and capabilities, while ensuring that commanders (and business leaders) have the most relevant, comprehensive intelligence and contextual information on which to base assessments and decisions.

Other areas that are likely to see rapid technological development in relation to the sea will be robotics, remote sensing devices, unmanned systems and nanotechnology. In terms of weapons, the armed forces of many countries in the developed world are likely to rationalise their traditional conventional munitions by employing a small range of common, tailored and adjustable weapons and systems that offer variable yields, detonation characteristics and degrees of precision. These advances will enable precise, discriminating activity in the realisation of objectives by single – or small numbers of – multirole platforms. In every envisaged scenario, assured access to Command, Control, Communications, Computers, Intelligence, Surveillance and Reconnaissance (C4ISR) assets will be vital to success, most notably those associated with space.

SPACE

The twenty-first century is likely to see Earth's near orbit teeming with satellites and other space vehicles, providing communications, sensor and weapon capabilities in both stand-alone and networked configurations. Any country not able to access space-based systems is unlikely to benefit from globalisation or have a capability to employ high-end warfare capabilities. This trend towards the industrialisation of near space will be aided by the development of cheaper, more flexible ways of launching satellites and installations into space and more sophisticated methods of accessing and controlling their functions and data. Improvements in optics will allow real-time imagery and persistent surveillance coverage over the sea once the technical problems associated with apertures and lens sizes are overcome.

The greatest innovations in the short term will be in the launch and exploitation of microsatellites, for both short-term contingencies and extended use as part of existing chains. Tactical Satellites (TACSAT) will be familiar capabilities, enabling replaceable communications links to relay electronic intelligence and maritime surveillance data, in the event of enemy action against normal satellite chains and to fill gaps in coverage, especially in remote regions like the Arctic.

Space will be a major arena for competition among the major powers, such as the USA, China, Russia and India, each of whom will continue to have weapon systems that will be able to disrupt or destroy an opponent's space communications and satellite systems. It is to be expected that other countries will acquire the technologies both to use space for their own ends and to be able to deny its use to others, if required.

ELECTRONIC DISRUPTION

It should be recognised that many of the technologies employed at sea today – the sensors, communications and information systems – operate in an electronically benign environment. However, increasingly, just as in cyberspace, it is likely that there will be increasing electronic threats from the armed forces of hostile states and some irregular groups. These will take the form of jamming, electronic manipulation and denial of service. In warfare, radars, communications and information bearers, as well as navigation and guidance systems, will have to operate in a much more hostile and prohibitive electronic environment. This largely neglected threat, which was an ever-present threat during the Cold War, will have serious implications for the integrity of the uplink and downlink of satellites, the operation of unmanned aerial and surface vehicles and a wide range of sensors, networks and communications across both military and civilian sectors.

In addition, portable jamming and electronic denial devices are available commercially from a wide variety of outlets, notably on the Internet. They will be used by criminals and terrorists to disrupt GPS signals and disable data and communications systems, especially short-range radio, wireless and mobile applications. Criminals in Brazil, pirates off Somalia and Taliban insurgents in Afghanistan have used these devices and it is reasonable to expect that their acquisition and use will proliferate. As a result, it will be necessary to incorporate more robust and resilient features and reversionary modes of operation into both military and civilian electronic systems. Even civilian port and marine infrastructure systems in high-threat areas of the world will need to be aware of the possible consequences of electronic denial of service and the need to harden their communications and information architectures.

UNMANNED VEHICLES

The most notable and immediately recognisable technological development of the twenty-first century has already arrived and is quickly transforming the way in which warfare and operations at sea are conducted. Recent years have seen the rapid proliferation of a host of unmanned vehicles of increasing capability, endurance and sophistication. Various vehicles and technologies enable operation above, under and on the surface of the sea.

Unmanned vehicles are generally *controlled* (with a human in the loop), *supervised* (with a human occasionally in the loop, for monitoring purposes) or fully *autonomous* (left to get on with things), especially when engaged in underwater applications. They are employed in 'dull, dangerous and dirty' as well as 'deep' tasks at sea (the 4 Ds) that humans would prefer not to do, or that they would not perform as well. These include repetitive, high-endurance roles and those in which there is a risk of injury, contamination or noxious effects, together with operations in the depths of the oceans. They are also useful in 'debatable' and 'deniable' activities, which human agency would wish to avoid, such as the covert or anonymous penetration of another country's sovereign territory, airspace or territorial seas. Indeed, the use of unmanned vehicles for more debatable and deniable activities is likely to expand, with increasing miniaturisation and stealth features being introduced as technology allows.

Unmanned aerial vehicles

Unmanned aerial vehicles (UAVs) are pilotless planes that do not carry a human operator, but can fly autonomously or be piloted remotely, either as expendable or recoverable assets. They can be fitted with a variety of electro-optic and infrared sensors, as well as radar and weapons, with imagery, video and intelligence relayed back in real time. They have roles in the provision of surveillance and targeting, as combat platforms, armed with missiles and other munitions, as logistics delivery vehicles and in a wide variety of law enforcement and civilian roles.

The use of UAVs was pioneered by Israel in its war against Syria in 1982, in neutralising enemy air defence systems. Oddly, UAVs took a while to come into their own. However, recent successes in campaigns in Afghanistan, Iraq and in the shadows of numerous counterterrorist operations have combined with advances in electronics and computing power to accelerate their development and popularise their use. They have provided extensive, persistent coverage, in terms of imagery and surveillance, as well as potent, generally precise attack capabilities. Their potential to reduce the costs of surveillance and the risks to human beings are incontrovertible and, despite fears associated with accountability, control and target discrimination, no self-respecting defence force would doubt their operational utility or a manufacturer their sales potential.

There are two categories of UAVs: those that operate autonomously; and those that are remotely piloted vehicles (RPVs), controlled by data link. Autonomous 'drones' fly in accordance with a pre-programmed flight plan before launch. Both system types usually consist of one or more aerial vehicles with various sensor or modular payloads and a ground control station (GCS), including the radio equipment to control the aerial vehicle and its systems.

Either operating as unmanned planes or helicopters, they come in a variety of roles, shapes and sizes. They can be hand-launched, with a range of about 3 km (2 miles), and operate up to 600 m (2,000 ft). They can be used by individual units out to 160 km (100 miles) and up to 5,500 m (18,000 ft). The more capable and expensive variants operate either at medium altitude with long endurance (MALE) over 200 km (125 miles) and up to 9,000 m (30,000 feet) or at high altitude, long endurance (HALE) out to ranges in excess of 14,500 km (9,000 miles) and beyond, and up to 18,000 m (60,000 ft).

One of the leading UAVs of recent years has been the RQ-4 Global Hawk, which has been used extensively by the US Air Force, the US Navy and NASA, which has flown them as far north as 85 degrees North latitude. It can cover as much as 100,000 sq km (40,000 sq miles) of terrain or sea in a day, staying in the air for twenty-eight hours and operating up to a height of 18,000 m (60,000 ft). It is a big beast, with a length of 14.5 m (47.6 ft), a

The RQ-4 Global Hawk unmanned aerial vehicle.

wingspan of 39.9 m (130.9 ft), wider than a Boeing 737, and costs $131.4 million ($222.7 million if R & D costs are included, equivalent to the price of two brand-new top-of-the-range Boeing 737s). Renamed the MQ-4 Triton, it will soon see service working in partnership with – or instead of – manned maritime patrol aircraft. A Canadian version, the Polar Hawk, will operate over the Arctic. Meanwhile, not to be left behind when there is technology to be copied, the Chinese have their equivalent, the Soar Eagle, for persistent surveillance of land and, more immediately, sea areas.

Another regular sight at sea in the future is likely to be the (Grim?) Reaper, which has been the main vehicle for conducting the popularly called 'drone' strikes against terrorists and insurgents, notably in Yemen, Afghanistan and Pakistan. The MQ-9 Reaper is capable of both remote-controlled and autonomous operation and provides a surveillance and immediate attack capability. With an effective range of about 1,850 km (1,150 miles), it carries up to fourteen air-to-ground missiles or a combination of missiles and precision-guided bombs. It will be fitted in future with air-to-air missiles, to shoot down other UAVs and helicopters.

In March 2013, the US Navy commissioned its first combined helicopter and UAV squadron, which incorporates eight MH-60R Seahawk multi-mission combat helicopters with ten MQ-8 Fire Scout unmanned helicopters. Both types of helicopters will deploy as composite packages onboard the LCS (littoral combat ships) from 2014. At a more modest level is a range of smaller UAVs, like the Scan Eagle, which can be launched and recovered by warships and auxiliaries to conduct surveillance and other patrol tasks by day or night, in conjunction with other ship-borne sensors and aircraft. In parallel, a wide variety of even smaller UAVs and micro-flyers are becoming available.

Meanwhile, the US Navy is also pioneering the use of unmanned combat air vehicles (UCAVs) from ships at sea, up to levels of sophistication and firepower associated with manned aircraft. Its pride and joy is the X-47B unmanned combat air system, which is the same size as a normal

An X-47B unmanned combat air system landing on the flight deck
of the aircraft carrier USS *George H.W. Bush.*

fighter-bomber. It has successfully completed several launch and recovery operations in the carrier USS *George H. W. Bush*. With a range of 3,400 km (2,100 miles) and a maximum operating altitude of 12,000 m (40,000 ft), the ship can carry 2 tons of bombs, munitions and sensors. Unlike other UCAVs, it has a pre-programmed mission profile, with minimal supervision by its operator. BAE Systems has just produced its own variant, Taranis, named after the Celtic god of thunder. The US Navy is looking for what it calls an Unmanned Carrier Launched Surveillance and Strike Aircraft (UNCLASS) to enter service by 2020.

Every country is now seeking to supplement its offshore surveillance with UAVs, either through purchase or indigenous production. It is likely that unmanned vehicles will be used for a variety of surveillance, monitoring and exploratory missions, especially in disputed and contested areas. They will be particularly useful in relation to claimed or actual sovereign jurisdictions. In fact, China has recently acquired considerable numbers of both armed and unarmed UAVs capable of providing surveillance over large areas of the East China and South China Seas and the Yellow Sea out to 1,600 nm (3,000 km). At the same time, Japan is also acquiring and deploying UAVs to conduct ocean surveillance of the areas in dispute with China and in particular its long chain of islands, which include the hotly disputed Senkaku Islands. They are also used extensively in the Indian Ocean in the hunt for pirates.

UAVs, like their land-based cousins, will be used for logistic supply. The Canadian Snow Goose is a combination parafoil or autogyro rotorcraft. Guided by GPS and launched from an aircraft, a ship or the land, it can place loads of just over 225 kg (500 lb) within 30 m (100 ft) of a pre-programmed point, before returning itself to base.

Of course, UAVs can be destroyed in the same way that manned aircraft can, with missiles and other kinetic weapons; in the future, they will be vulnerable to directed-energy weapons (DEWs – see page 197) and 'hunter-killer' UAVs, armed with missiles and lasers. In addition, guidance about how to build electronic devices to counter UAVs is freely available on the Internet, including jamming of the command link that directs its movements and controls the flow of data. It is likely that unmanned vehicles will need to be fitted with anti-jam technologies or pre-programmed to operate with artificial intelligence (AI) to ensure that they are autonomous as possible.

Unmanned surface vehicles

Rapid developments in digital processing and innovations in power management and systems engineering have led to a proliferation of unmanned surface vehicles (USVs) that are available for surveillance, logistics supply, combat and a range of warfare functions. USVs are designed to operate through radio control, a tether or autonomously, with the insertion of pre-programmed or downloaded mission packages.

At sea, they will increasingly be used to go in harm's way, with an expanding array of offensive weapons, including gun, missile and, later, directed energy (DE – see page 195) options. The Singaporean Navy has used a Protector armed USV to protect its major warships when on anti-piracy patrols. The Protector,[2] also used by the Israeli Navy and others, is a 9–11-m (30–36-ft) rigid inflatable boat, with a range of interchangeable modules that allow the fitting of various sensors and weapons depending on its task. It can be employed for unit and harbour protection, reconnaissance, in electronic warfare and in anti-submarine and anti-surface warfare. It has a radar, an electro-optical director (EOD), and a 360-degree camera, as well as a forward-looking infrared (FLIR) sensor and camera and an eye-safe laser range-finder (LRF). Its armament includes machine guns, a Gatling gun and a grenade launcher, as well as Spike anti-armour missiles. Protector needs two operators on a ship or ashore, one to drive the USV and the other to operate the sensors and weapons. Meanwhile, Zyvex Marine has produced the Piranha, which uses lightweight carbon nanomaterials in its construction, instead of the traditional fibreglass or aluminium. That means that the 16.5-m (54-ft) long vessel weighs only 3,810 kg (8,400 lb) and can carry a 6,800-kg (15,000 lb) weapon/sensor or cargo payload about 4,000 km (2,500 miles). In performance terms, that represents about eight times the range, three times the payload and 60 per cent fuel efficiency over vessels of similar size.

USVs will also be used for oceanography and mapping, probing unknown or disputed areas, testing responses and engaging in dangerous tasks, such as mine-hunting, jamming sources and offering themselves as decoys and distractions to confuse human operators and missile warning heads. They

[2] A joint development between Israel's Rafael, BAE Systems and Lockheed Martin.

are likely to increase in size, with suggestions by Rolls-Royce that even merchantmen could be unmanned ('drone ships'), relying on GPS, satellite technologies and centralised control to ensure their safe operation.

On land, in support of amphibious forces and in other operations against land targets, they will have similar roles, but with the addition of being able to assist both assault operations and general manoeuvre, fitted with a range of sensors and gun, missile and DE firepower. Other new technologies that will have significant impact are autonomous vehicles that can deliver logistics from sea to shore and conduct rescue and casualty evacuation tasks on land. They will operate with robotic bipeds (porters) and quadrupeds (mules), able to move across different types of terrain, which will supply ammunition, stores and other support material for troops operating on the ground. They are also likely to function as mobile communications bearers and in intelligence and targeting roles, especially in providing targeting for long-range fire from warships and land-based artillery. They will also be used for combat search and rescue of personnel under fire and in areas contaminated by chemical, radiological or other noxious agents.

Unmanned underwater vehicles

Unmanned underwater vehicles (UUVs) are used extensively by commercial operators for tasks associated with deep-sea exploration, resource exploitation and extraction, as well as maintenance, repair and inspection tasks with oil and gas platforms, pipelines and offshore installations. Military forces use them for mine countermeasures (MCM), operations in dirty or dangerous scenarios, to conduct environmental assessments and, increasingly, as surveillance assets and potential weapon carriers.

Current underwater remotely controlled vehicles rely on electrically driven propellers or water jets. They are normally tethered by an umbilical to a parent platform, such as a surface ship or submarine, in order to maintain control, data links and power input. More advanced models operate autonomously, like miniature submarines, exploiting battery power and basic artificial intelligence (AI) as part of a pre-programmed operational mission.

The momentum in UUV operations is being sustained by innovative vehicle design, improved software that allows autonomous operations and more reliable communications. However, significant improvements are required before they can rival the utility and effectiveness of their airborne counterparts, including vehicle agility, endurance, control and autonomous system integration. Also, whereas unmanned air systems can be controlled from thousands of kilometres away using satellite and radio links, a UUV can rarely operate without the close attentions of its parent. Future UUVs will have to rely on AI that confers a degree of autonomy and the ability to respond to what they find.

Despite their current limitations, UUVs could eventually contribute decisively to a key breakthrough in maritime warfare. Until now, the opaque nature of the sea has provided a comfortable stealth environment in which submarines could hide and operate with considerable advantages in relation to surface ships. The cost of detecting, deterring and destroying submarines, and in detecting underwater craft and mines has been disproportionate in resource terms. The evolution of UUVs is likely to mean that cheap (if necessary, disposable) unmanned vehicles can be deployed into high-threat areas.

As the century progresses and technology enables increased sophistication and reliability, it should be possible to develop surface and submarine unmanned systems that will be able not only to deploy independently into areas of known submarine activity, but also to detect, classify, track and report them. They will also be tasked tactically to provide defensive, detection and possibly attack options against underwater threats for groups of surface ships and submarines. On the basis that they are lose-able and therefore use-able, they will continue to be invaluable in the search for and elimination of mines and underwater obstructions, as well as for reconnaissance and covert operations. In times of tension and wartime, armed UUVs could be deployed to locate, mark and, if necessary, attack the submarines and ships of opponents. They would be limited only by their access to motive power and the requirement to refuel or re-programme. Even in peacetime, it is possible to envisage a situation in which long-endurance UUVs are used to locate and betray the positions of ballistic missile-carrying submarines. This development would have a significant impact on deterrence postures and calculations.

Research is pointing the way ahead. NATO's Centre for Maritime Research and Experimentation (CMRE) is trying to develop autonomous underwater vehicles (AUVs) that can talk to each other through acoustic modems, just as children would pass a message one to the other. It is called the – wait for it! – marine robotic system of self-organising, logically linked physical nodes (MORPH) project. So far, two surface and two underwater vehicles are cooperating. This collective approach is important because the slow-moving AUVs are, with their power limitations and sensor range, unable to keep up with modern fast-moving submarines. The idea is that several AUVs will be in a known submarine operating area, passing off target information to each other, before calling in a much faster weapon carrier, such as a maritime patrol aircraft or helicopter, to deal with the submarine or continue tracking and marking it. Alternatively, other on-station AUVs could be alerted ahead of the intended victim to continue the tracking.

The Defense Advanced Research Projects Agency (DARPA) has one of the most advanced unmanned programmes, Deep Sea Operations (DSOP), which has trialled vehicles down to 4,450 m (14,600 ft), beyond the depth that manned platforms can operate. Current challenges include ensuring that sensors can communicate targets of interest to other interested parties. There are also attempts to extend the endurance of these vehicles to achieve mission lengths of months and integrate them with wider underwater networks.

Project Hydra is looking at how to deploy UAVs and UUVs into areas of interest and into operations, with both based on a mother ship. Meanwhile, the large displacement unmanned undersea vehicle (LDUUV) will be an autonomous, long-endurance UUV that will cruise around offshore. It will use air-independent power systems and other technologies, to provide months of operationally deployed time, together with advanced autonomy, sensing and processing technologies to help it pick its way through a crowded environment. Basically, it is an unmanned submarine, with sensors and weapons for self-defence and offensive operations. With a large weapons and sensor bay, it will be able to act as the centre of a network of sensors, capable of detecting all types of vessels, and a range of mobile vehicles that can return to charge their power and re-programme.

The LDUUV is likely to be employed in conjunction with manned submarines in a supportive role, especially in avoiding mines and obstructions, if necessary taking a hit on their behalf. It would also be useful in mine-laying, where the mines, if mobile, could be (deactivated and) recalled to the LDUUV.

The LDUUV is likely to be used together with another emerging concept, the Persistent Littoral Undersea Surveillance (PLUS) project, involving the planting of arrays or networks of sensors in the sea and on the seabed, to enable the detection of quiet nuclear and diesel-electric submarines. During the Cold War, both NATO and the Warsaw Pact used so-called bottom arrays of passive sonar listening devices (typically the Sound Surveillance System – SOSUS) to detect the discrete frequencies of passing nuclear and other submarines. Most advanced countries still do so.

DARPA is on the case with its Distributed Agile Submarine Hunting (DASH) programme. Again, they are after quiet submarines, this time in deep waters. DASH is based on a networked system of passively listening, interconnected sensors and arrays that radiates and extends from the seabed and communicates information via an expendable 'surface node' (float) to its base. Once an initial detection is made, a UUV deploys to locate and track the submarine with its active sonar. This vehicle has already conducted satisfactory trials in the deep ocean.

An extension of this approach is the incongruously and idiosyncratically named 'upward falling payloads' programme. Secure pods would be positioned many years in advance in forward areas, especially in the deep oceans, which would lie dormant or hibernating for most of the time, allowing various elements or the complete network to be activated in time of need, to provide operational and situational awareness support to warships and submarines. The pods would contain unmanned vehicles, for surveillance, improved communications and rescue options, as well as deception and electronic jamming tasks. The vehicles would include underwater versions and others that rise to the surface and operate there and some would be armed.

Needless to say, there are some technical difficulties to be overcome, such as communicating with the pods to update the software and activate the unmanned vehicles, together with power supplies and dealing with the rigours of the ocean floor. There is also the matter of security; potential opponents and inquisitive explorers will be looking for them. Nevertheless, it is clear that these pods can be laid, just like mines, either well in advance or just ahead of operations, allowing a speedy response to a crisis ahead of the deployment of major forces. If successful, they could reduce the numbers of ships, submarines and aircraft that would be needed to be employed in harm's way in future operations.

Another UUV that is likely to proliferate in the future is the 'glider'. It uses small changes in its buoyancy in conjunction with its wings to convert vertical motion to horizontal speed. The hull compresses as it sinks, matching the compressibility of seawater. Gliders move through the water in a sawtooth profile, using changes in pressure and heat to reduce the power required to move at slow speed (about 1 knot). They use small amounts of electrical power (typically less than 1 watt), allowing the vehicle to achieve high levels of endurance and enabling missions of oceanic length and on-station times of up to three months. Some have already crossed the Atlantic and Pacific, while others have operated in the polar regions, recording and collecting biophysical and oceanographic data. As they rise to the surface, they deploy an antenna to communicate by radio or satellite, to send data ashore and receive new programming.

Most operate down to about 1,000 m (3,300 ft), although one glider has achieved regular depths of 6,000 m (20,000 ft). In November 2012, a Liquid Robotics Wave Glider set the Guinness World Record for the longest distance travelled on the Earth's surface by an unmanned system of 14,000 km (8,700 miles) on an autonomous mission of a year. Further technological development is likely to result in increased ranges, deeper diving depths and more sophisticated ways of operating, including more advanced missions.

Gliders are likely to be limited to open ocean operations in the near future. They lack the technological sophistication to deal with underwater obstacles and complex inshore environments, without human control and supervision. However, they are adept at remaining modestly and quietly on station, either in transit or on a pre-programmed profile. As such, they are likely to be employed in wide-area sampling tasks by civilian research organisations, but have clear future potential as low-cost (about $100,000) platforms and probes in support of other underwater sensors.

In the future, UUVs, some with endurance measured in weeks and months, will be cruising around the oceans on a routine basis collecting environmental data and, with their passive sonars alert and other non-acoustic sensors, attempting to locate actual or potential opponents' ships and submarines. Some will be gliders, others will run on pre-programmed patrol lines, but still more still will be sophisticated sensor platforms with the power, autonomous capabilities and range to be able to conduct wide-area surveillance and warning tasks.

Once in contact with an object of interest or to receive updated tasking, they are likely to communicate information with their base station either by rising to the surface to expose an aerial or by releasing a tethered or free-floating buoy. At the end of their patrol, they would return automatically to base or simply sink to the ocean floor in a pre-planned position, lying dormant until picked up, recharged and re-programmed. They will at some stage, and for specific missions, be armed with suitable weapons with which to engage hostile targets and installations, or even other unmanned vehicles. Alternatively, they could call in support from pre-laid pods or their wider sensor and weapon networks.

Within the coastal and littoral regions, defence and security tasks could be conducted by means of specially constructed seabed or offshore platforms that would deploy a range of unmanned vehicles to patrol coastal areas and respond to intrusions or attacks by hostile forces. They could also operate from specially configured or modular 'mother ships'. Indeed, in the second half of the century, it is possible that the majority of warfare and routine operational tasks will be conducted remotely by unmanned and robotic applications. Why go to sea and run all those risks if machines can do it all for you?

BALLISTIC MISSILE DEFENCE

Ballistic missiles pose a significant threat to populations, deployed forces and territories and are currently operated by about thirty countries, mostly with high explosive warheads. They were used extensively during the war between Iraq and Iran in the 'war of the cities' in the 1980s and by Iraq in the First Gulf War. Today, they are the prime launch and delivery vehicle of choice for nuclear-armed states, normally passing out of the atmosphere before the warheads descend almost vertically and at high speed onto their targets. The twenty-first century will see the proliferation of ballistic missiles, armed with conventional, chemical and nuclear warheads. Countering them will be an enduring preoccupation of the majority of countries.

Developed world countries lead the field in this area. At the NATO Summit in Lisbon in 2010, it was decided to create a comprehensive ballistic missile defence (BMD) capability to protect NATO European populations and territory. As a result, an existing programme – the Active Layered

Theatre Ballistic Missile Defence (ALTBMD) – will incorporate a range of command and control, radars and other detection and interception facilities to destroy incoming ballistic missiles. These will include a range of land, space and airborne sensors and weapon systems, as well as existing technology that is already deployed at sea, in the form of missiles and radar guidance systems.

The advantage of basing interceptor missiles in ships is that they can be easily moved around, not only to reduce the risks to the firing platform, but also to be able to concentrate firepower in the area of greatest threat and achieve the best radar coverage and intercept position. The Aegis Weapon System and the Standard Missile-3 (SM-3) interceptor (Block IA), carried in US cruisers and destroyers, are able to intercept capability against short- and medium-range missiles (launched from up to 3,000 km/1,850 miles). In all, the Aegis BMD system has achieved 23 successful intercepts from 28 attempts, with 20 successful hits out of 25 outside the atmosphere.[3] By 2020, it is planned that NATO countries will have complete coverage and a range of sensors and interceptors, by land and sea, including the Standard surface-to-air missile to deal with medium- and intermediate-range missiles.

The US Navy has 5 cruisers and 19 destroyers that are BMD-capable; these are expected to increase to 36 by 2018 and 94 ships by 2024. The Japanese are likely to add to their capability, too. Nevertheless, any ship deploying the appropriate missile system and suitable radars and data transfer equipment (several European countries) will be able to provide a similar intercept capability. Russia, China, India and other countries are working on similar systems.

In the future, improved versions of US naval missiles will be able to intercept ballistic missiles at every stage of their flight, while data links from ship to land-based systems will be able to incorporate other tracking data to cue land-based assets, such as the Terminal High Altitude Area Defense (THAAD) system[4] and emerging solutions based on Patriot PAC-3 missiles.

The ability to deploy highly mobile batteries of interceptor missiles and

---

[3] These included three successful intercepts in four attempts by ships of the Japan Maritime Self-Defense Force (JMSDF).

[4] A system designed to shoot down short, medium, and intermediate ballistic missiles in their terminal phase. It is probably less effective against intercontinental ballistic missiles (ICBMs).

their associated guidance systems by sea will continue to be a major component of anti-ballistic missile defence and, by extension, of diplomacy. It would enable a country to offer a tangible demonstration of political and military support through the provision of a powerful defensive shield. US Navy BMD-capable warships were deployed to protect friendly countries in the event of retaliatory ballistic missile strikes in response to US action against Syria in 2013. In addition, the future deployment of DE and other advanced intercept devices, especially in space, where they are markedly more effective, will further enhance the capability, along with improvements in the speed and integration of networks that enable cooperation between 'sensors and shooters', as the expression has it.

Improvements in BMD have implications for the future utility and effectiveness of both conventional and nuclear ballistic missiles, complicating deterrence calculations and leading to exploration of alternative delivery vehicles, new deterrent technology options and more sophisticated ways of countering BMD systems.

WARSHIP DESIGN

Life at sea has always been conditioned by the available technology that enables the mitigation of the effects and challenges of wind, wave and tide. Sailing ships relied on the expertise and experience, as well as the muscle power and practical skills, of a wide range of marine specialists, skills and human resources. The transition to mechanically driven vessels, powered systems and digital technologies led to substantial manpower substitution and dilution within both warships and merchant ships, although the external and eternal challenges of the sea remain. Even so, ships still have to be handled with competence and efficiency in constrained seaways, in complicated traffic situations and in conditions of extreme weather.

Modern ship designs often require a significant amount of technical and specialist skill among the crew. Despite the development of user-friendly technologies and automatic processing, the requirement to integrate a wide array of human and technological interfaces in fast-moving, complex scenarios remains. Combat at sea, in particular, introduces a very large number of variables, dislocated expectations and unintended consequences. As Nelson wrote before the battle of Trafalgar in 1805, 'Something must be left to chance; nothing is sure in a sea fight above all'.[5] In the modern world, life at sea can be considered predictable or routine compared to former eras, but crews still need to be prepared to deal with the unexpected and the challenges from the sea that are always at hand to trap the overconfident or unwary.

Warship design in the twenty-first century will change radically to reflect the need to incorporate new means of propulsion and power generation, novel weapon systems and revolutionary new composite materials. Warships will also reduce their vulnerability to detection by advanced missile and electronic sensor technologies through the application of stealth and emission control techniques. Most importantly, they will need to be able to absorb technological innovation at an even greater rate than in the past, if they are to maintain parity with the most advanced and technologically agile maritime countries of the future.

Modularisation

Modern warships have traditionally been designed around their principal weapon systems and sensor suites, based on their primary specialist role. For example, an air defence destroyer has had to accommodate the size and shape of its surface-to-air missile system and its associated sensors. In the future, navies will need their warships to be cost-effective and to remain operationally relevant, especially as the capital investment and through-life costs are substantial. It has often proved prohibitively expensive to reconfigure or adapt ships in the face of changing operational requirements or to incorporate technologies as they have emerged. However, the arrival of open systems architecture (allowing power and data to be connected seamlessly to a variety of mechanical, electrical and electronic systems, integrated weapon and sensor packages and fire-and-forget weapons), container-launched weapons and standardisation have led to the possibilities opened up by modularisation.

Modularisation is an operational concept that is based on ship designs

[5] In a secret memorandum to his captains about tactics to be employed in the event of a battle with the Combined French and Spanish fleet, written while on HMS *Victory*, off Cadiz, 9 October 1805.

that combine common hulls with 'mix and match' equipment, weapons and systems. Tailored mission packages and new technology modules can be 'slotted' into preformed housings, with electrical and data connections based on 'plug-and-play' common architectures.

It seems somehow appropriate that the country that produced Lego should have been the pioneer of naval warship modularisation. The Royal Danish Navy produced the Standard Flexible (StanFlex) design in the 1980s based on a common hull (the Flyvefisken-class patrol vessel) in which specialist warfare modules (offshore surveillance/pollution control; combat; MCM; and minelayer) were fitted onto dedicated slots and positions in the hulls. Today, the principle of modularisation is fully incorporated into Danish warships, notably the highly versatile and capable Absalon-class command and support ships and the Ivor Huitfeldt-class frigates. The modules (similar to containers) and deck fittings are precisely engineered to allow connections with power, cooling, communications, water and data supplies. The weapon system or sensor is mounted on or in the module, with the electronics, power machinery, magazine and supporting equipment inside. Modules range from anti-ship and anti-air missiles, guns and cranes to mine warfare equipment and anti-submarine sonars and torpedoes.

The US Navy has entered the modular game with two variants of its 3,000-ton littoral combat ship (LCS) – the mono-hulled USS *Freedom* (LCS-1) and the trimaran USS *Independence* (LCS-2). They are to have mine warfare (MW), anti-submarine warfare (ASW) and anti-surface warfare (ASUW) modules. The MW and ASW modules are sensor packages, with their weapons delivered by UAV or helicopter. The ASUW module – guns and short-range missiles – is structured to deal with pirates, small high-speed craft and other irregular opponents. As their name suggests, they were designed to operate in the littoral regions of the world, both in and out of harm's way against low-impact threats, while providing low-cost, transformable hulls capable of absorbing technology modules over time and of swinging between roles. However, with each vessel costing about $700 million, the ships have proved decidedly expensive – almost double the original estimate.

The LCSs have also been built to commercial standards, which reduces their overall protection and survivability levels in high-end combat situations. At present, there is clear potential for the LCS to be seriously outgunned by warships of similar size from other countries and by more aggressive and heavily armed criminals and terrorists. Outgunned they might be, but it will be difficult to outrun them. Although designed to use economical diesels for cruising, the LCSs have a useful turn of speed – up to 50 knots – courtesy of their gas turbine engine. No doubt a clean pair of heels will be useful in the future for getting out of unexpectedly awkward situations.

The danger is that modular ships can become jacks of all trade and masters of none. That is fine for appearance's sake in peacetime and situations other than conflict, but represents a very high-risk approach in combat. By contrast, the new Russian Steregushchy-class frigate (2,200 tons) is about 30 per cent smaller than an LCS and costs $180 million. For the money, it carries a 100-mm automatic gun, close-in defence Gatling gun systems (AK-630), medium-range surface-to-air missiles (S400 series), SS-N-25 anti-ship missiles, anti-ship and anti-submarine torpedoes and a helicopter. Export versions are heading for Algeria and Indonesia – and to China.

However, if cost-effectiveness, flexibility of use and minimum manpower are determining factors, it would appear that modularisation will be the way ahead for most major navies. Despite the eye-watering upfront cost of its LCS, the USA will no doubt make a virtue out of a necessity and ensure that the modules more than make up for the inadequacies of the original design concept. The simple truth is that, as with containerisation in civilian shipping, it took some time before operators learned how best to develop the supporting infrastructure and exploit the flexibility inherent in the concept.

The USA is also exploring the possibilities offered by modularisation and containerisation to deliver flexible operational and logistics capabilities from commercial containerships. The most ambitious modular project is the Tactically Expandable Maritime Platform (TEMP), which is being developed by DARPA, primarily for use in disaster relief and humanitarian aid situations. The TEMP programme will develop modular technologies and systems that take advantage of the standardisation offered by the use of ISO containers and its associated intermodal infrastructure. Initial applications are likely to include humanitarian assistance and disaster relief (HADR), but will extend to provide Modular Sea Depot and Modular Sea Base packages, all designed to produce floating offshore bases, without the need for a port.

The ultimate in modularisation is the provision of a quadruple launcher for the Russian 3M-54 Klub (Sizzler) missile in a container developed by the Novator Design Bureau. Normally, this missile is deployed in warships and submarines, but both anti-ship and land-attack versions (with ranges of up to 235 km/145 miles and 320 km/200 miles in each case) can be mounted and concealed, along with its control functions, on merchant ships in ordinary shipping containers. The roof is designed to retract, to enable the missile to be elevated and launched. The self-contained system can also be carried on a truck, a train, a merchant vessel or any type of warship with little requirement for any further system integration other than power supplies.

Therefore, where it is cost-effective and practicable, it is increasingly likely that states will invest in hulls that incorporate common power, electrical and data systems, coupled with the choice of a range of modular and interchangeable components in order to provide the best value for money and the most flexible use of the hull over time and over the vessel's entire life cycle.[6]

Electrical drive

Warships have traditionally been powered by main machinery – mechanical drive – to propel them through the water, with separate steam, hydraulic and pneumatic systems to provide other services and dedicated generators to power electrically driven equipment. An all-electric ship has a single group of engines to generate the electrical power required for both propulsion and auxiliary systems, producing a common pool of electricity for use by the ship's propulsion and non-propulsion systems. Integrated electrical power is particularly good at coping with the loads associated with a diverse range of electrically driven utilities, heavy electronic use and high-volume data processing. It also has the advantages of more coherent systems integration, the ability to produce surges of power on demand and more efficient use of fuel and power, typically between 10 and 25 per cent.

Cruise liners and increasing numbers of commercial vessels, in particular icebreakers, tankers, floating oil and gas platforms and ferries, already use this form of drive. For example, the RMS *Queen Mary 2*'s power plant consists of four sixteen-cylinder marine diesel engines capable of generating

---

[6] The British future Type 26 Global Combat Ship is a good example of where the broad capability parameters have been established, including sufficient space for choices to be made about capabilities, both before ships are built and after they enter service.

67.2 megawatts (MW) (90,100 hp), as well as two gas turbines, which provide a further 50 MW (67,000 hp). The output is channelled to the ship's propellers through four electrical motors each housed in external pods and powers all the other ship's services. The integrated electric propulsion arrangement delivers economical cruising at low speed, as well as the option to generate much higher speeds when required.

Even so, navies have been slow to take up this method of power generation and distribution, mainly because the electric drive components were considered too bulky and vulnerable to action damage for warships. Better late than never, Advanced Electrical Power Systems (AEPSs) are now being incorporated into warships, notably the US Navy's newest destroyer, the Zumwalt-class, the Royal Navy's Daring-class destroyers, the French Forbin-class frigates and the Italian Bergamini-class frigates. As an example, the Zumwalts have an all-electric drive with an integrated power system (IPS) based on 'permanent magnet-synchronous motors (PMMs)'. Distribution is based on a central bus bar (or distribution system), which passes direct current through the ship, with redundant back-up provision, alternative routeing and workarounds in the event of action damage or accidents.

The Zumwalt-class guided-missile destroyer USS *Zumwalt*,
the first of three Zumwalt-class destroyers.

The all-electric ship is capable of generating ten times the power of any current class in service. Electric drive also means that there are no drive shafts or reduction gears and significantly reduces the ship's acoustic signature, as well as making more power available for weapon systems and the ship's domestic services. Both the Zumwalts and the Lewis and Clark dry cargo ships will incorporate further developments to enable them to store electrical energy (radically improved fuel cells, batteries and capacitors) and use alternative fuels. Not surprisingly, parallel research and development is taking place to deal with the heat generated and to distribute and manage the power to a variety of weapon, sensor and human systems. This system will in the future have to cope with both continuous electrical loads and the need to release huge pulses of energy to support emerging high-power weapons. In the Zumwalts, it will enable its radar arrays to be steered electronically, rather than rotating, within a composite superstructure and mast.

The Zumwalt-class, whose 12,000-ton displacement rivals that of the German pocket battleships of the Second World War, may afford a glimpse into the future of major combat vessels. Originally supposed to number between eight and twelve hulls, escalating costs ($1.8 billion each and rising) led to only three being ordered, the first to be delivered in 2014, with the second and third in 2015 and 2018.

In appearance, the Zumwalt's most immediately evident and distinctive feature will be a 'tumblehome' design (the hull slopes inwards from the waterline), reducing its radar signature and improving its stealth characteristics. Its size means that it will combine traditional multidimensional sea warfare tasks with a significant ability to strike land targets accurately from distance.

Its weapons will be stored in twenty quadruple silos, known as a 'peripheral vertical launch system' (PVLS), spaced around the edge of the upper deck, rather than the traditional unified vertical launch system (VLS), so that they are not disabled by a single hit. These will hold Tomahawk cruise missiles and anti-air missiles capable of destroying aircraft, missiles and satellites. Its main gun system will fire a range of up to 920 advanced precision shells and munitions, including a GPS-guided long-range land-attack projectile (LRLAP), out to 63 nm (117 km) and beyond. It will also carry two helicopters and deploy a range of UAVs. As with its modularised cousins, it will incorporate open architecture, standardised software and

Arleigh Burke-class destroyers firing their missiles during an exercise.

commercial-off-the-shelf (COTS) hardware, linked to common data links and networked systems in other ships, aircraft and submarines. Most significantly, it will have a crew of only 142, including the aviation detachment, while an Arleigh Burke-class destroyer has 275–300.

Another recipient of enhanced electrical power and distribution will be the new nuclear-powered carriers of the Gerald R. Ford class, whose power plants will deliver three times the electrical output of existing carrier reactor systems. The supercarrier's most radical innovation will be the appearance of four electromagnetic aircraft launch systems (EMALS), which use a linear electromagnetic accelerator motor, as a successor to the traditional steam-driven catapults. The arrestor wires will also be tensioned and adjusted by electrical power.

The first two of the class will be commissioned in 2015 and 2019. At about 100,000 tons, they will have the same displacement as their predecessors, the Nimitz class, but will have about 500–900 fewer crew members, higher levels of automation and about 30 per cent less maintenance. They will also have markedly increased power generation (150 per cent) and wider distribution systems in order to service the catapult and arrestor systems and future high-energy weapon systems.

The Ford class will host about ninety aircraft, comprising the F-35C Lightning and F-18 Super Hornet fighter and maritime strike attack aircraft; all-weather airborne early warning and control aircraft; electronic attack and suppression aircraft; and Seahawk helicopters for a range of warfare tasks, including anti-submarine warfare. Air operations are planned for around 160 sorties a day, with a surge capacity of 220 (compared to 140 a day for the existing Nimitz class).

Nuclear-powered ships

Nuclear power is currently and extensively used in large warships (typically aircraft carriers), icebreakers and in submarines, but is also suitable for vessels that need to be at sea for long periods without refuelling or operate in remote areas. About 140 ships are powered by more than 180 small nuclear reactors.

Today, the political and public appetite for nuclear-powered ships is unfavourable, leading to restrictions on port access. Nevertheless, in forthcoming years, constraints on fossil fuel use, good nuclear safety records and the challenges of operating in remote areas of the ocean may bring marine nuclear propulsion into more widespread use. Nuclear power will continue to be the power source of choice for long-endurance nuclear submarines and large combatant warships, although civilian use will probably centre on customised, smaller power plants (25 MW of output instead of the 1,500 MW in traditional reactors). Large bulk carriers on oceanic passages would seem to offer the most scope, along with specialist towing ships that could shift large barges and loads over long distances, although proposals have been made for tankers and liquefied natural gas (LNG) carriers.

In particular, nuclear propulsion is likely to prove technically and economically necessary in the Arctic, where the local difficulties, such as the power required for breaking ice up to 3 m (10 ft) thick and the lack of refuelling facilities, are significant. Furthermore, as a result of having six nuclear icebreakers and a nuclear cargo ship, the Russians have increased Arctic navigation from two to ten months per year and, in the Western Arctic, to all year round. A new nuclear icebreaker, 173 m (568 ft) long, 34 m (112 ft) wide and displacing up to 33,530 tons, has been procured, which is designed to break through 3-m (10-ft) thick ice at up to 2 knots, ahead of ships up to 70,000 tons. It will be on station in 2017, with two more following in 2019 and 2020. A more powerful Russian nuclear-powered LK-110 icebreaker of 55,600 tons is planned.

Another innovation in this area will be the development of floating nuclear power generation platforms, moored in shallow waters, to take advantage of the high volumes of cooling water available from the sea and improve resistance to extreme events such as the earthquake and tsunami that induced three of the four reactors at Fukushima in Japan to go into meltdown. Russia has built the 21,500-ton *Akademik Lomonosov*, which is due to go into service in 2016. It will produce 70 MW of electricity or 300 MW of heat, to supply a community of 200,000 people.[7] At present, it is planned that the *Akademik Lomonosov*, along with seven other similar platforms, will be used to service remote communities and oil and gas infrastructure in the Arctic and along the Northern Sea Route. However, there seems little practical reason why the concept should not be capable of wider application and greater power generation (up to 1000 MW). Indeed, floating nuclear power generation plants might mitigate the potential danger that exists in East Asia in having so many nuclear installations sited in an area of significantly elevated risk (the Pacific 'Ring of Fire'), whose vulnerability to earthquakes, extreme weather and tsunamis should be a cause of international concern.

Self-healing and shape-shifting materials

Future ship structures and aircraft are likely to see the introduction of components comprising self-healing metals. Self-healing materials are materials that are able to heal or repair themselves automatically and autonomously without any external intervention, typically in reaction to corrosion. The promise of self-healing materials and the direction indicated by the nano-technology indicate that it might be possible to produce advanced composite

[7] It can be modified to produce 240,000 cubic m (8.5 million cubic ft) of fresh water every day.

materials, which are lighter, more flexible in use and more durable than existing materials.

These metals will have tiny balloons or nodules introduced during manufacture, while they are in molten or liquid form. If a plate or component is damaged, these balloons would burst and release materials that will heal cracks or action damage. In the early stages of its development, it is unlikely that this process would form a permanent repair, but is likely to suffice in an emergency. Bullet holes in metal and concrete have already been repaired with self-healing polymers, with only water and carbon dioxide needed to excite a response.

Coupled with polymers, complex barrier layers and other advanced materials, new compounds are likely to revolutionise the manufacture of most systems and vessels, leading to self-healing plastics, shape-changing composites, transparent aluminium and high-strength carbon-nanotube-derived wire and cable. At some stage, the flexible properties of nanoscale-impregnated surfaces are likely to be able to offer warships the opportunity to shift shape or give the impression of having done so.

NOVEL WEAPON SYSTEMS

The comparative technological advantage enjoyed by the USA and its allies in projecting conventional power abroad and at sea is being steadily eroded by the wide range of weapons and systems available to potential opponents. Known as anti-access and area denial weapons, these include increasing numbers of capable missiles, unmanned vehicles and cheap precision-guided munitions, as well as mines and mini-submarines.

Most importantly, these weapons are cheaper to produce than the systems that the USA and its allies have procured to counter them, enabling adversaries to impose significant costs on developed navies by forcing them to adopt expensive defensive measures. Currently, a missile used to shoot down an incoming missile costs about three times as much; what is known as the 'cost-exchange ratio' is considered distinctly unfavourable, especially in times of financial austerity. In particular, the USA has recognised that the ability to project power in distant waters, such as the western Pacific and the Gulf, is becoming not only more challenging, but infinitely more expensive. Advanced navies are therefore looking to achieve higher response times, increased lethality and resupply at significantly lower cost. Here electric drive is essential to a new generation of disruptive technologies, all of which will change the way in which warships operate and campaigns at sea are fought.

Weapons such as the electromagnetic rail gun and various high-power microwave (HPM) weapons and DEWs require instantly available and repeated bursts of concentrated electrical energy. These systems are in the concept, technology-proving and trials phases of their development, but current funding and progress suggests that they will be operational within the next decade or two.

Electromagnetic rail gun

Just emerging from its technical assessment and development phases, the electromagnetic rail gun has formidable potential, even though the idea has been around for about a century. Technology has had to catch up with the theory. Naval guns up to 5-in diameter (most of them) can only reach a range of 11 nm (21 km), although they can double that distance with rocket assistance. The rail gun would use grid-centred pulses of electromagnetic energy instead of explosive chemical propellants (like gas, rocket fuel or cordite) to fire up to 10 projectiles a minute at ranges out to 40–87 nm (80–160 km), although 200 nm (370 km) is considered theoretically achievable. It will engage anything from shore targets and fixed positions ashore to other ships and ballistic and cruise missiles and is likely to be operational by 2025.

To produce the necessary surges of energy, electricity is stored in a capacitor bank and released into the rail gun in milliseconds. The energy is passed through a pair of parallel rails and the current generates a series of highly charged magnetic fields, accelerating and launching an inert 18 kg (40 lb) projectile, which is positioned between the rails. The eye-catching element is that the rail gun will have a muzzle velocity seven times the speed of sound (Mach 7, or 8,575 km/h (5,328 mph)). Probably passing out of the atmosphere on its way, the projectile will be precision guided, by GPS or by another third party, in the final phase of its engagement. An impact velocity of Mach 5 – equivalent to thirty-two times the amount of kinetic force a 1-ton vehicle hitting at 160 km/h (100 mph) would exert – will do the rest, without the need for conventional explosives. Collateral damage at the target can be minimised, although it is envisaged that fragmentation munitions

– for dealing with land forces – could be dispensed just as it arrives at its target. In engaging cruise and ballistic missiles, the projectile would be an airburst round deploying tungsten penetrators to enhance the probability of a successful kill.

Apart from its fearsome firepower, the other main advantage of the rail gun is that it theoretically provides a large number of potential rounds, reducing significantly the space and support currently needed for the storage of missiles and other munitions (the rail gun would store about 1,000 rounds in current magazines). It also costs a lot less – the power generated for the 33-megajoule (MJ) electromagnetic rail gun shot at the Naval Surface Warfare Center was obtained from the local power utility, and cost about $7. Having access to a national grid is one thing; a ship will have to deal with the little matter of generating an awesome amount of electrical power in a very short space of time. Ranges over 175 nm (320 km) require a power surge of 5 million amps, while repeated attacks on targets 87 nm (160 km) away would demand a steady 1 million amps.

There are also some 'management issues' to overcome, which are being addressed by the US Navy's Office of Naval Research (ONR). The rail gun generates extremely high levels of heat and, to minimise component wear, infrared signature and damage to the host platform, effective cooling and thermal management processes are required, for which dedicated screening, ducting and cooling arrangements will need to be developed. The ship will also need to deal with the shock (the electrical equivalent of recoil). Innovations in the development of nanomaterials and composites are likely to help.

Then there is the development cost. These have already reached $260 million and the project is likely to need another $300 million over the next five years, just to produce a working prototype by 2018. As yet, the mechanism by which the rail gun stores, charges and pulses the power needed to hurl its projectiles over long distances has not been constructed.

The Zumwalt class has been specifically built with the power generation requirements for the rail gun and future DEWs in mind, as well as the electrical management system to allocate power where it would be needed. Other warships would have to be specially built or configured to take the rail gun, as each discharge requires 20–33 MJ of energy, more than most existing ships can deliver without seriously affecting their propulsion and other systems. One interim solution involves the storage of electricity in very dense, high-power cells, or specially constructed power storage modules that could be fitted to smaller ships.

ONR, with General Atomics (GA) and BAE Systems, is working on smaller advanced composite rail gun prototypes, in the hope that they prove suitable for smaller vessels than the Zumwalt. The modestly named 'Blitzer' is envisaged to be able to fit into the space occupied by the 5-inch gun on current destroyers. It would have an engagement range of up to 87 nm (160 km).

Another likely innovation, similar to the rail gun and for which the technology has been known since the 1930s, is the coil gun, which fires a projectile by means of one or more electromagnetic coils configured along a barrel. In fact, an experimental induction coil gun version of an electromagnetic missile launcher (EMML) has already been tested for launching Tomahawk missiles. Yet another new gadget is the light gas gun, until now an apparatus for conducting physics and space-based experiments, but whose potential is being developed to produce a gun capable of generating very high velocities and delivering devastating kinetic impact.

Directed energy

An area where life most closely imitates science fiction is in the field of DEWs. DE includes all types of device that can emit and focus electromagnetic radiation, including radio frequency, microwave, lasers and masers.[8] They also include particle-beam weapons and devices that use sound as a disorientating or disruptive agent. Of course, DE devices are not just used for disabling and destroying; they are used in a wide variety of industrial uses and for detecting and tracking objects – and for pointing and entertainment. Militarily, they include laser rangefinders and target designators used in guiding aircraft to conduct precision attacks. They have also been at sea at least since the 1980s, when they were used as dazzle weapons against personnel and those aircraft and ship systems sensitive to light.

---

[8] Microwave Amplification by Stimulated Emission of Radiation: a maser is a device that produces coherent electromagnetic waves through amplification by stimulated emission. It emits electromagnetic waves (microwave and radio frequencies) across a broad spectrum.

Laser Weapon System (LaWS): a laser is fired through a beam director on a Kineto Tracking Mount, controlled by a MK-15 Phalanx Close-In Weapons System.

A DEW emits brief high-energy pulses – in a beam of concentrated electromagnetic energy or atomic or subatomic particles – in an aimed direction without the means of a projectile. It transfers energy to a target at the speed of light, in order to disable or destroy it. In addition, the weapons can be precisely targeted and the power output controlled – high power for lethal outcomes and low power for non-lethal outcomes. The energy takes the form of electromagnetic radiation (lasers or masers); particles with mass, in particle-beam weapons (technically a form of micro-projectile weapon); and sound (sonic weapons). A 1 MJ laser pulse delivers roughly the same energy as 200 g (0.4 lb) of high explosive, and has a similar effect on a target. The primary damage mechanism is caused by reaction when the surface of the target is explosively evaporated. Generally, a 'hard kill' requires a concentration of about 10,000 joules per sq cm (64,500 joules per sq in) on a target.

DEWs are being developed with two main types. Solid-state lasers (SSL), able to focus 15 kilowatts (kW) of energy through a crystal, are already in existence and are common in factories where they are used for cutting and welding metal. They have been adapted for military purposes, but, although feasible against light aircraft and small craft, need hundreds of kilowatts to deal with a missile in the time available. A more suitable weapon in this regard is the free-electron laser (FEL), which in tests has already demonstrated the ability to produce an electron beam capable of cutting through 8 m (26 ft) of steel per second. It can also be tuned and scaled according to the prevailing conditions and is capable of reaching suitably high levels of power output. However, it will probably take until the 2020s before FELs are able to use even megawatt levels of energy.

Another kind of laser is the chemical laser, which was used on a Boeing 747 Airborne Laser Test Bed up until recently. It uses chemical reactions to produce the energy. The Advanced Tactical Laser (ATL) programme mounts a 100-kW-class chemical oxygen iodine laser (COIL) on an AC-130 gunship, which has a range of about 11 nm (20 km).

On trials, the USA has already demonstrated the capability of DE to disable and destroy USVs and UAVs. Two significant high-power SSL initiatives are under way in the USA: the Laser Weapon System (LaWS) and the Maritime Laser Demonstrator (MLD). An operational LaWS has already deployed to the Gulf on the USS *Ponce*, an amphibious assault and command ship, and it is likely that the US Navy will soon be able to install current-generation SSLs on its destroyers and as modular elements on their LCSs, to provide improved self-defence capabilities against air and missile threats, as well as swarms of small surface craft. BAE Systems and Boeing are producing a 10-kW SSL that can be fitted to a machine-gun mounting.

One significant drawback with DEWs is that they can only be used along a direct line of sight. This means that targets that are obscured or shielded by other objects cannot be engaged without the use of reflectors to reflect the beam onto the target. Consequently, their range needs to be significantly increased by the use of relay mirrors, which would also permit a single DE device to engage targets attacking from different directions and beyond the line of sight of the firing platform. Relay mirrors could be carried by an UAV or an aerostat.

DE can also be used to strike satellites and other targets in space, where their effectiveness is so much greater owing to the conditions outside the atmosphere. The beam is not subject to the same levels of dissipation, distortion and attenuation. In fact, a chemical laser was used by the US Navy to disable a US Air Force satellite in orbit in 1997 at a distance of 432 km (268 miles).

The advantages of DE weapons include high levels of reliability and the high number of shots or salvoes (up to 1,000), within the power that can be generated by the host platform. As with the rail gun, this could lead to a marked reduction in the number of conventional munitions that a ship has to hold. Another major advantage of DE weapons is that their power output can be scaled according to the operational circumstances, enabling naval forces to deal with a variety of security scenarios.

Nevertheless, DE weapons are unlikely to replace conventional missiles and munitions in the near term. But they are on their way and they will be introduced gradually to complement and reinforce existing systems, as development and technological innovation go forward. Within the next five to ten years, it may be possible to use mature laser technologies to create deployable, ground-based weapons to defend forward bases and deployed troops against aircraft, short-range munitions (like mortars and shells) and ballistic missiles. Because of their potential to overcome the size, weight and magazine-depth challenges posed by current technology chemical lasers and SSLs are likely to continue to be the most suitable for mounting on large mobile platforms such as surface naval vessels. Given sufficient resources, it may also be feasible in the midterm to develop HPM emitters for use by aircraft or cruise missiles that could degrade, damage or destroy the electronic hardware that allows ballistic and cruise missile guidance. The US Marine Corps will also probably exploit SSL development programmes to develop ground-based air defence systems and vehicle-mounted devices.

In the longer term (the next ten to twenty years), it is expected that innovative developments will reduce the volume, weight and cooling require-ments of high-power SSLs, so that they can be fitted to aircraft, ground combat vehicles and minor warships. However, by the late 2020s, it will be technically feasible to develop ship-based FELs with power outputs sufficient to deal with more hardened targets, including cruise and ballistic missile re-entry vehicles. These devices will be large and would have thermal conse-quences for the ship's company and other ship systems, for which shielding and dissipation of the waste heat would be required.

High-power microwave weapons

HPM weapons use electricity to power a microwave generator that emits very short pulses of microwave radiation (of nanoseconds' and microseconds' duration) at megawatt to gigawatt output levels. They would be either narrowly focused on a specific target, such as a missile or vessel, or used as area weapons to degrade, disable or destroy electronically dependent systems and weapons within range. One drawback of the area mode, of course, as with FELs, is that all unshielded electronic systems would be affected, including friendly forces, so care would be needed to ensure that collateral damage was not incurred. Nevertheless, with continuing investment, it is likely that HPM emitters carried by aircraft or cruise missiles could degrade, damage or destroy the electronic components in their opponents' systems.

Particle-beam weapons

Another DEW likely to make its appearance is the particle-beam weapon. The science is based on the ability to use electric and magnetic fields to accelerate and direct charged particles along a predetermined path. Electrostatic lenses would focus streams of electrons, protons and ionised atoms for collisions, to produce an electrically neutral beam of high-energy hydrogen atoms. As a result, a particle-beam weapon would disrupt or destroy a target's atomic or molecular structure – in other words, it would melt it from the inside out – through the use of a high-energy, intensely powerful beam of atomic or subatomic particles.

At first sight, particle beams would appear to be ideal DEWs. The pulsed particle beam could contain 1 gigajoule of kinetic energy or more and travelling at the speed of light would have immense destructive power. Once they strike a target, they have a high rate of penetration, which would rapidly break up internal components without the need to erode its outer or protective layers. Attempts to shield or harden targets would not be effective. Once stable propagation can be achieved, these weapons could have devastating destructive power. Indeed, their development only awaits the arrival of sufficient power and suitable particle accelerators to ensure their future employment as weapons of certain destruction. The major obstacle in developing a functional particle beam weapon has been the production of a power source that is light enough to put into operation and can produce millions of electron volts of power and tens of megawatts of discharge. Only a conventional power station would currently be able to meet these power demands.

So, in summary, technological progress will continue to reduce the volume, weight and cooling requirements of high-power SSLs into the 2020s, creating opportunities to integrate them into aircraft and smaller vessels. By the late 2020s, it should be possible to operationalise FELs and other DE devices on ships, with power outputs sufficient to cope with most incoming projectiles, such as anti-ship missiles, aircraft, ballistic-missile re-entry vehicles and even small calibre rounds. The arrival of particle-beam weapons would decisively overturn existing assumptions about weapons of mass destruction and the nature of strategic deterrence. Needless to say, the possibilities of DE and HPM weapons of all kinds are the subjects of extensive research and development in several major countries as well as the USA, including the European Union, Russia, China and a host of mid-sized powers. It is clear that they will be a distinctive feature of warfare at sea from now on and a defining element from the 2030s onwards.

Hypersonic missiles

It is perhaps just as well that DE and other advanced unconventional weapons are in development, because the possibilities offered by hypersonic missiles offer a substantial advantage to offensive capabilities against both land and sea targets.

One of the problems with current cruise and anti-ship missiles is that they fly at speeds just below the speed of sound (Mach 1). This means that they can take some time to reach their targets and are vulnerable to an increasingly sophisticated range of jamming, decoying and anti-missile systems. Similarly, the use of ballistic missiles with conventional warheads by nuclear powers gives the unfortunate impression that a nuclear strike might be in progress, which could invite nuclear retaliation, even though the missiles might be on their way to neighbouring non-nuclear opponents.

These factors have encouraged the development of more effective missile technologies, to enable penetration of modern defences and in countering offensive missiles. These improvements are necessary as the USA and its allies are widely believed to be losing the strategic advantage that stealth technologies confer, as other countries adopt stealth techniques and the ability to detect stealth platforms.

Defence companies and research organisations are attempting to develop hypersonic missiles that will enable longer-range, speedier reaction responses to incoming missiles and little time for opponents to react to attacks. Hypersonic missiles will make use of the upper atmosphere and reach speeds of five times that of sound (Mach 5), equivalent to around 6,200 km/h (3,800 mph) at sea level and 5,300 km/h (3,300 mph) at high altitudes (where the colder, thinner air means the speed of sound is lower). This makes them more like rockets, but more manoeuvrable and responsive, and their speed would seriously inhibit detection and interception. In addition, by providing a lower-cost means of reaching the upper atmosphere, they would also improve both civilian and military access to positioning other assets in space.

The challenge is to design an engine, which is totally different from the turbofan and turbojet engines that power jet aircraft, few of which can fly beyond Mach 2. One option is the ramjet, which reduces incoming air to subsonic speeds and is already used to power France's air-launched, nuclear-tipped Air-Sol Moyenne Portée missiles (ASMPA, an advanced medium-range air to surface missile) to speeds of Mach 3, or around 3,700 km/h (2,300 mph). Another option, which offers speeds of Mach 5 and above, is the scramjet, or supersonic-combustion ramjet, which uses supersonic air as part of the combustion cycle, rather like trying to strike and keep a match alight in a consistently high wind. Unfortunately, scramjets, like ramjets, have other combustion issues (blowing themselves up in flight) and need to be already moving fast to compress enough air for combustion. They therefore need to be accelerated by being launched from an aircraft or rocket. Clearly, the technology is still immature, but Russian, British, American and (no doubt) Chinese scientists are on the case. NASA achieved a controlled flight of 10 seconds at Mach 9.68 in 2008 and by May 2013, its X-51A Waverider completed a powered flight of Mach 5.1 for four minutes.

Other experimentation is concentrating on launching a hypersonic cruise missile vehicle on an intercontinental ballistic missile (ICBM) launched just into space, where it separates and glides back to Earth at speeds of about 20,000 km/h (12,400 mph) – sixteen times the speed of sound. Two tests of this approach, in 2010 and 2011, both achieved separation, but the cruise vehicle could not deal with the re-entry heat and trajectory. Solutions based on the Space Shuttle (which travelled at twenty-five times the speed of sound as it re-entered the atmosphere) seem to offer the way ahead in dealing with these issues.

The USA is now firmly committed to developing hypersonic missiles – and so are the Russians and Chinese. Given current trends, it would appear only a matter of time (and resources) before the technical difficulties are resolved. They will be coming – very quickly – to a place near you and me soon.

NON-LETHAL APPROACHES

Current trends suggest that alternatives to the threat and use of lethal force will be developed and deployed, not least because of the increased risks of confrontation, misunderstandings and conflict in the vicinity of disputed claims, of mistakes and of violations of human rights in relation to suspected criminals, terrorists and other malefactors.

Present devices include DEWs, tasers, stun grenades, various projectiles, gases and irritants. There is also a stingball grenade, deploying around one hundred hard rubber pellets, and green lasers that disorientate and dazzle. The US Marine Corps' Active Denial System, a focused high-frequency microwave (HPM) device capable of heating all living matter in a target area rapidly and continuously, causes transient – intolerable – pain, without permanent damage. The skin temperature of a person to a depth of a few millimetres heats to approximately 54°C (130°F) in as little as two seconds – the equivalent of more than a hot flush. The US Air Force's Personnel Halting and Stimulation Response (PHaSR) system, about the size of a rifle, incorporates two low-power diode lasers, one visible and one infrared. The laser light temporarily distracts or 'dazzles' the target person without permanent damage (apparently).

More sonic, microwave and DE applications are in the pipeline against various types of opponent, as well as nanosecond-long electrical pulse generators, designed to induce the loss of voluntary muscular control by electrical stimulation. Various levels and varieties of temporary disablement and disorientation can be expected to follow. Sonic devices are regularly employed against pirates and underwater intruders.

It is also anticipated that technological development will lead to more sophisticated methods for disabling ships and submarines. Measures to disrupt and degrade ships' propulsion and auxiliary machinery, especially with regard to electric drives, and warships' weapon systems will feature, in company with and in addition to the familiar cyber and electronic attack. These will include HPM transmissions to disrupt ship systems and disable small vessels. Unmanned vehicles will also be able to deploy a range of mechanical disabling and tagging devices, able to foul propellers and attach discreet transmitters and emitters.

Biomimicry

One of the most innovative and imaginative features of modern technological development is biomimicry. Biomimetics is the field of study for which animals provide the inspiration for engineering designs. Technology development has already recognised and applied examples offered by organic species in improving the design and performance of platforms and systems. It is no coincidence that the shape of nuclear submarines bears a passing resemblance to marine mammals. Similarly, the shark's ability to vary the shape and texture of its skin to minimise hydrodynamic drag has led to coatings for ship's hulls, submarines, aircraft fuselages and divers that potentially reduce the friction and energy use as they pass through water.

The shell of the scaly-foot gastropod (*Crysomalion squamiferum*) is a composite, made of three layers, each with different properties and made of different minerals. Its structure resists heat, prevents its constituent minerals leaching away in acidic water and the attacks of its predators, which include crabs, with the dexterity to penetrate and peel conventional shells. The iron-sulphide-infused outer layer disperses the energy of a blow or penetrating claw; the middle organic layer is soft and capable of absorbing shocks; the inner layer provides overall structural support and stops the shell from bending, especially in resisting the penetration of a crab's claw into the shell's aperture and breaking off chunks. Not surprisingly, the Massachusetts Institute of Technology (MIT) is looking at various armour and protective applications.

On an even more esoteric front, the Jacobs School of Engineering, at the University College of San Diego, has been studying the applicability of sea-horse tails as crush-resistant robotic arms, for underwater use. Meanwhile, researchers at the Virginia Tech College of Engineering have been working on a lifelike, autonomous robot that is modelled on the lion's mane jellyfish (*Cyanea capillata*), 1.7 m (5 ft 7 in) in length and weighing 77 kg (170 lb). The $5 million project is funded by the Naval Undersea Warfare Center and the ONR, which hope that CYRO will be used for surveillance, mapping and monitoring the environment. Powered by a rechargeable nickel metal hydride battery, it is being designed to operate autonomously for months. Movement through the water is by means of direct current electrical motors, which control mechanical arms in conjunction with a silicon mesoglea, the pulp of the fish's body, which contains the electronic components.

PARADIGM SHIFTS IN TECHNOLOGY

There are technologies already in development, which, once mature, will transform the ways in which commercial activity and warfare are conducted at sea. They include the electromagnetic pulse (EMP), which is a weapon of mass effect, as well as nanotechnology, quantum computing and nuclear fusion, three 'game-changers', which promise or threaten to introduce major discontinuities into the current ways of viewing international cooperation and competition.

Electromagnetic pulse

As the century progresses, it is likely that some countries will seek to develop and deploy EMP weapons. The possibilities for this weapon emerged when early nuclear tests revealed that high altitude atomic blasts produced an EMP of electrically charged matter, resulting in intense currents and powerful electromagnetic fields. These act effectively as electromagnetic shock waves, producing transient voltages of thousands of volts in exposed or unprotected electrical and electronic components and circuits.

Although living organisms are largely invulnerable to these effects, electrical and electronic equipment can be temporarily or permanently disabled. Ionised gases also block short wavelength radio and radar signals for extended periods. In terms of coverage – if an EMP device were exploded 320 km (200 miles) above the centre of the USA, its effects would be felt across the whole country. A similar effect could be produced by the use of a flux compression generator (FCG). This consists of a tube filled with explosives placed inside a copper coil. Just before the explosives are detonated, the coil is energised by charged capacitors, in order to create a magnetic field. As the tube flares on detonation, it touches the edge of the coil and creates a moving short circuit, resulting in a very high-power EMP.

If the EMP threat emerges in the twenty-first century (and some Chinese military academics are predicting its use), it will be necessary to shield and harden vital components in both military and civilian systems, with the most vital elements contained in an electrically conductive enclosure, known as a Faraday cage. However, all electrical equipment needs power – and, in many cases, data – and these connections introduce vulnerabilities, which can currently only be addressed by the use of fibre-optic cables or electromagnetic arresting devices. Hardening new equipment and systems in the face of this possible threat will add a substantial cost burden; older equipment and systems might be impossible to harden or screen properly and could require complete replacement. Hardening by design would be significantly easier and less expensive than attempting to secure existing equipment.

Nanotechnology

Nanotechnology is the manipulation of matter on an atomic and molecular scale, with at least one dimension sized from 1 to 100 nanometres. Just so that you know, one nanometre is one-billionth of a metre. By comparison, the smallest cellular life forms, bacteria, are around 200 nanometres in length. A nanometre compared to a metre is the same as the scale of a marble compared to the size of the Earth.[9]

Invented in 2004, graphene is a one-atom thick, tightly bonded layer of the mineral graphite, which is 200 times stronger than structural steel and a very efficient conductor of heat and electricity. It is normally arranged in a regular hexagonal pattern (like chicken wire) and is very light, with a

[9] V. Kohlschütter and P. Haenni, 'Zur Kenntnis des Graphitischen Kohlenstoffs und der Graphitsäure' in *Z. Anorg. Allg. Chem.*, 105 (1) (1918).

1-sq-m (11-sq-ft) sheet weighing only 0.77 mg. It is potentially as versatile in its application as plastic and can be manufactured as a composite, like carbon fibre.

The most important area for development involves carbon nanotubes, which are elastic, resistant to most chemicals and high temperatures, a better conductor of electricity than silver and a highly efficient heat conductor. They are also incredibly strong – a woven nanotube fibre, 1 cm (0.4 in) in diameter, would have the tensile strength to carry a load of 1,200 tons.

They are distinctly superior in electrical wiring – an ordinary copper wire burns out in response to 1 million amps per sq cm (6.5 million amps per sq in); a nanotube can withstand 1 billion amps. Nanotubes would allow faster electronic speeds, use less power, take up to one hundred times less space on a circuit and generate less heat, allowing fifty times greater computing speeds and lower cooling requirements. Computers built with nanotube-based circuits are expected to operate more than a thousand times faster (greater than 1 terahertz) very soon after the technology matures.

Already used in car components, tennis rackets, golf clubs and training shoes, nanotechnology is already being explored for its possibilities in the fields of filtration, water and chemically resistant coatings and cloaking devices. Mixed with fly ash (the residue from power stations), it can be made into lightweight, high-impact resistant composites. Nanotechnology is also likely to assist with the development of super-capacitors, which will enable the discharge requirements of rail guns and DE devices. Intriguingly, when electricity is run through graphene alternated with polymer, it makes the material expand and contract, offering opportunities for the creation of very strong artificial muscles and other motor functions.

With the current rate of progress, it seems possible that warships will in the future be able to discharge large numbers of active nanobots, in the same way that chaff clouds are dispensed as decoys today, in order to deceive both electronic and human sensors. Some might be programmed to deceive, confuse and seduce missile heads and radars by transmitting false signals and distorting received images; others might be programmed to swarm together like bees or other insects to present a coherent visual image in the form of the vessel or target that an opponent is seeking. Nanoparticles are also likely to be used for tagging or marking future targets for reacquisition or engagement with weapons. Dispensed from an aircraft or unmanned vehicle in the form of a powder or a cloud, with discrete markers and magnetic attractors, they would adhere to a surface and 'light up' targets for detection by lasers or other limited spectrum devices.

Of course, there is a snag. The cost of the material that makes up carbon nanotubes is $500–1,000 dollars per gram. Gold (9 carat) currently costs about $12 dollars per gram. The costs should reduce if current production processes are improved and economies of scale can be made.

Quantum computing

Further out is the distant prospect of quantum computing, which promises immense amounts of computing power through correlation of information at the subatomic level, as a result of the unusual properties of particles at the atomic level. The technology promises to permit extremely rapid, multiple calculations and the analysis of complex problems and situations. It has been assessed that if the world's most powerful computer today has the capability of the human brain, then a quantum-enabled laptop has the potential to compute using all the data known to mankind in a fraction of a second. Already, elementary quantum computers exist in laboratories that can compute 3,600 times faster than conventional computers.

Two technical problems remain. Quantum computers are extremely sensitive – small disturbances in their vicinity upset the delicate balance and coherence between atoms when they are vibrating in phase with each other to allow calculations. Also, quantum computers cannot deal in certainty, but thrive in the uncertainty that exists at the atomic level. Thus, they correlate rather than calculate in arithmetic terms and the result is achieved by averaging out a huge number of calculations. This makes it difficult for them to interface with other systems that require precise calculations.

Once solutions are found, quantum computing will transform every aspect of life. It would allow secure communications and data transfer, because of the infinite possibilities of quantum cryptography. Conversely, hardly any current digital code, from banking to the most closely guarded secrets, would be safe. At sea, algorithmic searching and factorising large numbers would be very fast, making multiple target acquisition, weapon allocation and engagement infinitely easier, together with the analytical functions associated with huge amounts of tactical and intelligence material. It would also assist in the operations of high-data-rate computational models and functions – for example, in underwater warfare, the analysis of the huge mass of acoustic data that is received by passive sonar sensors, such as towed arrays, multi-static arrays or sonobuoys, or low frequency active systems.

Nuclear fusion

Nuclear fusion occurs when atoms are forced together and fuse to form heavier atoms. During the process of fusion, substantial amounts of energy are released, delivering about ten times the amount of energy used to cause the fusion. Current, conventional nuclear power produces energy by atomic fission, by splitting of the already heavy atoms of uranium fuel.

The way it works is that fusion reactors – tokamaks – heat superheated, electrically charged gases of a mix of the hydrogen isotopes, deuterium and tritium, in plasma form, within a vacuum chamber. The idea is that plasma, held in a spinning vortex controlled by hugely powerful magnets to ensure that it does not interact with the sides of the tokamak, is heated under pressure to extremely high temperatures (at least 100 million°C/180 million°F), so that two hydrogen nuclei fuse to create helium, releasing virtually unlimited, sustainable and clean energy in the form of heat. Remarkably, unlike nuclear-fission power plants, fusion reactors do not produce high-level radioactive waste and use non-toxic fuel derived from water. Sadly, in existing tokamak (and other) magnetic fusion experiments, insufficient energy from fusion is produced to maintain the plasma temperature.

Expectations fuelled by the anticipated performance of nuclear fusion have been rife since its theoretical discovery in 1929 and practical demonstration in 1932 – the standing joke is that the commercial exploitation of nuclear fusion is always thirty years away. There are about twenty-six tokamaks in operation at present, but the most advanced and best funded is the International Thermonuclear Experimental Reactor (ITER), located in Provence in France and due to be completed in 2018. It is anticipated that the first commercial demonstration fusion power plant, named DEMO, will be built between 2024 and 2033, trialled between 2033 and 2038 and operated progressively up to full capability from 2040. That probably means that commercial reactors and power generation plants should be online at some stage from 2045.

Coupled with advances in superconductors, this development would rev-olutionise power generation and distribution. A superconductor is a material that conveys electricity or transports electrons from one atom to another with no resistance. This means no heat, sound or any other form of energy would be released at the temperature at which the material becomes superconduc-tive. Unfortunately, most materials need to be very cold in order to become superconductive and an excessive amount of energy is needed to cool them. This makes superconductors inefficient and uneconomical, but research is exploring compounds that could be superconductive at higher temperatures.

Where might this lead at sea? Firstly, this level of power generation would allow the construction and deployment of extremely powerful DE and other electrical charge weapons that would have a highly disruptive effect on the operation of various platforms at sea, in the air and in space, cued by exten-sive sensor fields and data exchange systems, as well as extremely high-capacity computing devices. On the seabed, superconductivity offers the prospect of highly efficient electrical power distribution and of energising wide networks of applications through sophisticated grids and distribution systems. The cold of the deep sea would also allow effective means of pro-viding cooling.

Land-based power generation by nuclear fusion on this scale would lead to the construction of interconnected seabed installations in the littoral regions of increasing scale, complexity and capability. They will be comple-mented by sensor arrays and powered by a web of electrical grids, linked to power generation on land and with power transmission losses mitigated by superconductors that utilise the cold water available in deeper water. Some facilities are likely to be set into the seabed itself or sited within enclosed sections of submarine canyons or seabed depressions, with advances into deeper waters as technology allows.

Owing to the increased emphasis on countries' EEZs in the future, it is possible to conceive of structures built on the seabed that act as energy and capability hubs, not only in directing and managing energy flows, but also in deploying inspection, environmental monitoring and law enforcement platforms. These might also extend to military installations in the event that countries lay claim to rights and sovereign jurisdictions within their EEZs. If they do, installations are likely to house, service and recharge and rearm unmanned and manned vehicles that will primarily deploy within the littorals and on continental shelves, and, for some missions, into international waters as well. In this sense, they will act as both garages and service stations, with smaller installations using remote, distributed weapon-launch platforms within an integrated defensive and offensive system and as nodes in wide-area sensor chains. As a result, the second half of the twenty-first century is likely to see the thorough technical and operational colonisation of the seabed.

Even without these major ground-breaking technologies, many other rapid advances in technology over the next twenty years, some of which have been introduced above, will significantly alter the ways in which warfare and commercial activity are conducted at sea. The main themes will include the rapid proliferation of unmanned and artificially intelligent vehicles at sea, the more diverse use of submarines and submersible platforms and the widespread possession of sophisticated, hypersonic and stealthy anti-ship missiles. These developments will be countered and the cost ratios between offence and defence altered by the arrival of DE and rail gun applications, by increasingly electronic disruption and denial technologies and an underwater environment made significantly less stealthy and opaque by the evolution of autonomous vehicles and seabed sensor networks. In all cases, there will be high levels of dependency on space-based technologies and solutions and significant wide area and mass destructive risks will exist in the development of particle beam and EMP weapons, with implications for existing deterrence theory. Nanotechnology is already offering new practical solutions at sea, with many more theoretically possible applications likely to appear as the century unfolds; graphene-based computing, 3D printing and new composite materials are in their infancy, but offer a coherent, credible route to future development and large-scale production. However, the arrival of quantum computing and nuclear-fusion-based power generation would fundamentally transform almost every aspect of human activity, with revolutionary possibilities for working, operating and living at sea.

CHAPTER SEVEN

Security at Sea

'He who lets the sea lull him into a false sense
of security is in very grave danger.'[1]

Many of the forces that will determine security at sea in the twenty-first century are still in motion and a settled, recognisable pattern has yet to emerge. The USA remains militarily dominant, particularly at sea, and China is the only trading power that has attempted to challenge US economic pre-eminence. However, the evident dispersal of both political and economic power away from the USA and Europe towards Asia – and other areas of economic growth, energy exploitation and capital accumulation – has constrained the ways in which the established powers can operate. The appetite in developed countries for military intervention has significantly diminished owing not only to the austerities required to get economies back in balance and flourishing, but also to the experience of Afghanistan and Iraq. State building under arms would appear to have had its day, for now. Nevertheless, the instability associated with these political and economic 'transitions' is likely to be accompanied by increased competition for resources and markets, which will, of course, test the resilience of the international system at sea.

Overall, the frequency and intensity of crises will necessarily be determined by the extent to which countries support the existing system of international trade and maritime law via the United Nations Convention on the Law of the Sea (UNCLOS). All states derive advantage and security from having a stable, peaceful and inclusive international trading system, within which their economies can thrive. After all, the 'Chinese Dream' of

---

[1] Hammond Innes, *The Wreck of the Mary Deare* (1956).

Xi Jinping (see Chapter 10) rides comfortably – and for free – on the back of the commitment of the developed world to maintain the freedom and security of the seas. However, when their national interests are at stake in areas where they can assert exclusive rights, the attitudes of countries tend to change. Rising powers that have become risen powers are reluctant to abide by rules that they believe they had little part in formulating. There is more than a hint that these powers – China, India, Russia (and possibly others if they had the chance) – are keen to make adjustments to the rules-based system in their favour. They imagine a strategic landscape more like that of the nineteenth century, where power belonged to the states with the economic and military muscle, with the balance of power provided by competing blocs or alliances.

In these circumstances, international relations would become a sliding scale of cooperation, competition and confrontation, depending on events and opportunities. China has a hybrid approach that aggressively claims exclusive rights in the South China and East China seas, yet loudly proclaims that the Arctic should be open to all states, in line with UNCLOS provisions. It has rules for its own backyard that conflict with its claims to universality elsewhere. Therefore, it will uphold an international system that suits its interests in maintaining favourable, secure trading links to its commodities and markets, but will contest the freedom of the seas where it conflicts with its 'territorial' ambitions at sea, such as in South East and East Asia.

Three features of the seascape that will be important to security are: increasing attempts by states to control activity and secure resources in their littoral regions; intensifying oceanic competition; and attempts to deal with the malware of the seas: pirates, criminals and terrorists.

LITTORAL COMPLEXITY AND CONTROL

More than three-quarters of the world's population, over 80 per cent of the world's capital cities and nearly all significant hubs of international trade and military power are concentrated in the littorals – basically the areas bounded by territorial seas and up to 160 km (100 miles) inland. By 2030, over 65 per cent of the world's population will live in urban areas, most of which will be susceptible to access, influence and attack from the sea. Critical air and sea routes from oceanic areas pass through coastal regions, trade routes intersect in the littorals and increasingly accessible and important sources of offshore oil, natural gas and seabed minerals are located in the adjacent waters. There will also be increasing pressure on the available sea-space from extensive land reclamation schemes, energy platforms and offshore construction projects. Expanding numbers of data and communications highways, research installations and energy grids will need to be powered, serviced and protected in the littoral regions.

As a result, states will seek to extend their jurisdiction, control and regulation over offshore areas up to the limits of their exclusive economic zones (EEZs), as they seek to exploit the resources that lie on and below the seabed and in the water column. They will also attempt to exclude interference by other states, prevent illicit activities and secure their maritime borders, in response to increasing levels of migration and bursts of criminality and terrorism. This will result in an aggregation of restrictions and regulations, along with more rigorous enforcement.

The need for security in the offshore zones will also lead to increasing control being exercised from the shore, with recourse to long-range patrol aircraft, long-endurance unmanned aerial vehicles (UAVs) and integrated coastal surveillance systems. This increased activity will eventually result in air and surface traffic over the sea being subject to permanent coverage, with the most intensive surveillance concentrated in the vicinity of ports, critical national infrastructure, energy installations and major coastal urban areas.

As part of this process, all sorts of reasons are likely to be advanced to inhibit the free passage of shipping through economic zones, as well as implications for the operations of foreign warships. These will range from maritime protected areas (MPAs) to mandatory traffic control schemes. In some cases, as in the Seychelles, where there are justifiable limits on the navigational routes by which the islands can be approached in the interests of fragile ecosystems, these will seem reasonable; in others, they are likely to be attempts to control legitimate movement and activity on the high seas. Others will use the pretext of suppressing criminality, illegal migration, terrorism and other threats as pretexts for extending their jurisdictions.

Consequently, we are likely to see the creeping territorialisation of these

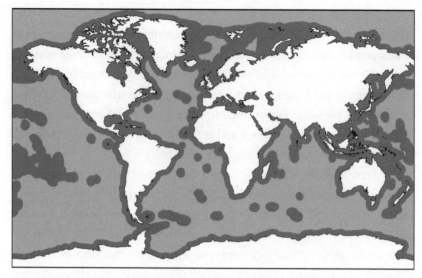

The proportion of the seas covered by exclusive economic zones.

littoral regions as states seek to extend their control and *de facto*, if not *de jure*, jurisdictions further out to sea, up to the limits of their current EEZ limits. In other words, exclusive *economic* zones will become simply *exclusive zones*, in which states will attempt to exercise national sovereignty and limit the activities of other states in those areas.

The obvious result of this process would be the establishment of formal shipping lanes, like airways, restricting the routes along which shipping could pass, either on the pretext of economic or environmental grounds, to enable states to control activity in their offshore zones. In fact, there are likely to be so many structures, platforms, MPAs and obstructions in the littoral regions and economic zones that ships operating there will have to obey control orders simply to negotiate the complex seascape of the future, not to mention a kaleidoscope of regulation and compliance.

In addition, for security and safety reasons, there will be increasing calls for ships to be identifiable and tracked in real time, wherever they are on the world's oceans. This is likely to involve satellite or other technology-based systems. Coastguards and other government marine agencies are already employing increasingly sophisticated technologies and techniques to detect intruders, with access to high-grade platforms and electronic devices, including unmanned vehicles.

Of course, on the high seas, the ability to track and identify vessels and determine their activities is very much diminished. Apart from voluntary measures, there has been little progress in tracking activity, despite clear evidence of criminal and illicit activity, including piracy, trafficking and illegal fishing. There have been reasonable calls for mandatory vessel identity and tracking procedures and the allocation of a unique and unchanging International Maritime Organization (IMO) identification number, which would reduce the advantages of using flags of convenience (FOCs) to evade regulation and legal obligations.

We have seen in Chapter 2 that the visibility of ships at sea going about their normal business has been significantly raised by technologies like the Automatic Identification System (AIS). Consequently, details of a ship's identity, position, course and speed, as well as its port of origin, destination and other vital statistics, are available within seconds to anyone with access to the Internet. In addition, it is possible to view and assess shipping densities and movements in detail in almost any part of the world.[2]

One weakness of the system, of course, is its universal accessibility. This means that pirates and other criminal or terrorist elements have been able to gain useful intelligence about shipping movements in order to plan attacks and hijackings. Software-defined radios, costing about $500 each, have also been used to hack into the AIS system and manipulate the data, generating false alerts (like emergencies to which ships might respond) and deceptive messages. The IMO issues guidance that, in 'high risk areas', 'the Master has the discretion to switch off the AIS if he believes that its use increases the ship's vulnerability'. Not surprisingly, warships are excluded from the mandatory requirement to transmit AIS information.

These measures could lead to a regime similar to the arrangements for air traffic, involving the reporting, live tracking and automatic electronic identification of all shipping movements in both the coastal zones and oceanic regions of the world. The system would be enabled by international regulation and cooperation, as well as by a worldwide chain of integrated radars, communications and satellite systems. In this way, the sea would soon assume the character of the air, where aircraft are fitted with identification, friend or foe (IFF) transponders, have to file a flight plan and pass

[2] For example, see www.marinetraffic.com/ais.

from nationally controlled sea-space, along mandatory seaways and then into oceanic reporting areas, before arriving in controlled sea-space again. The attractions for states wishing to exert tighter control over their EEZs and to exclude shipping from certain areas are evident.

There will be more constraints on the use of the sea by companies and states at the hands of ethically, ideologically and socially responsible motivated organisations. Some will take the form of pressure groups; others will seek to take direct action. The globalisation of protest enabled by the proliferation of Internet and related technologies will allow individuals and groups to connect with vast amounts of contextual and exploitative information. A wide range of civilian satellite-derived imagery, webcams and information-rich websites gives ordinary citizens a breadth, depth and fidelity of information that even the most active state intelligence organisations and corporations would have struggled to achieve twenty years ago. In 2013, researchers from the University of British Columbia used Google Earth to ascertain that there were 1,900 fishing weirs along the coast of the Persian/ Arabian Gulf during 2005, which caught approximately 31,000 tons of fish that year. The official number reported to the United Nations' Food and Agriculture Organization (FAO) had been 5,260 tons.

On the other hand, it is quite clear that some countries will not tolerate interference with their rights in their territorial seas and economic zones. Robust action by Russia against attempts by Greenpeace protestors to board an energy platform in the Arctic in October 2013 and the subsequent legal sanctions were an indication of how more assertive and sensitive regimes might respond. Protest of this sort will become more common as countries develop more of their offshore zones and introduce restrictions on what can and cannot be done on the high seas.

Security will therefore be characterised by a constant tension between the exercise of increasing control by states of their offshore zones and efforts to safeguard the global commons and freedom of navigation in the face of states or non-state entities seeking to subvert the existing arrangements for their own ends. In particular, the dominant issue relating to security at sea will be whether the principle of the freedom of the seas will prevail in the face of increasing claims by states to territorialise their offshore zones. The term 'littoral' is coming to mean the range at which a country can project its surveillance and enforcement power seawards rather than simply a geographical expression. Ironically, in the past, the territorial seas of a country were roughly determined by the range of a cannon shot (3 nautical miles/5.5 km); nowadays, the range might soon equate to that of an anti-ship cruise missile (most of which can nominally fly out to 200 nm/370 km).

OCEANIC COMPETITION

The sea, belonging to everyone and no one, has always been an ungoverned space. Unlike land and the air, it is barely policed, even today. The twenty-first century will witness a continuing 'scramble' and need, in the face of population pressure, human expectations and resource imbalances, to exploit the resources of the sea. These resources include oil and gas deposits; seabed minerals; the distillation of fresh water and other trace elements from seawater; the hunting or farming of food, in the form of fish and plant protein; and the use of wind, wave and tide as renewable energy sources. As such, the oceanic regions are likely to be colonised by expanding numbers of power generation, food production and extraction sites, as well as energy and power grids. These will have to be accommodated alongside proliferating numbers of MPAs and the increased protection of environmentally significant areas. All these trends mean that the sea will become more crowded and its use contested. The temptations to encroach on and acquire what until now has been seen as internationally shared space are likely to prove difficult to resist.

Consequently, states seem likely to extend their practical control and sovereign authority out to sea as far as legitimately and practically possible. Indeed, in the past, states have pressed for jurisdiction over varying distances from their coast. About 40 per cent of the world's oceans are contained within the 200-nm (370-km) limit that is the boundary for the EEZs and some states are pressing for more on the basis of the extended continental shelf entitlements, outlined in Chapter 1. This is a genie that was contained in the UNCLOS lamp.

Very soon, proprietary claims by states and extensions of jurisdiction will extend beyond their EEZs into the global commons, the high seas and the deep oceans, where control of access and resources will be key components of a country's soft sea power. Indeed, this process is already well under way, most blatantly with Russia's bid for the North Pole[3] and China's claims in the East China and South China seas. Given its newfound assertiveness, Russia might even seek to exert similar pressure on every part of its 'near abroad', especially in the Baltic and Black Seas. The UK is seeking to extend the territorial limits off its ocean territories where it has a discernible continental shelf; elsewhere, other powers, such as Brazil, Canada and Australia, are staking extended claims. A scramble for resources of this type has historically led to competition and confrontation and, in the absence of definitive international arbitration, agreement and regulation, is likely to need extensive surveillance and policing by responsible states and international organisations.

However, it will be necessary to ensure that legitimate projects involving resource extraction, power generation plants, fish farms and engineering activities on the high seas are covered by appropriate regulation. In the absence of clear guidelines and enforcement, there would be a risk of the establishment and assertion of private or sovereign rights. Otherwise, the field would be clear for open ocean opportunism (beyond that already practised) and entrepreneurial piracy, with the rights of the commons arrogated to private or national interests. In a highly competitive world, this might translate into arbitrary and contested actions by aggressive multinational companies and marginally democratic regimes to assert claims and prevent others from doing so. Once again, it would be the exercise of soft sea power in its purest form, with a hint of hard sea power to back it up, if necessary. We have already seen China's highly aggressive approach to fishing, with its subsidised investment in vessels and fuel. The problem is that there is generally no one authority to regulate behaviour and impose rules for the good of all. The global commons are wide open to all manner of pollution, exploitation and pillage of their resources, as well as systematic degradation of ecosystems and food chains, mostly out of sight of prying eyes. Even within some EEZs, there is little to prevent illegal and unauthorised activity

---

[3] In April 2014, President Putin authorised legislation that would allow Russian energy companies to establish armed response forces, ostensibly to protect platforms, pipelines and infrastructure from terrorists and other potential threats. The *Rossiyskaya Gazeta*, a Russian government daily newspaper of record, believed that this law would result in massive expansion of private corporate armies comprising sophisticated weapons and quasi-legal powers of enforcement. Experience would indicate that this move is likely to result in the expansion of Russian claims to jurisdiction in its EEZ and in the high seas as the ice recedes from Russia's Arctic coastline.

– who for example knows what is going on at this particular moment about 100 nm (200 km) off Pitcairn Island? Certainly not the British Foreign and Commonwealth Office, one would venture to suggest.

Mare liberum or *mare clausum* – the problem with China

Almost all aspects and themes associated with increased littoral control and oceanic competition are being played out in the Asia-Pacific region, where there are several extremely lively maritime demarcation problems. However, the most serious maritime security dispute involves China's determination to extend its sovereignty and jurisdiction well out into the South China and East China Seas, regardless of the rights and sensibilities of others under UNCLOS. It is effectively a test case.

In terms of geography, the South China Sea is bounded by China as the dominant geographical presence and regional power, but also by archipelagic and island countries, such as Malaysia, the Philippines and Indonesia, as well as Vietnam, all of whose geography creates constraining choke points along the routes that service China's lines of commerce, supply and deployment. The East China Sea is the major exit route to open waters and airspace, and access in the event of trouble with South Korea, Japan and, of course, Taiwan. Half of the world's merchant traffic by tonnage passes through the Strait of Malacca, Sunda Strait and Lombok Strait, with the majority continuing on into the South China Sea. Tanker traffic passing through the Strait of Malacca into the South China Sea is more than three times greater than Suez Canal traffic, and well over five times more than the Panama Canal. The costs for Japan and South Korea, for example, of routeing around this region would be significant.

Here, Chinese maritime strategy relates to the security of its immediate region and the protection of access to its increasingly global interests. Its interest in the South China Sea reflects the importance of its coastal provinces – notably its industrial, financial and population centres – to China's economic well-being and the energy resources that lie beneath the seabed. China's 'near seas' concept has three main components: a determination to neutralise the ability of any other power to project military power against the Chinese mainland; to isolate and absorb Taiwan; and to ensure the security of its shipping routes for oil, gas, commodities and, in return, its exports.

China's attitude to its regional neighbours and the strategic relationship between China and the USA, as the country most capable of – and most committed to – maintaining the current international system, are central to any understanding of security at sea.

China's maritime claims

The central issue revolves around historic Chinese claims to the waters of the South China and East China seas and the Yellow Sea, a claim it inherited from the Imperial period, but which was more recently reaffirmed from its Nationalist era. The Chinese Communist Party (CCP) has championed them with vigour, despite having implicitly surrendered historic rights when China signed and ratified UNCLOS III. From then on, as we have seen in Chapter 1, countries could claim their territorial seas and economic zones according to the criteria laid down in UNCLOS. Territorial seas extend to 12 nm (22 km) and EEZs out to 200 nm (370 km). Where one economic zone meets another economic zone within 200 nm (370 km) from the so-called territorial baseline, a median line is established. So, if two countries are 300 nm (560 km) apart, the median line would give each country an EEZ of 150 nm (280 km). If a country had an offshore island, broadly capable of supporting human life (not a rock, of course), the EEZ would be measured from there to a median line.

China does not like median lines and ignores them. Instead, it has produced a series of maps that show a roughly delineated (as if drawn with a pen) dashed line enclosing most of the East China and South China seas, a tongue-shaped area which is claimed as Chinese territorial seas. This 'ten-dash line',[4] appropriating huge expanses of the high seas and intruding deeply into the EEZs and entitlements of China's maritime neighbours, including Japan, Taiwan, Malaysia, the Philippines, Vietnam and South Korea. In particular, China has also adopted a decidedly proprietorial approach to the Spratly and Paracel islands within the ten-dash line, which are also claimed – and some occupied – by the other countries.

---

[4] The 'ten-dash line' appeared in 2013, as the previous maps (with a 'nine-dash line'), extraordinarily, did not include Taiwan. The new one does include Taiwan and appears in Chinese passports.

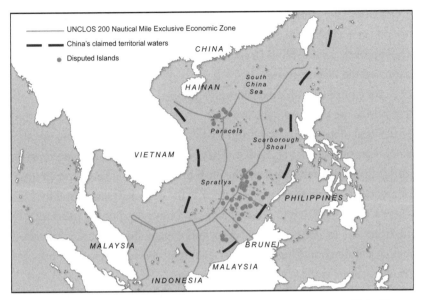

The disputed Asia-Pacific area, showing the conflict between the zones established by UNCLOS and China's maritime claims.

In 2009, China intoned that it had 'indisputable sovereignty over the islands of the South China Sea and the adjacent waters', together with the 'sovereign rights and jurisdiction over the relevant waters as well as the seabed and subsoil thereof'. China, as a predominantly land power views the sea in territorial terms, something to own and occupy. It attempted to include this notion in UNCLOS and has built extensive structures on some of the islands and established military facilities to assert and reinforce its claims. As seen above, UNCLOS distinguishes between islands and other features, such as reefs, sand bars and rocks. China is especially keen to prove that these navigational hazards, rocks and shoals are really islands, because they would bestow 200-nm (370-km) EEZs on the country to which they were ascribed.

South China and East China Seas

China's maritime surveillance and law enforcement services have been extremely active in support of its claims, notably in confrontations with the Philippines and Vietnam in the South China Sea and Japan in the East

China Sea. The 'China Maritime Police' is a unitary authority formed of several agencies, known, because of their uncoordinated and often competitive approach, as the 'Nine Dragons'. This rationalisation has significantly improved the responsiveness and efficiency of China's offshore operations. They are equipped with modern, well-equipped and robust coastguard vessels, which are working hard to ensure that possession of the islands and 80 per cent of the South China and East China Seas represents considerably more than nine-tenths of the law. They conduct continuous, wide-ranging patrols throughout the whole of the dash-line area, while naval and air units are frequently to be found in the vicinity of the disputed islands and in areas where China is seeking to extend its reach. China also puts its fishermen in the front line to assert historic rights and engage the maritime protection agencies of neighbouring countries, leading in several cases in the past few years, to confrontation, arrests and violence.

China's approach is to use military assets and the non-military elements of its sea power against weaker opponents in the South China Sea, with alternate policing actions and precisely judged shows of force. It normally deploys civilian and non-military assets to reduce the risks of escalation and ensure that disputes remain localised. Chinese provocations and intrusions are never enough for the USA or other outside powers to intervene directly, but are sufficient to legitimise Chinese presence and claims over time. Against regional rivals, the approach is designed to test resolve, probe weaknesses, wear an opponent down and erode the political will to resist. Indeed, its resources in terms of personnel and vessels are ideally scaled to conduct the maritime version of what might be called Chinese (sea) water torture.

The Japanese Maritime Self-Defense Force and Japan Coast Guard are certainly feeling the pressure. This is because the Chinese are particularly aggrieved about – and fixated on – the Senkaku Islands, to the north-east of Taiwan, which are administered by the Japanese as their sovereign territory. There are frequent confrontational episodes between Chinese and Japanese maritime and air assets, with Chinese vessels regularly entering Japanese territorial waters in the vicinity of the Senkakus, along with substantial numbers of fishing boats. China also routinely (and legally) sails its warships through the disputed waters en route to exercises, as well as conducting numerous warship and submarine deployments in the Philippine Sea south of Japan, as part of what the People's Liberation Army Navy (PLAN) calls 'core security-related interests'. In response, Japan, determined to uphold its sovereignty, has acquired twelve dedicated patrol ships, increased its defence budget by 23 per cent to 32.5 billion yen ($348.15 million) from April 2014, commissioned maritime UAVs and begun to build amphibious forces and marines. This is despite the fact that Japan and China have an interest in maintaining reasonable relations and in promoting stability in the region in supporting their $300 billion-a-year trade together.

Out of the blue, the situation deteriorated sharply in November 2013, when China unilaterally imposed an Air Defence Identification Zone (ADIZ) that not only covered the Senkaku Islands, but also obtruded into the South Korean ADIZ and took in a disputed islet. Essentially, the terms of the ADIZ mandated that all aircraft flying into and through the zone have to inform China's air traffic control system. Importantly, a 'zone' extends upwards from sea level as high as an aircraft can fly and the move is designed to assert Chinese *droit de seigneur* over the sea area as well. It obviously affects the operations of South Korean and Japanese aircraft, but also those of other countries, notably their military activities. The temperature was raised still further in a Chinese attempt to pillory the Japanese about the issue in January 2014, when Liu Xiaoming, China's ambassador in London, wrote, 'China and Britain are both victors of the Second World War. Our two countries have a common responsibility to work with the international community to oppose and condemn any words or actions aimed at invalidating the peaceful post-war consensus and challenging the international order.' One would hope that this sort of attitude would lead to more cooperative approaches by China in the East China and South China Seas. But with almost daily incidents in the vicinity of the Senkaku Islands, the situation is tense between China and Japan and could easily escalate into shows of force.

In all cases, China's navy and shore-based assets lurk in the background as an implicit threat, occasionally made manifest by incidents like that at the James Shoal off Malaysia in March 2013. Here, a Chinese naval task force, comprising a large amphibious ship and two destroyers, was sent to conduct a ceremony to 'maintain national sovereignty' at the shoal[5] located just 43 nm (80 km) off Malaysia's coast (130 nm/240 km inside Malaysia's EEZ and

---

[5] The group of rocks had previously seen the erection in 2010 of a stone structure declaring it to be the Chinese 'Zengmu Reef'.

970 nm/1,800 km from the Chinese mainland). This was the furthest south that Chinese warships had ventured to assert sovereignty. Unchallenged and initially unnoticed, this sort of incident is likely to recur with increasing frequency, as China continues to probe the limits of international and regional tolerance. At the moment, the Chinese are not doing a good job of heeding Deng Xiaoping's advice, 'Hide your strength, wait your moment.'

Other claims are ambitious, to say the least. Wang Yilin, chairman of the China National Offshore Oil Corporation (CNOOC), told an audience at CNOOC's headquarters in May 2012 that large-scale deep-water rigs are 'our mobile national territory and a strategic weapon'. Statements like this make a strong claim for Chinese sovereignty wherever its rigs might be located, whether in other countries' offshore zones or on the high seas. In May 2014, Chinese vessels repeatedly rammed and fired high-pressure water cannons at Vietnamese vessels attempting to prevent the installation of a Chinese oil rig at a point 140 nm (220 km) off the Vietnamese coast. China promptly and unilaterally announced an exclusion zone of 3 nm (4.8 km) around the rig. Yet again, creeping territoriality rears its ugly head. It seems likely at some stage in the future that China will deploy coastguard or naval units to protect its assets overseas and to offer assistance to those countries that cannot or will not maintain law and order in those EEZs where China has a commercial footprint.

A Chinese mare nostrum?

China has other motives for restricting activity in its EEZ. It wants to create a *mare nostrum* in the Yellow, East China and South China seas – a sort of exclusive maritime backyard. Indeed, the past four years have seen increasing numbers of Chinese cruise ships operating in these disputed waters, establishing the new normal in the minds of the Chinese people. Its public statements consistently support this line, 'Then why were Chinese warships sent to patrol the East China Sea and South China Sea? As you know, the Chinese government has sovereign power over the East China Sea and South China Sea. It is our stand to exert sovereign power in these areas. Therefore, it is right and above reproach for Chinese warships to patrol in the territory of China.'[6]

---

[6] Lieutenant General Qi Jianguo, Deputy Chief of General Staff, People's Liberation Army, at the Shangri-La Dialogue 2013, Fourth Plenary Session, as reported by IISS, 2 June 2013.

For its own part, China does not like foreign warships or government vessels operating in its EEZ, even though Article 58 of UNCLOS states that in an EEZ, 'all states, whether coastal or land-locked, enjoy, subject to the relevant provisions of this convention, the freedoms ... of navigation and overflight ... and other internationally lawful uses of the sea related to these freedoms, such as those associated with the operation of ships [and] aircraft'. China sees foreign military activities as an outrage to its national honour and opportunities for surveillance and intelligence gathering by those countries that would constrain its freedom of action and manoeuvre, both politically and militarily. Nor does China like foreign warships operating close to its own major units. A taste of things to come occurred in early December 2013, when the USS *Cowpens*, a guided missile cruiser, was operating in the vicinity of the Chinese carrier *Liaoning* in international waters in the South China Sea. In an episode reminiscent of the good old days of the Cold War, the *Cowpens* had to take evasive action to avoid a collision after a Chinese warship tried to prevent her moving close to the Chinese carrier. It was the most significant event at sea between the two navies since the harassment by five Chinese ships of the oceanographic research vessel, USS *Impeccable*, in 2009, also in the South China Sea.

The problem for China is that under UNCLOS – and certainly under customary law – the USA, or anyone else, can freely operate its warships right up to the Chinese 12 nm (22 km) limit, as well as exercising transit or innocent passage even within territorial seas.[7] Within an EEZ, they can mount simulated exercises and weapon firings, dive submarines, fly aircraft, conduct surveillance and reconnaissance operations and other intelligence-gathering activities, and collect military and marine data. China's characteristic approach has been to claim that military activities are in all cases prejudicial to the environment and the economic exploitation of its EEZ and therefore subject to its permission and regulation. The natural logic of the Chinese claims to exert territorial control over its EEZ would be to extend this prohibition out to 200 nm (370 km) and it would be an easy flip to include operating aircraft from aircraft carriers as well.

---

[7] Currently, international law does not allow the submerged transit of a submarine within another country's territorial seas, the operation of combat aircraft and other evolutions that detract from the status of the warship as innocent or transiting.

Meanwhile, without blushing, the Chinese media have been keen to let the USA know that PLAN has been 'making forays into the US EEZ' (probably Guam) since July 2013.

It is easy to see why China wants to control these areas of ocean. The South China Sea in particular contains a lot of oil and gas, as well as fish and other resources. Reasonable assessments suggest that there are more than 200 billion barrels of oil and 56 trillion cubic m (2 quadrillion cubic ft) of natural gas. It does not want any interference with its attempts to exploit these resources. There is also an issue relating to size, which matters to the Chinese as a budding great power. The extent of a country's EEZ is a virility issue. The USA heads the list with 11,351,000 sq km (4,382,646 sq miles), followed by France, Australia, Russia and the UK. China appears at number 33, with an EEZ of 879,019 sq km (339,391 sq miles), sandwiched between Peru and Somalia. With Mauritius, the Solomon Islands and the Federated State of Micronesia all above them, the Chinese view is likely to be somewhat jaundiced. However, once China's claims over Taiwan and the ten-dash line are included, China jumps up to an almost respectable number 11 (up there at the top table), with 3,879,666 sq km (1,497,947 sq miles).

Furthermore, militarily and strategically, China's achievement of sovereignty in the South China Sea would allow it to hold potential opponents at considerable range off its coast and intimidate and overawe its neighbours with the proximity of its navy's fighting power. It would also allow China to extend its control towards the strategic choke points of the Malacca, Lombok and Sunda straits. Needless to say, it would also make it more difficult for the USA, the UK or any other country to support its allies and partners in the region and the positions of Taiwan, Japan and South Korea would become increasingly precarious, constrained and threatened respectively. Control of the South China Sea would, as with the Japanese in the Second World War, permit easier access for the Chinese to deploy into the Indian Ocean and into the wide expanses of the Pacific.

There is a commercial aspect to China's desire to dominate the South China and East China seas. It has invested heavily in building up commercial and industrial linkages with the countries bordering the region and seeks to enjoy the advantages of being able to integrate its strategic, trading and commercial interests. China's approach in the area of the ten-dash line seems to be the creation of an exclusive strategic and economic space within which it sets not only the terms for security, but also the basis for dominating the sea lines of communication (notably to Taiwan, South Korea and Japan) and control of economic exchange. When seen from its own perspective and in the light of its considerable investment in the region and its own strategic pre-occupations, this seems logical and sensible. It also looks a lot like the tributary system familiar to Zheng He and the emperors in the fifteenth century.

China's approach is coloured by its conception of itself as a (past, present and future) great power against which all other countries are calibrated. China's elites demonstrate a marked contempt for what they view as little powers (almost everyone) and for liberal notions of individual rights, equalities and freedoms, in contrast to the 'logical' approach favoured by the Chinese regime. Difficulties with the Chinese may also be the result of cultural characteristics wrought by the conflict of these two political-social philosophies. David Shambaugh, in a recent book on China,[8] described 'a society composed of self-seeking, power-maximising individuals, who are dismissive of domestic social responsibilities and public goods, are certainly in no position to embrace arguments concerning international responsibilities and public goods'. He went on to write about China's preference for 'a regional hierarchy of asymmetric interstate relations centred on itself'. We should not doubt that for China, trade and maritime acquisition is an extension of war by other means. The worry for those seeking to maintain the international order is that, if China gets its way, other states will seek to bend the existing rules as well.

Future regional prospects

As we have seen, while China is able to devote plenty of assets and manpower to assert its claims and probe responses, regional states are unlikely to be able to react to every Chinese incursion, still less deter or counter its claims. The various claimants are not able to match China either individually or collectively. Collaboration is needed to share the burden of surveillance, intelligence and information and to strengthen common ownership of the high seas. Their best hopes lie in resolving the disputes with China

---

[8] *China Goes Global: the Partial Power* (2013).

on a multilateral basis within the Association of Southeast Asian Nations (ASEAN), which is attempting to develop a Code of Conduct, and by keeping the USA engaged. Without the direct involvement of major maritime powers, such as the USA, Japan and Australia, China would be able to browbeat and coerce its neighbours. The Chinese are not remotely keen on combinations that are directly or obliquely designed to level a playing field in relation to them. They prefer to settle disputes on a bilateral basis, rather than on a collective basis with a combination of states, and reject any role or involvement for outside powers. The Chinese attitude is that 'might is right' and should be respected. Some of the regional countries have taken the hint and have begun to acquire both platforms and skills to resist the pressure. Vietnam, Malaysia and Singapore continue a wary naval expansion, while avoiding opportunities to annoy the Chinese. Conscious of this need to stiffen resolve, Japan has provided the Philippines with twelve new patrol boats and the USA assists with capacity building.

Nevertheless, there is a broader problem for regional countries. China has committed up to 60 per cent of its outward direct investment in South East and East Asia and taken care to promote close bilateral commercial relationships. Regional countries are caught on the horns of a dilemma, with China coercing, intimidating and seducing (through economic stick and carrot tactics) other countries into acquiescing in its demands to extended sovereignty. Indeed, when challenged to stand up for their rights under UNCLOS, some countries are reluctant to confront China and speak of the 'Asian Way' of seeking compromise. It is by no means certain that anyone has passed China the script outlining how the 'Asian Way' would be applied to China's claims. The USA, in its own interests, has wanted to be involved and settle things, but has found itself excluded: Congressman Randy Forbes, writing in the US Naval Institute Newsletter in August 2013 summed up US experience: 'I think there are some real opportunities; you just have to be careful. I have not historically seen us do a very good job negotiating with the Chinese. They normally walk out of the room with the cake and we end up with the plate.'

The US position in the Asia-Pacific region has since the Second World War rested on a pattern of political and military alliances and partnerships, including specific security guarantees to Japan and South Korea. Taiwan, of course, remains a special (in other words, ambiguous) case. It seems certain that the USA will maintain and extend its current system of regional and bilateral alliances and agreements with other countries, while encouraging countries to build their own capacity, both for regional contingencies, including those involving China, and in local support of the international maritime system, with the assurance it will reinforce and support them if the going gets tough or the threat too powerful to handle. These arrangements need to be linked to an integrated regional maritime surveillance programme that is able to track, report and, when necessary, cue assets to intercept and mark Chinese naval and maritime security activities, which Japan already provides for its own waters.

In the current environment, China is likely to keep the disputes in the South China and East China seas bubbling along, by maintaining an appropriate level of tension and containing the risks of escalation. It will be alternately robust and conciliatory, seeking to confuse and obfuscate until in a position to enforce its claims. Chinese policy appears to be one of constant encroachment and testing of the limits of tolerance, never enough to provoke a reaction, but sufficient to assert a right. It is the use of insistence and persistence as a means of overcoming resistance. In these circumstances, it will be necessary to resist attempts by China to obtain undisputed rights by default and for regional countries to continue to reinforce their presence in disputed areas.

In reality, and as will be seen in the next chapter, China still lacks adequate military means to make the South China Sea a Chinese lake and permanently exclude rival navies from its 'near seas'. It probably needs about ten years to acquire a capability at sea that is able to overawe its neighbours and attempt to prevent outside interference. However, a modest increase in Chinese capability would increase its relative power at sea in the region, sufficient to bully its neighbours and hold outside powers at bay if they sought to intervene.

The ghost at the wedding of US–China relations is likely to be Russia. Russia has its own worries about China, most notably the distinct demographic imbalance along its long border with the Middle Kingdom, the vulnerability of its sparsely populated, resource-rich eastern territories and China's substantial presence and influence in Central Asia. Its navy would be concerned about Chinese control of the sea approaches to the Russian Far East, as well as the potential for China to dominate the strategic choke point of the Bering Strait, once the Arctic becomes commercially viable as a shipping route. Another notable and, from the Chinese point of view, uninvited outside power with an interest in the region will be India, with its extensive investments and trading connections in South East Asia, notably a growing commercial presence in Malaysia and Indonesia.

In this atmosphere, most Asia-Pacific countries will strive to contain US–Chinese rivalry and to preserve the stability and security that have been the context and cornerstone for regional prosperity and growth. They will have calculated that, as long as the USA remains engaged and honours its treaty obligations (and Japan and Australia continue to maintain their strategic stance), the security framework in the Asia-Pacific region will hold. There were signs, too, during the tour of Asia by President Barack Obama in April 2014, that the USA is getting its act together. He confirmed that the dispute over the Senkaku Islands would be subject to the terms of the existing USA/Japan Treaty of Mutual Cooperation and Security in the event of an armed attack. Even though the USA is not supporting anyone's claims to the islands, it would uphold Japan's rights to administer them. President Obama also signed a ten-year defence agreement with the Philippines, which included the re-establishment of military bases and the stationing of forces there, and South Korea and Malaysia received similar soothing assurances.

However, it is vital US forces are at suitable readiness to support America's friends, deter attempts at Chinese coercion and respond credibly to incidents that threaten to escalate beyond local capacity. In addition, the situation will require the vigorous assertion of the freedom of the seas and the rights of transit and innocent passage in accordance with UNCLOS and customary international law. This means operating in times and places of their choice rather than anyone else's choosing and may require going, potentially, in harm's way. This type of operation was something that the USA routinely exercised during the Cold War in relation to the Soviet Union, with frequent close quarters situations between US warships claiming their international rights and their Soviet counterparts trying to see them off the premises. Since 1991, the US Navy has conducted more than 300 'freedom of navigation' exercises to challenge exaggerated claims by fifty-three countries; in 2013, it challenged the claims of, among others, China, Indonesia, Iran, Malaysia, Oman, Taiwan and Vietnam. Conversely, it will be important for illegal and illegitimate probes by Chinese military and maritime security forces to be resisted if the regional basis for stability and assurance is to be maintained.

One can see why China's attitude makes the USA wary of ratifying UNCLOS; it would encourage similar behaviour by other countries and perpetuate a maritime regime, which has already proved too vague, suscep-tible to legal manipulation and prone to exploitation, to provide assurance for a superpower that relies on the freedom of the seas for both its trading and defence needs. If China got its way over the South China Sea, it is likely that other states would follow suit and the current international rules would become unsustainable, as China would have demonstrated the power to modify in its favour the existing international rules and effectively rein-troduce the concept of *mare clausum*. There might also be moves to revive the 1970s' idea of 'littoral clubs' whereby those states that have a coastline fronting onto a particular ocean or sea would have pre-eminent rights over its overall use and jurisdiction. This is certainly a line which is being pushed by China. In these circumstances, it would be game over for *mare liberum*.

The situation in the Asia-Pacific region may eventually be determined by the success of several trade patterns that are emerging, especially those that should lead to regional free trade agreements. ASEAN is seeking to align the economies of its members by 2015, building on the progress achieved by ASEAN and its six free trade partners (Australia, China, India, Japan, Korea and New Zealand) in launching the Regional Comprehensive Economic Partnership. These initiatives look likely in future to be replaced by success in agreeing the Trans-Pacific Partnership between twelve members, headed by the USA, which will represent a free trade area of some 800 million peo-ple and a GDP of $27 trillion.[9] Crucially, it requires the operation of *mare liberum* to work and, pointedly, China has not been invited to join the party.

The issues at stake in the South China Sea represent a significant test case, as do, at a lower volume, the disputes between the USA and Canada about the status of the Northwest Passage, and between several countries in the Eastern Mediterranean region. Claims to sea areas are likely to become territorial in their application and interpretation. The more that states think of their maritime boundaries in the same terms as land borders, either

---

[9] However, at present the Trans-Pacific Partnership is being held up because of fears in Asia about the protection of local tariffs, economic advantages and industries.

for economic or homeland security reasons, the more investment in the apparatus of security and sustainability they will need and seek to impose. If these disputes are not resolved peacefully, future naval conflicts are likely to revolve around and result in a 'land grab' at sea, just as land campaigns in the past were fought to acquire land and assets. Great powers have an interest in defending a world that either serves their interests or universal values – or both. The question is, is China an outlier or the leader of a pack, each of which is watching closely how events unfold before making its move?

THE MALWARE OF THE SEA

We have seen how complex and cluttered the littoral regions of the world will be in the future, not least because of continuing urbanisation, economic development and high levels of human activity. In all cases, states will need assured and uninterrupted access to and from their ports and areas of economic production and wealth. At the same time, maritime sovereignty and borders, as well as offshore zones and high-value ports, need to be safeguarded against intrusions and violations by state-based and proxy actors, terrorists and criminals. Their integrity will also be challenged by illegal immigration, the trafficking of people, drugs and weapons and the changing topographies and conditions brought about by sea level changes, while good environmental status and sustainable ecosystems will need active management if they are to thrive.

For those states that do not invest in maritime border security, there would appear to be extensive opportunities for terrorists, traffickers and pirates to operate in the littoral regions of the world. Trafficking and other criminal networks already parallel and exploit the extensive access provided by an open maritime trading system and resource-constrained enforcement agencies. Coastal raiding by criminals and pirates, for private gain, has only been seen in recent years in small-scale, local scenarios, mostly in East Africa and in the Sri Lankan struggle against the Liberation Tigers of Tamil Eelam (LTTE). However, in the absence of suitably effective deterrence, detection and defence measures, these opportunistic crimes are likely to increase, both in frequency and geographic scope.

Similarly, the concerted, highly lethal 2008 attack on Mumbai by terrorists and the cross-border raid by an Al-Shabaab sponsored group in the

Westgate shopping centre in Nairobi in September 2013 demonstrated the vulnerabilities of civil, lightly guarded societies to this kind of attack and the opportunities that they present. Israel faces the problem all the time. As population, economic activity and wealth continue to expand in the littoral regions, the opportunities and temptations for criminals, terrorists and small, armed groups operating at and from the sea are likely to expand substantially. As societies have become more interconnected, interdependent and 'wired', they are likely to become more susceptible to systemic breakdown and small, targeted amounts of violence and military-level force.

Terrorist elements, in particular, have recognised that they can achieve significant impact, profile and leverage if they can threaten or disrupt international sea lanes and major maritime hubs. Needless to say, a successful attack on a major port or energy complex is likely to lead to operational and commercial disruption on a large scale, possibly leading to losses of millions or billions of dollars. Even a credible threat or hoax would fundamentally dislocate and restrict the operations of a port or other critical shore side infrastructure. Meanwhile, the extended reach of Somali pirates over 1,000 nm (1,850 km) into the Indian Ocean through the use of fishing vessels employed as 'mother ships', shows the potential scope and scale for further criminal activity at sea.

Terrorism

In the modern era, terrorists have launched attacks at sea and from the sea against the land. They have successfully attacked ships (notably in the cases of the USS *Cole* in 2000 and the MV *Limbourg* in 2002), oil and gas platforms (Iraq's Al Basrah Oil Terminal (ABOT) and the Khawr Al-Amaya Oil Terminal (KAAOT) in the northern Persian Gulf) and urban populations (Mumbai). Terrorists also use the sea to transfer weapons, explosives, people and other illicit goods between locations, through well-established networks, including fishing vessels (in the case of the IRA), dhow traffic (Al Qaeda and its affiliates) and a combination of both (the Tamil Sea Tigers).

Before they were forcibly suppressed, the Sea Tigers of the LTTE demonstrated ingenuity and improvisation in their struggle against the Sri Lankan Navy, between 1984 and 2009. They developed a range of fibreglass suicide craft and attack boats, up to 15 m (50 ft) long and armed with heavy machine guns, grenade launchers and mines. As well as attacking shore installations and anchored ships, as part of a sustained sabotage and bombing campaign, they destroyed at least twenty-nine Sri Lankan inshore patrol boats and one freighter. They had also built three semi-submersibles by the time the war ended in 2009.

Terrorist attacks on littoral and maritime targets are unlikely to diminish in the future. The logic of what could happen (imagination- and vulnerability-based assessments) rather than what is likely to happen (intelligence led) suggests that a variety of options exist at sea for future exploitation. The possibilities have not yet been exhausted. These will include attacks on vulnerable and remote coastlines, especially against urbanised areas and energy installations and facilities; the use of 'phantom'[10] and hijacked ships to penetrate – and block approaches to – ports and terminals or international straits; assaults on cruise ships and other high-value, prestige shipping and, underutilised until now, the widespread use of improvised explosive devices (IEDs), both as mines in congested shipping lanes and carried on unsuspecting ships. Above all, terrorists, criminals and traffickers are likely to exploit the opportunities offered by unmanned vehicles and technologies in the land, sea and air environments, as well as exploring the possibilities of the underwater dimension, especially against static targets.

Terrorists are likely to absorb emerging, available technology as part of their capability into the future. Together with sophisticated electronics and communications enablers and jammers, they will have access to more advanced weaponry and data systems to support their ventures. As the Israelis discovered in 2006, some will have access to sophisticated weapons provided by states. Iran supplied anti-armour weapons, rockets and C-802 Yingji-82 anti-ship missiles to Hezbollah. One of these sank an Egyptian coaster, while another struck the Israeli frigate *Hanit* while she was enforcing a naval blockade off Beirut. Hezbollah has also demonstrated its ability to employ an, as yet, unsophisticated UAV.

---

[10] Phantoms are ships that use false papers, registrations and identities to engage in criminal and terrorist activity. Many pass through complex chains of ownership and certification; some have their configuration and appearance altered.

Criminality

Criminality at sea ranges across several areas of operation, from piracy and armed robbery at one end of the spectrum to petty smuggling and breaches of fishing regulations at the other. It includes toxic dumping and illegal fish exploitation on a massive scale by organised criminal organisations, with access to wide networks of financing and distribution. It extends to the trade in illegal armaments, drugs and the materials required for developing weapons of mass destruction, as well as the illicit movement of migrating people and the trafficking of human beings. Yet again, much of this criminal activity thrives on the fact that the sea is largely unpoliced, as well as on the weak institutions and corruption of certain states, allied to imaginative use of FOCs, a largely opaque international system for the transfer of financial resources and inadequate intelligence.

Criminals are likely to continue to view the sea as an area for exploitation wherever there are weaknesses in the international system and gaps in national jurisdiction and responsibility. Indeed, as we have seen with Somalia and several other countries, it is the failure by states to fulfil their sovereign responsibilities with regard to their borders, territorial seas and economic zones that provides the incentive and pretext for criminals and pirates to operate. It seems reasonable to believe that the twenty-first century will continue to see the extensive use of the sea by criminals, traffickers and terrorists.

The twenty-first century is also seeing the blurring of the definitions between terrorism, criminality and trafficking. Criminals, including pirates, will use terrorist tactics; terrorists will resort to crime to fund their activities and traffickers will cooperate with both criminals and terrorists in terms of traded goods, including weapons and explosives, and protection for their networks. As has been seen with a variety of terrorist groups, including the FARC and the IRA, the symbiotic relationship between terror and crime allows the threat or use of violence for both political advantage and economic gain.

Another aspect, routinely exposed by the financial assurance experts, Thomson Reuters and others, will be the widespread use of shell companies, front organisations and third parties to shield illicit operations from intelligence and law enforcement agencies. These will include both complicit and unknowing partners, who will provide the appearance of financial, legal and institutional respectability, as well as the means by which transactions can be concealed and legitimised. These services will take in money laundering, the transfer of contraband of all kinds, including black market weapons and systems, and the corruption and infiltration of official organisations, enforcement agencies and institutions. They will also make extensive use of cyber opportunities. Europol reported in October 2013 that criminals had hacked into the control, logging and monitoring systems that managed container traffic in the port of Antwerp between 2011 and 2013. This enabled them to traffic cocaine and heroin concealed among legitimate containerised cargoes from South America.

Needless to say, the use of ships flying FOCs will continue to play an important part in this process, from the petty to the serious, as will the extensive regional traffic centred on fishing vessels (almost everywhere) and dhow traffic (in the Indian Ocean and Horn of Africa). Similarly, many pirates, especially those in East Asia, belong to organised crime networks, comprising corrupt officials, port workers, hired hands and businessmen who dispose of the proceeds. In West Africa and Asia, underpaid maritime security personnel have been found to be complicit, with some actively involved in criminal activity and armed attacks.

Although these elements will continue to be the preserve of intelligence and law enforcement agencies, one can anticipate, as has been seen above, the likely proliferation and diffusion of sophisticated weaponry onto the international black market, mostly as a result of the collapse of well-armed regimes into failed states. Navies currently assist in the detection and apprehension of criminals and terrorists, as well as in the prevention of trafficking and illegal migration. When law enforcement agencies become overmatched in terms of the violence that can be offered, military force will increasingly be required to deter, detain and defeat malefactors.

This is because criminals are also gaining access to increasingly effective weaponry and systems. Russian and Chinese companies offer for sale on the Internet a wide range of disruptive and disabling devices, ranging from compact communications and GPS jammers to hand portable wireless and mobile telephone suppression devices. Online expertise, guidance and component ordering provide solutions for neutralising surveillance activity and devising novel attack methods, as well as the means of manufacturing underwater improvised explosive devices (UWIEDs), semi-submersible vehicles and counter-UAV jammers. Future terrorists and criminals will very soon build or acquire unmanned vehicles. The days of the human bank robber and the suicide bomber might well be over.

In the 1980s, aircraft and fast boats were the smuggling vehicles of choice for Colombian drugs cartels, but more and more were being detected by radar. They were replaced by semi-submersible, low visibility 'narco-subs', the first of which was detected in 2006 off Costa Rica. By 2008, an average of ten per month were detected, each carrying several tons of cocaine. As their crews would scuttle them on interception, very few were captured, but it was estimated that about 330 tons of cocaine were being moved every year. Costing about $2 million to build, a single trip was thought to generate revenue of about $100 million. Commercial manned and unmanned vehicles are also available. Manned underwater vehicles, such as the DeepFlight *Super Falcon* and DeepFlight *Aviator* developed by Hawkes Ocean Technologies near San Francisco, are capable of descents to 450 m (1,500 ft).

These technologies are reminders that, as authorities and agencies introduce more sophisticated surface surveillance and intercept capabilities, terrorists and criminals are likely to seek to exploit the underwater environment in their attempts to conduct attacks against prestige targets and expose vulnerabilities – and increase costs and overheads – for both national infrastructures and the international trading system. Mines and UWIEDs can be laid on the seabed or attached to structures and vessels. It is already common practice for drugs, illegal materials and arms to be smuggled in externally mounted pods ('parasites') below the waterline of ships' hulls.

One other trend will emerge in the near future. Technology will enable states and groups to take offensive action against their targets and rivals anonymously. We have already seen the potential of unmanned vehicles to provide anonymity for a variety of actions and perpetrators. Consequently, the incidence of 'accidents' is likely to increase, as is the use of unmanned vehicles across the board for the transfer of illicit or trafficked goods. Why take the risk of accompanying the merchandise yourself, when a decent navigation system or artificial intelligence can do it for you? Drugs traffickers are employing 'narco-torpedoes'. Consequently, as with mines, it will become increasingly difficult to determine responsibility for acts of violence at sea.[11]

Piracy

With antecedents that reach back to classical times, piracy thrived in various troubled parts of the world for most of the twentieth century and survived into the early years of our present century. The most notorious trouble spots today are the Strait of Malacca, the Gulf of Guinea in West Africa and, until recently, the Horn of Africa and the Indian Ocean. However, the problem of piracy and armed robbery (which is technically what takes place in national jurisdictions) is universal and can be found in the Bay of Bengal, the Caribbean and many parts of South America. Because the perpetrators live on the land and rely on its support, piracy is paradoxically a land problem with a maritime dimension. Common piracy is usually opportunistic and sporadic (banditry), while organised piracy is endemic and defined by the range and sophistication of the links that sustain it, the context within which these networks are able to operate and the effects that criminalised activity has on local political, economic and social landscapes.

Piracy has flourished wherever there have been assets worth seizing, international and national governance and law enforcement have been weak and a suitable business model has presented itself, in preference to other alternatives. Most pirates want to be able to live long enough to enjoy the fruits of their illicit labours. It is seldom a long-term career choice in the conventional sense and still less a way of life that many would follow if they had something better to do. In fact, it is a classic example of an occupation that is characterised by the constant interplay of opportunity and risk.

The costs to legitimate business are substantial. Møller-Maersk increased its piracy risk surcharges from $110 to $170 per 40-ft equivalent unit on routes threatened by pirate action, those between the Indian subcontinent, the Middle East, Europe and Central/South America. At their height, average ransoms paid to Somali pirates in 2011 rose to $5.4 million from $3.4 million

---

[11] A conspiracy theory arose from the BP Deepwater Horizon disaster, reinforced by a Russian 'eyewitness', that it had been torpedoed by a North Korean submarine, which might be a speculative foretaste of things to come.

in 2009, although the record was $9.5 million for the release of the *Samho Dream*, a South Korean crude oil tanker. Oceans Beyond Piracy reckoned that the overall cost of piracy in 2011 was $7 billion, with 80 per cent of the cost borne by shipping companies and the rest by governments. The report estimated that between $339 million and $413 million was paid in ransoms off the Somali coast between 2005 and 2012.[12] The average haul was $2.7 million. Ordinary pirates usually received $30,000–75,000 each, with a bonus of up to $10,000 for the first man to board a ship and for those bringing their own weapons or ladders.[13]

Modern piracy ranges from incidents of petty larceny on the high seas to extensive business enterprises involving the capture and detention of ships and their crews (as off the coast of Somalia and well out into the Indian Ocean) and their subsequent release for ransom. In the latter case, countries, companies and counter-piracy operations initially struggled to achieve a post-modern consensus on how to deal with a pre-modern threat. Neglecting the convenience of classifying these pirates as 'common enemies of all mankind', the differing interpretations of international and national law were allowed to obstruct and delay the implementation of proven measures to deter and disrupt pirate activity. The problem was partly exacerbated by the fact that the few genuine and many more self-appointed piracy 'experts' rapidly and substantially exceeded the numbers of active pirates. They continue to do so. Another escalating factor was the willingness of shipping companies to pay ransoms, in the interests of the crews' safety in some cases or hard economic logic in others, such that a profitable business model emerged for the pirates that tilted the risk–reward calculation excessively in favour of the reward aspects.

By the start of 2014, piracy off Somalia had been virtually, but not fully, eradicated, by a combination of concerted action by international naval forces, the presence of armed guards on transiting vessels and the disruption of pirate infrastructure and networks ashore. Measures to protect transiting

---

[12] At their peak, in 2011, Somali pirates are estimated to have collected as much as $156 million in ransoms. Ironically, it has been calculated that the amount spent in 2013 on private security arrangements and other measures significantly exceeded the sums paid out in ransoms since 2005 ('The Pirate Economy', by Joe Pinsker in *The Atlantic*, 16 April 2014).

[13] 'Pirate Trails: Tracking the Illicit Financial Flows from Pirate Activities off the Horn of Africa', World Bank, the UN and Interpol, 4 November 2013.

merchant ships and other civil users of the sea in the Indian Ocean and Gulf of Aden include a range of physical ways of countering the threat: ships are fitted with obstructions that prevent and deter boarding; many have secure refuges or citadels where the crew can hide in the event of a successful boarding; and most transit through threat areas at higher speed (and cost) than normal. Also, the majority of major shipping companies employ armed response teams and close protection for their ships in areas of high risk and many states have contributed warships to international efforts to discourage and suppress piracy off Somalia. Other countries, including Japan, China, India and Korea, offer convoy facilities for transiting ships. All counter-piracy operations are enabled by wide-area surveillance derived from satellite, aircraft and UAVs, linked to a comprehensive information sharing and reporting network. The wonder is that these common-sense measures were not put in place before and with more urgency.

During the time of the greatest number of pirate attacks off Somalia, there had been a clear breakdown in the exercise of sovereignty by the coastal state and distinct indifference by the international community. It is interesting to speculate what the reaction to a similar breakdown of sovereign jurisdiction on land, with all its attendant miseries, would have been. The likelihood would have been that an international effort would have been made to at least assist the failing or failed state and that a peacekeeping force would have been assembled and deployed. It is worth asking why the same impetus is not applied to breakdowns in law and order and violations of sovereignty offshore, especially when the impact is felt by not only the coastal state but also the international system of law and trade.

Piracy and the counters to it are a function of the context in which it takes place. A comparison between the recent business models and examples of piracy off Somalia and the situation off West Africa represents a case in point. The West African model is predominantly based on the theft of oil and cargo, but also includes the widespread kidnapping of hostages, especially Europeans, for ransom or exchange with human trafficking and third-party networks. This enables the armed robbers to operate more autonomously and more cheaply than their more organised and structured Somali counterparts. It also allows them to work more quickly, avoiding long negotiations that tie up resources. According to the International Maritime Bureau (IMB), 966 seafarers were attacked by pirates off West Africa in 2012, with over 200 taken hostage. As of 30 September 2013, 90 separate attacks were reported against shipping vessels in the Gulf of Guinea resulting in seven hijacking incidents, 132 persons held hostage aboard hijacked vessels, and 34 seafarers and oil workers kidnapped and held on shore. Hijackings target refined product tankers from which the pirates steal a proportion of the cargo to sell on the black market. Hostages are typically held for an average of four days (the time it takes to off-load the cargo). There is also a greater degree of violence in the initial attack.

A recent UN report[14] acknowledged the steep decline in pirate attacks off Somalia and the Horn of Africa, but noted that the pirate networks remained active. It highlighted the way in which criminal networks and individuals had diversified their business model interests by seeking alternative employment. These included the provision of armed protection to vessels involved in regional trading and illegal fishing activities[15] and the trafficking of arms, narcotics and people. Weapons and explosives were available through clan contacts with Al-Shabaab and operations were conducted in association with criminal elements in Yemen and with wider networks in the Gulf States and Iran.

It is important that the world does not become complacent about piracy or believe that it is an isolated phenomenon harking back to a former age or occurring in undeveloped areas of the world. Piracy is going on all the time, as a single snapshot of a typical week's activity in March 2013 illustrates, when the following seven piracy incidents were reported worldwide. Pirates in a small launch fired at a tanker off Nigeria, but did not board it. Off Somalia, a fishing vessel was attacked and robbed, while a merchant ship 57 nm (105 km) off the coast was attacked by eight pirates in a skiff, but deterred by an embarked armed security team. In the Bay of Bengal, a gang of twenty or so pirates had attacked thirty-four fishermen in three trawlers. The crews were beaten, had their arms and legs bound, and then thrown overboard. Three of the crew escaped and were saved by other fishermen, but all the others were lost. At Dumai and Adang Bay anchorages in Indonesia,

---

[14] *Report of the Monitoring Group on Somalia and Eritrea Pursuant to Security Council Resolution 2060 (2012): Somalia*, 12 July 2013.

[15] In April 2013, Puntland Maritime Police Force (PMPF) arrested 5 illegal fishing boats and 78 Iranian nationals illegally fishing off the coast along with 12 Somalis who were protecting the illegal fishing boats.

robbers in boats attacked a tanker and a bulk carrier respectively, while near Singapore a tug was boarded and robbed.

In the future, piracy, as with other forms of lawlessness at sea, will thrive wherever governance and enforcement are weak, incentives are strong and opportunities for private gain present themselves. Its character will vary according to the context in which it takes place and solutions will have to be tailored to the circumstances of each individual case. Often, the solutions will require resolution of the conditions that enabled or caused piracy to occur in the first place through a combination of measures that will range from incentives (to make the rewards of good behaviour more attractive than the risks associated with piracy) and coercion (to deal with the intractable, irreconcilable elements). Sea power can only deal with the manifestations of pirates at sea and protect ships and coastlines from their attentions; it can seldom eradicate the causes of piracy, which are on land, unless it is to neutralise or destroy the bases from which pirates operate by means of a decisive projection of naval or amphibious power. However, the overwhelming lesson from counter-piracy operations in the past fifteen years is that, in the absence of suitable restraining authority, the violence associated with piracy can only be deterred and defeated by the threat or use of violence to prevent attacks. Convoys, routeing and self-protection measures all have validity, but are not sufficient in the face of determined, desperate and experienced criminals operating over wide expanses of sea. Ships have to look to themselves – that's why, as we have seen, the merchantmen of the British East India Company had rows of cannon.

Migration and people trafficking

Persistent imbalances in wealth, social progress and economic development, together with political instability, demographic trends and climate change are likely to lead to increasing numbers of migrants at sea in the years to come. Many of these will attempt to travel by sea, as land borders become progressively less porous in response to the need of states to control population flows in the interests of their own social and economic stability. Almost all developed countries, notably the USA, Australia and the states of the EU, have had to establish both individual and collective maritime border security arrangements. Owing to the length of coastlines and complex geography of some states' jurisdictions, these efforts have only been partially successful. The problem is particularly acute in the Mediterranean where there is a marked disparity in wealth, opportunity and social provision between the northern and southern shores. North Africa is also a major transit area for those fleeing persecution, conflict and demographic pressures in the Middle East and Africa, as well as for economic migrants from sub-Saharan Africa.

Criminal and entrepreneurial activity has sought to capitalise on the human urge to flee persecution or seek better life opportunities. As an example, the International Centre on Migration Policy Development (ICMPD) estimates that between 100,000 and 120,000 migrants and persons cross the Mediterranean Sea every year without necessary authorisation or documents. Almost 900 migrant Search and Rescue cases were reported off Europe's southern maritime borders between 2011 and 2013, involving almost 50,000 people in distress. The tragic loss of life at sea, in several incidents in the Mediterranean in late 2013, on the passage between North Africa and Lampedusa and off the Atlantic coast is an indication of the scale of future migration and the pattern of criminal exploitation.

Closely linked to migration is the trafficking of people, which is generally defined as the procurement of an illegal entry or illegal residence of a person, into or in a country of which that person is not a national or permanent resident, for the purpose of financial or other material benefit. However, according to the UN, only about 10 per cent of people trafficked go by sea. Women account for 55–60 per cent of all trafficked victims detected globally, with women and girls together accounting for about 75 per cent. Twenty-seven per cent of all victims detected globally are children, of which two out of three victims are girls. Trafficking for sexual exploitation is more common in Europe, Central Asia and the Americas, whereas trafficking for forced labour is more frequently detected in Africa, the Middle East, South Asia, East Asia and the Pacific. The trafficking flow originating in East Asia remains the most prominent transnational flow.

The issue of trafficking and forced labour are particularly acute in the commercial fishing sector. Pressures associated with overfishing, illegal fishing and the use of low-cost workers have resulted in extensive abuse, forced labour and violence. Those trafficked often lack training, language proficiency, safety assurance and basic labour standards. These practices are often linked to other forms of crime, such as organised fisheries crime, other forms of trafficking and corruption.

Until the causes of migration and trafficking are addressed, the solution for Europe (and elsewhere) needs to be a comprehensive, multidisciplinary approach based on collaboration and cooperation between all sending and receiving countries and relevant international and national agencies. It will require extensive, integrated surveillance, intelligence and intercept facilities, allowing a comprehensive link to highly responsive vessels and aviation resources. Europe already has the European Agency for the Management of Operational Cooperation at the External Borders of the Member States of the European Union (FRONTEX for short). Its role is to 'promote, coordinate and develop European border management in line with the EU fundamental rights charter and apply the concept of Integrated Border Management'. However, it is likely to require additional resources, including military assets and inter-agency support, to cope with the increased flows of people fleeing conflict, economic hardship and persecution.

Also, with increased numbers of crossings taking place, often in unsound vessels or relying on the receiving country responding to distress calls, it is clear that some form of forward defence of a country's frontiers might be required, if necessary right up to the 12-nm (22-km) limit of potential sending countries. This would enable the interception of vessels before they had the chance to make the crossing, especially in unsafe vessels and practices. Operationally, it is likely that increased investment in satellite and both manned and unmanned aircraft, as well as ground-level human intelligence, will be required to maintain a coherent, comprehensive maritime picture of migratory traffic.

The measures needed to deal with migration and trafficking are indicators of the sophisticated, integrated surveillance systems that will be required to cope with risks and vulnerabilities in increasingly complex littoral regions. Navies and law enforcement agencies are already facing the prospect of having to confront criminal and terrorist groups able to acquire and operate military grade weapons and systems, enabling them to outrun and outgun the more modest patrol capabilities of official agencies. RPGs and light weapons no longer seem to do the trick. This process will be aided by the steady leakage of weapons and systems of increasing sophistication from the stockpiles of failed states, and through an extensive and thriving black market. Most recently, these countries have included Libya and Syria, but also extend to any country with weak controls and corruptible officials.

Comprehensive surveillance and coverage

The 'malware' situation at sea will mean simply that there will need to be suitable deterrent, detection and disruptive systems – both technological and human – in place to counter these types of attempts and attacks. Similarly, intelligence organisations will need to be attuned to the detection, identification and tracking of distinctive components and the associated expertise, just as specialist bomb-makers are tracked today. Having said that, the components for the narco-subs deployed by drugs cartels in Colombia and the mini-subs developed by the Tamil Tigers were largely manufactured with components that were at hand, available for order on the Internet or accessible through channels indistinguishable from normal activity.

Many countries have built chains of radar stations along their coasts (vaguely reminiscent of the watchtowers and beacons of ancient times) and introduced measures to be able to identify and track vessels operating in their territorial seas. The widespread use of AIS has greatly facilitated this process, along with various reporting and traffic management schemes. Following the Mumbai bombing in 2008, which used a fishing vessel hijacked on the high seas, Indian authorities made tracking equipment mandatory on fishing vessels and other craft in their national waters. India has also developed the notion of an 'electronic fence' around its coast and islands, with a comprehensive system of coastal surveillance, radar sites and protection. Its integrity and coverage have recently been threatened by the theft of components from some of the remotely operated sites. Many countries are now considering the mandatory fitting of identification and real-time tracking devices to vessels operating in their offshore zones, as well as increasing investment in maritime patrol aircraft, unmanned vehicles and radar chains. Turkey has started to institute a combined electronic reporting, automatic identification and maritime patrol regime around its extensive, accessible and complex coastline. In the USA, all states whose boundaries include maritime harbours and ports are taking decisive steps, backed up by legislation, to put in place surveillance and security measures to deter, detect and defeat the threats associated with criminal and terrorist activity at sea.

Much of this surveillance is now extending well into EEZs as countries seek to provide protection of their offshore platforms and assets not only against criminals, terrorists and (in some countries, such as South Korea) hostile incursions by another state, but also against migration, resource piracy and waste dumping. Other countries, such as China, which are particularly irritated or nervous about the innocent passage of foreign warships and research vessels within their territorial seas – and the exercise of their military functions in international waters just beyond these – have extensive surveillance, identification and targeting networks that extend well beyond the requirements of EEZ protection.

FUTURE PROSPECTS

For the near future, shared equitable access to common resources and the sea lines of communications around the world are likely to be guaranteed, in principle, if not always in practice. Nevertheless, there is a possibility, in the event of a global economic downturn, that protectionism and regional groupings could emerge as regimes attempt to preserve their mandate to govern, in authoritarian, 'managed' and democratic societies. In this scenario, the sea would become an increasingly contested space, with the emphasis on regional and local production, consumption and trade flows, and with regional security arrangements, possibly resulting in competing trade and security blocs. Re-shoring and the establishments of manufacture and production closer to home could also appear as a result of emerging technological shifts, such as 3D printing and nanotechnology.

The path to the future is likely to lie between these two extremes, with countries and companies taking advantage of international maritime law when it is in their interests to do so, but exploring the means to subvert or avoid its provisions when compliance does not suit their national or commercial interests. It is likely to be a world of self-interest and zero-sum games. Compete where you can, cooperate when you must.

Therefore, security at sea will be characterised by states' attempts to assert territorial rights to their offshore zones and the determination of other states to resist encroachments on the freedom of navigation and the global commons as enshrined in UNCLOS. Just as footpaths as rights of way in England traditionally have to be walked at least once in a year and a day for them to be sustained, so states will need to continue to assert their rights to freedom of navigation in contentious, but legally defined sea areas. The USA is the foremost champion of the rights of freedom of navigation, but it will need practical assistance and moral support from its allies and partners in order to maintain the sea as the global commons. As a result, those countries that have an interest in retaining the global commons will have to invest resources in maintaining their continued existence and operation. Mostly this will involve policing, asserting and enforcing international agreements and conventions. Just as multinational coalitions of the willing were established to deal with piracy off the Horn of Africa and the Indian Ocean, it is increasingly likely that multinational efforts will be required to deal with issues and problems that lie beyond national jurisdictions.

At the global level, security will essentially revolve around the protection by states of individual sovereign rights and of the integrity of an international system that ensures economic activity and productive exchange between suppliers, manufacturers and markets. This means that those countries and areas that produce the raw materials and energy and those that drive industrial production and economic growth, together with the states that dominate the routes between them, will determine the way in which the system is shaped and managed. For three centuries, the world has become accustomed to the (largely) benign stewardship and dominance of the oceans by the British and the USA, in succession. Their currencies have also been the dominant unit of exchange. For most of that time, the global system has been one that has been predisposed, and has tended towards, an open trading culture and a free market philosophy. On those occasions when that dominance has been aggressively challenged and the global system threatened by individual states, the circumstances have led to world wars and a Cold War.

It is clear from past experience that monopolies in trade and exchange and regional constraints in a globalised system, which translate into tariffs and preferential trading schemes, rarely survive. Spain and Portugal tried to dictate the terms of trade with the Americas and the Indies in the late fifteenth and early sixteenth centuries and found themselves beset by interlopers, various maritime entrepreneurs and an assortment of privateers, pirates and opportunists. It did not help that its own citizens and colonists were complicit in the process, in order to gain the goods and services (slaves mostly) at a price and convenience level that they were prepared to afford. The lesson from history is that inclusive trading systems are better regulated and policed for the benefit of all legitimate users, than exclusive, excluding systems that tend to attract and encourage bad behaviour, such as smuggling and trafficking, that often leads to confrontation and conflict, especially when it involves the interests of states or elites. Exclusive systems also involve significant overheads for the enforcing authority. The imposition of sanctions, blockades and embargoes often incurs similar problems in their application, with the incentives and rewards of infraction often outweighing the risks for the perpetrators and making the costs for the enforcers prohibitive.

Global governance

It will by now be apparent to the reader that global governance is sadly lacking at sea; it either has to be something in which every state participates or is controlled by one particular country. The UN has no direct operational role in being able to implement or enforce UNCLOS, despite the authority granted to organisations such as the IMO, the International Whaling Commission and the International Seabed Authority (ISA) to encourage compliance with various aspects of UNCLOS.

On the high seas, there remain considerable gaps in legal definition and effective, multilateral enforcement. Where so much activity is currently unregulated and largely unobserved, national institutions are likely to enforce law and order only in their areas of jurisdiction and when it is in their interest to do so. The freedom of the high seas only works on the principle that states are more concerned to preserve their own unrestricted access than in denying the access of others. In these circumstances, it is probable that most countries will generally adhere to the stability and security of a global system that operates to their advantage, but will continue to involve themselves in disputes that affect their interests locally or regionally. Thus, in general there will be cooperation at the global level and competition at local level, although some countries will consider it advantageous to pressure the international system for individual reasons, while others will either tolerate – or fail to deal with – various criminal or terrorist elements operating in their vicinity. So far, the indications are that competition is not a sound basis for ensuring that the seas remain safe, secure and sustainable. Safeguards and mechanisms for cooperation are inadequate in the face of pressures from both commercial and national interests that seek to exploit the seas for their own benefit.

Pressure for improved governance in those areas beyond national jurisdictions is likely to be maintained by increasingly powerful and influential non-public bodies like the Global Ocean Commission (founded in February 2013) and the World Bank's Global Partnership for the Oceans (launched at Rio+ in Singapore in 2012). The latter is an association of more than one hundred governments, international organisations, civil society groups and private sector interests committed to addressing the threats to the health, productivity and resilience of the world's oceans. It aims to deal with problems like overfishing, pollution and habitat loss, in order to promote more productive, sustainable uses of the sea. Unfortunately, it is significant that the issue of the sea as the global commons is scarcely considered in any depth at gatherings such as the World Economic Forum at Davos every year, even though, as we have seen, the sea is so vital to the functioning of globalisation.

Even so, there is general agreement that more sophisticated institutional arrangements are required to regulate the oceans outside national jurisdictions, balancing the idea of the global commons and the rights of sovereign countries. UNCLOS is not a bad basis on which to start. It already provides a reasonable basis for the demarcation of national and international rights and obligations and has made a start with the management of ocean resources with the establishment of ISA. The vast majority of countries have ratified it, except for a few outliers, most notably the USA (see Chapter 1). However, while the USA generally adheres to its provisions, China, which has ratified UNCLOS, ignores its provisions when it is in its interests to do so.

The problem is that UNCLOS appears to be running out of steam, and although the UN has been active on providing peacekeeping forces for conflicts and disputes on land, it has dragged its feet with regard to the seas. What is required is a single international body, with the authority, resources and legitimacy to manage and regulate the different aspects of use, and abuse, of the global commons, in the interests of all states and future generations.

One might think that this should be the role of the IMO. Unfortunately, for most of the time of its operation, it has signally failed to live up to its grandiose title. Because of its need to attract the support of states, the IMO has been particularly ineffective in providing leadership and frameworks for dealing with a wide variety of maritime security issues, notably piracy trafficking and counter-drugs enforcement. Throughout the escalating piracy crisis off Somalia, it did little except wring its hands, express pious hopes and claim that the issue was too complex and legally constrained. In its defence, one has to remember that it was established in 1948 to deal with pollution at sea, not issues of security. There is something to do with more than hot air here. How about the IMO being more international in its effect, more comprehensive and organised in its approach to maritime issues? Safe, secure and sustainable – how many of those terms does it cover? Similarly, UNCLOS also offers a pretty feeble way in which to resolve territorial and natural resource disputes through the International Tribunal for the Law of the Sea (ITLOS).

It is clear that a single entity needs to absorb the functions of the many different and competing organisations and pressure groups. It would develop, establish and enforce agreed policy on the sustainable use and development of the oceans on behalf of the international community. It should establish common standards for every aspect of the use of the sea, from the extraction of minerals and managing MPAs to fishing and the welfare of seafarers, taking responsibility for both the seabed and the water column of the high seas, beyond national jurisdictions and economic zones. With suitable authority and enforcement powers, it should be able to balance and integrate the competing claims of environmental, economic and state activity in the interests of sustainable development and the global community. Most importantly, it would develop a Code of Conduct, established by the UN, to which all users of the high seas should adhere, and it should have sufficient teeth, both legal and practical, to enforce its decisions, either by calling on the resources of individual countries or having dedicated mechanisms of its own.

The organisation should also be able to coordinate the resources and assets that would be needed for the UN to be able to undertake the temporary control of a country's territorial sea and EEZ, in the event of the inability of a country to maintain its rights and responsibilities with regard to its offshore zone (as in the case of Somalia). It would in these circumstances coordinate capacity building, training and the establishment of the institutional framework to allow fragile countries to be able to safeguard their offshore zones.

This single authority would need to be reinforced by – and linked to – an institution that allows the equitable resolution of maritime disputes, the further codification of international maritime law and the settlement of other legal issues at sea. A universally recognised and equitably constituted international court, which would replace the currently hobbled ITLOS, would need to be able to settle disputes, establish case law and precedent, impose penalties and sanctions and have access to the means to enforce its decisions. One hardly dares to hope for the ability of an international body to call upon the armed forces and law enforcement agencies of states to enforce the decisions of an international court at sea, wherever states, groups and individuals might be in breach. The idea of an International Admiralty Court system that could deal with all aspects of maritime law, from disputes arising from the interpretation of UNCLOS to the arraignment of pirates and other criminals on the high seas, has been frequently raised. It would need to have the prestige, independence and acceptability to be able to pronounce definitively and authoritatively on maritime issues.

The fact that a couple of decisions have been made by the International Court of Justice (ICJ) has been encouraging in this regard. In January 2014, the ICJ gave a compromise judgment that equitably settled a maritime border dispute between Peru and Chile that had been simmering and niggling since 1883. Both countries have decided that they will abide by the decision. The ICJ also gave a judgment in 2013 about a similar dispute between Colombia and Nicaragua, ruling largely in favour of the latter. Unfortunately, Colombia has not been quite so keen as Peru and Chile to comply.

In advance of a single joined-up maritime management organisation and court, it is possible that regional approaches might prove a reasonable and pragmatic way of building consensus. This approach is already working with regard to fisheries and emissions control, reflecting, of course, regional attempts to control pollution, overfishing and other noxious and nefarious practices, as well as piracy, without the impulse to overextend to the global level. However, it is important that regional approaches do not abandon the universal principles underlying global treaties, but find regional ways of implementing them, consistent with their context and requirements. For example, while putting to one side the issue of conflicting claims, regional politico-economic approaches to asset exploitation and dispute resolution might be formulated that were acceptable to both or all parties and in accordance with international law and principles. This approach would appear to be suited to the circumstances of the dispute between the UK and Argentina in the South Atlantic and for those situations, such as the South China and East China seas and the eastern Mediterranean, where the proceeds from exploitation are needed to stimulate or sustain growth and development.

MARITIME SECURITY: AN ONGOING CHALLENGE

A glance at any military or coastguard directory demonstrates how much attention is being paid to the issue of maritime security, especially within EEZs. In addition, almost every country with a coast is building or acquiring specialist offshore patrol vessels, designed and equipped to operate at low cost and with smaller ship companies. Turkey, France, the Netherlands, Malaysia and Indonesia are among a host of countries that are investing in this type of vessel, incorporating innovative systems and approaches to minimise overheads and maximise on task time. However, as we have seen, marine agencies will need to be careful that they continue to overmatch, in terms of platform performance, sensors and weaponry, the capabilities that criminals, terrorist and traffickers are able to acquire. In many cases, sophisticated criminal and terrorist groups will have the resources to outrun and outgun the more modest patrol capabilities of official agencies. It is noticeable that Russian and Chinese equivalents are significantly more heavily armed, possibly being ready for a serious fight if matters should escalate, either with states seeking to assert alternative rights or irregular groups equipped with military levels of capability.

Irregular activity will continue to be a widespread feature of the future strategic landscape and maritime scene. Increased vigilance and awareness of traffic in the littoral waters of states and in the vicinity of offshore installations will be required to deter, detect and defeat this illicit activity. Future systems of coastal protection will, in the majority of countries, ensure that security and control begins far from shore, with wide-area surveillance, to detect both threats and anomalies. Comprehensive cover would rely on the efficient exploitation and integration of a range of sensor platforms, comprising manned and unmanned aircraft, ship and static detector systems, to ensure that proportionate, timely responses to threat warnings and incidents can be cued and directed. Similarly, natural events and marine accidents, as seen in recent hurricanes and earthquakes, will need suitable warning, contingency planning and rapid, effective responses.

Ports and coastal infrastructures in particular will be integrated more closely with emergency services and associated agencies through communications/information technologies to manage maritime approaches and intermodal activity. These will include marine AISs, together with secure information systems and penetrative, spectral analysis and infrared capabilities that enable the detection of unusual or dangerous cargo, including the presence of chemical, radiological and nuclear materials. New sensor technologies will appear that will rapidly and efficiently assess whether incoming or transiting vessels are carrying threatening materials, illegal goods or contraband additions to the underwater sections of hulls. Other remote technologies will incorporate sensors to ensure environmental and regulatory compliance by visiting or transiting vessels.

A range of political, economic, technological and climatic trends means that the sea will become more crowded and, in some places, more contested – between states, between commercial concerns and between law enforcement agencies and terrorist and criminal activity. With activity at sea increasingly concentrated on a decreasing number of major ports, routes and choke points, modern maritime armed and law enforcement forces will need to remain vigilant and enabled in order to ensure security and the rights of access and trade. In a joined-up, interdependent world, which enables the globalisation of illicit as well as legitimate activity, enforcement operations will require regional engagement and international cooperation, together with long-term commitment, training resources, local capacity building and suitable investment in intelligence and technical support. All these features will be contained within a comprehensive, multidisciplinary approach to minimise the incidence and impact of corruption and local networks, as well as mitigate the fact that most illicit groups and individuals are able to operate within the fabric of local littoral societies.

In the wider world, armed forces, in conjunction with their associated maritime agencies, will have to act in those circumstances where foreign states or international authority are weak or ineffectual, in response to the threats from irregular activity, lawless behaviour and naturally induced extreme weather or other catastrophic events. Finally, in resisting attempts by some states, notably China, to assert sovereign rights over the global commons, the willingness and capability of states to uphold the existing international system will determine whether the principle of the freedom of the seas established 500 years ago will continue to prevail.

CHAPTER EIGHT

Strategic Competition

'The whole art of war is being transformed into mere prudence, with the
primary aim of preventing the uncertain balance from suddenly shifting
to our disadvantage and half-war from developing into total war.'[1]

The twenty-first century, far from seeing the 'end of history' and the triumph of liberal democracy and free market theory, will be characterised by the clash of varying forms of capitalism and a dynamic interaction between democratic, authoritarian and 'managed' regimes. There are enough points of difference amid developed, developing, emerging, failing – and flailing – states to suggest that crisis, confrontation and possibly conflict lie ahead, based on the need for governments and regimes to maintain legitimacy in a politically and economically competitive world. For countries, the sea will act as both a barrier, keeping problems and competitors, however imperfectly, at arm's length, and as a bridge, not only to engender cooperation in solving regional problems and differences, but also as the medium across which states, alone or together, will project military power and threaten force in support of national interests. Some states will seek to establish the barrier as far as possible from their coasts, while others will seek to maintain the sea as a bridge over which all can freely pass, echoing John Adams: 'Neither nature nor art has partitioned the sea into empires. The ocean and its treasures are the common property of all men.'[2]

In *Some Principles of Maritime Strategy* (1911), Sir Julian Corbett set little store by the ability of commentators and professionals to determine the

---

[1] Carl von Clausewitz, *On War* viii (1832).
[2] Letter to Richard Rush dated 5 April 1815, in *The Works of John Adams* (1856).

future of warfare in the face of rapid technological and geopolitical change. Reflecting on his own experience, he wondered whether, 'the whole naval art has suffered a revolution beyond all previous experience, and it is possible the old practice is no longer a safe guide'. Amid strategic tensions and the rapid technological advances of the twenty-first century, one has some sympathy with this view. However, much about sea power is enduring. Despite changing geopolitical and technological contexts, Alfred Thayer Mahan's observation about 'the unchangeable, or unchanging, order of things, remaining the same in cause and effect, from age to age'[3] has particular relevance for warfare at sea. Contexts, like the tide, ebb and flow, but the sea itself is constant.

As we have seen, the enduring theme of maritime warfare in the twenty-first century will be the maintenance of the freedom of the seas in the face of attempts by states to control access to various parts of the high seas. As always, success in warfare will be determined by the ability of states to generate sufficient combat power to maintain relative superiority in any particular situation, along with the political will to use force – if necessary – in support of political ends.

For most countries in the developed world, the danger of invasion from any quarter is remote, as long as the international system holds together and the USA remains engaged (that is to say, has vital interests at stake). However, in many parts of the world, insecurity will continue to be caused by the effects of climate change, resource imbalances, societal instability, migration and demographic pressures. In addition, crises will continue to occur around the rest of the world as a result of the interplay of geopolitical rivalries, resource competition and transnational pressures.

Since no country or political grouping can be insulated from these issues, maritime forces in the twenty-first century will be primarily concerned with containing the scale and consequences of crises that threaten to escalate into confrontation and conflict. It is clear that the interconnected and interdependent character of the global community and the transnational profile of most risks have reinforced the links of economic and military interdependence. Consequently, most significant military action will be undertaken at the behest of the United Nations or within the frameworks provided by

---

[3] *The Influence of Sea Power on History 1660–1783* (1899).

multinational permanent alliances, such as NATO and the EU, regional organisations, like the African Union and the Arab League, and ad hoc coalitions.

RESTRAINTS ON LARGE-SCALE CONFLICT

Those looking forward to global fleet actions between rival navies and other maritime forces are likely to be disappointed. Future warfare at sea seems set to be restricted to local or, at worst, regional, level by a number of factors.

Firstly, the possession of nuclear weapons by the world's main maritime powers currently sets a limit on the level of escalation that a confrontation might reach. The sea has been the medium of choice for the positioning of strategic nuclear deterrence capabilities based in ballistic missile submarines, notably by the USA, the Soviet Union/Russia, France and the UK. Nuclear warheads can be delivered by a variety of land-based missiles and aircraft, but the vastness and opaqueness of the ocean confer concealment and invulnerability. In addition, the (as yet) extreme difficulty of intercepting the missiles and their (often) multiple warheads mean that the ballistic-missile-firing submarine will continue to be operated well into the twenty-first century. The USA, the UK, France, China and Russia[4] rely on them as their prime means of nuclear deterrence, with successor systems, combining submarine and ballistic missile elements, already being planned and programmed, to remain in service until 2045 and beyond.

Secondly, as previously discussed, the sea is maintained as a permissive environment: its freedom and security are currently underwritten in strategic terms by the military power of the USA and its partners, in both the general and the local sense, linked to an international system of conventions and legal instruments that seeks to harmonise competing jurisdictions, contain ambitions and settle disputes.

Of course, US maritime power has been exercised, until now, in the absence of any significant threat to its dominance, very reminiscent of the experience of the Royal Navy in the long century after the Battle of Trafalgar in 1805. It is true that, at the moment, China and Russia probably lack the necessary capability and lethality to defeat the USA at sea, except in small

---

[4] And India by 2017.

encounter situations. Although America might reasonably anticipate some nasty surprises and losses, its collective capabilities and technological superiority would most probably defeat the bulk of conventional threats that the Chinese and the Russians would, individually, be able to pose. Also, Chinese nuclear submarines are noisy, at levels associated with their Russian equivalents twenty years ago, making them much more readily detectable than their US, UK (and Russian) counterparts.

Nevertheless, the force imbalance is likely to change as China acquires more capable modern platforms and systems in large numbers and Russia modernises its fleet of surface ships and submarines. China, as we have seen, deploys an integrated network of surveillance systems and weapons (predominantly missile- and submarine-based) designed to neutralise an opponent's (for which read the USA) air, space and network capabilities, as well as supporting, with increasingly precise and discriminating weapons, long-range, accurate attacks on sea and land targets. Chinese operations are also designed to deny America information derived from surveillance systems, satellites and other reconnaissance platforms, partly through sophisticated communications and network disruption techniques.

There is another factor preventing naval warfare on a large scale. Very few states – notably the USA (with its NATO allies), India, China and Russia – will have the economic capacity, industrial strength and demographic momentum to maintain significant state-on-state capability and (theoretically) the ability to fight wars on an industrial scale, as well as the ability to manufacture all that is needed to sustain modern, high-tempo combat over time. Even for the major states, self-sufficiency would not be straightforward after decades of economic and technological interdependence. Future combat at sea will be conditioned by the need to fight with the resources that one has at the start of a conflict. Without the ability to gear up industry to produce large numbers of replacement hulls and to integrate sophisticated weapons systems, it is unlikely that any country could sustain a war for long or with high levels of attrition.

EMERGING CHALLENGES

Given its geographic spread and its expanding span of ambition, its oil and gas wealth and rapidly modernising maritime capability, it would be remiss to exclude Russia from the scene. China and Russia are set to lead a significant challenge to the hegemony of the USA and to all open economies and democracies, in commercial, geopolitical and military terms. Their 'managed' economic and political models will both compete and cooperate with developed and developing countries in the interests of their respective power-elites, drawing to them all those countries that have similar politico-economic models or regimes that have authoritarian aspirations.

So, the twenty-first century is likely to see Russia, China and India beginning to extend their reach and grip, not only to exploit the very obvious economic and resource benefits, but also to project power and influence in support of national interests, initially in their respective maritime 'near abroads'. Russia seems determined to regain its brooding influence over the Baltic and Black Seas, as well as asserting its *droit de seigneur* in the northern polar region and reasserting its presence in the Mediterranean. Similarly, China is seeking to strengthen its perceptual and actual hold on the South China and East China Seas, in order to press its claims to the Spratly and Paracel islands, and to extend its strategic influence to the so-called first and second chain of major islands in East Asia. India, as its carrier and submarine programmes complete, will want to secure regional ascendancy in the Indian Ocean, from the Gulf to the Strait of Malacca. All three will want to ensure the continued security of their lines of economic supply across the world's oceans. They will also want to compete for allies, markets and overseas bases. Consequently, it is likely that their capacity and appetite for more forward presence, intervention and expeditionary operations by sea will grow.

In addition, Russia, China and India have well-established and technically sophisticated defence industrial facilities, capable of producing modern warships, missiles and combat systems across the whole range of maritime warfare activity and requirements. All three are manufacturing carriers and nuclear-powered submarines, as well as a wide range of unmanned vehicles, space systems, sophisticated aircraft and increasingly innovative electronic technologies. It is likely that, in the future, their industry and technological expertise will have the capacity to surprise. Also, the fact that few emerging powers have the financial and technological resources and skills to absorb cutting-edge capabilities into their defence–industrial base or their front-line

SUPER HIGHWAY

forces, despite their geostrategic aspirations, means Russian, Chinese and possibly Indian derivatives are likely to proliferate.

A complicating factor for China and Russia is the continuing health and relevance of NATO, whose political and military commitment to collective defence and action has persisted for more than sixty years, long outliving the purpose for which the alliance was originally intended. The defensive and deployable warfare capabilities of the European pillar of NATO (and other 'Western' powers as a whole) are formidable in their own right, including, in France and the UK, two nuclear-capable powers. They represent, in aggregate, the most powerful and capable maritime forces after the USA and, both individually and collectively, are among the best equipped and trained in the world.

A major strategic objective for both China and Russia is likely to be the weakening of the NATO alliance and various Asia-Pacific region partnerships, together with the detachment of at least some its members from their allegiance to the USA, by means of commercial, energy and economic investment inducements, not to mention outright bullying on occasions. They will have recognised a divergence of views over Iraq, Afghanistan, Libya and Syria and the consequent recriminations, as well as the reluctance to commit forces to counter adventurism. At the very least, they will want to introduce a dilemma in some NATO countries and force hard choices about the relative importance of their strategic and economic priorities. They will also be conscious that in the Western world not only is there less bang for the buck available, but also the bucks themselves are diminishing. The cost growth and inflation of platforms, equipment and personnel are continuously rising, in contrast to potential opponents who can build and operate ships and aircraft at greatly reduced rates, not least because their manpower overheads are proportionately lower. In addition, the countries of the developed world have navies that are reduced to the bare minimum required to conduct their peacetime tasks, with precious little spare capacity preserved for war. In conflicts not involving the USA, these 'come as you are' navies will have to fight with what they have, or play for time. Nor is it certain whether the 'arsenal of democracy' would or could provide the necessary surge to replenish war stocks at short notice.

In the near future, the USA, China and Russia will benchmark their military and maritime capabilities against each other, while other countries will adjust their capabilities, in order to support, oppose or counter one or the others. India is likely to enter the equation in the early 2020s with regard to its strategic position in the Indian Ocean. Other countries – the UK, France, Europe as a whole, South Korea, Australia and Japan – will possess substantial stand-alone capabilities in their own right, while most others will have maritime denial and varying levels of power projection capabilities, predominantly configured for use in their own region or vicinity. However, it is unlikely that any would seek to risk confrontation or conflict involving any one of the big three without the active backing or tacit support of at least one of the others.

THE USA AND CHINA

The critical axis of competition in the first part of the century will be between the USA and China. One wishes to retain, the other to attain, great power status. Whatever is said in public statements and despite the pronounced disparity in capabilities, each views the other as a likely opponent. The USA and its allies take at face value the bland assurances about China and its peaceful rise. They should heed the view of Mahan in his own time: 'The habit of mind is narrow which fails to see that a navy such as Germany is now building will be as efficacious for other ends than those immediately proposed'[5] Chinese capabilities are benchmarked against the USA and America increasingly calibrates its requirements in relation to China. The relationship is complicated by the economic codependence of the two countries, but, in strategic terms, it is likely to define the leading edge of maritime warfare in the early quarter of the twenty-first century, one which could easily assume the proportions of an arms race.

And we should always expect the unexpected. Norman Angell, the author of *The Grand Illusion*, wrote before the First World War that war between the great powers then was implausible and unlikely because of their interdependence and the integration of the world's economy. In the modern world, this is – apparently – why conflict cannot break out between the USA and China. Unfortunately, the lesson of history is that if an event is not strictly impossible, then it is in fact entirely possible. The phenomenon

---

[5] *Naval Strategy.*

of globalisation merely raises the entry threshold, the exit costs and consequences for great power competition and conflict, but does not preclude them, as was seen between 1910 and 1918.

The Chinese perspective

The Chinese, as we have seen, want to exclude US influence and fighting power from the Asia-Pacific region and secure their lines of commerce and economic supply to their markets. However, in doing so, China will be cautious in forcing its claims in the South China and East China seas and will not want to risk the integrity of its lines of economic supply or push the Association of Southeast Asian Nation (ASEAN) countries into the arms of the USA and Japan.

China is now dependent as never before on the rest of the world to keep it going. Until the mid-1990s, it was more or less self-sufficient within the scale of its economy and consumption. Now it relies on other countries for oil, copper, iron ore, soya and many other commodities, without which it could not sustain its development or satisfy its people's rising aspirations. For example, China produces half the world's steel, but is heavily reliant on imports of iron ore produced by BHP Billiton, Rio Tinto and Vale, the three major global miners. It is critically dependent on the Gulf for its oil and gas, which is why its ties to Iran remain strong, as witnessed by continued investment following the agreement to $120 billion's worth of contracts with the Iranian hydrocarbon sector between 2007 and 2013. Similarly, more than half of Saudi Arabian oil passes to Asia, compared with 14 per cent to the USA. Saudi Aramco owns refineries in Qingdao Province and Fujian, while Chinese firms have begun investing in Saudi Arabian infrastructure projects.

Overall, the Chinese in the twenty-first century will seek to exact profit and monopolise trading arrangements, with a clear interest in the maintenance of stable and profitable conditions in the markets and geographic areas in which they wish to operate. Therefore, the Chinese will not want to risk the security of the routes to and from their primary markets, initially to the Gulf, the USA and Europe, but also to Africa and South America. The Arctic also features at some stage from about 2025.

China is painfully aware that all of these routes are capable of interdiction by the USA and its allies, or by India, but also conscious that the USA, with its shale gas and unconventional oil windfall discoveries, might depart the scene and leave a security vacuum in its wake. No strategic competitor, aspiring regional hegemon or rising power is likely to feel comfortable with this situation, but China has a choice: either to cooperate within the existing system or compete so that it can dictate how the system operates on its own terms, to harmonise its strategic and economic interests. In fact, China has assessed that its energy security is too important to be left to the benevolence of US security guarantees and market forces alone and has classified the issue as a matter of national security. In safeguarding its energy supplies, China is using its large foreign-exchange reserves to invest in foreign energy markets and programmes, to secure future supply and to promote interdependence, so that energy suppliers will be disinclined to withhold oil exports in the event of an international crisis, one possibly engineered by China. It is also increasing its investment and presence in what would appear to be a new maritime Silk Road stretching up to the Gulf and beyond to the greater Middle East, as well as a major overland pipeline system through Myanmar (Burma), to bypass the Malacca Strait.

At the same time, the People's Liberation Army Navy (PLAN) is keen to promote itself as the guardian of China's economy, its overseas interests and Chinese people working abroad. Consequently, it is adopting a more expansive attitude and an expeditionary mentality, both to deter rival claims in certain areas and to provide secure lines of maritime commerce and supply. Senior Chinese admirals talk about the country's economic interests being inseparable from PLAN's to protect China's access to the sea and the security of its major sea routes. This attitude is a demonstrable shift in its emphasis, from a 'near seas' to a 'far seas' approach, which was signalled in China's Defence Strategy in 2008: 'the Navy has been striving to improve in an all-round way its capabilities of integrated offshore operations, strategic deterrence and strategic counterattacks, and to develop its capabilities of conducting cooperation in distant waters'. The announcement of the strategy was immediately followed by the dispatch of Chinese warships to anti-piracy patrols off the Horn of Africa in 2008.

It seems likely that the events of the past six years and the expectations of the Chinese Communist Party (CCP) and people that China should become a great power will stimulate and fuel further investment in rather

Jiangkai II (Type 054A), Chinese frigate.

harder-edged 'far seas' capabilities. In 2010, the PLAN hospital ship *Peace Ark* embarked on a major medical aid 'Harmonious Mission' to countries worldwide, including Africa. PLAN warships also deployed to the Gulf for the first time. Since 2011, PLAN's presence in the Middle East and North Africa (MENA) has increased. In February 2011, the PLAN frigate *Xuzhou* was deployed to 'support and protect' the evacuation of Chinese nationals from the Libyan civil war, while in March, *Maanshan* provided the first Chinese armed escort for the UN World Food Programme in Somalia. Other frigates have been deployed to participate in anti-piracy patrols and convoys in the Indian Ocean. At the beginning of 2014, the frigate *Yancheng* joined Russian warships in escorting Danish and Norwegian ships transporting chemical weapons out of Syria. China's willingness and capability to cooperate were seen in its response to the Malaysia Airlines flight MH370 disappearance in March 2014, when it contributed satellite data, several major warships and surveillance aircraft to the search for the stricken airliner.[6]

China is also strengthening its diplomatic relationships with regimes and countries that lie along the most important sea routes. This approach parallels the gaining of access to several commercial port and airport facilities

---

[6] The incident also inadvertently revealed the extent and sophistication of Chinese satellite surveillance capabilities.

on the routes across the South China Sea and the Indian Ocean, known popularly as its 'string of pearls', and in Europe at places like Piraeus and Antwerp. These are a combination of straightforward commercial hubs and support arrangements, with evident potential, at least in the Indian Ocean, for extending those access arrangements to military bases and support. At this point, they are what the USA terms 'places, not bases'. However, to the historian, they look suspiciously like a mirror image of the 'treaty ports' (Hong Kong, Shanghai, Nanjing and a lot more)[7] that used to operate along the coast of China in the colonial era.

This footprint reflects China's security interests, especially those sea lines of communication through the Indian Ocean, as well as the sources of its mineral and hydrocarbon resources, including to the 'four seas' (Red, Black, Mediterranean and Caspian). China will be seeking further opportunities to enhance its participation in international security operations. The most likely deployment ships will be the Type 054A Jiangkai II class of which sixteen were in commission by the end of 2013, with others under construction. In order to provide logistics for distant operations, two new 23,000-ton Type 903 Fuchi-class replenishment ships were acquired in 2013, with the likelihood that more similar vessels will follow.

China has also seen – and has experienced at first hand – what Britain and the USA as great powers have demonstrated and achieved with their naval capabilities, and wants to emulate them. History has taught that the possession of a powerful navy keeps predators away from your shores, protects your economic base and permits you to coerce countries that conflict with your world vision. It has hardly noticed that it helps of course if you are either an island or a continental power with 4,800-km (3,000-mile) oceans to the east and the west.

As the Chinese discovered on repeated occasions – and still need to remember today – an extensive land border has countervailing disadvantages, as France found to its strategic cost in relation to Britain throughout most of modern history. China is still psychologically and militarily a continental Eurasian land power that frets about its land borders and the

---

[7] Treaty ports were Asian ports, especially in China, that were opened to foreign trade in the mid-nineteenth century because of pressure from Britain, France, Germany and the USA, as well as Japan and Russia. In China, the ports were first opened to British traders in 1842 after the first Opium War (1839–42).

possibility of internal unrest. China will be mindful of the key lesson from Zheng He's voyages. They took place when the Chinese were the only significant sea power in South East Asia and the Indian Ocean. Then, as now, protection of their land borders took priority over the need to maintain the sea lanes that were vital to China's strategic and economic dominance. In addition, the Long March – of disgruntled, frustrated people, not benefiting from economic growth – is not a distant memory, but an ever-present insecurity.

China will also have to contend with Japan and India, both of which have significant maritime trade interests in South East Asia and increasingly powerful maritime forces. With regard to India, China needs to ensure the security and stability of its trade and energy supply across the Indian Ocean, to the Gulf, to Africa and to the greater Middle East and Mediterranean. It has reduced its dependence on sea routes through the archipelagos and choke points of South East Asia (notably the Strait of Malacca) by the use of the Karakoram Highway, linking China and Pakistan through Xinjiang and on to the Gulf. It also has access through the Irrawaddy Corridor that connects Yunnan, Myanmar (Burma) and the Bay of Bengal and the ability to transfer gas from Myanmar's offshore terminals to Yunnan Province. Chinese investments in port facilities in the Indian Ocean (notably at Gwadar in Pakistan) and the Bay of Bengal supplement these maritime escape routes.

The current scale of Chinese activity is unlikely to provoke the USA and it seems inconceivable that the strategic objectives of the CCP would put at risk the conditions within which China's economic growth, and by extension its social harmony and political stability, so crucially depend. It is not in China's strategic interests to encourage the USA, either into intervening with a significant footprint in the Asia-Pacific region any more than it does today or to alter what has been (from China's point of view) an extremely beneficial, cost-effective and profitable exchange and trading arrangement. Meanwhile, it is likely to continue modernising its armed forces, in particular its maritime capabilities, so that it can be seen to be powerful enough to counter and, if necessary, confront the USA in its 'near abroad'. It can also maintain the pressure on other countries in its own region in support of its maritime claims, by the commitment of paramilitary and civilian vessels, unmanned aerial vehicle (UAV) and maritime patrol activity and occasional coat-trailing forays by naval units to gauge resolve and test responses.

The simple fact is that China will seek to exclude the USA from operating in the Asia-Pacific region, either by suborning or intimidating its potential allies or by holding the USA at range and at risk by virtue of its military capability. It will not attempt to match the Americans in every warfare discipline, but simply to employ low-cost capabilities to exclude decisive US combat power. The USA has to be able to control the sea lanes and protect its allies; the Chinese simply have to deny it the ability to do so. That is why China's naval modernisation is centred on long-range cruise missile armed forces, submarines and a range of land- and air-based anti-access and area denial weapons. They are designed to neutralise local US superiority and keep US forces, predominantly the US Navy and its carriers, out of China's area of Asia-Pacific interest.

For now, there seems little doubt that, in the short term, China will concentrate on dealing with issues of sovereignty and security in its immediate region, while ensuring that its actual or potential interests (as in the Arctic) in the wider world are not unduly constrained. However, PLAN would move to fill gaps left by the indifference, inattention or insolvency of the USA. Currently, it is clear that PLAN procurement strategies are designed to exclude unwelcome and uninvited intruders; it is scarcely capable of asserting any kind of sea control. Its surface ship modernisation programme introduces largely like-for-like replacements and its new carrier would struggle to deal with modern opponents. Indeed, most of its serious air power at sea will be deployed from the land in the near future.

The US perspective

The US strategy in relation to the Asia-Pacific region is designed to show that it intends to remain a major contributor to regional stability and security, while demonstrating that it has the military might to deal with an aspiring superpower that attempts to dictate the terms of international engagement and economic exchange there. In its absence, countries in the region would have to choose whether to defy or accommodate China. The USA will also have calculated that its presence is necessary to reassure allies and other non-aligned countries and, in its own interests, to preserve a collective system open to free market exchange and trading. The alternative is to allow China to establish a preferential trading and military system in the region, which would exclude free competition and significantly damage US strategic and economic interests.

The USA is pursuing a twin-track policy in response to China's challenge. In the first place, it is confronting the Chinese legal and physical encroachment on the global commons and other country's exclusive economic zones (EEZs) directly. The USA will continue to champion the idea of the freedom of the global commons (space, cyberspace and the sea), as the basis of an open trading system and as the prime mediums for the projection of its own national power. In particular, its armed forces will be prioritised towards ensuring its continued ability to maintain the sea as a global commons, together with the airspace above.

Simultaneously, its careful, patient construction of trans-Pacific and transatlantic free trade agreements are clear indications that it intends to promote free trade, if necessary to the exclusion of China. In this way, it can also bring to bear the economic and diplomatic instruments of national power to most effect, both in its own interests and those of its allies and partners. In doing so, the continued ability of the USA to control the commons and sustain free trade will keep the world safe for globalisation.

By sea and by air

Militarily, an indication of how the USA might deal with the China issue seemed to be heralded by the 2010 *Quadrennial Defense Review* (*QDR*). It described how 'air and naval forces will integrate capabilities across all operational domains – air, sea, land, space, and cyberspace – to counter growing challenges to US freedom of action'.[8] It claimed that it had no particular opponent in mind, other than 'adversaries across the range of military operations, including adversaries equipped with sophisticated anti-access and area denial capabilities'.[9] There are no prizes for guessing who the opponent was.

Since then, the USA has considered which forces are the most suitable for operation in the restricted waters and inshore zones of the Asia-Pacific region. Its response has been the Air-Sea Battle Concept (ASBC), designed to

---

[8] Department of Defense, *Quadrennial Defense Review Report* (Washington DC: Department of Defense, 2010).
[9] Op cit.

deal with far-flung problems that need US involvement and to signal to Asia in general and China in particular that it intends to remain a major player in the region. The idea of the ASBC is not exactly new. In broad terms, it formed the basis of most of the campaigns of the Second World War, notably in the battle of the Atlantic and during the US-led drive across the Pacific.

However, it cannot view its operations in the Pacific as a rerun of the Second World War. The context is different and the USA and its allies will not have to island-hop, recapturing and regaining territory from an entrenched enemy. US planning will need to involve all those diplomatic, economic and military instruments that are required to uphold and protect its interests in Asia and to bring the most appropriate combination to bear on the maritime environment. Above all, it should carefully consider which forces are most suitable for containing what might turn out to be a competitive, opportunist power on the rise, while assisting with the maintenance of stability and security in the Asia-Pacific region, just in case China prefers a cooperative relationship.

In the event of conflict, the ASBC anticipates a lengthy campaign that would include the interdiction of lines of supply and commerce to the target country and a rapid mobilisation of logistics and munitions to front-line forces. The plan was followed up in early 2012 by the Joint Operational Access Concept (JOAC), which was, essentially, an updated version of shock and awe, based on the comprehensive obliteration of an opponent's cyber and space capabilities and the destruction 'in depth' of all capabilities threatening the free passage of US and allied forces in the Asia-Pacific region. The US Air Force and Navy would be on hand to neutralise an opponent's surveillance and strike capabilities at source (in his country), as well as provide high levels of defensive assurance to deal with his attacks against both US and friendly forces. This reflects the consideration that the ASBC would need to take in regional allies, like Japan, Singapore and others, if basing rights, operational integration and effective logistics supply were to be forthcoming. In particular, the USA would need to show that it could sustain a convincing deterrence and, if necessary, combat posture, in order to reassure allies and partners, who otherwise would have to make an accommodation with the unnamed regional threat.

Whether this scale of effort is militarily deliverable or politically acceptable, particularly as it involves the precision destruction of scores of military facilities and possibly involves action against a nuclear power remains open to question. It is also clear that a short and sharp campaign would not necessarily suit the USA. Nevertheless, it represents about the closest one can get to devastation without pressing the nuclear button and would give any potential opponent pause for reflection. In that sense, it could provide a credible balance of terror and deterrence. The question that begs in the mind of US planners (and presumably that of the 'opponent') is whether he could conduct a similar campaign against their forces.

The results of this competition will come down to the resources that are available to maintain assets that are able to deter and prevail at sea, both militarily and commercially. China is driving up the costs of maritime dominance for the USA by its investment in anti-access and area denial weapons, linked to wide-area sensors and a range of launch platforms that are optimised for combat in the South China and East China seas and among their encircling island chains. Just as the choke points of the Lombok, Sunda and Malacca straits constrain exit for China, so they also inhibit entry for the USA and its allies.

In this respect, an anonymous US gaming blog, active in 2012, gave what appeared to catch the mood, if not the verbal precision and elegance expected from an armed forces Staff Course appraisal:

> History tells us big armadas do bad in confine waters
> The third world countries are building navies just for that
> Will be interesting to see the whipping we'll get
> My computer games are not the easy ones of the past
> My favorite is the China Wars and Iran Wars
> You only win if you get them away from the backyard.

In addition, it is clear that the Chinese are modernising rapidly and are now seeking to adopt more joint approaches to warfare, integrating all elements of fighting power within a coherent combined arms doctrine. They are not simply stuck in the groove of anti-access and area denial and look set to graduate to the more sophisticated offensive and power projection approaches favoured by Western countries. Critically, China is planning to have four aircraft carriers by 2022 – a statement of significant intent alongside their other modernisation programmes.

We do, however, need to consider timescales. China is already one of the world's most prolific military shipbuilders in the world, but, in the near future, is not going to be able to take on the USA in a general war, to compete militarily in absolute, aggregate fighting power. It could, though, credibly establish superiority and possibly control in local or regional terms and hold out. One day, at current rates of progress, it might just be able to take on the USA.

To be fair, the ABSC as a concept seems to reflect the requirement for US intervention forces pretty much anywhere in the world where US interests, allies or partners are threatened. It also gives notice to all potential opponents that what is good enough for containing, deterring and, if necessary, combating (let's face it) China is pretty much capable of doing the same in Europe, in the eastern Mediterranean, the Gulf or anywhere else. It represents a decisive shift away from low-impact, high-footprint (Afghanistan and Iraq) to high-impact, low-footprint forces, which would be highly agile, less vulnerable to strikes by potential opponents and less exposed to interdiction on their way to a combat zone.

As such, the USA will be looking for allies and partners to pull their weight in their various regions of the world, to act as hubs or nodes in preserving the international system and in deterring and confronting state opportunism, aggression and adventurism. America will provide capacity-enhancing, collective training and strategic intelligence support, as well as arms and systems transfers, but successive administrations, both Republican and Democrat, will expect their partners to 'man up', in policy, capability and resource terms. As has been seen in recent episodes in Libya, Syria and Ukraine, the USA will not always be available as the force of first – or even last – resort, unless its vital interests or treaty obligations are at stake.

CAN THE USA COPE?

In this regard, it is reasonable to ask whether the USA will have the resources and appetite to intervene at sea to provide the force of last resort in defence of the international system in the future. The US Navy plans to maintain around 290–300 warships in the near future and to have 306 battle-ready warships by 2043. This means acquiring a total of 266 ships, of which 220 would be combat ships and 46 combat logistics and support ships. A comparison of the US Department of Defense 2014 shipbuilding plan with the Congressional Budget Office assessment of its likely resources makes this cheery total look less convincing. The simple message is that the US Navy has 15 per cent less available revenue than it thinks it has and, unless it gains a substantial uplift in resources over the next thirty years or significantly alters the way in which it operates, it will not be able to fulfil, by a long way, its current and envisaged range of tasking.

The British experience in the American War of Independence (1776–83) is a salutary reminder of how a power that is engaged globally at sea cannot always apply sufficient relative power to prevail in one particular theatre of operations, especially when resources and commitments do not match. Owing to a coalition of maritime powers (France, Spain and the Netherlands) ranged against them and their possessions in virtually every ocean, the British were unable to concentrate enough fighting power to support land operations in America or to deal with over 1,700 American and allied privateers that severely interrupted and damaged British commerce.

If the strategic landscape is initially characterised by regional powers with both regional dominance and global influence, but limited maritime reach, US power will remain strong in overall terms. However, it is no longer able to concentrate and guarantee sufficiently decisive combat power in every part of the world simultaneously, and will rely much more on the efforts of its allies to provide forward presence and deterrence in their own geographical vicinity. It looks very much like the USA will need to decide whether it wants to sacrifice its global footprint in favour of a national force of last resort that can deter threats to its vital national interests and prevail against any likely peer competitor or combination of competitors. It will have to pick its fights wisely and heed Emperor Augustus's admonition that great powers 'should not go fishing with a golden hook', in terms of risk-benefit analysis.

Importantly, the USA will rely more on the close engagement and involvement of its allies and partners in providing niche capabilities and force multipliers, as well as platforms and capabilities, to undertake regional surveillance and security operations. This means that its allies and like-minded socio-economic fellow travellers will need to take more forward-leaning responsibility for an international system that operates for the good of all and in their security and economic interests. Already, the burden of anti-piracy operations in the Indian Ocean has been taken up by a wide diversity of countries that have a distinct interest in maintaining law and order at sea. However, this has proved a low-risk scenario for the participants and allies of the US will need to be prepared to take more risks on behalf of international solidarity and security if the present system is to be preserved in the absence or non-availability of US assets.

The means by which this wider maritime cooperation might be achieved first surfaced in 2005, when the then US Chief of Naval Operations Admiral Mike Mullen proposed the 'Thousand-Ship Navy' (TSN) concept, essentially a cooperative enterprise that would supplement the US Navy's efforts, and ease its burden, in providing global maritime security. Mullen saw the TSN as a global maritime partnership that united maritime forces, port operators, commercial shippers and international, governmental and non-governmental agencies to counter risks and threats on the high seas and to address mutual concerns.

The implementation of the TSN would have incorporated another major US-led initiative, that of Maritime Domain Awareness, which sought to provide as much visibility and information as possible about the positions and activities of vessels at sea, which was greatly assisted by the adoption of the Automatic Identification System (AIS). Similarly, traffic reporting systems were set up, such as the Virtual Regional Maritime Traffic Centre, an Italian initiative that tracked merchant traffic in the Mediterranean and Black seas. Nevertheless, many smaller vessels, particularly those engaged in fishing, leisure and, of course, illicit activities, chose not to use AIS or similar systems – nor did warships, government vessels and others seeking to avoid surveillance and identification.

The TSN initiative never really caught on. Countries had already started – and continue – to cooperate and exchange information as part of a wide range of maritime security and contingent operations. Also, countries generally resisted the formal arrangements that made it look as if they were being invited to join a posse, with the USA as sheriff and chief beneficiary. However, fast-forward to the second decade of the twenty-first century and the concept would appear to still have some legs. The USA is encouraging countries to take responsibility for international norms in their particular regions as it concentrates on its Asia-Pacific pivot and attempts to trim its huge defence budget in the wake of the fiscal and economic crisis of 2007–8.

276 | SUPER HIGHWAY

Forward presence and the demonstration of 'force withheld' in every part of the world are unlikely to be a sustainable (that is to say, affordable) or even desirable strategy. Instead, it is probable that US maritime power will be configured to enable and impose maritime control at specific times and places of political choice. The USA will still wish to take on all comers, support its allies and maintain its treaty obligations, but will be more selective and discriminating about where and how it chooses to threaten, employ and confront opponents.

Current thinking centres on regional and local forces providing the capabilities and networks to respond to immediate threats and emerging risks, with the implicit assurance that America will assist whenever the going gets tough. Thus, the USA is likely to build a network of relationships with those countries that have an interest in maintaining an open trading system and the freedom of the high seas. It will cooperate and integrate its capabilities with local partners, especially its allies in Europe and the Asia-Pacific regions. Rather than instituting a posse, as in the past, it seems that the new arrangements would rely on the cavalry riding to the rescue.

MAINTAINING STRATEGIC HARMONY

History is replete with examples about the problematic relationship between established powers, which defend and exploit an international system from whose continuation they derive political and economic advantage, and aspirational powers, which challenge the status quo and seek to induce change for their own benefit and continued rise. Also, in global terms and in the Asia-Pacific region, two ideologically different political and economic philosophies compete. For sixty years, US power has provided the security and economic framework within which Asian countries have produced the most rapid economic growth in history. It is not surprising that China would want to order things in its own image; it suspects that the USA will not be as accommodating to a strategic and economic peer competitor as it has been to a trade partner and an emerging economy. Again, it would be mindful of the circumstances of Sparta's successful challenge, as a land power, to Athens pre-eminence as a maritime power in the Greek world; in particular, Thucydides' observation that, 'the rise of Athens and the fear that this inspired in Sparta made war inevitable'. Indeed, in the vast majority of cases in the modern era when a rising power has challenged or rivalled an existing power, it has resulted in war.

Some commentators are sanguine about China's growing power at sea, taking at face value China's claims about its peaceful rise and believing that it simply reflects the natural requirements of a country on the way to (responsible) superpower status. More worldly-wise naval planners, when thinking about China's modernising navy, generally recall the rise of the German and Japanese navies in the nineteenth century. This period showed that a country does not need to have a maritime tradition or heritage to establish a formidable navy. It needs political will and resources to energise and incentivise society to deliver the skills and manpower required.

The other problem is that battle fleets tend to run into each other eventually. German naval officers toasted 'Der Tag', the day when they could test their ships and capabilities against the established power and reputation of the Royal Navy. Their Japanese counterparts, after their smashing victories over the Russians at Port Arthur and Tsushima, similarly welcomed the chance to take on the USA and clear it from the Pacific.

In history, when war has not resulted, it has been the identification of common interests – or shared opponents – that has ensured that a suitable convergence of political accommodation and cultural understanding was reached. Most commonly, it has required major concessions and attitudinal shifts on both sides. It is perhaps worth bearing in mind that the USA was extremely bullish in its own hemisphere as it rose to global power status at the end of the nineteenth century, threatening, or actually using, force to get its way. It threatened both Germany and Britain and engineered a war with Spain. As late as the 1930s, it still retained notional plans for war with Britain. However, it was the understanding by Britain that its interests in the western hemisphere would be safeguarded by the rise of US sea power that enabled the Royal Navy to reduce its force levels across much of the western hemisphere. However, even if the USA and China are able to manage their strategic relationship, it will be important for other countries not to be caught in the crossfire or to find that they have been disadvantaged by a strategic compromise that merely makes the world safe, secure and prosperous for the USA and China.

The likelihood of conflict between China and the USA will be determined by the extent to which disputes in the Asia-Pacific region evolve into armed confrontations between China and those countries with whom the USA has a security treaty or understanding, most notably Japan and South Korea. It will also hinge on Chinese ambitions in relation to the ten-dash line (see Chapter 7) in the South China and East China seas and whether the US and the countries in the region will acquiesce in the wholesale territorialisation of the high seas and the flouting of the United Nations Convention on the Law of the Sea (UNCLOS). Nevertheless, as long as China has more to lose than to gain from a breakdown of the international system of law and trade, the current grudging acceptance of the status quo seems set to continue, punctuated by a sequence of minor spats and disputes in the margins of UNCLOS.

As such, the first half of the twenty-first century in the region is likely to witness a series of tests of will and resolve as both the USA and China probe and assess each other's responses to incidents on the ragged edge between Chinese 'territorial' claims and US insistence on the freedom of the seas. Only the commitment of credible maritime forces and solidarity among like-minded countries are likely to prevent breakdowns in the international system. Countries will probably have to decide on a case-by-case basis whether it is worth risking confrontation and conflict in order to preserve their offshore integrity and the freedom of the seas. Those that possess decisive military capability are likely to be able to threaten or use force to insist on their claimed rights or the maintenance of the status quo. Those that cannot deploy forces or call allies in aid will be forced to back down in the face of encroachment or exploitation. Unless the USA stands behind them, speaking softly and carrying a big stick, the 'Melian Dialogue' from the Peloponnesian War will probably apply: 'the strong do as they can and the weak suffer what they must'.

CHAPTER NINE

Maritime Warfare

'A good Navy is not a provocation to war.
It is the surest guarantee of peace.'[1]

'War is not so much a matter of weapons as of money, for
money furnishes the material for war. And this is especially true
when a land power fights those whose strength is at sea.'[2]

Assessments about the future of warfare are a risky undertaking for any commentator that values his reputation, owing to the high number of variables that exist in both the geopolitical and military spheres and to the uncertain, uneven impact of technological development. However, equipment has to be procured, people have to be trained and investment committed based on a plan that anticipates future trends and events. The long lead times associated with platform and system development and the acquisition of individual and collective skills, together with the need to assess and make sensible budget allocations, mean that some approximation of the future context for warfare at sea is necessary. Most important of all, a view of the future is required in order to develop a coherent national and maritime strategy that harmonises policy aspirations, resources and military and commercial practicality.

One of the most obvious factors is the rising challenge being presented to the established maritime powers. Both China and Russia are significant regional maritime powers, with extensive reach into the wider world, while

---

[1] President Theodore Roosevelt, in his second annual message to Congress, on 2 December 1902.
[2] Thucydides, in the *The Peloponnesian War* (circa 404 BCE).

India is also building a substantial maritime capability, which will enable it to dominate the Indian Ocean. All three are procuring formidable combat capabilities and, in regional terms at least, seek to match those of the USA. By the mid-2020s, their aircraft carriers, nuclear submarines and amphibious capabilities will be vying with those of America for the world's attention and responding to a substantial bow wave of national expectation and investment. As we have seen in Chapters 3 and 8, there is also a notable build-up of naval capabilities in the Asia-Pacific region, where states are attempting to calibrate where their interests, opportunities and vulnerabilities lie in the ambiguous geopolitical space between the USA and China.

Elsewhere, most other states also recognise the importance of the sea in preserving their access to globalisation and enabling them to protect and exploit the resources of the sea within their offshore zones. They are acquiring modern maritime capabilities, with sophisticated sensors and weapon suites, to deter state opponents, but also to deal with terrorists, criminals and traffickers. Some countries will also want to be able to project power beyond their immediate neighbourhoods to promote and protect their interests and to contribute to multinational law enforcement or humanitarian missions.

In general terms, it seems likely that major maritime powers will cooperate in some areas, in maintaining stability, security and the viability of the international system at sea in general terms, but will compete, either passively or actively, in areas of specific national interest or dispute. We are likely to see states progressively extending control over their exclusive economic zones (EEZs), while some may also claim jurisdictional rights over areas of ocean that are considered the high seas under international law. Unless these claims are contested, they are likely to pass into international law on the basis that practice – and the exercise of armed force to reinforce it – tends to result in permanent changes to existing conventions and agreements (in an *ex post facto* legitimisation process).

The risks and costs of fighting on land will lead to a decrease in such conflicts; instead, there will be clashes associated with 'land grabs' at sea, both for sea-space and for resources. The incidence of confrontation and conflict will be determined by the willingness of those states committed to the notion of the freedom of the seas to challenge states that seek to 'own' their EEZs and close down areas of the high seas in their own interests. We will have the unfamiliar prospect of naval forces 'holding ground' in the form of presence and patrol operations to ensure that others, both state and commercial players, do not encroach, either on national jurisdictions and entitlements or on the global commons.

In general terms, warfare at sea will continue very much as it does today, with warships and auxiliaries going about their familiar business: the maintenance of maritime security, the promotion of a country's interests, the protection of its sovereignty and the projection of national power. Those countries that can afford, in human and material terms, to acquire and operate advanced technologies, specialist warships and other sophisticated maritime capabilities will do so. Significantly, the two most recently ordered Arleigh Burke destroyers cost nearly $1.5 billion each and the Zumwalt programme cost has been estimated at $12.069 billion for three ships.[3] Great powers at sea will be defined, in their own eyes and those of potential opponents, by their ability to operate major battle groups, to sustain substantial deterrent forces and to project power beyond their respective regions. However, mere possession of these capabilities will not be sufficient; what is important is how they are used. Posturing is not a suitable substitute for the calibrated threat and use of force within a carefully calculated and considered strategy. Nor is narrative a substitute for carefully considered policy.

As technology develops, the freedom of action of great, medium and small states will be constrained, in comparison with the past, by the sophisticated maritime denial capabilities acquired by many countries over recent years. The economic convergence between the developed and developing countries in the past two decades has been paralleled by a marked convergence in terms of the technological sophistication and availability of maritime warfare technologies. These include, among others, quiet, high-endurance submarines, powerful anti-ship missiles, modern mines, unmanned vehicles and access to commercial space-based intelligence products.

We have seen in Chapter 6 the range and scale of changes that new technologies will have on the future of warfare at sea. Many of them will take time to enter into service and not all will be available to every country simultaneously, despite the pirating of technology. Today, there is a rough

---

[3] Congressional Research Service: *Navy DDG-51 and DDG-1000 Destroyer Programs: Background and Issues for Congress*, dated 8 April 2014.

equilibrium of technologies and capabilities, despite differences in force levels, training and performance. Past experience suggests that unexpected innovations and technological surprises will emerge as the century progresses. The future discovery and development of breakthrough technologies by a single country or group of states would upset the current balance and would transform the conduct of warfare at sea, until the rest of the world caught up.

We also need to remember that the availability of technology enables irregular groups and individuals to access military levels of capability, which could be used for both legitimate and illicit purposes. States will not have a monopoly on the instruments of coercion and the use of force. Criminals, terrorists and other sub-state groups will have access to the means to inflict significant damage on civilian populations, armed forces and law enforcement agencies.

JOINT AND COOPERATIVE APPROACHES

One of the defining features of the period ahead will see accelerating technological developments and advanced communications breaking down the divisions between land, sea, subsurface and air environments. As a result, many more military capabilities will be brought to bear at sea, beyond those provided by navies and sea-based assets. In the future, a range of land-based weapons, systems and aircraft will participate as components of joint (or 'integrated' as the current argot has it) approaches to warfare at sea, just as naval forces will increasingly contribute to successful campaigns on the land, in space and in the air. Capabilities associated with space, cyberspace and the electromagnetic spectrum will be critical enablers, notably in providing actionable intelligence, communications, precision positioning and timing for weapons systems, but also for disrupting and disabling the systems and sensors of opponents.

Meanwhile, what is known as Networked Enabled Capability (NEC) is being developed, which involves the near real-time gathering, processing and diffusion of information and decisions to allow the linking up of a broad range of sensors and weapon systems, over considerable distances. It also enables sensors and 'shooters' in different ships, aircraft and other units to be integrated as a common capability against an opponent's war-fighting assets, with multiple individuals and organisations having direct and simultaneous access to information and to each other.

This trend will not only allow weapons and systems to be used across disciplinary boundaries, but also enable widely dispersed military units to operate as reconfigurable, mix and match 'communities of operational interest' or as modular components in a cohesive network, allowing closer coordination of engagement and tactical manoeuvre. Satellite systems and space imaging, the proliferation of advanced surveillance and data systems and integrated communications technologies will also enable the cueing of an array of responses to situations, as well as access to space-based and other command, control, communications and surveillance assets.

This integrated capability will allow sea combat in the future to be conducted at the greatest range possible from an opponent, with reliance on wide-area and unmanned surveillance assets and long-range attack systems. Just as opposing aircraft carriers tended not to be in contact with each other in the Second World War, warships today and tomorrow will probably never encounter their opponents within visual or even radar ranges. Cooperative and networked systems will mean that an attacking unit will generally be firing its weapons based on cueing and targeting information provided by the sensors in another platform.

This type of cooperative engagement capability has already been demonstrated. In the US Navy Integrated Fire Control-Counter Air (NIFC-CA) concept, a warship fires a missile well beyond the range of its own sensors, on the basis of information received from a carrier-based E-2D Hawkeye airborne early warning (AEW) aircraft, which tells the missile where to find its target. The Standard SM-6 missile uses its active seeker head to acquire and home in on the target. In other situations, the sensors involved might be mounted in warships or aircraft, but also in submarines, aerostats, satellites and unmanned vehicles. Artificial intelligence (AI) will in the future allow ever more remote identification, classification and neutralisation of targets, based on rigorously coded criteria and rules of engagement. The techniques would also allow minor warships to confront larger and more powerfully armed opponents by calling in firepower from elsewhere. Even if parts of the enabling systems and networks are degraded or destroyed, redundancy will be provided by temporary bearers and proxies in the form of mini- or tactical satellites, unmanned vehicles and other temporary solutions, such as aerostats.

UNMANNED SYSTEMS

We have seen in Chapter 6 that the proliferation of unmanned systems, by land, sea and air, will continue, for both combat and combat support functions, as well as for a wide spectrum of law enforcement tasks. They will be staple, indispensable items in the inventories of all maritime powers.

Apart from their undoubted operational benefits, their use will encourage states to be more forward-leaning and less cautious in their dealings with their rivals and competitors, especially in situations in which states probe the edges of tolerance in relation to claims and disputes. Without a human in sight, the first unmanned aerial vehicle (UAV) to approach a US or Chinese carrier group is likely to be shot down, as it will be difficult to assess whether it is on a surveillance or attack mission (or both).

It would also be difficult to assess whether it was a state-owned or terrorist-operated vehicle. Unmanned and robotic applications enable criminals and terrorists to de-risk a significant proportion of their activities. Narcotics, armaments and many other forms of contraband can be transported without direct risk to the perpetrator, and so the use of unmanned vehicles by non-state groups is expected to increase rapidly. Hezbollah has used UAVs in the past, and in March 2014, two small UAVs from North Korea crashed just south of the border with South Korea, carrying high-resolution cameras, which had taken photographs of the South Korean presidential compound and some military facilities. This proliferation will have significant implications for terrorism and counterterrorism, as well as the monitoring of unmanned vehicles. Protocols and rules of engagement will need to be established in order to ensure that ownership and missions can be readily identified, as well as procedures for when unmanned vehicles malfunction and misbehave.

Within a decade, technologically advanced or progressively upgraded manned and unmanned attack and surveillance aircraft, together with armed rotorcraft, will become more widely available at sea, often linked to other integrated surveillance and targeting systems. Unmanned vehicles will be in the forefront of surveillance and attack, starting with aerial variants and progressing to surface and underwater options. All types will be able to benefit from networked operations (particularly targeting) and advances in anti-ship cruise missile technology.

Consequently, significant resources and research will be devoted to finding ways to counter unmanned vehicles, notably through manipulation and interruption of their control mechanisms and data links. This will apply not only to the systems of state-based opponents, but also to the unmanned vehicles used by all kinds by terrorists and criminals.

SPACE

Maritime warfare will in the future be extensively supported by space-based services, especially in terms of the ability to locate, track and identify activities taking place at sea, both in peace and conflict. In addition, satellite communications will be significant enablers of data bearers and information networks, control systems for a range of unmanned vehicles and, of course, for providing accurate positional information for a wide range of precision munitions and military applications. Thus what happens in space is increasingly relevant to activity at sea. The simple message is that if you are not in space, you are unlikely to be conducting much warfare.

The Outer Space Treaty[4] of 1967 governs the use of space for military and other purposes. As well as designating space as the common heritage of mankind, its relevant articles banned the use of space, Earth's orbit or any other celestial body for the stationing of nuclear weapons or weapons of mass destruction. The treaty does not prohibit the deployment of conventional weapons in orbit;[5] this will probably lead to the future stationing of weapon systems in space, not only for use against ballistic weapons, satellites and vehicles in the exo-atmosphere, but also in engaging targets on the surface of the Earth.

The principles underlying the future use of space are similar to those that apply to the use of the sea. Space power is a function of the extent to which a country or group of countries can exploit the use of space for its own benefit, while either protecting access for all countries or denying its use to

---

[4] Formally, the Treaty on Principles Governing the Activities of States in the Exploration and Use of Outer Space, including the Moon and Other Celestial Bodies. By March 2014, 101 countries were states parties to the Treaty, while another 27 had signed the Treaty, but had not completed ratification.

[5] The launching state retains jurisdiction and control over any object that it projects into space and is liable for any damage that it causes.

an opponent. Consequently, in view of how critical space-based services and platforms will be to every aspect of future warfare, space will be subject to competition and conflict. It is also an area that criminal and terrorist groups have already started to target for disruption and exploitation.

There will be progressive attempts to deal with the surveillance threat from space. The proliferation of anti-ballistic missile technologies will be accompanied by anti-satellite systems, which will hold at risk all existing space platforms and services. In time of conflict, it would have to be assumed that some or all services provided by space-based systems, such as communications, navigational, guidance and surveillance might be unavailable.

Another consideration is that, as the exo-atmosphere becomes more cluttered and disputed – and anti-ballistic missile systems become more effective – it is likely that ballistic missiles will lose some of their vaunted invulnerability. Other forms of strategic deterrence based on the ability to conduct denial of service attacks on integrated, interconnected and fragile infrastructures could emerge, together with space-based systems and other methods of strategic coercion, possibly based around directed energy (DE – see Chapter 6), electromagnetic pulse or enhanced cyber options.

The major powers – the USA, Russia and China – already have proven anti-satellite capabilities, and now India is developing its own ability to disable and destroy objects in space. They and other states, as well as sub-state operators, will discover ways of jamming and manipulating the uplink and downlink elements of satellites and compromising the physical, optical and electronic integrity of space systems, with lasers playing a major part, as well as masers, when technology allows. In the future, it is highly likely that there will be 'killer satellites' stationed in space, in the event of conflict. The advent of hypersonic missiles and civilian space travel will increase the risks to space-based services and complicate things still further.

In response, states will need to have ways not only of protecting their space assets, but also of mitigating the destruction or disabling of satellites and other space enablers. In some cases, this will be achieved by the launching of replacement mini-satellite chains, perhaps from existing or former ballistic missile submarines, and the substitution of disabled satellites by unmanned or manned aircraft, aerostats or airships to act as communications bearers, re-transmit facilities and network enablers. The loss of positional information for navigation, targeting weapons and other tactical systems would have particularly serious consequences.

CYBER AND ELECTROMAGNETIC WARFARE

Navies currently operate in a generally benign electromagnetic environment, which is largely clear from electronic interference. This is not likely to continue into the future as both state-based and irregular opponents develop and bring into operation technologies that disrupt communications, sensors and networks. These devices and systems are likely to be able to degrade or allow manipulation of terrestrial and satellite communications, data exchanges and guidance systems. China, North Korea and Russia already field a substantial number of high-power jamming and disruption systems, ranging from tactical-level electronic countermeasures up to large-area and dedicated systems designed to deal with cruise missiles, GPS-guided munitions and satellite communications. Unmanned systems are likely to have a particularly hard time of it.

In this respect, it is by no means certain that the sensors, communications and systems of US and allied maritime forces have incorporated the necessary robustness and agility to maintain operational effectiveness in a situation involving heavy electronic suppression. Consequently, more attention will be needed to ensure that existing and emerging systems have sufficient hardening, resilience and redundancy to survive in an electronic environment characterised by high-intensity and high-power electronic jamming and spectrum denial systems. These will be primarily deployed by military operators, but, given the range of systems available on the open market today, the necessary technologies are also likely to be acquired by criminals, terrorists and other groups. Mobile and wireless signals will be particularly vulnerable.

Similarly, great emphasis is placed on the potential for the devastating effects of cyber-attacks in future military campaigns. As computing power increases, as silicon-based circuits give way to graphene and as more of the world's population gains access to Internet technologies, through an increasing variety of mobile, wearable and linked devices, the range and intensity of activity in cyberspace will expand, for good and ill. States and armed forces will constantly probe for vulnerabilities in both peacetime and wartime, in order to gain critical intelligence, deny opponents the use of, and confidence in, networked products and exploit the medium, for their own benefit and the exclusion of others. Cyberspace will see the development and operationalisation of a vast range of offensive and defensive measures, capabilities that in virtual terms will mirror and complement the hard capabilities available in the real world. At the same time, opponents will target and selectively destroy the physical infrastructure, connections and bearers of fixed and mobile Information and Communications Technologies (ICT), notably masts, servers and routing mechanisms. Transoceanic fibre-optic communications cables will be subject to either compromise or severance.

Networked systems that are carelessly linked to other networks, with insufficient redundancy, imperfect safeguards and permeable firewalls, will always be vulnerable to manipulation and degradation. Increasingly, dedicated, stand-alone networks, backed up with sophisticated counter-intrusion mechanisms and voluminous databases, will be created to ensure the integrity of future operations. These will be operated independently of existing servers, cables and telecommunication linkages, to avoid compromise and virus attacks.

ABOVE-WATER WARFARE

The twenty-first century will be characterised at sea by an intense desire to know where everything is, whether for trade, exploitation or war. The tracking of one's own and a military opponent's (or commercial competitor's) assets and assessments of his likely intentions are crucial to success. In the last fifteen years, technological advances, particularly in satellite imagery, radars and UAVs, have enabled much greater coverage of oceanic areas and the location of potential threats. In the future, a wide range of military and commercial satellites will determine the position and identity of individual ships, through optical, radar and electronic means. The increasingly sophisticated sensors of maritime patrol aircraft, wide-area UAVs and land-based systems, coupled to increasingly powerful and capable data analysis, management and exchange networks, will make the task of concealment even harder. Ships and other maritime assets have become more visible and identifiable. It is likely that there will be a revival of the use of underground facilities.[6]

The second major issue relates to vulnerability. It has been seen that technology is balancing the odds in tactical terms. Most notable in this regard is a diversity of extremely capable anti-ship missiles that can be fired from land, sea or air, as well as by submarines. These are generally variants of a type known as cruise missiles, which travel a certain distance from launch at predetermined heights before locating their targets by active radar or passive homing onto radar, infrared or jamming emissions. The USA and its allies have a range of sophisticated, proven anti-ship missiles: notably Harpoon, the Naval Strike Missile and three generations of Exocets.

Other capable missiles are finding their way to potential adversaries. For example, the Russians produce the 3M-54E Klub, known as the SS-N-27 or Sizzler to NATO – an anti-ship (or land-attack) missile fired either by surface ships or submarines from a range of 100–160 nm (200–300 km). It cruises at Mach 0.6–0.8 and then fires at 13 nm (25 km) from the target supersonic 'kill' vehicle, which accelerates to Mach 2.9. Not to be outdone, the SS-N-26 Yakhont is launched at ranges up to 160 nm (300 km) and flies at Mach 2.6 at a height of 8 m (26 ft) above the sea. Terminal attack speed is reported to be 0.6 km/s (0.4 miles/s). The challenge from hypersonic missiles, as we have seen, is even greater.

As well as anti-ship cruise missiles, the Chinese have a particularly threatening missile called the DF-21D Dong Feng, with a range of 1,500 nm (2,700 km). Because of its trajectory and steep, rapid terminal dive phase and the possibility that the missile would be launched in salvoes or deploy multiple re-entry warheads, the Dong Feng presents significant difficulties for conventional missile defences. It is able to hit a static land impact area roughly the size of an American aircraft carrier. Whether it can repeat the trick with a highly manoeuvrable target that has a significant incentive in not being hit is another matter. In the future, it will be guided to the vicinity of

---

[6] During the Cold War, several countries built underground facilities for their navies. Sweden, for example, constructed a huge underground complex at Muskö inside a rock face of solid granite, capable of housing submarines and a range of warships up to destroyer size. Today, the Chinese naval base at Yulin on Hainan Island has an underground facility that hides up to twenty nuclear submarines from surveillance and satellites.

its intended target by land-based radars, UAVs and satellites, as part of the Chinese Naval Ocean Surveillance System (NOSS) satellite chain.

In the immediate future, the balance of advantage in high-end warfare is likely to lie with offensive systems, in both missiles and submarine-launched torpedoes. Their precision, lethality and ability to discriminate between various targets will improve still further, especially when linked to sophisticated surveillance and networked systems. As a result, ships will require increasingly capable and expensive anti-air and anti-missile systems, as well as greatly improved anti-torpedo provision, if they are to perform their operational functions.

The need for counters to this increased visibility and vulnerability will result in additional investment in three main areas of development. Firstly, as described above, capabilities, sensors and weapons will be widely dispersed in various ships, platforms and systems, as part of a network, often separated by large distances. The idea is that in the event of loss or damage to one or more elements of the network, there is sufficient redundancy and duplication to allow several solutions to be found to provide the sensor, system or weapon that is needed in any particular situation.

Secondly, there will be increased investment in reducing the electronic signatures, radar cross-sections, visual profiles and emissions of surface vessels and increasing their 'stealth' characteristics. All these measures will be designed to prevent detection and identification in the first place and, if unsuccessful, reduce to a minimum the chances of a successful engagement by a weapon. This trend will encompass conventional ways of reducing radar signatures through design and material measures. It will also extend to employing artificially intelligent decoys and altering received images, as well as the innovative use of visual disruption, camouflage and composite materials, electronic and physical obscurants and nanotechnology. Unmanned applications will be used for confusing and distracting incoming missiles. These will include novel ways of jamming and manipulating radars and other electronically based sensors, coupled with capabilities to deceive and distract imagery, electronic intercept and radar satellites. The use of increasing numbers of unmanned and off-board devices will confuse and distract incoming missiles and nanotechnology will deliver nanobots and micro-flyers that can swarm and generate false signals and images to satellites, surveillance sensors and missile-targeting radars.

Thirdly, it is likely that more capabilities will be carried in increasing numbers of submersibles and hulls, to take advantage of the inherent stealth properties of the underwater dimension. Submarines will be the prime beneficiaries, with increased investment applied to make them even more versatile. As we shall see below, their size and displacement will grow as they incorporate more systems and acquire new roles. These might include some functions currently associated with surface combatants, such as air defence (firing missiles from submerged positions against targets detected by a third party), as a mother ship for a variety of unmanned applications and for assault force insertion.

Navies will also look at the possibilities offered by semi-submersibles. The Iranian Revolutionary Guard Corps (IRGC) is operating a number of these craft at a small scale and it would seem possible that larger variants will follow. These would have the bulk of their structure under the water, like a submerged submarine on the surface, with a low freeboard section above the water, comprising light, low-observable composite materials, which would limit detection opportunities for a wide range of sensors. It would have access ports for both manned and unmanned vehicles, missiles and communications bearers, including aerostats. This arrangement would prevent or limit potential action damage to vital parts of the vessels, with the section above the water being readily replaceable or repairable.

However, submarines do not have the versatility, the range of sensors and weapons or, except for nuclear submarines, the agility, speed and endurance of surface ships and are not yet suited to controlling oceanic areas. They are much better at denying access to them and through them. In most situations, surface vessels will be required to conduct those functions that require visible presence and seamless communications connectivity. These will include aircraft carriers and major amphibious units designed to provide deployable air and power projection capabilities, together with other surface vessels, which deal with all those situations requiring direct human engagement, from humanitarian relief to coercive action. In particular, surface vessels will continue to be needed to transport large quantities of combat material and support the movement of men, equipment and supplies in bulk and over distance. They are also the most suitable types of vessel for a wide range of diplomatic tasks, including forward presence and assurance to allies and friends.

In addition, surface combatants (cruisers, destroyers and frigates) are needed to provide sensor platforms, weapons delivery and protective coverage for larger ships, with systems that enable them to engage in above-water warfare against missiles and aircraft, underwater warfare against submarines and on the surface against other ships. Some are able to launch cruise missiles against the land, while others are equipped to engage ballistic missiles and satellites. All are able to host significant communications and data transfer facilities, as well as helicopters and UAVs. Their sensors will be a combination of hull-mounted, towed, streamed and unmanned variants; they will have the ability to remain acoustically and electronically silent, while off-board and cooperative sensors (in other units) perform warning, targeting and electronic countermeasure tasks. In the light of increasing offensive missile capabilities, the trend will be towards multipurpose platforms that can combine the most utility and firepower with the most stealth characteristics to go in harm's way. As Alfred Thayer Mahan said, 'the backbone and real power of any navy are the vessels which, by due proportion of defensive and offensive powers, are capable of giving and taking hard knocks'.[7] The guiding principle in the twenty-first century will be that if an asset is not lose-able, in support of strategic and operational objectives, it will not be use-able. It will not be a case of what you have, but what you can use.

In the future environment, we are likely to see the emergence of two main types of surface warship. The first is a large surface mother ship capable of hosting a range of manned and unmanned systems, each providing defensive, offensive and routine functions and networked capabilities, either within its hull or in association, much like the submarine and destroyer depot ships of the early to mid-twentieth century. Pirates and large fishing enterprises have already realised the potential of mother ships for operations in the open ocean. As it happens, the US Navy is introducing Afloat Forward Staging Bases (AFSBs) in 2015. The bases are designed to provide in-theatre logistics support and act as a forward staging base for mine countermeasures (MCM), amphibious and special operations missions. The AFSB has been developed from a BP tanker design and built to commercial standards. It costs about $500 million – compared to about $2 billion for an Arleigh Burke-class destroyer. They are not warships of course, but the application

---

[7] *Naval Strategy* (1911).

of generic hulls is likely to be extended as more unmanned and autonomous combat vehicles and modular sensor systems become operational. The US Military Sealift Command (MSC) has already taken delivery of two Mobile Landing Platforms, auxiliary support ships, which will provide an offshore in case onshore bases are not available or contested. The hulls will be used to support HADR and amphibious operations, as well as complementing the US Navy's Joint High Speed Vessels (JHSVs) (essentially adapted high speed civilian ferries designed to deploy troops into action quickly) and other types of landing craft.

The second type will be composite, 'mix and match' and multi-role warships, which, as we have seen, will increasingly be configured around generic hulls, with modular sensor and weapon applications, allowing them to switch roles and undertake a wide range of missions, with the ability to form part of a wider network of sensors and weapon platforms. They will also be fully integrated within joint structures, enabling them to access – and contribute to – wider capabilities that can be brought to bear at sea, through participation with air and land forces and the exploitation of intelligence, surveillance and targeting information. Only major navies will retain the capacity and appetite to operate a balanced range of specialist warships.

There will also be consolidation of the trend towards cooperative networks of platforms and systems, both manned and unmanned technologies, able to absorb damage and reconfigure rapidly and providing redundancy and alternative routeing in the event of failures and disruptions. Therefore, warfare will be characterised by a desire and ability to engage threats from the greatest possible range and with the highest degree of precision. This will require, and is leading to, as we have seen, an extensive array of surveillance and targeting resources, linked to dispersed weapon platforms that are part of a sophisticated network of sensors and 'shooters'.

Aircraft carriers

One of the biggest changes in warfare in the twenty-first century will be in the employment of the US Navy's supercarriers and other large carriers (and possibly those of other countries). Until now, they and their battle groups have been at the heart of the US policy of deterrence and guardians of the post-Cold War environment. They have epitomised the US policy of

The aircraft carrier USS *Nimitz*.

forward presence, able to provide reassurance to friends and a potent warning to would-be aggressors and adventurists that the USA is serious about
a region or an issue. US carriers are in-your-face mobile concentrations of
raw coercive power, designed to deter and frighten off opponents.

The main point of a carrier is to deliver fighting power beyond the reach
of land-based aircraft or in situations where land-based aircraft transit times
do not allow a high enough sortie rate consistent with the tempo of a campaign. It also serves as a less vulnerable means of deploying aircraft than
a static airfield, which may be subject to ballistic missile, conventional air
and irregular forces attack. In terms of sustainable reach and the ability to
intervene across a range of warfare disciplines at a time and place of political
choice, its agility and capacity are unmatched. When combined with a range
of other vessels in a battle group or task group, it offers a significant range
of power projection, offensive and defensive capabilities.

However, modern US carriers have never been put directly in harm's way,
nor are they likely to be in the future. They are emphatically not designed
to take on enemy battle fleets in the same way that their Second World

War predecessors did. The cost–benefit ratio associated with placing a US supercarrier in danger is simply becoming too weighted in favour of the cheap, high-impact missiles and torpedoes available today and increasingly tomorrow. As a previous US Secretary of Defense, Robert Gates, said, the new Ford-class carriers with their full complement of combat aircraft, 'would represent potentially $15 to $20 billion worth of hardware at risk'. Like nuclear-powered ballistic missile submarines, if you have to use them in anger, you have probably failed. Carriers spend most of their time in service keeping the peace, so that they will not have to fight, as in the Falklands War when the two British carriers stayed well to the east of the combat zone and provided aircraft at range to support combat air patrol and land-attack missions. It was also the case at the battles of the Coral Sea and Midway in 1942, and more recently in both Gulf Wars. The advent of unmanned combat air vehicles (UCAVs) will further encourage the carriers' distance from the riskier parts of the ocean. Consequently, the likelihood is that carriers will probably stay on the edge of harm's way, generating significant amounts of combat air power well away from the main action.

This is causing an interesting transition to take place in the use of US naval power. In the past, a US president's first recourse in the event of a crisis was to reach for a carrier battle group, with the implication that it would be the carrier-based aircraft that would provide the coercive combat power. In recent crises, it has been other elements in the battle group, previously regarded as defensive assets for the carrier itself, that are assuming greater importance. While providing multi-threat protection for the carrier, the cruisers and destroyers carry cruise missiles to attack land targets with precision and provide in most cases an integral anti-ballistic missile capability. These have proved eminently usable in coercing proscribed regimes and reassuring allies. The importance of these roles is likely to increase. Similarly, as has been noted, the use of the US Ohio-class missile-firing submarines has demonstrated the ability to launch ordnance from distant and concealed locations.

Meanwhile, the entry into service of UCAVs, with the range and firepower to match those of manned aircraft, as well as an improved clutch of long-range precision weapons, is likely to accelerate this transition. With networked solutions available, it is doubtful whether it is necessary to concentrate so much combat power, investment and human resource in a single super-platform. On the other hand, if the electromagnetic spectrum is going to become less permissive, the need to maintain access to aircraft and combat power that can operate regardless will be essential.

Therefore, on balance, it is likely that advanced powers will need two types of carriers. Those that can afford them will seek to acquire large supercarriers, which would typically provide impressive power projection platforms, capable of asserting national interest and dominating most situations short of high-impact conflict and war, as well as a maritime strategic reserve and forward-deployed hub in war well back from the front line.

In conflict, the serious fighting will be done by smaller 'flat tops' that will deploy aircraft, unmanned options and other force elements right up to the front line and will actively go in harm's way, backed up by longer-range manned and UAVs/UCAVs from the supercarriers. This is clearly the role that will be played by the current generation of large aviation-capable amphibious ships, which already operate AV8-B Harriers and tilt-rotor V-22 Ospreys, and will soon see the introduction of the F-35B Lightning II. Thus, it will be a return to the Second World War philosophy of a combination of large carriers and 'jeep' carriers – the cheap and cheerful vessels that provided close support for convoys and amphibious assaults, updated to the twenty-first century for use as street-fighters in harm's way. Other countries are likely to follow suit.

It seems likely that the first half of the twenty-first century will see a proliferation of these medium-sized ships with flight decks, both traditional amphibious ships and new, multipurpose aviation-capable hulls, with modular applications that would enable them to operate a range of manned and unmanned vehicles, in the air, over and under the sea and ashore. These vessels will be both depot ships – providing basing and maintenance facilities – and operational platforms, able to integrate organic, deployable and networked sensors and weapons, for both offence and defence. They will be low-cost, lean-manned mother ships, able to operate up-threat with both surveillance and attack vehicles, providing networked firepower, communications nodes and sensor packages.

It is important that concepts take into account that large hulls (and in particular, aviation-capable 'flat-tops') are inherently flexible and adaptable in their potential for use, because of their size, shape and stowage arrangements, together with the 'lift and shift' virtues of their aviation assets. This means that carriers can operate throughout the spectrum of crisis from combat operations to humanitarian relief, as demonstrated admirably by US carriers off Indonesia (USS *Abraham Lincoln*) and Haiti (USS *Carl Vinson*) in 2005 and 2010 respectively. This flexibility should also extend to accommodating and deploying joint elements, platforms and personnel; in coalition operations, the carriers and other large vessels are likely to include providing the only means by which smaller, less capable partners are able to contribute force elements. They need to be multipurpose maids of all work rather than single-role behemoths.

It therefore seems likely that the USA will continue to invest in its super-carriers, at least as long as the current programme delivers. However, they are unlikely to be going in serious harm's way any time soon and, starting with the Ford class, it is anticipated that there will be marked reduction in the number of supercarriers, for both fiscal and operational reasons.

AMPHIBIOUS WARFARE

The freedom of the high seas gives sea-based, especially amphibious forces unrivalled opportunities to influence events and decisions on land, especially when they are positioned in good time and deployed from high readiness. As long ago as 1759, a pundit wrote: 'A military, naval, littoral war, when wisely prepared and discreetly conducted … comes like Thunder and Lightning to some unprepared part of the world.' He added: 'Happy for that People who are Sovereigns enough of the sea to put it into execution!'[8] Basil Liddell Hart was even more emphatic: 'Amphibious flexibility is the greatest strategic asset that a sea power possesses.'[9]

The sea is the only medium that will enable any operation that requires persistence or the transport of significant amounts of materiel, particularly ground forces. Amphibious forces can act immediately on arrival without infrastructure or resources in place, and they can offer immediate impact in modern conditions, both in their own right and as part of a wider joint campaign or operation.

Most countries will want to deter aggression and defend as far forward

[8] Thomas More Molyneux, *Conjunct Expeditions* (1759).
[9] B. H. Liddell Hart, *Deterrent or Defence* (1960).

The amphibious assault ship USS *Saipan*.

and away from their countries as possible, in order to ensure the survival of sophisticated, fragile infrastructures, densely occupied cityscapes and the stability of societies that are all highly dependent on safe, secure means of production and supply. As a result, if the future is going to be characterised by limited conflicts rather than general wars, in which coercion rather than invasion and total war is the predominant feature, the projection of power against the land by navies, in conjunction with air and other expeditionary elements, would seem to be coming into its own again. However, even against modest sea denial opponents, the range of emergent risks involved in approaching hostile or even moderately unfriendly shores and the acquisition of advanced technologies by potential opponents mean that traditional methods of conducting assaults against the land need to be revised. With a diminished chance of surprise, amphibious forces will have to stand further out to sea until the environment is sufficiently shaped and hostile forces suppressed to enable them to come close inshore and ashore to exploit opportunities. Instead of previous, large-scale amphibious landings, a more dynamic, flexible joint approach is necessary that capitalises on the surprise and speed generated by maritime forces poising offshore and ranging at will along a coast. In other words, it is unlikely with the level of surveillance available from both military and civilian systems that operational level surprise will be achieved. The accent will then be on generating high levels of operational tempo and achieving tactical surprise in many places simultaneously. In this way, operational 'bubbles' of opportunity, defined by time and area, would be established, secured and sustained for the minimum time necessary and subsequently collapsed around those objectives to which force was to be applied to achieve the desired effect.

For most of the last century, there has been a fixed assumption that 'boots on the ground' are always required to bring conflict to a successful conclusion and that ground has to be occupied to secure military objectives. However, in emerging situations and in the future, there is likely to be more careful consideration of the idea that it is the effect of military action that needs to be felt on the ground rather than the activity itself. Mobility, cooperative firepower and high-speed information processing are likely to allow military action to take place from increasingly long-range locations, while reducing the 'footprint' on the ground.

In emerging concepts, these are beginning to be discussed in terms of 'high-impact, low-footprint operations', prioritised towards the achievement of operational objectives with the minimum of effort and risk. It means the least exposure of combat forces in time and space to the actions of an opponent or hostile forces. In an era in which the cost-effectiveness of denial weapons substantially trumps the costs of suppressing them, a lower footprint is essential. In terms of boots on the ground, this approach could be likened to the reduced weight of precision-guided munitions bombs that is needed to destroy a target compared to previous 'dumb' bombs.

A commander's calculation should, in the future, centre on how few troops he or she needs to complete a mission, rather than concentrating as much human force as possible. It is likely that 'occupying ground' will in future be seen as a very blunt way of achieving these objectives, one that is unlikely to be employed, except by forces that lack the technical sophistication to engage in low-footprint, high-impact operations, in peace support activities and in situations involving total war. In effect, assets will be required to isolate and shape a target area, so that small groups of attackers can achieve their objectives, with the aim of reducing the numbers of humans in direct contact with an opponent.

This approach will place a premium on special forces and dedicated assault formations, with high levels of mobility, agility and the ability to access firepower, both integrated within their own force and on call from a wide range of other platforms, including ships, aircraft, missiles and long-range gunnery and land-attack munitions. For example, the Zumwalt-class destroyer has an Advanced Gun System (AGS), which fires a 155-mm rocket-assisted, GPS-guided long-range land-attack projectile (LRLAP) accurately out to 63 nm (117 km) and beyond. Technological progress with GPS- and laser-guided munitions, as well as experience with land-attack missiles, has led to more sophisticated and effective ways of conducting fire support against the land.

One of the most progressive areas of development in this regard will be the introduction of fire support to ground forces ashore, based on loitering and persistent munitions. These are weapons, such as Tomahawk Block IV Tactical Cruise Missile (TLAM), which, like armed UAVs, are able to linger over areas, waiting for targets of opportunity or guidance by forces on the ground or another unit. This is the concept of a 'fire basket' into which munitions are fired or parked and then guided to the precise point of impact by designation (by troops, UAVs or aircraft, for example) or by integral terminal guidance, such as automated target recognition or infrared seekers, in precise time slots in response to requirements. To these are likely to be added aircraft and a range of time-critical, loitering and fly-through munitions that are provided by ships at sea, yet guided to their targets by the troops on the ground, possibly through laser designation or direct steering of the weapons as they arrive over the battlefield. These developments are likely to reduce the logistical footprint and increase the agility of ground forces significantly.

In these circumstances, the specialist amphibious ships can be employed more as fighting platforms in their own right, with marines or troops employed as the weapon systems of those ships. Added emphasis can then be given to making ground precarious and untenable for the enemy rather than occupying it. This means that instead of the traditional amphibious landing, with its heavy footprint and slow build-up, assault forces would undertake a range of lower-footprint, dispersed, but high-impact operations over a wider area supported from the warships offshore. They can go by high speed vertical take-off and landing (VTOL) and tilt-rotor aircraft, helicopter, assault craft and amphibious vehicle straight to their objectives to facilitate surprise and permit inshore threats to be bypassed or minimised. Thus, it would be possible to exploit more fully the mobility, protection and infrastructure facilities available afloat and to deploy from the ships, with men, equipment and vehicles returning on completion of missions and spending the minimum time ashore. The ships also provide a 'reverse slope', if it is necessary, to recover as part of a rolling campaign of assaults, or if it is required to reconfigure or retire in the face of overwhelming force or the use of chemical weapons.

However, on the basis of 'never say never', it has to be recognised that a traditional assault landing (such as D-Day or across the Pacific in the Second World War) might still be needed, but it is highly unlikely that this type or scale of operation against a contested shore or with similar levels of attrition will take place again. Direct assault in the teeth of the enemy is distinctly out of fashion and, in view of modern technologies, may not be necessary. More likely would be the forcible isolation and defence of a point of landing by assault forces and the subsequent transportation of troops and materiel through a rapid build-up ashore in a relatively secured and benign environment.

UNDERWATER WARFARE

Underwater warfare will evolve in response to increasing numbers of functions being stationed in underwater platforms to take advantage of the stealth and secrecy opportunities provided by the sea. Nuclear attack and hunter-killer submarines, and their conventional diesel-electric cousins, will remain important elements in most war-fighting navies in the early twenty-first century. Nuclear submarines, in particular, are the hallmark of a navy with regional power and aspirations to global influence and will retain their status, with aircraft carriers, as the capital ships of the twenty-first century. Their flexibility, endurance, high-speed advantage and inherent stealth, survivability and ability to surprise make them formidable opponents, along with their global reach and sustainability. The presence or mere indication of the proximity of a nuclear submarine dramatically shapes the geometry of a tactical situation and the perceptions of opposing commanders.[10] They will continue to host a variety of anti-ship and anti-submarine weapons, as well as land-attack missiles, backed up by increasingly sophisticated communications and data transfer systems.

Less expensive but having many of the same advantages as nuclear submarines are those equipped with air-independent propulsion (AIP), which enables them to remain submerged without recharging their batteries for anything up to three weeks, such as the German Type 214 submarine and the Chinese AIP submarine types – the Yuan class and the Song class.

Submarines are proliferating rapidly, with most maritime countries investing in either nuclear or AIP variants. Submarines will be more than just ship sinkers (their instinctively preferred role) and will be increasingly employed for other functions, both as multitasked, jacks-of-all-trades (descendants of the current hunter-killer submarines) and as specialist platforms (the heirs of the ballistic-missile-firing submarines and the modern cruise-missile-firing Ohio class). They will also deploy unmanned vehicles for self-protection, surveillance and attack, as well as manned vehicles for covert operations and insertion. In particular, autonomous and tethered unmanned underwater vehicles (UUVs) will scout out ahead of submarines to detect mines and other submarines, and to conduct covert reconnaissance.

In early December 2013, the US submarine, USS *Providence*, successfully launched a UAV while submerged, which then landed safely ashore. This development will expand significantly the tactical horizon of submarines, which hitherto has been limited by what could be detected by a submarine's periscopes, sonars and masts and the information provided from external sources. They can now send UAVs to locate and confirm suitable targets by land and sea.

In future, more dedicated attempts are likely to be made to match the stealth cover provided by the sea with the versatility associated with surface warships in areas of high threat to aircraft and surface vessels. This might include the deployment of anti-air missiles from a submerged position in

---

[10] For most countries, the experience of the Argentinian Navy, as reflected in its lessons from the Falklands War, will resonate: 'the British nuclear submarines constituted a threat with which the Argentinian Navy could not cope'.

response to targeting and guidance information from a third-party platform. As such, the weapon and mission bays of submarines – and their discharge systems – will need to adapt, to reflect the increasing range of roles and to avoid the limitations imposed by standardised pressure hulls and torpedo tubes.

A submarine's key vulnerability is the noise radiated by its machinery and the hull. Conventional submarines are very silent when running on electrical power; nuclear-powered boats have engineering components, which, if not precisely manufactured and suppressed emit distinctive noise frequencies that can be detected and classified. The need for low levels of detectability will be extended to both noise and emission control. For nuclear submarines, this is likely to mean increased investment in noise cancelling and suppression measures and technologies and AIP for conventional boats, together with, in both nuclear and conventional variants, improved anechoic coatings, decoys and disruptive systems. These are likely to include various autonomous vehicles, pre-programmed with signatures and other deceptive devices.

In addition, further measures and technologies will be developed to minimise the detection opportunities for potential opponents. Some of the most remarkable future advances are likely to include the development of acoustic masking-fluid cloaking methods, based on hundreds of tiny water jets designed to degrade the detection capabilities of sonars and radars. The acoustic cloak will also be made using 'meta-materials', which would absorb and suppress incoming sonar transmissions. A fluid cloak would reduce the hydrodynamic disturbance around submarines, to ensure that wake and turbulence indications are lowered to undetectable levels.

Another vulnerability is the risk of visual, electro-optic, radar or electronic detection whenever submarines or one of their masts breaks the surface (thus removing the cloaking property of the sea) to access intelligence and other information, or to use periscopes for assessing their immediate vicinity. This normally entails them being close to the surface, in order to raise their communications masts, usually satellite systems and long-haul terrestrial radio, or use trailing wires. In the future, it is anticipated that submarines will have masts with extremely low probabilities of visibility and detection. The trend is towards optronic masts that barely breach the surface, which house several sensors, such as high-definition low-light, infrared and heat-sensing cameras, as well as systems that support navigation, electronic warfare and communications. It is also likely that sensors and communication devices will be mounted on towed buoys and remotely operated vehicles (ROVs) that can be controlled and accessed via a tethered fibre-optic cable while remaining deep.

Another technological application that is set to tilt the balance of advantage still further in favour of submarines is the introduction of anti-aircraft missiles such as IDAS, a short-range missile that can be launched from a submerged submarine. Four missiles will fit in a container in one torpedo tube that can be guided by fibre-optic wire to a range of about 11 nm (20 km). Another application is a 30-mm mast-mounted gun system that can be used when the submarine is at periscope depth.

As a result, future submarines are likely to need to change their traditional configuration and shapes, to accommodate new sensors and weapons. In particular, they will need alternatives to torpedo tubes, especially for housing and releasing unmanned vehicles that will operate as sensor and weapon platforms and as communications nodes.

At the other end of the scale, increasing use of mini-submarines is likely. They already exist in the inventories of countries such as Iran, North Korea and Pakistan, alongside semi-submersible craft. They are typically used for covert and clandestine operations and penetration of coastal areas by special forces. At the military level, they are useful for proxy and deniable actions, while providing a low-cost, difficult-to-detect sea denial capability. The *Sea Dagger* series of submarine, produced by Kockums of Sweden, is a typical example, displacing 55–72 tons, with a length of 16–20 m (52–66 ft), a height of 3.6 m (12 ft) and a diameter of 2.5 m (8 ft). It has a sonar, communications systems, a navigational radar, an optronic mast and a range of mission modules. Most importantly and usefully, it comprises six configurable modules: generic bow and stern sections, with the remaining four carrying specific mission packages for anti-submarine warfare, reconnaissance and mining. It has a crew of four and can remain on task for eight days.

However, new technologies mean that submarines are unlikely to have it all their own way in the new environment. Increasingly, anti-submarine forces will develop novel tactics, techniques and technologies that will assist in mitigating and, in the event of a technological breakthrough, minimising the threat from submarines. Initially, these will be manifested in a range of acoustic sensors and arrays, which will be positioned on the seabed and deployed from aircraft, other submarines and ships. Submarines are also likely to find themselves beset, not only by other capable submarines, but also by swarms of dormant or mobile underwater vehicles, both autonomous and manned and linked to networks of sensors, which will only have ears for them. The UUVs will have the luxury of being able to use their active sonars with impunity and will be able to bring more capable helpers to the scene. The presence of unmanned vehicles in these quantities may have the effect of significantly reducing the opaqueness of the sea. Large, high-endurance UUVs fitted with active sonars that activate when passive sensors indicate an object of interest will patrol wide areas of ocean on an autonomous basis. They will make the task of ballistic missile-firing submarines, whose prime motivation is to remain undetected, considerably more challenging.

In addition, armed forces will look to take advantage of the benefits of stationing more of their assets in the stealthy undersea domain. It is feasible in the future that there will be underwater bases, both for protective and operational reasons. As long ago as 1966, the US Navy recognised that large undersea installations with a 'shirt sleeve environment' could exist under the continental shelf. The technology now allows, using off-the-shelf petroleum, mining, submarine and nuclear equipment, the establishment of permanent manned installations within the sea floor that do not have any air umbilical with the land or water surface, yet maintain a normal one-atmosphere environment.

Similarly, the drive by states to increase control in their offshore zones, particularly in the EEZs, will lead to the proliferation of networks of underwater detection, recording and response systems. Based around both passive and active acoustic sensors, with integrated analysis and processing facilities, these networks will be linked to anti-intrusion and alerting mechanisms, as well as mines and dormant weapons. Even now, a wide range of civilian applications is unwittingly collecting sensitive acoustic data, including discrete frequencies associated with submarines. These sensors range from academic sampling by fixed and mobile devices and acoustic sensors that sample and test whether marine energy platforms represent an environmental and ecosystem risk.

Also, this move towards the underwater operation of warfare capabilities at sea is likely to be accompanied by the increased exploitation of the seabed as a base for sensors and weapon systems, particularly, but not exclusively, in the more protected and controlled littoral regions of the world. These systems would be built into the seabed or masked for concealment and will remain largely dormant, as with the 'upward falling payloads' initiative, until activated by command or pre-programmed cues. They are also likely to be laid, as with mines, ahead of an operation, such as in mounting or resisting an amphibious approach, in order to shape a prospective operating area or to reduce the freedom of action of a potential opponent. Submarines are likely to find them a significant challenge.

Submariners do not like mines[11] at all – unless they have laid them themselves.[12] Improvised explosive devices (IEDs) have been the means by which major powers have had their freedom of manoeuvre constrained in recent campaigns in Iraq and Afghanistan, and Israel in Lebanon. The lesson will not have been lost. IEDs and mines will continue to be developed for use at sea and become even more widely available, where increasingly sophisticated variants will target specific platforms and employ advanced counter-detection and counter-clearance measures. They are particularly effective against submarines. They are also attractive as an asymmetric option in the littoral, where even primitive mines pose a significant sea denial capability and a substantial threat to maritime forces, including amphibious forces and inshore submarine operations. In addition, IEDs operated remotely or in a suicide attack will pose a threat to major platforms transiting choke points and when in port.

In the twenty-first century, the desire by states to control more of their EEZs is likely to lead to an increased use of defensive mines, both in wartime and in peacetime, to deter and defeat approaches by hostile, competitive or inquisitive states. In particular, they are a simple, cheap way of denying an opponent sea-space and deterring vessels from exercising their rights of innocent or transit passage through waters over which a country wants to exercise jurisdiction. Furthermore, it would be a reasonable, legal and politically irritating tactic for a country, seeking to exclude traffic from a sensitive

---

[11] A very high proportion of submarines, from all countries, was sunk or damaged by mines in both world wars.

[12] Even then they are not safe. A Pakistani submarine, which was laying mines ahead of the departure of the Indian carrier *Vikrant* from Chittagong harbour during the 1971 Indo-Pakistani War, managed to detonate one of its own carefully placed mines.

zone, to declare minefields at regular intervals, through which vessels would pass at their own peril. If so, incidents similar to that in the Corfu Channel in 1946 are possible, when British warships exercised the right of innocent passage through the strait, but were attacked by Albanian shore batteries. Two destroyers were mined and badly damaged in a subsequent transit.

In the future, mines with greater detection ranges and target discrimination are likely to be made of composite materials that will be difficult to detect by sonar alone, such as non-metallic and anechoic coatings. They will incorporate the facility to bury themselves in the seabed. Far from being static, they will become increasingly mobile, able to engage targets through the use of rocket or torpedo technology, pioneered by the US Mk 60 Captor mine, which lay dormant until a target was detected on acoustic sensors, whereupon a homing torpedo would be released. Unmanned vehicles, as well as being used for countermeasures, will increasingly be employed as mobile mines.

Most effective in protecting vital areas, such as ports, bases and access routes, mines are likely to be linked to extensive arrays of sensors, both acoustic and non-acoustic, which will be positioned on the seabed and within the water column. They will be collocated with sampling and other multidisciplinary sensing tools, able to detect anything from tsunamis to penetrations by submarines.

However, weakness and vulnerability to mines are likely to be addressed in the twenty-first century through the development of active 3D close-range sonar imaging and through the more intensive use of UUVs. In particular, it is likely that all warships will have tethered and autonomous unmanned[13] vehicles that will deploy ahead of their parent ships to establish whether an area is clear of mines and the coast is clear. Currently, as the saying goes, every ship can be a mine-hunter – once.

NUCLEAR WEAPONS AT SEA

There are a substantial number of nuclear weapons at sea, most of them fitted to intercontinental ballistic missiles in nuclear submarines. They are designed to deter would-be opponents from launching an overwhelming

---

[13] Autonomous vehicles, such as the 3.6-m (12-ft) long Knifefish, will enter service with the US Navy in 2017 to replace the previous use of marine mammals as mine detectors.

attack on a country, either nuclear or conventional. The logic is that the costs to an opponent should outweigh any possible advantage that he might gain as a result of his actions.

Other notable maritime nuclear weapons are those that are fitted to Russian naval missiles and torpedoes,[14] and it is possible that the Chinese have some deployed at sea as well. These arrangements suggest that they are not simply deterrent weapons. However, apart from the bellicose rhetoric of North Korea's regime, none of the nuclear powers in the current geostrategic balance of advantage seem disposed to contemplate, threaten or emphasise their potential for nuclear war-fighting.

Nevertheless, in 2005, a People's Liberation Army general, Zhu Chenghu, told a *Wall Street Journal* reporter, 'If the Americans target their missiles and position-guided ammunition on China's territory, I think we will have to respond with nuclear weapons.' When China fired missiles in the direction of Taiwan in response to a visit to the USA by Taiwan's president in 1995, America dispatched a carrier battle group to the region, and General Xiong Guangkai promptly said that China would attack the USA – possibly with nuclear weapons – if a confrontation over Taiwan occurred. He added, 'In the end, you care more about Los Angeles than you do about Taipei.'

As these officers were neither dismissed nor publicly reprimanded, it is clear that the Chinese Communist Party (CCP) is content to promote uncertainty about its intentions with respect to its nuclear release plans. In reality, China remains weak in relation to the USA in overall conventional combat power and needs to trail the potential use of nuclear weapons while it finds the means to deter and defeat the USA in conventional encounters and engagements.

Even so, there would appear to be significantly more risk of a nuclear device being used at sea than against land targets. The regime of a regional power with nuclear weapons that is in future threatened with the over-whelming conventional firepower of the USA could resort to nuclear weapons to offset its conventional inferiority. Such might be the case in response to the deployment of carrier battle groups or large concentrations of war

[14] Hans M. Kristensen, *Non-Strategic Nuclear Weapons*, Federation of American Scientists, Special Report No. 3 (May 2012), page 53, http://www.fas.org/_docs/Non_Strategic_Nuclear_Weapons.pdf.

materiel in transit to an operational theatre, especially in circumstances (at sea) where the potential perpetrator might believe the effect and subsequent political (and physical) fallout to be containable.

Another aspect of the nuclear issue is that the debate and theory about nuclear deterrence use have until now been conditioned and framed by the strategic relationship that existed during the Cold War, between the USA and NATO on the one hand and Russia on the other. With new players, such as India, Pakistan, China, North Korea and potentially Iran, that calculus might have changed without anyone noticing, or refining the original model.

Where the international community has found difficulty has been in dealing with a rogue regime, or elements within it, which commits an offence against accepted norms of behaviour between states, but possesses nuclear weapons. It is worth remembering that on 26 March 2010, a North Korean submarine torpedoed and sank a South Korean warship (the *Cheonan*), killing forty-six of its ship's company. By any standards, this would normally be considered an act of war, following on from the numerous incursions by North Korean mini-submarines into South Korean territorial seas (exemplified by the wreck and capture of one in September 1996). However, it is significant that international responses, led by the USA, sought to defuse tensions with an acknowledged nuclear-capable regime and to apply further sanctions. One is left to wonder whether this approach would have been adopted if the regime had not possessed nuclear weapons, or whether Iran – in its present non-nuclear posture – would have been treated in the same way in similar circumstances.

The worry must be that states, particularly those with an authoritarian and confrontational approach to international relations, would seek to commit various acts with impunity, including the encouragement of terrorism and proxy forces, under the cover of their nuclear capability.

TOWARDS 2025 AND BEYOND

Warfare at sea will be very much as one might expect in the short term – the future will be very much 'like the present, only more so',[15] as developing world capabilities converge with those of the developed world. The next

---

[15] In Colin Gray's memorable phrase.

fifteen or so years will see several countries acquire major warships such as aircraft carriers, nuclear submarines and powerful amphibious capabilities, allowing them to deploy outside their immediate region for large-scale exercises and extended operations, which may present substantial regional challenges to established maritime powers.

Advanced technologies will be available to those states and groups able to pay the appropriate price; an increasing variety of fire-and-forget and autonomous systems will obviate the need for specialist training and tactical acuity. Warfare will be characterised by weapons and systems that will deny naval forces access to parts of the ocean, which will only be overcome with prohibitive levels of resources, attrition and loss of operational tempo. In addition, a major challenge will be to maintain weapons and sensor effectiveness in the face of increasingly capable and powerful electronic denial and disruption systems.

The period towards the mid-2020s will be dominated by the use of unmanned vehicles and cooperative technologies, along with access to space-based services for surveillance and targeting. The use of precision munitions will mean that it will be possible to strike vessels and targets at extended ranges, with accurate and increasingly destructive weapons. Traditional forms of force protection and projection will become obsolete in the face of advanced technologies: increasingly lethal ballistic, cruise and supersonic missiles; more silent, high-endurance nuclear and AIP ocean-going submarines and a range of unmanned, anti-access and sea denial systems. Nor should the threat from chemical, biological and radiological weapons be discounted, especially when linked to compound materials and nanoscale features.

As such, the first half of the twenty-first century looks set to be an age of strategic brinkmanship at sea, punctuated with periodic episodes of confrontation over disputed claims and unilateral attempts to close down the freedom of the seas by existing and emerging powers. The international system of conventions and legal instruments that exists to harmonise competing jurisdictions, contain ambitions and settle disputes will also come under pressure.

However, the balance of capabilities in the various regions of the world, including the substantial power of the USA, and the considerable risks of escalation, mean that general war and fleet actions between the major powers are unlikely. No one will be able to deliver the knock-out blow. In spite of this, there are probably going to be a series of 'encounter' actions that will involve confrontation and armed exchanges between individual units and groups of units engaged in testing the limits of national tolerance with regard to assumed rights to resources or sea-space. In these circumstances, it is likely that there will be frequent altercations between, and losses of, unmanned vehicles in the front line of maritime disputes. One can envisage bloodless confrontations in which the direct combat functions are between machines. More traditional conflict is possible between regional rivals, most immediately in the Asia-Pacific region, but also in relation to unresolved issues in the greater Middle East and Africa.

If it comes to blows, the operational imperative at sea in the future will be on holding potential opponents at risk at the greatest distance possible – a consistent trend in naval warfare since the early days, when ramming and boarding were necessary tactics as ships were incapable of elaborate manoeuvres and the range of firepower was limited. In modern conflicts, distance can be kept through the use of long-range surveillance assets and weapons capable of dealing with hostile platforms and launch systems before they are able to engage, to the extent that opponents at sea are increasingly unlikely to see each other in the future. This trend will be accelerated and enabled by integrated surveillance and weapon systems located in a wide variety of locations and vessels.

It seems probable that the trend for warship design will be for simple, cheaper hulls with common propulsion and power generation modules, as well as plug-and-play electrical and data highways that can accept a wide range of modular applications, also allowing the use of manned and unmanned vehicles. This approach would also allow warships to be configured more appropriately and cost-effectively for peacetime and wartime roles. They will be complemented by large-hulled mother ships, some of which will be carriers and large amphibious ships, capable of deploying a range of well-armed manned and unmanned vehicles, as well as sensors.

Also, increasing numbers of warfare functions will be based in submersible or semi-submersible platforms, in order to reduce the vulnerabilities of surface ships to highly manoeuvrable transonic and hypersonic missiles. Conversely, it is probable that submarines and underwater craft are likely to find that their ability to remain undetected below the surface will be challenged by the presence of a range of unmanned vehicles, denial systems (predominantly mines and other barrier systems) and wide-area sensor arrays. These will include both dormant and active elements, some with the ability to track, classify and engage when necessary.

From about 2025 to 2030, things will begin to change radically at sea. New technologies will dominate the design and operation of surface ships, with increased power generation available to a wide range of energy-hungry systems. Greatly increased computing and processing power will enhance the performance and fidelity of sensor systems, such as radars, electro-optical devices and sonars. The introduction of directed-energy weapons (DEWs), electromagnetic rail guns and possibly coil guns (see Chapter 6) is likely to enable the cost-effective engagement of a wide range of high-performance offensive missiles and projectiles. Unmanned, hypersonic and space-based defensive systems will have proliferated and nanotechnology will provide solutions to both protective and deceptive requirements, in the form of non-reflective coatings, composite materials and swarming off-board decoy devices. These new technologies will have a transformative effect on the offensive and defensive capabilities of warships in the above-water environment, with the balance of advantage shifting towards defence.

The generation and storage of large amounts of electrical power will possibly lead to the development of active force fields, as well as mirrored and other reflective surfaces and coatings that will deflect the impact of DE. There will also be disruptive technologies such as high-endurance, autonomous underwater vehicles (AUVs), anti-satellite options and electromagnetic and cyber penetrators. Meanwhile, the seabed will be used extensively for the basing of a wide range of weapons, communications and cooperative networks, as well as the site for power grids and sensor arrays.

All this will result in fewer people being at sea in the future, just as the numbers of personnel required to man a warship in the days of sail were dramatically reduced once the transition to mechanically powered vessels was completed. In the first place, a great many roles currently carried out by sea-based platforms will be conducted from the land, in particular functions such as routine surveillance, traffic control and the identification of vessels that do not identify themselves on automatic information systems. UAVs in particular will take over many of the functions associated with maritime patrol and remote sensor operation. The application of automation, AI and robotics will further drive down numbers. The effect will be to de-risk a wide variety of functions for human beings, especially in the categories of 'dull, dangerous, deep and dirty' tasks.

No one has yet demonstrated the ability to predict the future accurately, especially in relation to warfare and technological progress. However, many of the trends that will dominate maritime warfare in the twenty-first century are already under way and will frame any unexpected technological or operational breakthroughs that occur. Throughout the transition from the Age of Sail to that of Steam, to that of Information, the conduct of warfare at sea has been in the process of constant evolution and refinement, punctuated by bursts of revolutionary change in times of war. There is no indication that the pace at sea is going to slacken in any way as the world moves beyond the Information age to whatever awaits it in the next era.

A lesson from the past is that it is important for established maritime powers to maintain at least technological parity, if not superiority, if they are to sustain a favourable situation at sea, as the British found out in the early twentieth century, when it no longer had the resources to defend every part of an empire built and sustained by sea power. The successes of Japanese offensives at the start of the Pacific War in 1941 were a direct consequence of Britain's failure to remember that sea power needs investment and attention to the changing strategic context. During the course of the twenty-first century, the danger for developed countries will be that they cede dominance at sea in the same way that the Ming dynasty chose to turn away from the sea, leaving the way clear for the Portuguese, the Dutch and other European powers to exploit the subsequent power vacuum.

CHAPTER TEN

What's a Country to Do?

'If a man does not know to what port he is
steering, no wind is favourable to him.'[1]

'Sailors, with their built-in sense of order, service, and
discipline, should really be running the world.'[2]

We are all used to viewing the world from the perspective of the Prime Meridian – the Greenwich Meridian – on which almost all maps and charts are based. However, we need to start paying more attention to the International Date Line , exactly on the other side of the world, where it runs irregularly down through the Pacific. Viewed from this angle, the strategic seascape of the twenty-first century is much clearer. Asia, particularly China, and the USA face each other across the Pacific in the same way that the USA and the Soviet Union used to face each other across the Atlantic. This perspective places the Middle Kingdom – appropriately – in the middle and consigns Europe and the UK to the furthest reaches of the left-hand side. Britain is, as the Romans viewed it, ultima Thule, again on the very edge of the known world.

This strategic geography will be the context within which a complex, multi-layered relationship of cooperation and competition will flow around the major powers of the twenty-first century. With strategic deterrence based primarily on financial and commercial codependence, China and the USA

---

[1] Seneca, *Letters (Epistolae), LXXI, 3.*
[2] Nicholas Monsarrat, accessed from http://www.bluemooners.com/sailingquotes.htm 23 April 2014.

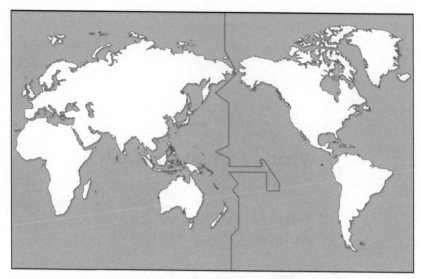

The world map, from the perspective of the International Date Line.

will compete at every other level of engagement: for markets, for influence, for resources and for strategic advantage. Other powers will try to accommodate their interests into this duopoly as best they can, within a constantly shifting assessment of risk and opportunity in support of national interest. Some of this complexity is apparent already. Countries such as Australia, Malaysia and Singapore have had to adjust and reconcile the balance of their commercial and strategic interests dynamically, as political circumstances and their economic interests dictate. It is difficult when China is your biggest trading partner and the USA the protector of your political independence.

The reverse perspective is also striking for another reason. With the vast expanse of the Pacific taking centre stage, the colour of the map is overwhelmingly blue, emphasising the continuing importance and relevance of the sea. Commentators casually speak of the Great Game[3] that is anticipated in the Arctic or as a revived sport in its traditional stamping ground of Central Asia. The Great Game is already being played out in the twenty-first century, not in the remote North or in Central Asia but at sea.

A state or community, and its individuals, choose to go to sea, mostly for profit, sometimes for pleasure or as a result of compulsion, and always

[3] Traditionally, the Great Game referred to the conflict between the British and Russian empires for supremacy in Central Asia during the nineteenth century.

in expectation. Of course, by virtue of its nature, the sea is generally less amenable and accessible to humans than the land; it takes some effort to be there. Being at sea is a temporary accommodation with a medium, which, if not hostile, has infinite ways of expressing why mankind should perhaps not be there. Engagement with the sea has always been, and will remain, a fine judgement about the shifting balance of risk and reward.

In the past, there were significant technical barriers, including that of access to the requisite vessels and skills, to intervening much beyond the shorelines or inshore waters of the world. Today, and increasingly in the future, technology will lower the entry level and enable more states, groups and individuals to operate at sea, both legitimately and illegally. An example has already been seen with the network-enabled pirates off Somalia, who have been enabled to operate far out to sea by GPS, Internet technologies, mobile phones and satellite communications, at distances up to 1,200 nm (2,220 km) from their coast.

The constantly repeated lesson of history is that control over – or guaranteed access to – the resources vital to human development (energy, food, water and raw materials) and the routes along which they travel remain vital strategic interests for states, if they are to prosper. It is not necessary to possess the resources themselves, but essential to retain the ability to obtain them at reasonable prices, take them away, add value through manufacture and convey them to markets. Also, any country that wishes to exert hard power and influence in the world needs to maintain secure access to the sea, either on its own or through its allies, in order to deploy its military instrument of power, its armed forces. As the relative importance of resources and routes change over time, so too should strategic priorities and investment.

Consequently, states will need to be watchful to ensure that their decisions about geostrategic priorities and investment of their national, human and material capital are in harmony with emerging trends and future contexts. As has been seen, the discovery and exploitation of vast quantities of shale gas and other unconventional sources will diversify the sources of high-calorie energy products. This trend alone will significantly alter the familiar pattern of geostrategic relationships and determine the relative importance of various trade routes. It will also alter long-held perceptions about geostrategic alignments and priorities. The USA, with projected energy self-sufficiency and a substantial energy export sector by 2035, is likely to find its focus on the Gulf firstly blurring and then weakening, once its dependence on oil and gas from the region diminishes, and its interest in other areas growing. Other regions and countries have also found – and will continue to find – energy sources closer to home, with implications for manufacturing and markets. Assumptions will also need to change with regard to basic human energy security, such as food and water, whose growing importance to the global economy is likely to result in the emergence of new shipping and trading patterns. Other critical sea routes might be less apparent to the casual observer. In the future, underwater pipelines, integrated electrical grids and distribution networks and extremely high-volume data-bearing cables will also be the routes by which globalisation is demonstrated, exploited and extended. Most will be sited at sea. These will need protection and regulation in much the same way as the traditional sea lines of communication.

The security and stability of the sea are conditioned by the simple fact that it belongs to no single state and gives unhindered access to almost everywhere in the world. The key attribute of sea power is that it is possible for states to control all or parts of the sea for their own benefit and deny it to others. Although the USA has maintained security at sea since the end of the Second World War, its ability to continue in this role in the face of challenges from rising and regional powers, not to mention corporate and criminal raiders, is open to question. If the open system of trading is to be protected and sustained, the USA will have to forge coalitions with the willing (and able) among both commercial concerns and states. It simply cannot cover all the bases on its own and will necessarily concentrate its power on prevailing in those circumstances where its national interests are at stake. To continue the analogy, others will have to step up to the plate.

When they do, there will be a more even balance of military power across the world. Dominant powers in various regions will assert themselves, while other countries will accommodate their interests in either cooperative or competitive ways, depending on the advantages to be gained or the risks mitigated. Nor should we take globalisation for granted because we are living in a 'globalised' present, based on the existing free circulation of goods, peoples, ideas and technology. We cannot assume that people, institutions and things will relate to each other in the same way in the future. Past experience, especially the last much-trumpeted period of globalisation (between

1870 and 1914), proves that those whom God has joined together, the tide of history has an unhappy knack of putting asunder. In these circumstances, where regionalisation superimposes itself onto globalisation, significant benefits will, of course, accrue to those countries able to project hard sea power beyond their immediate area, in the form of expeditionary capabilities, to assist and support friends, build commercial relationships and to deter and coerce potential opponents. They will also gain political advantage and broader influence by their contributions to regional security, their role in development and their responses to humanitarian relief and development programmes. The appearance of USS *Abraham Lincoln* off Banda Aceh in response to the tsunami of 2004 transformed the American-Indonesian relationship.

In the second decade of the twenty-first century, the sea is assuming a renewed importance in the deliberations and decisions of states. Mainly, this reflects the massive expansion of trade and economic activity, which, together with the resources of the sea, offers opportunities and routes to prosperity and, for some countries, recovery and sustained growth. That is because the sea is a manoeuvre space for business, for soft sea power, as well as deterrence and warfare, with more flexibility for investment and innovation than on land, coupled with less regulation and oversight. Its remote and restless character enables those operating there and mastering its moods to transcend some of the less dynamic processes associated with the bureaucracy of states and economic communities. 'Who are so free as the sons of the wave?', as the traditional British naval anthem 'Heart of Oak' has it.

As the twenty-first century unfolds, governments, regimes and companies will seek to secure and exploit the resources of offshore zones to an unprecedented degree. In addition, they will compete with other states and companies in identifying and exploiting the resources of the open oceans and take advantage of the access provided by the sea to engage aggressively in global trade. Countries will continue to guard their sovereign rights jealously, discharge their responsibilities to their advantage and protect their political and economic interests in their offshore zones in an era of increasing maritime encroachment and intensifying competition. Meanwhile, there will be a concerted drive by responsible states and communities of interest to invest to a greater or lesser extent in technologies and practices that encourage sustainable development and diversification of economic supply, in a world whose growing population will continue to consume huge amounts of both organic and inorganic resources.

In response, each state will need to plot a course through a complex pattern of fluctuating international allegiances, resource pressures and complex trade patterns. States will compete economically with allies and fight wars alongside competitors, when circumstances and national interests demand. We have seen that the next ten years at least are likely to be characterised by a largely secure and permissive international system at sea, in which states will generally cooperate, but compete for strategic and regional advantage both within – and around – the edges of international maritime law. States will seek to secure and exploit the resources of their economic zones, while maximising the opportunities provided by the sea to promote trade, conduct warfare and provide security for their societies. In addition, in conjunction with commercial concerns, they will compete to secure rights over the resources of the wider global commons. In these circumstances, it will be important for those states that benefit most from globalisation to continue to assert the rights of the commons and demonstrate their commitment to the principles of the freedom of navigation and innocent and transit passage, right up to the limits of territorial seas prescribed by the United Nations Convention on the Law of the Sea (UNCLOS). It will be necessary to preserve *mare liberum* and resist the attempts at imposing *mare clausum*.

GRAND STRATEGY

In order to thrive in the twenty-first century, a country with an interest in the use of the sea needs to develop and implement a coherent maritime strategy – galvanising the sea power of the state and society. A national maritime strategy defines fundamentally a state's long-term future relationship and engagement with the sea and involves the comprehensive integration of all those elements and partnerships – military, commercial and institutional – that can advance its interests. This strategy should identify the risks and opportunities that lie ahead and bring together all aspects of the country's maritime activities, ambitions and aspirations in a comprehensive, joined-up vision. Only then can priorities for investment – the numbers of warships, the size of a fishing fleet and energy projects – and the scale of national effort be legitimately established.

But, before tackling a maritime strategy, a country needs to develop a Grand Strategy, one that establishes across government and society the sort of country that its people want and how it intends to shape its future. A Grand Strategy should be a joined-up, comprehensive approach to determining and championing a country's future interests by all government departments and national interests, based on a reasonable and reasoned assessment of the future context within which a country will operate. In practice, a country can only in the most general sense make itself ready for the future, which will be shaped by long-term trends, some of which are only partly visible and recognisable from day-to-day, amid today's international and strategic situation.

A country that does not attempt to view the future as accurately as possible is unlikely to have a future that is worthwhile in the long term. Like any successful company, it has to have a vision. This requires an intelligent analysis of likely futures, along with an assessment of likely risks and opportunities across the whole range of national interests. It is simply not good enough, in either strategic or military terms, to just take an interest as far as the horizon, which for politicians in democratic societies is effectively the next election. The need to provide a coherent assessment of the future is not so that anyone can fool people that they can predict the future; there are simply too many variables and unforeseeable factors. Nevertheless, it is necessary to provide a frame of reference within which decisions in the national interest can be made in response to events, risks and opportunities.

Examination of this future context will enable governments to establish what policies are viable, what resources are available and what is practicable in political and strategic terms. A government should attempt to reconcile ends (what the public and politicians want), means (what they can afford) and ways (the ability of the country to deliver, in human, practical and technological terms). Countries need take into account the outcomes that its population or regime seek to achieve, the human, geographic and material resources available and the practical measures and instruments of state power that can be exploited to create and sustain geopolitical advantage. This approach also identifies where additional investment (means) should be directed, such as skills, infrastructure and technological development, to achieve the ends that the contextual analysis of the future suggests are desirable and possible. When these elements (ends, ways and means) are out of balance, programmes and public spending tend to be incoherent and wasteful and investment misdirected. Ultimately, the issue is the balance between policy, resources and capability. If a country does not have agile, capable and coherent instruments of state power at its disposal, it will not be able to respond to the world's opportunities and risks, let alone cope with the strategic shocks that seem likely to punctuate a complex, fast-moving strategic landscape in the future.

For example, a modern British Grand Strategy that started from first principles would most likely identify that the country's vital national interests lie in an open world economy and access to international trade and investment. Its outlook is instinctively global – a welcome legacy of empire, its economic interests and its investments – and 8 million of its citizens are to be found all over the world. It already has the advantage of English as the global language for international exchange and association, as well as being the most widely used means of expression on the Internet. The UK also has a range of connections and cultural ties with what can loosely be termed the Anglo-sphere – Canada, Australia, New Zealand and many other instinctively Anglophone territories – and its trade with the Commonwealth is thriving, with member states collectively exporting more than £1.5 trillion ($2.52 trillion) of goods and services each year. However, one cannot simply turn one's back on established links. In an era of globalisation, the relationships with Europe, the Gulf and the USA magnify UK influence with Beijing, Brasília, New Delhi and Singapore. A country needs to recognise that reaching out to a globalised world of possibilities lies at the heart of a mentality that sees opportunities in every corner of the Earth.

A coherent Grand Strategy ensures that squabbling government departments and vested interests can be tamed; ambitious officials and self-seeking military officers will have their scope for personal manoeuvre restricted and resources can be allocated where they best suit the achievement of the strategic aim, which should always be the national interest. Grand Strategy also means that there is always a reference point for decision-making and a heading to which the ship of state can be returned if it is knocked off course by unexpected crises or events.

Within the armed forces, a strategic approach can damp down the inter-Service squabbles that simmer during normal times and ignite during periodic defence reviews. At such times, the national interest is frequently subordinated to atavistic loyalties and vested interests (both military and industrial), which can result in levels of competition approaching those of sectarian warfare. Another major weakness with the system is the lack of military expertise at the political level, which results in there being no 'intelligent customer', able to weigh the quality and impartiality of military advice. All too often, officers tell politicians what they think they want to hear, and politicians fail to ask the right questions about what they are told.

Finally, there may be a case for taking some strategic issues out of the rough and tumble of 'here today, gone tomorrow' democratic processes for those important national issues like health, energy, transport and defence that require a long-term view rather than one shaped by party political considerations. Perhaps the task could be given to an impartial, independent body[4] and kept under constant review to assess its continued relevance and balance of ends, ways and means. In the case of defence, politicians and military grandees would then deliver against the strategic plan, while everyday politics sorts out the associated policy, resource allocations and achievement of the required outcomes. This approach might also stimulate a more intelligent and engaged public debate and a degree of true democratic consensus. Otherwise, a defence strategy is likely to change with every new administration or government, with the consequent uncertainties in defence procurement, capability and manning levels.

DEVELOPING A MARITIME STRATEGY

Countries often assess their opportunities and risks in relation to the sea in discrete, stove-piped terms. Thus, the naval aspect is addressed by Defence; shipping and ports by Transport; energy by Energy (and Climate Change), fishing by some vague Environment and Food ministry and so on. This fragmentary, disjointed and a-strategic approach is compounded by the fact that in most cases the separate departments and ministries are competing for scarce resources and preserving existing power-bases.

As with Grand Strategy, a coherent maritime strategy identifies and establishes the ends that are sought by engagement with the sea, the resources

---

[4] In the UK, it might be a Royal Commission or a Special Committee of the Privy Council.

that can be committed to achieve them and the distinctive ways in which they can be realised in the face of stiff competition and opposition. Above all, a country's approach to sea power should accurately reflect its distinctive culture and attributes, which include its physical assets, its heritage and national mythology. Specifically, a maritime strategy should determine and propose how best to ensure that a country's territorial seas and economic zone are to be managed and exploited in a secure, responsible and sustainable way. Those countries that can provide secure, stable offshore zones and maintain coherent regulatory, taxation and legal regimes for their exclusive economic zones (EEZs) are likely to attract inward investment and enterprise. This not only applies to substantial oil and gas reserves, but extends to other resources, such as leisure and tourism, fishing and renewable energy, as well as clean water, sustainable ecosystems and resources such as shallow water in which to build settlements and offshore infrastructure. The issue of invulnerability from the worst that Mother Nature can inflict, in the form of rising sea levels, extreme weather events, earthquakes and tsunamis, will also be a major consideration.

With respect to the wider world, a maritime strategy should identify the country's interest in where it could most profitably and effectively exploit the sea, both as a highway and as a resource. It also needs to be remembered that the residual overseas possessions of the USA, the UK and France (and others) all confer extensive EEZs and other proprietary rights, which are often regarded as anachronisms, as self-indulgent outposts and relics of empire. Some are military bases and stepping stones that allow strategic reach (such as Gibraltar and Ascension Island, for the UK, in supporting the Falkland Islands), while Guam and other Pacific island territories will form the basis of US strategic engagement in that region for some time to come. However, these overseas territories (and their EEZs) are also commercially and economically exploitable assets, as has been seen with hydrocarbon discoveries off the Falklands and French Guiana, which require more than passing quixotic interest, in the form of presence, involvement and investment. Who knows what might be going on behind your back? In some cases, it is a lot of illegal fishing.

Once again, the harmonisation of ends (outcomes), ways (practicality) and means (resources, both human and material) can determine the extent to which investment in the sea can benefit a country. Its influence should impart a strategic approach to the programmes in every sector of society and the economy to ensure a properly joined-up coherent plan for the future that incorporates environmental, economic, social and security factors. Maritime, especially naval, capability does not exist in isolation; it translates directly into – and links with – political, diplomatic and economic influence. The requirements emanating from different departments or ministries can be harmonised, prioritised and de-conflicted, with a rigorous scrutiny of what best suits a maritime strategy and the return that the country would receive by investment.

Britain has shown in the past how a strategic approach can work. The coherent administration of naval and military logistics in the long eighteenth century, from food supply to arms manufacturing, was crucial to military and strategic success. Despite the weaknesses of the political system, the British state had the necessary reservoir of bureaucratic and administrative ability to harness its national resources, including its fleet, and link them to the support of trade. By contrast, neither France nor Spain gave shipping and commerce sufficient priority, in part because merchants and shipowners, excluded from political power, were unable to influence policy or resource allocation. The key to Britain's success was the unique engagement between the state, the commercial sector, the maritime community and the sea during the emergence of an integrated state and society that was at one with the sea.

In essence, a country should be able to examine the strengths of its human, physical, material and informational resources and determine where they might best be applied to make the most of the sea. In particular, it should identify those key trends that lead into the future and should apply technology and intellectual effort to those areas that will be the most suited to innovative and market-leading approaches. Today, one might consider emerging requirements, such as coastal engineering, subsea infrastructure, polar operations and unmanned systems, as suitable areas for development and exploitation, as well as in pioneering areas of naval technology. Overall, in those areas where it can compete, a country should, with vigour; but just as in commerce, if another country's assets can do something cheaper, more productively or efficiently, then it makes sense to accept that and use them.

Needless to say, at a time of extreme and accelerating technological development, it is necessary for governments and commercial concerns to continue to invest in targeted research and development, not only in support of innovation, but also in providing the capacity to counter decisive and disruptive technologies that are likely to emerge, both as competitive commercial products and in the military sphere. Research and investment need to be accompanied by active intelligence and data-gathering operations that target the sources of emerging threat technologies and industries, as well as the commercial competition. We are in a world characterised by crowdsourcing, whistle-blowers and open architectures, an environment in which few secrets are safe.

A maritime strategy that translates into real political, diplomatic and economic benefit nowadays is one that enables a country to exploit the advantages of globalisation in all its forms. As well as providing the ways in which threats to the country are deterred and defeated, armed forces are actively used to further a country's commercial and national interests in the wider world. If necessary, this means demonstrating commitment to one's friends (and by extension the markets they represent), however temporary the relationship might be, and standing with them, in harm's way if necessary, in the face of the armed flouting of international maritime law or of imminent aggression.

In this regard, it needs to be remembered that the willingness and preparedness to use force are vital components of deterrence, particularly in those circumstances, to recall Trotsky's memorable phrase, when you might not be interested in war, but war might be interested in you. Unless 'might is right' is to return as a familiar principle of international relations, its practice has to be confronted. A key issue for governments is whether, in the twenty-first century, they would be prepared to use their navies in support of economic activity in a less than benign environment, in the way both Dutch and British warships were needed in the seventeenth century to protect their respective fishing fleets during peacetime. In the 1980s, the transit of neutral shipping was threatened by Iran seeking to exert pressure on the international community by controlling access through the Strait of Hormuz. The US reaction was unhesitatingly straightforward, involving the re-flagging of eleven Kuwaiti ships as American, with US crews, and their escort through the disputed waters in the face of armed Iranian opposition. These choices will probably need to be made again in the future. Wherever there is trouble, the USA will be looking for its allies and friends to support its protection of the international system and those countries that do not volunteer are likely to find themselves marginalised not only politically and economically, but also in US military counsels and markets. Countries in the Gulf region are looking round for friends as the greater Middle East region looks pregnant with crisis possibilities.

Clearly, there are also close, mutually reinforcing links between national security and economic well-being. A healthy economy underpins stability and security and facilitates the pursuit of national interests through all instruments of state power: diplomatic, economic and military. Paul Kennedy's understanding was that a country's sea power was a function and result of its economic strength.[5] That is perhaps too simple an assessment and there is a more intricately woven relationship between the two, with the reverse being equally true. Strength at sea remains critical to supporting national economic advantage and strategic influence. If managed wisely, the mutually reinforcing relationship can offer pretty good value for money over the long term.

LOOKING THROUGH THE WRONG END OF THE TELESCOPE

As indicated above, most countries have a major stake in the security of the sea, by virtue of its status in international law, as a free and secure trading system that delivers 95 per cent of goods traded by volume and as the means to support allies and friends. The need for a navy is obvious to societies when threatened with invasion, blockade or price inflation with regard to staple goods, such as oil and food, caused by disruptions in the global seagoing supply chain. It rarely occurs to them that the use of the sea is the most politically flexible, economical and least offensive way (for most of the time) of providing support to friends and allies. As we saw in Chapter 3, in threatening or using force, a navy allows a graduated choice of responses from presence to war that can be escalated or relaxed indefinitely, according to events and circumstances.

In recent years, Western democracies have sought to reduce the proportion of public expenditure afforded to defence in the face of burgeoning costs

[5] Paul Kennedy, *The Rise and Fall of British Sea Power* (1976).

of government, social programmes and national infrastructures during the significant global economic recession in 2007–8. The harsh fiscal climate means that armed forces will have to demonstrate continuing relevance to the outcomes that a national Grand Strategy requires. They will have to demonstrate their affordability and cost-effectiveness against other forms of political influence and justify the considerable resource investment in human skills and hard-edged capability. Armed forces should be smarter at showing how they deliver outcomes and 'turn a profit' in strategic terms.

Part of the problem lies in the fact that, in many states, although politicians and public are aware of the nominal input costs of defence and naval provision, they are generally ignorant of the output benefits, in economic terms. Sea power, in particular, is perceived as an overhead or a cost, rather than an enabler of so many other political, diplomatic and economic benefits. Certainly, politicians take a keen interest when national policy affects their constituencies and (re-) electoral chances. Both in the USA and in the UK (and in many other countries), both procurement and infrastructure decisions are an uneasy and not always satisfactory balance between the requirements of national defence, value for money and local electorally loaded and influenced considerations. More than ever before, countries will need to identify the output benefits that are gained by investment in armed forces and, in particular, in the use of navies and other joint assets used at sea. Some benefits will always, inevitably, be unpredictable and unforeseen, because that is the way of the future, but cost and benefit analyses are not difficult and should lie at the heart of public accountability, even, or perhaps especially, in the areas of security and defence. If those outputs are not precisely calibrated, articulated and understood, it is a sure sign that the process of strategic thought and development has been imperfect.

For European navies in particular, ground needs to be made up. The slow drawdown from the Cold War and a succession of wars of choice by US and other leading democracies diverted attention away from the sea. This strategic myopia was compounded by the way in which developed world governments introduced largely incoherent defence reductions, with little regard for strategic coherence and the balance of forces. An atmosphere of structural disarmament by successive governments, unrelated to objective strategic assessments of risks and opportunities, still lies heavily on many

European countries and threatens the USA as well. The 'peace dividend' was spent a long time ago and, in some cases, many times over.

It is argued here that, instead of reducing the capacity of navies, governments should realise the extent to which naval capability translates directly into political, economic and diplomatic power. Any country with maritime forces is able to deploy and intervene at times and places of choice in order to advance its interests. As such, a navy should be seen and used as an investment, just as any other insurance policy sometimes can lead to a tangible benefit. Properly coordinated with other instruments of national and maritime power within a coherent Grand Strategy, it offers a versatile, cost-effective means of influencing decisions and events across the world and a vital enabler for national resilience, reach and prosperity in an increasingly competitive and uncertain world.

'SEA BLINDNESS'

Nevertheless, navies themselves need to do a better job of selling themselves to the public whose interests they represent. Navies find it extremely difficult to explain how peace and order at sea do not keep themselves and how, if they did not exist, it would be necessary to invent them. It is assumed by public opinion in many countries that because nothing untoward occurs at sea, it is its natural and normal state. In reality, the sea is the world's greatest expanse of unregulated space. It is often a case of out of sight, out of mind and what in the UK is called 'sea blindness', an inability to see the opportunities and risks represented by the sea. American Admiral John S. McCain said in 1964, 'You seldom hear of the fleets except when there is trouble, and then you hear a lot'.[6] Some would say that armed forces justify themselves, their size, shape and money expended on them, solely by their role in deterring and defeating threats. As Thomas Hardy wrote, 'War makes rattling good history, but peace is poor reading.'[7] The situation is made worse by the inability of the average citizen to appreciate what goes on beyond the horizon. For the British, this is especially surprising as the dominance of

[6] In the *Norfolk Star Ledger* of 4 August 1964. Admiral McCain is the father of the John McCain, who is a US naval air veteran, Senator for Arizona and Presidential candidate in 2008.
[7] *The Dynasts* ii (1906).

British sea power depended on a distinctively deep well of public support across the whole of society and on the country's strong attachment to a stirring view of its actual and mythical past. But often, 'it is customary in democratic countries to deplore expenditures on armaments as conflicting with the requirements of social services. There is a tendency to forget the most important social service a government can do for its people is to keep them alive and free.'[8]

By way of contrast, it is instructive to recall that the Athenians in 483 BCE discovered an extremely rich vein of silver within their territory at Laurium – a significant windfall, akin to the discovery of oil and gas today. Leading politicians offered the people a choice between spending the proceeds on a fleet of 200 triremes or distributing it among the people, in a classical equivalent of a modern social and welfare programme. The people chose the trireme option, just in time to defeat the superpower of the day, Persia, and form the basis for the Athenian seaborne empire. It might be argued that similar choices are likely to have to be made by governments in Western countries if they are to continue to enjoy and exploit the influence and freedom that they have enjoyed for centuries on the sea.

There is another problem. The senior officers (indeed all officers) of navies in democracies are constrained in their ability to take part in public discourse by anxious politicians and overzealous communications officials. They are required to be 'on-message' or to resign. As a result, precious little original thinking or public discourse about future maritime strategy – as opposed to policy – emerges, leaving navies politically and perceptually vulnerable to the siren calls of a-strategic views of the future. As a result, they have to resort to behind-the-hand techniques, which include using retired officers (and their online blogs) as mouthpieces, academic frontmen (and women) and broad, unattributed hints to the media. One almost longs for the time when Jacky Fisher, as First Sea Lord, threatened to turn the Cabinet Ministers' 'wives into widows, their children fatherless and their homes into dunghills'[9] if they did not support his plans for additional battle-cruisers.

Public ignorance of the consequences of decisions made for political rather than strategic reasons means that electoral choices about defence

---

[8] Sir John Slessor, *Strategy for the West* (1954).
[9] As recounted in Winston Churchill's *The World Crisis, 1911–1918* (2005).

rarely involve reasoned debate about the key issues. Navies do most things well for most of the time, normally with a positive, 'can-do' attitude, even in the face of severe resource pressures, but even a temporary hiatus in resource allocation or a 'capability holiday' (for example, when the UK chose not to have carriers between 2011 and 2020) for just a few years can have disproportionately damaging consequences for the preservation of scarce collective and individual skills and the capacity for success on operations.

In the absence of an overwhelming threat of invasion and instant devastation (and with the comforting assurance provided by a strategic nuclear deterrent), the way seems clear for the UK to return to a role in which it has proved singularly effective over the centuries, that of being strong at sea, in both commercial and naval senses. The return on investment would be privileged access to globalisation, a close partnership with a reviving superpower and the ability to protect and promote national interests worldwide. It is the only way any country can claim or reasonably aspire to be a global player and maintain more than regional influence in the twenty-first century. Indeed, one of the first political poems in English, 'The Libel [or little book] of English Policy' in 1436 began by *'exhortynge alle Englande to kepe the see enviroun'*.

RELEASING THE INNER PIRATE

The individual and society also have roles to play in response to the opportunities provided by the sea. Sections of modern society and commercial companies need to release their 'inner pirate', to apply entrepreneurial flair, impetus and innovative solutions to the emerging challenges at sea. There is money to be made in the front line of maritime commerce and in the vanguard of new services and industries, dealing with gaps in the emerging market at sea, whether that is in mining, environmental control or security.

The 'inner pirate' is evident in the way in which private security companies sprung up and thrived in response to the threat from pirates in the Indian Ocean and elsewhere. While the international community and institutions were wringing their hands and countries were distinctly slow in responding, a range of responsible – as well as some less savoury – companies responded to the need to upset the risk and reward calculus of the pirates. Similarly, the British marine services group Gardline, based in Great

Yarmouth in eastern England, showed admirable buccaneering spirit in establishing a strong position and reputation in the maritime sector. Starting with a single converted trawler some thirty years ago, it now sports a diverse group of companies that support and service a wide range of marine activities worldwide, notably ocean surveillance, maritime security and technical support. Meanwhile, a host of companies and academic institutions in the north-east of England are in the forefront of providing technical solutions, mostly in the field of unmanned vehicles, to the task of exploiting the underwater and deep-sea environments.

More widely, the simple fact that a market sector is already dominated by a particular country or company should not deter attempts to penetrate the market and exploit opportunities that might be available. The cruise business is an interesting example of where the trade has been dominated by three major companies: Carnival, Royal Caribbean and Norwegian Cruise Line. Today, smaller, more agile competitors offering specific cruises base on themes (Disney), age group (over 50s or families) or nationality (Chinese, German, Portuguese) are breaking in and taking market share based on a critical assessment of future trends while the traditional companies stuck with what they knew and did best. A country might also consider that its strengths lie in innovation and technological development; if that is the case, this is where the focus and investment should be. Alternatively, its advantage is in the provision of world-class training and expertise or in specialist niche areas, such as boatbuilding, subsea technologies or offshore engineering. The rule should be that, consistent with a country's resources, nothing should be ruled in and nothing should be ruled out.

For established maritime powers, releasing the inner corsair of entrepreneurial activity that lies at the heart of making a good living from the sea involves innovative approaches to the world's opportunities and problems and putting in place the investment in capital and skills that addresses current and future opportunities. History shows that this can only happen through a close partnership between governments and private initiative. Without the one, there are insufficient safeguards, public commitment and assurances to mitigate geopolitical and commercial risk; without the other, there is unlikely to be access to the agility and innovation necessary for success in a competitive, sometimes cut-throat environment. In this respect, the shipping companies of developed countries will need to look for significant efficiencies and cost containment if they are to compete with leaner operations by companies from China and developing countries that can benefit from state support and less scrupulous compliance with international labour, emissions and shipping standards.

Meanwhile, politicians and diplomats could assist by insisting on a more level playing field. As the century is unfolding, the international system is becoming progressively less equitable in the way in which the benefits of globalisation are being delivered. In some countries, national legislation and collective agreements have been made, which, although enacted with the best of intentions, severely constrain competition and create an uneven trading floor. In this respect, the enforcement of common standards by governments to enable fair competition, free market access and safety provision – in the face of regional or local protectionism, prejudicial regulation and beneficial subsidies – will be essential. This is nowhere more important than in the harmonisation of labour rights and responsibilities of seafarers and the numerous loopholes perpetuated principally by flags of convenience (FOCs). Similarly, environmental and emission limits, which add substantial costs to shipping, need to be universally applied, if they are to be effective and equitable. Even with technological improvements, fuel-saving measures and operational efficiencies, the process of making shipping green is in danger of putting many shipping companies in the red, with limits on sulphur dioxide emissions proving especially difficult and expensive to implement.

JOINED-UP COMPETITIVENESS

Public and political support is always likely to lag behind entrepreneurial urge and commercial initiative, but another important aspect of successful sea power is the extent to which the state chooses to translate the combined resources of a country into usable and exploitable power at sea. It must make a conscious decision to turn to the sea as a means of economic growth and political influence; it cannot simply be left to private initiative and simple calculations about return on investment and political advantage. More than ever, in the face of strategic competition from states, notably China, that provide direct political, financial and national support to their state-based and state-owned oceanic ventures, the 'flag', in the form of government, has to support 'trade', which, in turn, repays the debt in the form of taxation and economic growth. Lobby, industry and trade associations do not have the political leverage and, anyway, too often have to represent multinational corporations or sectoral interests. Conversely, governments are generally too focused on the short-term horizon to be able to think or act in an integrated fashion at the strategic level. Without political leadership and a strategic approach to engagement with the sea, a country is unlikely to be able to prevail in the highly competitive environment of the twenty-first century. Indeed, historical experience has shown that no country can be strong at sea in any area without government championship that extends beyond moral support and platitudes. The best arrangement would seem to be a public–private partnership, in which entrepreneurial activity is encouraged to thrive within a conducive, protective and joined-up strategic framework provided by the state.

However, government initiatives and policies that simply encourage individual aspects of a country's approach to the sea are unlikely to be effective. As indicated above, they rarely take a comprehensive view of the sea and largely divine recommendations and objectives within narrow sectors. Someone needs to bring all these strands together and establish priorities for action and investment within a comprehensive strategy. It looks like a job for a fully empowered Minister of Marine; it is simply not good enough to have the sea relegated to a subset of a parent department, such as Transport. Strength at sea relies on the integration of all those instruments and elements of national power that can deliver wealth and advantage at sea, with a careful assessment of the balance of soft and hard sea power.

States, companies and individuals will have to compete much harder and strive for competitive advantage in the modern world, overcoming the sense of entitlement and culture of risk avoidance that seem to beset most developed world approaches to demonstrations of enterprise at sea. Willie Sutton, a reasonably well-known American bandit, was once asked why he robbed banks; he supposedly replied: 'Because that's where the money is.'[10] Any country wishing to make its way in the world would do well to remember this simple logic with regard to the sea. Employment and reward

---

[10] Often mistakenly attributed to Jesse James.

are matters of risk-taking, endeavour and initiative, not entitlement that derives from easy choices and basking in the reflected glory of a maritime heritage – dwarfs standing on giants' shoulders need not apply. A maritime tradition, more especially a naval heritage of battles won, stirring deeds and vibrant commerce, should be a source of inspiration, emulation and confidence, a 'golden thread' that runs through a culture or society. Most countries would like very much to have the maritime tradition inherited by the UK. As Napoleon once remarked, 'Wherever wood can swim, there I am sure to find this flag of England.'[11] With these advantages, you would think that a country might do better for itself in a world largely cast in its image. If it does not, as history has shown, others will.

THE CHINESE APPROACH

It is worth considering the Chinese approach to sea power. China wants to be a great power on the global stage and produce what Xi Jinping calls the 'Chinese Dream' – 'national rejuvenation, improvement of people's livelihoods, prosperity, construction of a better society and military strengthening'. Within a 'managed' society and economy, the Chinese have developed an integrated maritime geostrategy, with every instrument of state power geared towards supporting both military and commercial success. Through its state-controlled shipping, shipbuilding and construction companies, China invests considerable sovereign wealth in extensive oil and gas, port development and offshore infrastructure. Its ability to mobilise low-cost manpower enables it to compete aggressively in all areas of marine activity, especially in overseas port construction, shipping, fishing and shipbuilding. Its navy is being expanded not only to deter and defeat threats to its sovereignty, but also to extend exclusive rights as far as possible in the East China and South China seas and to secure its sea lines of communication with its markets and sources of supply.

The country's integration into global trade and production networks has increased the potential for a spillover of civil technology to the military, particularly in dual-use technologies and production techniques. State monopolies, including those in the defence sector, have been restructured

---

[11] At Rochefort, July 1815.

to fit a more corporate mould, encouraging greater levels of competition and allowing for improved integration with China's growing civilian research and development sector, such as state-funded science and technology universities and research institutes. Meanwhile, the development of China's domestic financial markets and state-controlled banks has allowed state-owned defence firms to acquire funding. China's diplomatic footprint and military activities directly support the assertion of what it considers to be its sovereign rights, in the Asia-Pacific region and in those parts of the world where it might have a commercial interest, both now and in the future. Its oil platforms are claimed as forward sovereign presence for the country's strategic interests and it has declared a national interest in the future development of the Arctic.

Again, the British have been this way before. The intimate connection between finance and sea power was demonstrated by Britain's experience of globalisation at the start of the twentieth century. The world of commerce was dominated by the free trade paradigm, an expanding global economy and attempts by most countries to remove tariff barriers and protectionist measures. The British merchant marine, backed up by the security guarantees of the Royal Navy, was the pre-eminent carrier by sea, giving traders the confidence that their goods would be shipped and delivered on time.[12] In addition, the availability of credit on the London market and the ability to conduct transactions and communicate on a global basis on undersea cables permitted more flexible and reliable means of exchange. Such was Britain's joined-up maritime power, it was noted at the time that the British government could coerce a foreign country or belligerent by blocking access to British merchant ships, credit and the undersea cables, without the necessity of a blockade.

[12] Lord Dundas, speaking to the UK Parliament in 1801, seemed to know what to do with sea power in a competitive world, 'I must observe that, from our insular situation, from our limited population not admitting of extensive continental operations, and from our importance depending in so material a degree upon the extent of our commerce and navigation, it is obvious that ... the primary object of our attention ought to be, by what means we can effectually increase those resources on which depends our naval superiority, and at the same time diminish or appropriate to ourselves those which might enable the enemy to contend with us in this respect.' He added, 'I need not attempt to prove to this house what must be obvious to all, that upon the possession of distant ... commerce the extent of our trade must in a great degree depend.'

There was also a cultural aspect. The rise to supremacy of British sea power depended on a wide public consensus, from politicians to the humblest labourer, that the sea was Britain's natural environment and national speciality. This in turn aroused expectations and a concentrated sense of purpose, both in anticipation of military victories, and in relation to commercial success. It also instilled the confidence to assert rights and invest resources in capabilities and enterprises that would produce naval and commercial results. Given that the modern globalised economy, too, relies on access to reliable banking and the assured flow of both capital and cargo, countries have a number of coercive options short of war. The more cards that a country holds, in the form of hard and soft sea power, the greater the potential there is for effective coercion.

In the first half of the twenty-first century, China appears to be implementing a commercial and military model that was prevalent in the centuries of European ascendancy. Once again, we are witnesses to a high volume of commercial and maritime activity – powered by state-endorsed monopolies and enterprising entrepreneurs, seeking to dominate the trading routes and access to the far-flung markets of the world. Whether or not China sees itself in the role, it is replicating many of the structural and cultural features of the aggressively expanding trading systems of the eighteenth century. Indeed, the strategy looks a lot like the expansion of British commerce at sea in the eighteenth and nineteenth centuries, with its integrated industrial production, trading and military approach, and one cannot help thinking that China has implemented the process in reverse – the British seaborne empire with Chinese characteristics perhaps. Indeed, the coordinated activities of the Chinese state-run companies, with their extensive investments in overseas ports, projects and markets, closely resemble those of the British and Dutch East India Companies. With warships following, trade and flag would appear to be almost, as they say in China, in harmony.

There may be an 'invisible hand' guiding the implementation of this strategy, in harmonising the commercial, military and strategic components in the national and Party interest. China is nothing if not a vast international conglomerate. However, the reason that China's approach to sea power looks so like that of the British is that the human approach to the sea as the primary strategic medium for trade and interaction between countries endures over time. The lesson from the British experience is that if a country is to mitigate the risks and shocks that occur at sea, exploit the opportunities and see off challengers, it must bring together interlocking, mutually supportive governmental, commercial and military elements that can be used to compete as part of an agile, pragmatic and single-minded strategy. In the twenty-first century, a country needs to harness the sea power of the state as a whole to compete on a global scale.

STRATEGIC CHOICES

The central issue for any country in the twenty-first century is to maintain the sea as a super highway, one that continues to connect each country and community with each other and allows free trade to underpin global economic growth. Does a country like Britain really want to revert to its former status of an insignificant group of islands off the north-west coast of an equally insignificant Europe – ultima Thule – pushed out to the left of the page on a projection and strategic map based on the International Date Line? The Elizabethan seafarers would have sought to burst out of those surly bounds and seized the opportunities presented by globalisation. Elizabeth I herself observed in a letter: 'the use of sea and air is common to all; neither can a title to the ocean belong to any people or private persons, forasmuch as neither nature nor public use and custom permit any possession therof'.[13] They would have understood the enduring importance of the sea and the freedom to navigate and trade; they would have appreciated the new Spanish Main represented by the economies of the Asia-Pacific region.

The Chinese left the maritime scene in the middle of the fifteenth century because they chose to devote more resources to the defence of their northern frontier and the immediate threat from pirates off their own coasts at the expense of their sources of prosperity and sustained success. During the course of the twenty-first century, the danger for developed countries is that they follow suit and cede dominance at sea, leaving the way clear for others – the modern day versions of the Portuguese, Dutch and English – to exploit the subsequent power and commercial vacuum.

---

[13] In a letter to the Ambassador of Philip II of Spain in 1580.

FUTURE TENSE OR FUTURE PERFECT?

The global community, such as it is, is going to have to manage and navigate a complex land and seascape in the twenty-first century. It will be necessary to resolve the tensions inherent in a highly competitive, regionally unpredictable, but broadly stable and interconnected world, as each country seeks to deal with the challenges and consequences of uneven global economic growth, modernity, paradigm shifts in technology, changes in resource allocation and a progressively demographically unbalanced population that will increase to at least 9 billion by 2045.

A shift in the prevailing geostrategic dynamic is already under way towards a renewed focus on the maritime environment, the security of which for some time has been largely taken for granted while it has been in the safekeeping of the USA. Consequently, many commentators believe that the twenty-first century will be a maritime century. This is not exactly a revelation; every century since the age of Columbus and da Gama has been a maritime century. Throughout the modern era, the sea continues to be the crucial enabler of human, economic and societal development; only in times of war and crisis that have threatened to disrupt its free flow have governments and peoples noticed how vital the super highway is to economic health and peaceful development.

Even now, new areas of 'colonisation' are opening up for the global economy in the twenty-first century. The convergence of Africa and South America, alongside the spectacular rise of the major Asian economies, with the developed economies of the West and the Anglo-sphere, fuelled (literally) by the newly discovered resources of the sea – notably unconventional oil and deep-sea gas – is likely to lead to unprecedented volumes of trade, which will rely on the sea for their distribution. Although, in Thomas Friedman's judgement, the world appears flat as far as virtual goods (finance, information and communications) are concerned, the reality is that the physical world, the world of people, commodities and manufactured goods, remains, as Columbus knew only too well, steadfastly – defiantly – round. With so many states, commercial companies and groups seeking to impose their version of sea power, the requirement for stability, security and equal shares for all along the routes of the world's super highway will be as urgent as ever. Countries will have to commit resources and forces, for the common good or in support of their own interests.

In an ideal world, a country would probably want its ships designed by the Italians and built in South Korea, its systems provided by the USA and innovation by the Israelis, its shipping lines run by the Danes, within a naval heritage provided by the British and a resource base by the Gulf states, all integrated within a maritime strategy devised by the Chinese. However, in the real world in which commercial and national power are diffused, sea power in the twenty-first century, as in any century, is likely to lie with those countries that combine powerful navies, which are able to enforce claims, with commercial power to exploit the carrying trade, the ocean routes and the resources of the sea. Indeed, where they possess and orchestrate within a coherent strategy both soft and hard maritime power, they are likely, as history reminds us, to control the strategic and economic levers of world power and influence.

The prize for maritime dominance in the twenty-first century, as at any other time since the fifteenth century, is control of the engine of globalisation, which enables a country or group of countries to set the global agenda in its own image and interests, with regard to every aspect of human activity, interchange and security. We return to where we started: 'Whosoever commands the sea, commands the trade; whosoever commands the trade of the world commands the riches of the world, and consequently the world itself.'[14] It was Britain in the nineteenth century, the USA in the second half of the twentieth century and in the early twenty-first century. Whom should we trust with the trident of Neptune – and the sceptre of the world – for the rest of this century?

---

[14] Sir Walter Raleigh, 'A Discourse of the Invention of Ships, Anchors, Compass, &c', in *The Works of Sir Walter Ralegh, Kt*, vol. 8.

Select Bibliography

This book contains deductions and assessments based on the synthesis of a great many sources. It also reflects personal experience of over thirty-five years of working in the maritime environment and the insights gained from developing policy and operational concepts at a senior level in the UK Armed Forces. As well as some original thought, the sources on which much of the analysis relies – in particular, the web-based resources – are too numerous and diverse to mention.

I have therefore included below those works that I believe readers would enjoy and that would expand their knowledge of what they have read in this book. They have been selected on the basis of their content, insight and direct relevance to the subject in question. I hope that friends and former colleagues will not be aggrieved or disappointed if their works have not been included and they feel that they should have been; it is not a reflection on their scholarship or wisdom.

INTRODUCTION

Sir John Fisher, *Memories* 1919 (reprinted by Forgotten Books in 2012).

Sir Walter Raleigh, *The Works of Sir Walter Ralegh, Kt.* 1829 (reprinted 1965) and *The Works of Sir Walter Ralegh, Kt: Miscellaneous Works* (Ulan Press, June 2011).

Grotius, Hugo, and Robert Feenstra, *Mare Liberum, 1609–2009* (Boston: Brill Academic, 2009).

Selden, John, and Marchamont Nedham, *Of the Dominion, or, Ownership of the Sea* (Clark, NJ: Law Book Exchange, 2004).

CHAPTER 1: GLOBALISATION AND SEA POWER

Appleby, Joyce, *The Relentless Revolution, A History of Capitalism* (New York: Norton, 2011).

Baer, George W., *One Hundred Years of Sea Power* (Stanford University Press, 1993).

Boxer, C. R., *Portuguese Conquest and Commerce in Southern Asia 1500–1750* (Farnham: Varorium, 1985).

Dreyer, Edward L., *Zheng He: China and the Oceans in the Early Ming dynasty, 1405–1433* (New York: Pearson Longman, 2007).

Mead, Walter R., *God and Gold: Britain, America, and the Making of the Modern World.* (London: Atlantic Books, 2007).

Menzies, Gavin, *1421: The Year China Discovered the World* (London: Bantam, 2002).

Ferguson, Niall, *Empire: How Britain Made the Modern World* (London: Penguin, 2004).

Hale, John R., *Lords of the Sea: the Epic Story of the Athenian Navy and the Birth of Democracy* (London: Penguin Books, 2010).

Herman, Arthur, *To Rule the Waves: How the British Navy Shaped the Modern World* (New York: Harper Perennial, 2005).

Paine, Lincoln P., *The Sea and Civilization: a Maritime History of the World* (London: Atlantic Books, 2014).

Parry, John H., *Trade and Dominion* (London: Cardinal/Sphere Books, 1971).

Parry, John H., *The Age of Reconnaissance,* (London: Cardinal/Sphere Books, 1973).

Raban, Jonathan, *The Oxford Book of the Sea* (Oxford Paperbacks, 1993).

Scott, David, *Leviathan: the Rise of Britain as a World Power* (London: Harper Press, 2013).

Wheeler, James S., *The Making of a World Power: War and the Military Revolution in Seventeenth-Century England* (Stroud: Sutton Publishing, 1999).

Wilson, Ben, *Empire of the Deep: the Rise and Fall of the British Navy* (London: Weidenfeld & Nicolson, 2013).

CHAPTER 2: THE GLOBAL SUPER HIGHWAY

Bernstein, William J., *A Splendid Exchange: How Trade Shaped the World* (London: Atlantic, 2008).

Blum, Andrew, *Tube: Behind the Scenes at the Internet* (London: Penguin, 2013).

Clare, Horatio, *Down to the Sea in Ships: of Ageless Oceans and Modern Men* (London: Chatto & Windus, 2014).

Conrad, Joseph, *The Collected Works of Joseph Conrad*, Volumes 1 and 2 (BiblioBazaar, 2009).

George, Rose, *Deep Sea and Foreign Going: Inside Shipping, the Invisible Industry that Brings you 90% of Everything* (London: Portobello Books, 2013)

Jephson, Chris, and Henning Morgen, *Creating Global Opportunities: Mærsk Line in Containerisation 1973–2013* (Cambridge: Cambridge University Press, 2013).

Levinson, Marc, *The Box: How the Shipping Container Made the World Smaller and the World Economy Bigger* (Princeton: Princeton University Press, 2008).

Lloyd's Maritime Atlas of World Ports and Shipping Places (Oxon/New York: Informa Law from Routledge, 2014).

Mahbubani, Kishore, *The New Asian Century* (New York: PublicAffairs, 2008).

Norris, Pat, *Watching Earth from Space: How Surveillance Helps Us – and Harms Us* (Chichester: Springer Praxis, 2010).

Saul, John R., *The Collapse of Globalism* (London: Atlantic, 2009).

United Nations Conference on Trade and Development (UNCTAD), *Review of Maritime Transport 2013*, available on unctad.org/en/publicationslibrary/rmt2013_en.

CHAPTER 3: SEA POWER TODAY

Angell, Norman, *The World's Highway: Some Notes on America's Relation to Sea Power and Non-Military Sanctions For the Law of Nations* (New York, 1915).

Bell, Christopher M., *Churchill and Sea Power* (Oxford: Oxford University Press, 2013).

Corbett, Julian S., *Some Principles of Maritime Strategy.* (Mineola, NY: Dover Publications, 2004).

Gray, Colin S., *Perspectives on Strategy* (Oxford: Oxford University Press, 2013).

Jackson, Paul A., *IHS Jane's All the World's Aircraft, 2013–2014* (Coulsdon: IHS Jane's, 2013).

Mahan, Alfred Thayer, *The Influence of Sea Power on History 1660–1783* (London: Sampson Low and Co, 1889).

Mahan, Alfred Thayer, *Naval Strategy* (London: Sampson Low and Co, 1911).

Padfield, Peter, *Maritime Supremacy & the Opening of the Western Mind: Naval Campaigns hat Shaped the Modern World, 1588–1782* (London: Pimlico, 2000).

Rothwell, Donald, and Tim Stephens, *The International Law of the Sea* (Oxford: Hart Publishing, 2010).

Saunders, Stephen, *Jane's Fighting Ships 2013–14* (Jane's Information Group, 2013).

CHAPTER 4: A CHANGING SEASCAPE

Emmerson, Charles, *The Future History of the Arctic* (London: Vintage, 2011).

Fairhall, David, *Cold Front Conflict Ahead in Arctic Waters* (London: I.B. Tauris, 2010).

Hallwood, Paul, *Economics of the Oceans: Rights, Rents and Resources* (Abingdon, Oxon/New York: Routledge, 2014).

Inter-Governmental Panel on Climate Change:

  Working Group 1, Climate Change 2013:

    The Physical Science Basis http://www.ipcc.ch/report/ar5/wg1/

  Working Group 2, *Climate Change 2014: Impacts, Adaptation, and Vulnerability* http://ipcc-wg2.gov/AR5/wg2/

Newell, Peter, *Globalization and the Environment: Capitalism, Ecology and Power* (Cambridge: Polity Press, 2012).

Pyne, Stephen J., *The Ice: a Journey to Antarctica* (London: Phoenix, 2004).

Ridley, Matt, *The Rational Optimist: How Prosperity Evolves* (London: Fourth Estate, 2011).

Roberts, Callum, *Ocean of Life: How Our Seas Are Changing* (London: Allen Lane 2012).

Smith, Laurence C., *The New North: the World in 2050* (London: Profile, 2012).

CHAPTER 5: NEW OPPORTUNITIES

Kurlansky, Mark, *The Last Fish Tale: the Fate of the Atlantic and Our Disappearing Fisheries* (London: Jonathan Cape, 2008).

Laughlin, Robert B., *Powering the Future: How We Will (Eventually) Solve the Energy Crisis and Fuel the Civilization of Tomorrow* (New York: Basic Books, 2011).

Sale, Richard and Potapov, Eugen, *The Scramble for the Arctic: Ownership, Exploitation and Conflict in the Far North* (London: Frances Lincoln, 2010).

CHAPTER 6: NEW TECHNOLOGIES

Buderi, Robert, *Naval Innovation for the 21st Century: The Office of Naval Research Since the End of the Cold War* (Annapolis, MD: Naval Institute Press, 2013).

Coker, Christopher, *Warrior Geeks: How 21st Century Technology is Changing the Way We Fight and Think About War* (London: Hurst, 2012).

Schmidt, Eric, and Jared Cohen, *The New Digital Age: Reshaping the Future of People, Nations and Business* (London: John Murray, 2013).

CHAPTER 7: SECURITY AT SEA

Kilcullen, David, *Out of the Mountains: the Coming Age of the Urban Guerrilla* (London: Hurst, 2013).

Klein, Natalie, *Maritime Security and the Law of the Sea* (Oxford: Oxford University Press, 2011).

Oceans Beyond Piracy, *The Economic Cost of Somali Piracy 2012* (http://oceansbeyondpiracy.org)

Parker, Geoffrey, *Sovereign City: the City-State Through History* (London, Reaktion, 2004).

CHAPTER 8: STRATEGIC COMPETITION

Barnett, Thomas P., *Great Powers: America and the World after Bush* (New York: G P Putnam's Sons, 2009).

Cropsey, Seth, *Mayday: the Twilight of American Naval Superiority* (London: Duckworth, 2013).

Erickson, Andrew S., Lyle Goldstein, and Nan Li, *China, the United States, and 21st-Century Sea Power Defining a Maritime Security Partnership* (Annapolis, MD: Naval Institute Press, 2010).

Fenby, Jonathan, *Tiger Heads and Snake Tails* (London: Simon & Schuster, 2012).

Friedberg, Aaron L., *A Contest for Supremacy: China, America, and the Struggle for Mastery in Asia* (New York: W. W. Norton & Co, 2011).

Friedman, Thomas L. and Michael Mandelbaum, *That Used to Be Us: What Went Wrong with America – and How it Can Come Back* (London: Little, Brown, 2011).

Kane, Thomas M., *Chinese Grand Strategy and Maritime Power* (London/Portland, OR: Frank Cass Publishers, 2002).

Kaplan, Robert D., *Monsoon: the Indian Ocean and the Future of American Power* (New York: Random House, 2011).

Kaplan, Robert D., *Asia's Cauldron: the South China Sea and the End of a Stable Pacific* (New York: Random House, 2014).

Lucas, Edward, *The New Cold War* (New York: Bloomsbury, 2008).

Shambaugh, David L., *China Goes Global: The Partial Power* (Oxford: Oxford University Press, 2013).

Sieff, Martin, *That Should Still Be Us: How Thomas Friedman's Flat World Myths Are Keeping Us Flat on Our Backs* (Hoboken, NJ: Wiley, 2012).

Smith, Martin A., *Power in the Changing Global Order: the US, Russia and China* (Cambridge/Malden, MA: Polity Press, 2012).

Till, Geoffrey, and Patrick Bratton, *Sea Power and the Asia-Pacific: the triumph of Neptune* (London/New York: Routledge, 2013).

CHAPTER 9: WARFARE AT SEA

Childs, Nick, *Britain's Future Navy* (Barnsley: Pen & Sword Books, 2012).

Gray, Colin S., *Another Bloody Century: Future Warfare* (London: Phoenix, 2006).

Morris, Ian, *Why the West Rules – For Now: the Patterns of History and What They Reveal About the Future* (London: Profile, 2010).

Richmond, Admiral Sir Herbert, *Statesmen and Sea Power* (Oxford, 1947).

Strachan, Sir Hew, *The Direction of War: Contemporary Strategy in Historical Perspective*, (Cambridge: Cambridge University Press, 2013).

Till, Geoffrey, *Seapower: A Guide for the Twenty-First Century*. (New York: Routledge, 2013).

CHAPTER 10: WHAT'S A COUNTRY TO DO?

Durande, Rodolphe and Jean-Philippe Vergne, *The Pirate Organization: Lessons From the Fringes of Capitalism* (Boston: Harvard Business, 2013).

Friedman, Thomas L., *Hot, Flat, and Crowded: Why the World Needs a Green Revolution – and How We Can Renew Our Global Future* (London: Penguin, 2009).

Gorshkov, Sergeï, *The Sea Power of the State* (Oxford: Pergamon Press, 1980).

Hattendorf, John B. and others, *British Naval Documents 1204–1960*, (Navy Records Society, 1993).

Kennedy, Paul, *The Rise and Fall of the Great Powers* (London: Unwin Hyman, 1988).

Kennedy, Paul M., *The Rise and Fall of British Naval Mastery* (London: Fontana, 1991).

Sharma, Ruchir, *Breakout Nations: in Search of the Next Economic Miracle* (London: Allen Lane, 2012).

Slessor, Sir John, *Strategy for the West* (London: Cassell, 1954).

Strowger, Roy, *Gardline: The First 40 Years*, (Bodmin, UK: MPG Books Group, 2009).

Acknowledgements

I want to thank the Royal Navy for giving me enough challenges and memorable experiences, in peace and war, to fill a lifetime and more. I have sailed every sea and visited every continent, proud and privileged to be in the company of good people whose only thought was to do their duty for their country and the Royal Navy. I cannot think how I could have had a more rewarding career.

I am most grateful to Lorne Forsyth for proposing the subject of this book in the first place and to Tim McClement for passing me the ball at an opportune moment. It has been a distinct pleasure working with the highly professional team at Elliott and Thompson, whose support and assistance have been invaluable. I am deeply appreciative of the patience, encouragement and guidance of Olivia Bays, from the first word to the last, as well as Pippa Crane's tireless exertions, unerring judgement and firm control of the author's enthusiasms and time management during the editing process.

I owe a special debt to a great many people, with whom I have served and whose example I cherish, notably Lords Boyce and West, Peter Abbott, Tony Bagnall, Roy Newman, John Coward and Geoff Biggs (who is sadly no longer with us). I very much value the lifelong friendship of Rob James and Chris Craig, as well as the academic guidance and kindness I have received (and continue to enjoy) from John Walsh and Colin Gray.

Finally, I would like to record my gratitude to my wife, Jackie, and my children Abigail and Jonathan, for their forbearance, love and understanding while I have spent long hours, public holidays and sunny days in my study rather than with them.

Picture Credits

Images reproduced courtesy of:

Page 54: Maersk

Page 73: Ministry of Defence, Crown Copyright.

Page 85: US Navy

Page 93: by Schekinov Alexey Victorovich (own work) [CC BY 3.0 (creativecommons.org/licenses/by-sa/3.0/legalcode)], via Wikimedia Commons

Page 117: © catolla/Shutterstock

Page 147: by Kiselev d (own work) [CC BY 3.0 (creativecommons.org/licenses/by-sa/3.0/legalcode)], via Wikimedia Commons

Page 156: by Jeff Milisen © Kampachi Farms, LLC

Page 173: US Navy by Erik Hildebrandt, courtesy of Northrop Grumman

Page 174: US Navy by Mass Communication Specialist 2nd Class Tony D. Curtis

Page 189: US Navy, courtesy of General Dynamics

Page 191: US Navy

Page 198: US Navy

Page 266: US Navy

Page 294: US Navy

Page 298: US Navy

Index

Page numbers in *italic* denote illustrations.

50 Let Pobedy 147, 147

Abu Dhabi 72, 108, 136
acidification 111–13, 132–133, 165
Adams, John 257
Adang Bay 243
Aden, Gulf of 96, 242
Admiral Kuznetsov 93
Afghanistan 26, 78, 170–73, 213, 262, 273, 306
Afloat Forward Staging Bases (AFSBs) 292
Africa 15, 23, 38, 57, 58, 61, 82, 95, 96, 97, 245, 245, 264, 266, 311, 339; East 2, 21, 12, 45, 137, 138, 147, 234; sub-Saharan 245; West 58, 136, 150, 238, 240, 242; *see also* North Africa; South Africa
African Union 259
Age: of Information 313; of Sail 22, 313; of Steam 313
Air Defence Identification Zone (ADIZ) 88, 225
aircraft 67, 68, 69, 84, 92, 98, 129, 168, 172, 174, 180, 193, 197, 199, 200, 202, 208, 225, 227, 239, 242, 254, 282, 284, 286, 292, 295, 300, 300, 302; Eagle 87; early warning (AEW) 283; electromagnetic aircraft launch systems (EMALS) 191; fighter 71, 84, 98, 87, 89, 192; Harrier 296; Lightning 89, 192; maritime patrol 97, 247; *Neptune* 98; Orion 89; Osprey 296; *Poseidon* 91, 98; Protection of Military Remains Act (1986) 129; Shenyang J-15 84; Skyhawk 101; Sukhoi 90; Super Hornet 192; Tracker 102; unmanned 246, 254, 284, 286; Unmanned Carrier Launched Surveillance and Strike (UNCLASS) 175; vertical take-off and landing (VTOL) 301; X-47B 174, 174

aircraft carriers 75, 77, 79, 83, 84, 93, 97, 101, 122, 138, 168, 174, 192, 227, 283, 289, 293–97; Ford-class 191–92, 295, 297; Nimitz class 191–92
Air-Sea Battle Concept (ASBC) 270–71, 273
Akademik Lomonosov 193
Al Basrah Oil Terminal (ABOT) 235
Al Qaeda 235
Alaska 140, 146, 166
Alcatel-Lucent 44
Al-Duqm 57
Alert 46
Aleutian Islands 162
Alexandria 45, 46
Algeria 187
Allianz 118
'All Red Line' 46
Allure of the Seas 52
Al-Shabaab 234, 243
America(s) *see* USA
American: Civil War 131; Revolution 21; War of Independence 22, 274
Angell, Sir Norman 65, 263
Angola 136, 137
Annapolis River 158
Antarctic 102, 112, 114, 142–43; Convention for the Conservation of Antarctic Living Resources 142; Treaty 142; West Antarctic Ice Sheet (WAIS) 114
Antwerp 238, 267
aquaculture 154–57; aquapods 155–56
ARA *General Belgrano* 77
Arab League 259
Arab Spring 94
Arabia 57, 162
Arabian Sea 39
Archimedes Principle 110
areas beyond national jurisdiction (ABNJ) 152, 251
Arctic 60, 93, 94, 95, 103, 113–14, 137, 140–42, 145, 145, 146, 147, 165, 170, 173,

192, 193, 214, 218, 220, 232, 264, 269, 316, 336; Basin 114; Circle 114, Circle 137; Council 140; East Antarctic Ice Sheet (EAIS) 114; ice 1, 110, 114, 133, 140, 145

Argentina 77, 102, 135, 142, 143, 254

Armada 15, 20

Arne, Thomas 22

Artificial intelligence (AI) 175, 177, 178, 212, 239, 283, 290, 312

artificial islands 29–30, 52, 108, 109, 134

Ascension Island 30, 153, 324

Asia 19, 23, 36, 38, 45, 53–58, 81, 85, 141, 143, 146, 149, 151, 213, 233, 238, 264, 271, 315; Central 99, 101, 231, 245, 316; East 11, 12, 39, 89, 193, 214, 230, 238, 245, 261; South 245; see also South East Asia

Asia-Pacific region 24, 25, 56, 69, 80–102, 103, 104, 116, 221, 223, 230, 232, 233, 262, 264, 268–71, 275–77, 280, 311, 336, 338

Association of Southeast Asian Nations (ASEAN) 80–81, 86, 87, 230, 233, 264

Athens 276

Atlantic 9, 10, 11, 14, 15, 16, 19, 20, 21, 25, 24, 26, 39, 43, 44, 45, 94, 95, 101, 111, 124, 228; South 102, 135, 254

Augustus 274

Australia 36, 38, 46, 80, 83, 91–92, 121, 136, 138, 139, 142, 147, 153, 164, 220, 230, 232, 233, 244, 263, 316, 322; Joint Defence Force 91

Automatic Identification System (AIS) 61, 217, 247, 255, 275

Azerbaijan 136

Bab-el-Mandeb 39

Bacon, Admiral Sir Reginald 167

BAE Systems 175, 176, 197, 199

Bagamoyo 57

Bahamas 14, 49, 51

Bahrain 72

Baltic Sea 21, 25, 26, 39, 92, 93, 94, 103, 124, 128, 157, 158, 220, 261

Banda Aceh 319

Bangladesh 57, 97

Barents Sea 25, 150

Beijing 322

Beirut 236

Belgium 142

Bengal 22; Bay of 243, 268

Bergen 76

Bering Strait 146, 232

biomimicry 205–6

Biscay, Bay of 30

Bismarck 128

Black Sea 9, 10, 25, 26, 39, 83, 92–95, 103, 124, 220, 261, 267, 275

Bob Douglas 137

Boeing 199

bombs: atomic 168; 'dumb' 299; munitions 299

Bonin Islands 83

Bosporus 39

Boxer, C R. 19

BP 137, 139, 292; Deepwater Horizon disaster 240

Brasília 322

Brazil 32, 52, 101–2, 121, 136, 137, 159, 170, 220

Bremenports 140

Britain 10, 19, 21–25, 31, 32, 36, 46, 47, 58, 77, 85, 225, 267, 277, 313, 325, 337, 338

British Columbia, University of 218

Brittany 158

Broome 138

Brunel, Isambard Kingdom 168

Burundi 57

Busan 57, 146

Buzzards Bay, Massachusetts 156

Bynkershoek, Cornelius 18

Byzantine Empire 11

Cable & Wireless Worldwide 44

cables 48, 127, 159, 318; Apollo 44; fibre-optic 44–46, 207, 288, 304; high-voltage direct current (HVDC) 159; submarine 43, 44; transatlantic telephone cable connection (TAT-1) 43–44; underwater 42–47

Cadiz 185

Cairo 46

Cameron, David 163

Campos Basin 136

Canada 21, 25, 51, 136, 139, 140, 144, 146, 166, 220, 233, 322

Cape Colony 22

Cape Horn 139, 44

Cape of Good Hope 14, 39, 66, 82

Caribbean 22, 122, 124, 240

Carnival Cruise Lines 50, 332

Carolina, North 119

Caroline Islands 83

Caspian Sea 39, 83, 92, 99, 136, 267

Celtic Sea 30

Centre for Maritime Research and Experimentation (CMRE) 178

Cheonan 88, 309
Chile 101–2, 142, 143, 253
China 4, 5, 7, 11, 13, 14, 23, 30, 32, 36, 38, 39, 41, 45, 49, 52, 55, 56–60, 65, 69, 79–90, 92, 95–98, 100, 102–5, 136, 138, 139, 140, 141, 144, 146, 149, 158, 159, 163, 164, 166, 168, 170, 175, 183, 187, 202, 213, 214, 220, 222–23, 226–29, 231–34, 242, 248, 251, 256, 259–62, 271–73, 276–80, 286, 287, 308, 309, 315, 316, 333, 334–38; and USA 263–76; Maritime Police (Nine Dragons) 224; National Offshore Oil Corporation (CNOOC) 138, 139, 141, 226; Chinese Communist Party (CCP) 77, 81, 222, 265, 268, 308; Chinese Naval Ocean Surveillance System (NOSS) 290
Chittagong 57, 306
Churchill, Winston 330
Clarkson, Jeremy 76
Clausewitz, Carl von 257
climate change 6, 109–14, 120, 121, 127, 133, 148, 258, 323; Intergovernmental Panel on (IPCC) 115, 120
Clipper Shipping 66
CLOV project 137
CMA CGM 55
Coen, Jan Pietersz 19
Cold War 5, 18, 26, 27, 47, 76, 92, 95, 170, 180, 227, 232, 249, 289, 297, 309, 328
Colombia 247, 253
Colombo 57
Colorado: River 161; University of 113
Columbus, Christopher 9, 14, 339
Command, Control, Communications, Computers, Intelligence, Surveillance and Reconnaissance (C4ISR) 169
Commission for the Limits of the Continental Shelf (CLCS) 30, 31
Confucianism 12–13
Congo, Democratic Republic of the 57
Conrad, Joseph 35
Constantinople (Istanbul) 9, 13, 21,
containerisation 40–42, 47, 56, 57, 146, 168, 185, 187, 238
Cook Islands 162
Copenhagen 52
Coral Sea, Battle of the 295
Corbett, Sir Julian 63, 257
Corfu Channel 307
corvettes 84, 87, 89, 90, 100
Costa Rica 239
criminality 237–40
Cromwell, Oliver 75

cruisers 77, 87, 93, 95, 183, 227, 292, 330
Crusades 11
CSCL 54
Cuba 95
Cummins, Anna 125

Danube, River 124
Darwin, Charles 33
Davos, World Economic Forum 251
D-Day 301
Deep Sea Operations (DSOP) 179
Defense Advanced Research Projects Agency (DARPA) 179, 180, 187
Delaware 51
Deng Xiaoping 226
denial 68–69, 79, 99, 263, 194, 212, 298, 304, 310
Denmark 31, 49, 107, 140, 141, 157, 158
Derby 73
destroyers 84, 87, 89, 95, 183, 185, 292; Arleigh Burke-class 191, *191*, 281, 292; Daring-class 189; Kolkota-class 98; Zumwalt-class 189, *189*, 190, 196, 197, 200, 281
dhows 235, 238
DigitalGlobe 62
directed energy *see* weapons, directed-energy
Diu, Battle of 16
Doyle, Sir Arthur Conan 4
DP World 41, 57
Drake, Francis 20
drugs 4, 50, 234, 238, 239, 284
Dubai 108; Logistics City 57
Dumai 243
Dundas, Lord 336

East China Sea 82 83, 87, 135, 214, 220–26, 228, 231, 254, 261, 264, 272, 278, 335
East India companies 66; British 244, 337; Dutch 16–17, 337
East Siberian Sea 166
Ecuador 162
Egypt 45, 46, 58
El Niño 121; El Niño–Southern Oscillation Phase (ENSO) 121, 125; *see also* La Niña
electromagnetic pulse (EMP) 206–7, 212, 286
Elizabeth I 19, 338
emission control 125–27; areas (ECAs) 126
Emma Maersk 54
Engels, F. 27
England 18, 20, 23, 65, 114, 116, 248, 332, 335

English Channel 20, 39, 52, 158
Eritrea 243
Eternal Peace 77
European Union (EU) 27, 78, 80, 140, 150, 152, 153, 202, 244, 246, 259
exclusive economic zones (EEZ) 28–31, 37, 82, 86, 93, 94, 101, 102, 123, 127, 130, 132, 142, 146, 149, 157, 162, 164, 166, 211, 215, 216, *216*, 218, 219, 220, 222, 223, 225, 226–28, 248, 252, 254, 270, 280, 305, 306, 324
ExxonMobil 137, 139
Eykon Energy 141

Falkland Islands 30, 143, 153, 324; 77, Falklands War 77, 295, 302; South Georgia 30, 153
Faraday cage 207
Faroe Islands 31, 140
Faroe-Rockall Plateau 31
Fast Combat Support Ships 80
Felixstowe 41, 57
ferries 48, 61, 293; Ro-Ro 95
Finland 140
Finna Fjord 140
First World War 18, 24, 25, 46, 66, 263
fish/fishing 6, 64, 67, 74, 111, 133, 135, 148–57, 217, 219, 243, 245–47, 251, 253, 324, 335; areas beyond national jurisdiction (ABN) 152; fish farms 48, 154–56, 220; illegal, unreported and unregulated (IUU) 50, 150, 152; maximum sustainable yield (MSY) 153; regional fisheries management organizations (RFMOs) 152; *see also* aquaculture
Fisher, Admiral Jacky 3, 167, 330
Five Power Defence Arrangements (FPDA) 80–81
flags of convenience (FOCs) 49, 50–51, 150, 217, 237, 238, 333
floating houses 117, *117*, 119
flux compression generator (FCG) 207
Foch 101
Forbes, Randy 230
France 30, 31, 78, 79, 142, 203, 210, 228, 254, 259, 262, 263, 267, 274, 324, 325
Friedman, Thomas 339
frigates 87, 88, 91, 99, 100, 101, 122, *266*, 292; anti-submarine- 90; Bergamini-class 189; Forbin-class 189; *Hanit* 236; Ivor huitfeldt-class 186; stealth 90, 98; Steregushchy-class 187; *Xuzhou* 266; *Yancheng* 266
Fukushima 45, 118, 193

Galápagos Rift 162
Galveston, Texas 118
Gama, Vasco da 9, 15, 339
Gardline 331
gas 37, 48, 52, 56, 74, 89, 92, 96, 99, 100–2, 107, 108, 132, 134–41, 143, 144, 147, 159, 160, 163, 165, 177, 188, 189, 195, 215, 219, 221, 228, 260, 264, 265, 317, 318, 324, 335, 339; liquefied natural (LNG) 47, 56, 60, 127, 136, 137–38, 144, 192
Gates, Robert 295
Gazprom 141
General Atomics (GA) 197
geoengineering 132–33
Geoje shipyard 138
geopolitics 66–67, 139, 258, 279, 321, 332
George H. W. Bush 174, 175
Georgia, Russia 94
Georgia, USA 113, 131
geostrategy 5, 66–67, 317, 335, 339
Germany 46, 49, 59, 263, 267, 277; Nazi 10
Gibraltar 324; Strait of 39
Global Ocean Commission 251
globalisation 2, 5, 7–33, 22, 20, 40, 62, 74, 77, 218, 270, 317–18, 320, 322, 326, 333, 340; beginnings of 13–16; maritime and economic 32–33; the emergence of modern 23–25
Glomar Challenger 143
Google 38, 62; Earth 218; Ocean 62
Gore, Al 107
Gray, Colin 309
Great Britain *see* Britain
Great Depression 24
Great Game 316
Great Yarmouth 332
Greece 49
Greenland 9, 114, 140, 141, 146
Greenpeace 218
grenades 176, 204, 236
Groningen 117
Grotius, Hugo 17
Guam 83, 161, 228
Guiana, French 324
Guinea, Gulf of 240, 242
Gulf 11, 39, 58, 79, 81, 82, 96–99, 100, 105, 136, 147, 194, 199, 243, 261, 264, 265, 266, 268, 273, 318, 322, 327, 340; Wars 77, 182, 295
guns 13, 99, 177, 186, 190, 199, 236, 304; Advanced Gun System (AGS) 300; Blitzer 197; coil 197, 312; gas 197; Gatling 176, 187; rail 195–97, 208, 212, 312

Gwadar 57, 97, 268

Haenni, P. 207
Hainan Island 62, 77, 289
Haiti 122, 297
Hambantota 57
Hamburg 28
Hatton Area 30
Havana 95
Hawaii 155, 161, 164
Hawkes Ocean Technologies 239
Hawkins, John 20
helicopters 87, 98, 100, 122, 172–74, 186, 187, 190, 292, 301; anti-submarine warfare (ASW) 89; Sea King 101; Seahawk 192
Hezbollah 100, 236, 284
high-resolution photography or imagery (IMINT) 61
hijackings 66, 217, 243 247
HMS *Ambush* 73
HMS *Sussex* 131
HMS *Victory* 75, 131, 185
Hong Kong 45, 49, 57, 108, 267; Disneyland Resort 109; International Airport 109
Hormuz, Strait of 38–40, 65, 99, 103, 326
Horn of Africa 100, 238, 240, 241, 243, 249, 265
Human Development Index 37
humanitarian: aid 64, 187, 291; assistance and disaster relief (HADR) 68, 97, 187, 293
hurricanes 116, 255; Great 120; Haiyan 120; Katrina 119, 120, 122; Sandy 119, 120, 122
Huxley, Thomas 148
Hyundai Heavy Industries 54, 88

Iberian Peninsula 9
icebreakers 146–47, 188, 192–93
Iceland 9, 31, 140, 141; 'Cod Wars' 77
identification, friend or foe transponders (IFF) 217
India 11, 20–22, 32, 38, 39, 41, 45, 52, 79, 80, 87, 96–99, 100, 103, 104, 136, 140, 163, 166, 170, 183, 214, 232, 233, 240, 242 247, 259–61, 265, 268, 286, 309; -Pakistan War 306
Indian Ocean 1, 11, 12, 15, 16, 21, 39, 57, 66, 82, 94–99, 103, 105, 111, 116, 121, 124, 164, 167, 175, 228, 235, 238, 240–42, 261, 263, 266, 267, 275, 280, 331
Indies 17, 249; East 14, 17; West 20, 21

Indonesia 11, 39, 79, 80, 81, 83, 90, 97, 121, 122, 139, 149, 162, 187, 221, 232, 243, 254, 297
Industrial: Period 112; Revolution 21
Information and Communications Technology (ICT) 168, 288
Inmarsat 62
Innes, Hammond 213
Integrated Fire Control-Counter Air (NIFC-CA) 283
intelligence 46, 47, 171, 209, 217, 293; artificial (AI) 175, 177, 212, 283; measure and signature (of emissions) (MASINT) 61; signals (SIGINT) 61
International: Convention for the Safety of Life 61; Court of Justice (ICJ) 27, 253 ; Date Line 315, *316*, 338; Labour Organization (ILO) 50; Maritime Bureau (IMB) 242; Maritime Organization (IMO) 28, 49–50, 61, 125–26, 133, 146, 157, 217, 251–52; Seabed Authority (ISA) 28,163, 250, 251; Thermonuclear experimental Reactor (ITER) 210; Tribunal for the Law of the Sea (ITLOS) 28, 250, 252–53
Internet 7, 35, 36, 38, 42, 43, 44–46, 62, 170, 218, 247, 287, 317, 322
IRA 235, 237
Iran 39, 77, 99–101, 103, 104, 182, 232, 236, 243, 264, 304, 309, 326; Iranian Revolution (1979) 99; Iranian Revolutionary Guard Corps (IRGG) 99, 291; -Iraq War (1980–88) 51, 52
Iraq 26, 78, 100, 172, 182, 213, 235, 262, 273, 306; Ian-Iraq War (1980–88) 51, 52
Ireland, Northern 158
Irish Sea 158
Irrawaddy Corridor 268
Israel 101, 168, 172, 176, 235, 306
Isua field 141
Italy 11, 78

Jamaran 101
James Shoal 225
Japan 1, 10, 32, 38, 39, 49, 58–59, 79, 80, 82–84, 86–89, 95–97, 104, 105, 108, 140, 142, 144, 146, 158, 162, 163, 166, 168, 175, 193, 221–25, 228, 230–33, 242, 263, 264, 267, 268, 271, 278; Coast Guard 87, 224; Eastern Tanakai Trough 166; Maritime Self-Defense Force (JMSDF) 87, 183, 224; Marine Corps 87; Sea of 144; USA/Japan Treaty of Mutual Cooperation 232

Jebel Ali 57
Joint High Speed Vessels (JHSVs) 293
Joint Operational Access Concept (JOAC)
    271

Kailua-Kona 161
Karachi 57
Karakoram Highway 268
Kennedy, Paul 32, 327
Kermadec Islands 164
Khawr Al-Amaya Oil Terminal (KAAOT)
    235
Knifefish 307
Kobe 146
Kockums 304
Kohlschütter, V. 207
Kola Peninsula 25
Konsberg Joint and Naval Strike 60
Korea 77, 233, 242; North 80, 88, 105, 284,
    287, 304 308, 309; South 32, 39, 54,
    57, 59, 80, 82, 84, 88–89, 97, 104, 138,
    140, 146, 158, 163, 166, 168, 221, 222,
    228–30, 232, 248, 263, 278, 284, 340
Kristensen, Hans M. 308
Kuril Islands 86, 95
Kuwait 45

La Niña 121; see also El Niño
Lagos, Makoko community 119
Lampedusa 245
lasers 197–98, 200, 204; Advanced Tactical
    (ATL) 199; chemical oxygen iodine
    (COIL) 199; free-electron (FEL) 199,
    200, 201, 202; laser range-finder (LRF)
    176; Laser Weapon System (LaWS) 198,
    199; Maritime Laser Demonstrator
    (MLD) 199; Solidstate (SSl) 198–200,
    202
Laurium 330
Law of Nations 17
law, international maritime 16–18, 26–31
Lebanon 97, 306
Lepanto, Battle of 13
Levant 11
Liaoning 84, 85, 85, 227
Liberation Tigers of Tamil Eelam (LTTE)
    234, 235
Liberia 49, 51
Libya 77, 247, 262, 273
Liddell Hart, Basil 297
Lisbon 182
littoral complexity and control 214–19
Liu Xiaoming 225
Liverpool 41

Lockheed Martin 161, 164, 176
Lombok Strait 39, 221, 228, 272
London 41, 44, 115, 336; Gateway 41, 57
Long Beach 36
Long March 268
Los Angeles, LAX airport 36
Lysekil 158

Maanshan 266
Mackinaw 147
Madras 22
Maersk Eleanora 53
Magellan 9
Mahan, Alfred Thayer 63, 73, 258, 263, 292
Makei Ocean Engineering 171
Malacca, Strait of 39, 96, 221, 228, 240,
    261, 265, 268, 272
Malawi 57
Malaysia 11, 39, 79, 80, 81, 82, 90, 221,
    222, 225, 230, 232, 254, 316; Airlines
    62, 87, 124, 266
Maldives 97, 116
Malta, Siege of 13
Manifa 136
manned vehicles 291, 302; underwater
    vehicles, Aviator 239; Super Falcon 239
mare: clausum 7, 8, 18, 221–34, 233, 320;
    liberum 8, 221–34, 233, 320
Mariana Islands 83
marine: conservation zones (MCZs) 153–54;
    protected areas (MPAs) 132, 153, 215,
    216, 219, 252
maritime: forces and power 67–69;
    Heritage Foundation 131; Labour
    Convention 50
Marjan 136
Marshall Islands 49, 51
masers 197–98
Matsuyama, Chunosuke 2
Mauritius 22, 57, 97, 228
McCain, Admiral John S. 329
McClean, Tom 30
McKinney-Møller 54
McLean, Malcolm P. 40
measure and signature (of emissions)
    intelligence (MASINT) 61
median line 88, 222
Mediterranean 9, 10, 11, 13, 15, 25, 39,
    71, 83, 93, 94, 95, 100, 101, 109, 124,
    135, 233, 245, 254, 261, 267, 273, 275;
    Shipping Company 55
MENA 266
Menzies, Gavin 11
methane hydrates 165–66

Mexico 164; Gulf of 55, 136, 137

Miami 38, 115, 118

Micronesia, Federated State sof 164, 228

Midway, Battle of 295

migration 215, 234, 244–48, 258; European Agency for the Management of Operational Cooperation at the External Borders of the Member States of the European Union (FRONTEX) 246; International Centre on Migration Policy Development (ICMPD) 245

Military Sealift Command (MSC) 293

mines/mining 28 69, 161–65, 168, 178, 179, 186, 194, 239, 264, 306, 307; Captor 307; mine countermeasures (MCM) 87, 89, 91, 177, 292; mining vessels 89, 91

Ming Dynasty 11, 12, 313

missiles 69, 84, 95, 168, 171, 173, 175, 177, 185, 186, 187, 194, 208, 227, 259, 260, 283, 290–92, 304, 308; Aegis Weapon System 183; Air-Sol Moyenne Portée (ASMPA) 203; anti-air 87, 186, 290, 302, 304, anti-ballistic 87, 184, 284, 295; anti-missile systems 290; anti-ship 84, 90, 100, 186–88, 202, 212, 219, 236, 289; Arihand-class 97; ballistic 62, 71, 77, 84, 93, 97, 100, 178, 182–84, 195–96, 200, 202, 203, 259, 284, 292, 294, 302, 305, 310; BMD 183, 184; Brahmos 90; boats 89, 90; C-802 100; cruise 67, 68, 71, 79, 84, 195–96, 200, 287, 295, 302, 310; Dong Feng 84, 289; electromagnetic missile launcher (EMML) 197; Exocet 289; Harpoon 289; Hawkeye 283; hypersonic 202–4, 212, 286, 289, 311; IDAS 304; Jin class 62; Khalij 100; missiles, Klub-S 90; Naval Strike 289; Noor 100; Patriot 183; scramjet 203; Sizzler 187–88, 289; Spike 176; Standard 183, 283; supersonic 310; Tactical cruise (TCM) 300; Terminal High Altitude Area Defense (THAAD) system 183; missiles, Tomahawk 190, 197, 300; transonic 311; Waverider 203; Yakhont 90, 289

Mississippi Delta 123

Møller-Maersk 42, 52, 53–55, 66, 89, 126, 240

Moluccas 20

Molyneux, Thomas More 297

Monaco 109

Monsarrat, Nicholas 315

Mont see Seawise Giant

Monterey 107

Moscow 95

Mozambique 97, 138

Mullen, Admiral Mike 84, 275

Mumbai 98, 234, 235, 247

munitions 79, 194, 200, 287, 299, 300, 310

Muscovy 20

Musko 289

MV Amoco Cadiz 50

MV Erika 50

MV Limbourg 235

MV Prestige 50

MV Sea Empress 50

Myanmar (Burma) 57, 97, 265, 268

Nairobi 235

Namibia 164

Nanjing 267

nanotechnology 55, 193, 207–9, 212, 248, 290

Napoleon 335

NASA 172

National: Ocean Conference 107; Security Agency (NSA) 47; Snow and Ice Data Center 113

Nautilus Minerals 164

naval: power 69–76; Surface Warfare Center 196; Undersea Warfare Center 206

navies 4, 63, 69, 70, 74, 75–76, 79, 103, 122, 189, 194, 279, 287, 291, 298, 301, 327, 328, 329, 330, 331, 340; Argentinian 302; Chinese 62, 265, 335; Danish 186; German 277; Indian 97, 98; Iranian 100, 101; Israeli 176; Japanese 24, 277; People's Liberation Army Navy (PLAN) 83, 84, 224, 226, 227, 228, 265, 266, 269, 308; ROK 89; Royal 3, 23, 24, 66, 77, 122, 189, 259, 277, 336; Russian 95; Singaporean 90, 176; Soviet 26; Sri Lankan 235; 'Thousand-Ship Navy' (TSN) 275; US 5, 24, 27, 47, 76, 78, 99, 80, 122, 172, 173, 174, 175, 183, 184, 186, 196, 199, 200, 232, 269, 271, 273–75, 283, 292, 293, 305, 307

Navigation Acts 23

Nelson, Horatio 63, 72, 75, 184

Neptune Minerals 164

Netherlands 16, 85, 108, 115, 116, 119, 254, 274

Networked Enabled Capacity (NEC) 282

New Delhi 322

New Orleans 115, 122

New South Wales 22
New York 38, 44, 118
New Zealand 80, 91, 142, 162, 164, 233, 322
Newfoundland 136
Nicaragua 253
Nigeria 116, 119, 136, 138, 139, 243
Ningbo-Zoushin 57
North Africa 13, 245, 266
North America 20, 21, 25, 38, 46, 56, 136, 163, 168; Great Lakes 119, 147
North Atlantic Treaty Organization (NATO) 25, 26, 78, 92–94, 103, 104, 178, 180, 182, 183, 259, 260, 262, 289, 309
North Pole 43, 111, 144, 147, 220
North Sea 117, 154, 158
Northern Sea Route (NSR) 39, 94, 114, 140, 141, 144, 145–46, 193
Northwest Passage (NWP) 39, 144–46, 233
Norway 60, 127, 140, 142, 144, 146, 160
Norwegian Cruise Line 332
Norwegian Sea 25
Nova Scotia 136, 158
Novator Design Bureau 187
nuclear fusion 210–12
Nuestra Señora de las Mercedes 131

Obama, Barack 81, 232
ocean thermal energy conversion (OTEC) 160–62
Odyssey Marine 131–32
Office of Naval Research (ONR) 161, 196, 197, 206
oil 39, 42, 47, 48, 52, 56, 74, 89, 92, 96, 99, 100, 101, 107, 108, 134, 135, 136–39, 140, 141, 143, 144, 159, 163, 165, 177, 188, 215, 219, 221, 228, 260, 264, 265, 318, 324, 327, 335, 339; Al Basrah Oil Terminal (ABOT) 235; Barrel of Oil Equivalent (BOE) 139; China National Offshore Oil Corporation (CNOOC) 138, 139, 141, 226; China National Petroleum Corporation (PetroChina/ CNPC) 139; China Petroleum & Chemical Corporation (Sinopec) 139, 141; Khawr Al-Amaya Oil Terminal (KAAOT) 235
Okhosk, Sea of 144
Okinawa 87
Oman 38, 97, 99
Opium War, first 267
Ottoman Empire 9

P3 network 55

Pacific 2, 20, 24, 26, 39, 43, 55, 83, 93, 95, 111, 116, 118, 121, 124, 147, 161, 162, 164, 181, 193, 194, 201, 228, 245, 271, 277, 313, 315, 316; Great Pacific Garbage Patch 124; South 121, 149
Pakistan 45, 57, 96, 97, 105, 173, 268, 304, 309; India-Pakistan War 306
Palm Islands 108
Palmerston, Lord 104
Panama 49, 51; Canal 23–24, 39, 51, 52, 56, 143–44, 147, 221; Canal Authority (ACP) 144
Papua New Guinea 164
Paracel Islands 89, 222, 261
Paris 31, 44; Memorandum of Understanding on Port State Control (Paris MOU) 51
Peace Ark 266
Pearl Harbor 24
Peloponnesian War 278, 279
Persia 20, 330
Persian Gulf 218, 235
Peru 121, 228, 253
Peter the Great 93
Pevensey 114
Philip II of Spain 338
Philippine Sea 224
Philippines 49, 79, 80–82, 87, 162, 221–23, 230, 232
Pinsker, Joe 241
pipelines 37, 60, 177, 265, 318
piracy 4, 11, 15, 20, 62, 65, 69, 74, 82, 94, 100, 150, 170, 176, 186, 205, 214, 217, 235, 237, 240–44, 248, 249, 252, 253, 265, 275, 317, 331; Oceans Beyond 241
Piraeus 267
Pitcarin Island 53, 221
Plimsoll line 51
pollution 123–27, 186, 220, 251–53; Convention on the Prevention of Marine Pollution by Dumping of Wastes and Other matter (1972) 133
Port Arthur 277
ports 36, 41–42, 55–58, 101, 102, 234, 307, 335; Paris Memorandum of Understanding on Port State Control (Paris MOU) 51; 'treaty' 267; see also named ports
Portsmouth 75
Portugal 10, 16, 19, 65, 85, 249
Prelude FLNG 138
Project Hydra 179
Provence 210

Puntland Maritime Police force (PMPF)
243
Putin, Vladimir 220
Pyne, Stephen J. 142

Qatar 51, 97, 138
Qi Jianguo, Lieutenant General 226
quantum computing 209–10

radar 61, 84, 171, 190, 206, 208, 247,
288–90, 303
Rafael 176
Raleigh, Sir Walter 3
'Reconquista' 9
Red Sea 10, 11, 39, 83, 162, 267
Regional comprehensive Partnership 233
registries 48–51; United Nations
Convention for Registration of Ships 48
remotely operated vehicles (ROVs) 46,
138, 304
Richmond, Sir Herbert 67–68
Rio de Janeiro 251
RMS Queen Mary 2 188
Rochefort 335
Rockall 30
Rolls-Royce 73, 177
Rongsheng Heavy Industries 60
Roosevelt, Theodore 279
Rosneft 141
Ross Sea 143
Rotterdam 41, 57, 146
Royal Caribbean International 52, 332
Royal Fleet Auxiliary 79
Rubio, Marco 77
Runciman, Walter 63
Rush, Richard 257
Russia 32, 79, 80, 86, 90, 92–95, 100,
104, 103, 136, 140, 141, 144, 147, 163,
168, 170, 183, 193, 202, 214, 218, 220,
228, 231, 259–62, 267, 279, 287, 309;
Northern Fleet 25, 94, 95; Pacific Fleet
94, 95, 100; see also Soviet Union
Rwanda 57

Safaniya 136
Sakhalin 136
Samho Dream 241
Samsung 89; Heavy Industries 138
San Diego, University College of 206
San Francisco 41, 239
Santa Barbara Basin 136
Santa Catarina 16–17
Santos Basin 136
São Paulo 101–2

satellites 43, 61, 62, 115, 168, 170, 177,
181, 190, 199, 218, 242, 246, 266, 283,
285–90, 292, 303; anti-satellite systems
284; mini- 286; QuickBird 62; Tactical
Satellites (TACSAT) 169
Saudi Aramco 264
Savannah 131
'sea blindness' 329–31
sea lanes and routes 143–48; Transpolar
Route 144
sea levels, rising 108, 110, 114–19, 133, 134,
166, 234, 324
sea power 2, 4, 5, 9, 10, 12, 18–23, 32, 33,
62, 63–105, 139, 244, 318, 320, 327, 334,
336–38; and empires 18–23; hard 4, 26,
64–68, 319, 337, 340; soft 4, 26, 64–68,
135, 148, 319, 337, 340
Seaspan 54
Seawise Giant 52
Second World War 10, 18, 24, 25, 58, 76,
77, 86, 123, 190, 225, 228, 230, 271, 283,
294–96, 301, 318
security 7, 47, 68, 79, 213–56, 274, 318,
320, 332, 336, 340; see also National
Security Agency (NSA)
Selden, John 18
Seneca 315
Senkaku Islands 86, 87, 175, 225, 232
Seven Years' War 21
Sewol 61
Seychelles 57, 97, 215
Shakespeare, William 20
Shambaugh, David 229
Shanghai 56, 57, 267; Cooperation
Organisation 95; Shangri-La Dialogue
226
Sharjah 99
Sheerness 117
Shell, Royal Dutch 137–39
Shenzen 57
shipbuilding 52, 58–61, 74, 88, 89, 273,
274, 332, 335
shipping 47–56; routes 147; lines 52–55;
UK Chamber of 126
ships 47, 48, 97, 122, 180, 199, 226, 227,
235, 236, 288, 296, 300; Absalon-
class 186; cable repair 48; container
47; fishing vessels 247; floating,
production, storage and offloading
(FPSO) 137; Flyvefisken-class 186; Fuchi
class 267; Jiangkai class 267; large
aviation-capable specialist ships (LHDs)
91; littoral combat (LCS) 174, 186–87,
199; Lewis and Clark dry cargo 190;

littoral combat (LCS) 186; MCM vessels 87, 89, 91; nuclear-powered 192–93, 303; Open Water (OW) 145; 'phantom' 236; Piranha 176; Polar class 144–45; Protector 176; registries 48–51; Ro-Ro 48, 127; support 87, 89, 186, 273, 293; surface 100, 177, 178, 200, 269, 291; TI class 52; Triple-E-class 52, 54, 89; unmanned 292; *see also* corvettes; cruisers; destroyers; dhows; ferries; frigates; icebreakers; tankers; warships

Siberia 146

Sichan Xinue Mining 141

Siemens 160

Sierra Leone 22

Singapore 16, 39, 56, 57, 80, 90, 140, 168, 230, 244, 251, 271, 316, 322

slavery 19, 23, 28, 249

Slessor, John 330

Smith, Adam 14

Snowden, Edward 47

Solomon Islands 228

Solwara I project 164

Somalia 65, 66, 170, 228, 237, 241–43, 252, 266, 317

Song Dynasty 11

South Africa 142, 164

South America 38, 52, 58, 101–2, 121, 147, 163, 238, 240, 264, 339

South China Sea 5, 12, 39, 62, 82, 83, 86, 87, 89, 90, 135, 137, 139, 175, 214, 220–28, 231, 233, 254, 261, 264, 267, 272, 278, 335

South East Asia 11, 45, 58, 95, 96, 136, 214, 230, 232, 267, 268; Association of Southeast Asian Nations (ASEAN) 80–81, 86, 87, 230, 233, 264

South Pole 43, 111

South Sandwich Islands 30, 153

Southampton 57

Southern Ocean 143

South-South trade 58

Soviet Union 25–27, 47, 76, 92, 142, 232, 259, 315; *see also* Russia

space 169–70, 199, 212, 260, 270, 271, 282, 283, 285–87; Shuttle 204; Outer Space Treaty 285

Spain 10, 16, 19, 20, 30, 46, 65, 85, 131, 249, 274, 277, 325

Sparta 276

Spratly Islands 89, 222, 261

Sri Lanka 57, 97

SS *Gairsappa* 131

SS *Republic* 131

St Kilda 31

St Petersburg, Florida 118

Statoil 160

submarines 44, 77, 79, 84, 87, 90, 92, 97, 99, 100, 102, 168, 176, 177, 180, 192, 212, 240, 259, 260, 283, 289, 291, 292, 301, 302, 301–5, 307, 310; Adula-class 98; air-independent propulsion (AIP) 89, 302, 303, 310; anti-submarine sonars 186; anti-submarine torpedoes 187; anti-submarine warfare (ASW) helicopters 89; anti-submarine-frigates 90; Astute-class 73, 73; Borei-class 93, 93; Distributed Agile Submarine Hunting (DASH) programme 180; German U-boats 25, 131; Kilo-class 89; mini- 88, 100, 194; nuclear 83, 203, 205, 303; Ohio-class 295, 302; *Sea Dagger* series 304; Shishumar-class hull 98; Sindlughosh-hull 97; Song class 302; Type 214 302; Yuan class 302

Subsea Works Inspection and Maintenance with Minimum Environment ROV (SWIMMER) 138

Sudan 101

Suez Canal 23–24, 39, 52, 144, 146, 147, 221

Sulla 71

Sunda Strait 39, 221, 228, 272

supertankers 52, 62

surveillance 186, 246–48, 266, 274, 275, 283, 284, 286, 289, 290, 293, 299, 332; Chinese Naval Ocean Surveillance System (NOSS) 290; Persistent Littoral Undersea Surveillance (PLUS) project 180; Sound Surveillance System (SOSUS) 180

Sussex 114

Sutton, Willie 334

Sweden 140, 158, 289, 304

Syria 71, 95, 97, 101, 172, 184, 247, 262, 266, 273; Assad regime 100

Tactically Expandable Maritime Platform (TEMP) 187

Tahiti 121

Taiwan 45, 82, 83, 84, 86, 90–91, 166, 221, 222, 224, 228, 229, 232, 308

Taliban 170

tankers 47, 97, 188, 292; International 51; supertankers 52, 62

Tanzania 57, 97

Tartous 94

Taushima Strait 88

ten-dash line 222–223, 223, 228

'ten-year rule' 24

terrorism 4, 67, 69, 214, 215, 217, 235–36, 239, 248, 280, 282

Thailand 80, 116

Thales Optronics 73

Thales Underwater Systems Ltd 73

Thames: Barrier 117; Estuary 41, 117; River 57, 117–18

Thomson Reuters 237

Thomson, James 22

Thucydides 276, 279

Tianjin 57, 138

Till, Geoff 1

Titanic 128

tonnage 51, 59, 144, 155, 221; deadweight (DWT) 51; gross (GT) 49, 52, 61, 104; IMO Tonnage convention 49

Tordesillas, Treaty of 16, 18, 20

torpedoes 88, 89, 99, 100, 186, 240, 304, 307, 308; anti-ship 187; anti-submarine 187; narco- 239

Total 138, 160

trade 5–8, 11, 12, 15–23, 37, 38, 39, 39, 41, 42, 48, 55, 56, 57, 63, 64–65, 66–69, 76, 79, 82, 87, 92, 96, 100, 101, 136, 139, 143, 213, 215, 225, 228, 229, 243, 248, 317–20, 327, 334–37, 339, 340; South-South 58; *see also* United Nations Conference on Trade and Development (UNCTAD)

Trafalgar, Battle of 184, 259

trafficking/traffickers 4, 28, 50, 69, 217, 234–37, 239, 244–47, 280

Trans-Pacific Partnership 233

Trinidad 22

Tsushima 277

Turkey 32, 59, 78, 99, 254

Tuvalu 116

twenty-foot equivalent unit (TEU) 40, 42, 53–57

Uganda 57

Uist, North 31

UK 30, 31, 41, 44, 49, 57, 78, 79, 80, 129, 135, 136, 142, 153, 158, 163, 168, 228, 254, 259, 260, 262, 263, 315, 322, 324, 328, 329, 331, 335, 336; Royal Fleet Auxiliary 79; Seabed Resources 164

Ukraine 94, 273

Ultra Electronics 73

underwater: cultural heritage (UCH) 127; improvised explosive devices (UWIEDs) 239; vehicles 304

United Arab Emirates (UAE) 57, 99, 108

United Nations (UN) 125, 50, 142, 157, 243, 250–52, 258, 266; Conference on Trade and Development (UNCTAD) 38, 48; Convention on the Law of the Sea (UNCLOS) 27–30, 37, 48, 81, 128, 130, 152, 163, 213, 214, 219, 221, 222, 223, 223, 227, 230, 232, 233, 248, 250, 251, 252–53, 278, 320; Educational, Scientific and Cultural Organization (UNESCO) 130, 132; Food and Agriculture Organization (FAO) 151, 154, 218; World Food programme 266

unmanned aerial vehicles (UAVs) 84, 87, 90, 92, 98, 171–75, 190, 199, 215, 225, 236, 242, 268, 284, 288, 289, 292, 296, 300, 302, 312; Magic Eye 90

unmanned systems 284–85, 312, 325

unmanned vehicles 171–82, 194, 208, 212, 216, 247, 285, 291, 307; autonomous underwater vehicles (AUVs) 138, 178–79, 312; 'drones' 172, 177; gliders 181; Global Hawk 172, 173; large displacement unmanned undersea vehicle (LDUUV) 179–80; long endurance (HALE) 172; marine robotic system of self-organising, logically linked physical nodes (MORPH) 179; medium altitude with long endurance (MALE) 172; Polar Hawk 173; Reaper 173; Scan Eagle 174; Seahawk 174; Snow Goose 175; Soar Eagle 173; Triton 173; Unmanned Carrier Launched Surveillance and Strike Aircraft (UNCLASS) 175; unmanned combat air vehicles (UCAVs) 174, 175, 295, 296; unmanned surface vehicles (USVs) 176–77, 199; unmanned underwater vehicles (UUVs) 177–82, 302, 305, 307

US: Air Force 76, 172, 200, 271; US Air Force Personnel Halting and Stimulation Response (PHaSR) 204; Army 76, 78; Coast Guard Cutter (USCGC) 147; Geological Survey 137, 143; Marine Corps 76, 78, 200; US Marine Corps Active Denial System 204; National Research Council 115; Naval Institute 230; Naval Service 80

USA 4, 5, 7, 10, 14, 15, 18–20, 23–27, 32, 36, 47, 49, 51, 55, 56, 65, 69, 71, 72, 76–78, 80–88, 92, 97, 100, 103–5, 107, 108, 118, 119, 130, 136, 139, 140, 142, 143, 146, 152, 159, 167, 170, 184, 187, 194, 199, 202, 204, 207, 213, 222, 224, 227–28, 230, 232, 233, 244, 245 247, 249, 251,

258–62, 271–78, 280, 286, 287, 289, 294, 297, 308–10, 315, 316–18, 317, 322, 324, 326, 328, 329, 339, 340; and China 263–76; Central 240; East Coast 55, 143, 144; Gulf Coast 122, 143, 144; USA/ Japan Treaty of Mutual Cooperation 232; *see also* North America; South America
USS *Abraham Lincoln* 122, 297, 319
USS *Bataan* 122
USS *Carl Vinson* 122, 297
USS *Cole* 235
USS *Cowpens* 227
USS *Freedom* 186
USS *Harry S. Truman* 122
USS *Impeccable* 227
USS *Independence* 186
USS *Nimitz* 294
USS *Ponce* 199
USS *Providence* 302
USS *Saipan* 298
USS *Zumwalt* 189

Vanuatu 164
Veerman, Cees 117
Velella Project 155–56, 156
Venezuela 136
Verizon 38
Vietnam 81, 87, 89–90, 90, 95, 97, 221–23, 226, 230, 232; War 77
Vikramaditya 98
Vikrant 989, 306
Vindeby 157
Virginia Tech College of Engineering 206

Wang Yi 86
Wang Yilin 226
warfare 25, 77, 168, 186, 258–60, 279–313, 319, 320; above-water 288–97; amphibious 297–301; cyber and electromagnetic 287–88; underwater 301–7
Warsaw Pact 180
warships 67, 70, 72, 71, 74–76, 78, 79, 84, 92, 94, 97, 100, 168, 184–88, 192, 200, 208, 226, 227, 248, 266, 75, 281, 283, 289, 292, 301, 309, 311, 312, 320, 337; Advanced Electrical Power Systems (AEPSs) 189; design 184–94, 31; modularisation 185–88

Washington Naval Treaty 24
Washington DC 44
Watling Island 14
weapons 28, 70, 100, 185, 190, 191, 194, 195, 197, 200, 234, 237, 238, 282, 290, 302, 310; directed-energy (DEWs) 175, 176, 177, 184, 195, 196, 197–202, 204, 208, 211, 212, 286, 312; high-power microwave (HPM) 195, 201, 204, 205; improvised explosive devices (IEDs) 236, 306; nuclear 259, 307–9; of mass destruction 202, 237; particle-beam 201; Shkval 100; underwater improvised explosive devices (USIEDs) 239; *see also* grenades; guns; munitions; torpedoes
weather, extreme 120–22, 324
Weir, Strachan & Henshaw, Bristol 73
William the Conqueror 114
Wilson, Woodrow 26–27
wind farms 157–59
Woods Hole Marine Biological Laboratory 156
World Bank 241; Global Partnership for the Oceans 251
World Islands 108
wrecks 128–32; Abandoned Shipwreck Act (ASA) 130; Ancient Monuments and Archaeological Areas Act (1979) 129; Convention for the Protection of Underwater Cultural Heritage 130–31; Merchant Shipping Act 129; Protection of Wrecks Act (1973) 129

Xi Jinping 82, 214, 335
Xinjiang 268
Xiong Guangkai, General 308

Yellow Sea 82, 175, 222, 226
Yemen 173, 243
Yulin 62, 289
Yunnan 268
Yuri Dolgorukly 93

Zambia 57
Zheng He 11, 82, 83, 229, 268; voyages of 12
Zyvex Marine 176